Edexcel BTEC
First
Public Services

Edexcel BTEC First Public Services

Textbook

Nick Cullingworth

Published in 2003 by:
Nelson Thornes Ltd
Delta Place
27 Bath Road
CHELTENHAM
GL53 7TH
United Kingdom

04 05 06 07 / 10 9 8 7 6 5 4 3 2

A catalogue record for this book is available from the British Library

ISBN 0 7487 6161 6

Illustrations by Oxford Designers and Illustrators and Rupert Besley

Page make-up by GreenGate Publishing Services, Tonbridge, Kent

Printed and bound in Great Britain by Scotprint

Contents

Introduction

Foreword

This book is written for students doing the new BTEC First Diploma in Public Services. It is based on the new specifications: *BF011696 Guidance and Units for the Edexcel Level 2 BTEC First Diploma in Public Services – issue 1 – May 2002*.

The book covers all 14 units of the qualification, and deals with them outcome by outcome. Students will therefore find information, ideas and skills guidance on all parts of the syllabus.

There is also explanation on assessment and grading, and on the integrated vocational assignment (IVA) – a new, externally assessed feature of the syllabus.

Introduction for students

Using this book

This book is for you – students who are following the new BTEC First Diploma in Public Services. It gives you information on all parts of the course, together with ideas and guidance to help you with your assignments. It also explains what the outcomes (sometimes called 'grading criteria') are about and what they are looking for.

It should be stressed at the outset that the aim of this book is not to do your work for you, but to help you to do your own work. Studying public services is all about doing your own research, asking your own questions, and finding your own answers. You should use this book as a starting point, then go on to do your own investigation in directions related to your own interests and the public service career you hope to take up.

How the book is organised

This book is divided in the same way as the syllabus. It starts with the three core units – the ones you must do – and then covers the eleven specialist units (from which you choose three only). Each chapter covers one unit.

The sub-headings are the same as the grading criteria in the specifications (syllabus) which you and your tutors have to follow. In the book these grading criteria are called 'outcomes', because the word is easier to use, and because they all refer to things you have to do to get your BTEC First Diploma in Public Services. The system of grading is explained on page xii.

If you are set an assignment you will find helpful information and ideas under the sub-headings which deal with the same outcomes as the assignment.

Special features

There are some special features in the book which give you useful information, skills guidance, or ask you relevant questions. These are:

FOCUS – examples of relevant facts and figures

CHECKPOINT – questions to make you think, or ideas for research

SKILLPOWER – advice on how to understand and cover outcomes

PROFILE – examples of how you could approach certain tasks

SUPERGRADES! – introduces sections dealing with merit or distinction outcomes, and tells you how to get these higher grades

LINK! – directs you to another part of the book to find useful information

COOL SITES – good starting points for getting information off the internet.

About the BTEC First Diploma in Public Services

This is a one-year full-time course for people who are interested in the public services and the work they do. It does not guarantee entry into any public service, but it tells you what the public services do, why they do it, and what careers they offer. The course also gives you skills and knowledge which will help you to apply for public service work, and to succeed when you get in.

The course is divided into units. For a First Diploma you have to do three core (compulsory) units and three specialist units – six units in all. In theory you can take any three out of the eleven specialist units on the syllabus – but in practice it is best to take the ones offered at your college!

Assignments

Most of your work will take the form of assignments. These will be tasks set mainly by your tutors, based on situations related to public service. They might be reports, role-plays, presentations, mock interviews, problem-solving exercises or research assignments. You may do them in groups or as individuals. Whatever form the assignments take, they will be based on the outcomes printed in the syllabus (sometimes called the 'specifications').

Assessment

There are no examinations on the BTEC First Diploma in Public Services. But one of the core units will be assessed using an assignment which is not set by your tutors, but by Edexcel BTEC. At present, that unit is Unit 1: The Public Services. All the outcomes for Unit 1 will be covered in one big assignment which you will do in the second term. There is more about this Integrated Vocational Assignment (IVA) on page xiii.

Systems of setting and marking assignments vary from college to college and from tutor to tutor. What often happens is that you do one big assignment or several smaller assignments for each unit. You may well get graded on each assignment. But these assignment grades are not the grades that really matter. They are used to help tutors and assessors to give you an overall grade for the unit.

The grades you can get for each unit are Pass, Merit or Distinction. There is a new points system in which Pass = 2 points, Merit = 4 points and Distinction = 6 points.

The exception to this is Unit 1, which carries twice as many points as the other units. For Unit 1 a pass = 4 points, a merit = 6 points and a distinction = 8 points. All the points for Unit 1 come with the Integrated Vocational Assignment (IVA).

To get your BTEC First Diploma in Public Services you must:
- attempt six units
- fail no more than one of them
- gain at least 12 points in all.

This means:
- if you get a pass in all six units you get a pass overall
- if you pass Unit 1 and four other units you will pass overall
- if you fail Unit 1 you must get at least a merit and four passes in your other units.

If this isn't clear, look at the table below.

Student	Core unit 1	Core unit 2	Core unit 3	Specialist unit	Specialist unit	Specialist unit	Points gained	Pass or not?
Andrew	P	P	P	P	P	P	14	P
Cath	P	P	P	P	–	P	12	P
Jaffar	–	P	P	P	P	P	10	–
Kylie	P	M	M	–	–	D	18	–

Andrew and Cath both pass because they have passed five or six units and have 12 points or more. Jaffar doesn't pass because although he has passed five units he doesn't have enough points. Kylie has more than enough points but not enough units – so she doesn't pass either.

Overall grade

You now get an overall grade for your BTEC First Diploma, based on the points you score for each unit. This will be decided by your tutors using official BTEC guidelines.

FOCUS

The Integrated Vocational Assignment (IVA)

- Integrated means it covers all the outcomes of the unit (and may include some material from other core units).
- Vocational means it is linked to public service work.
- Assignment means you are set a series of tasks to do over a period of time.

The IVA is not an examination, but it is not a normal assignment either. It is written by people outside your college and sent to your college in Term 2. You will get it in January and your college will set a deadline, probably in April.

From around September onwards you will find an exemplar (example) of an IVA on the BTEC website. This is for guidance only – it is not the real thing! In January your college will give you your own copy of the real IVA. This is the one you must work from.

As a student you will receive printed instructions for your IVA. You must study the instructions carefully. The main points are shown below, in simplified language, but *they may be changed*, so they are given for general guidance only.

- The IVA is compulsory.
- Your college will give you a deadline and the study time and facilities you need.

- Discuss anything you don't understand about the IVA with your tutors at the earliest possible date!
- All the work you hand in for your IVA must be your own work.
- If you work in a group, it must be clear that each individual in the group has covered the outcomes.
- You must make it clear where your information comes from.
- You can use any suitable format for your work (e.g. writing, word processing or video), but check with your tutor first!
- You can use witness statements to show you have met an outcome, but this must be arranged with your tutor first!
- Work must be 'concise and focused'. Don't put in rough work. Leave out any leaflets or handouts which are not written by you. Quality is better than quantity.
- List all your sources (who or where you got your information from) at the end.
- Make sure you have an official cover sheet, and that it is filled in and signed by your tutor when you hand in your IVA.

After your IVA has been handed in at your college it will first be marked by your own tutors. But they will not be able to give you a definite grade, because it will then be sent off to BTEC to be remarked by an outside examiner.

The marking will in both cases be done to a marking scheme provided by BTEC.

Format of the IVA

The IVA will consist of;
- A scenario or setting describing a situation which can be met with in the public services. This scenario will be about things which are mentioned in the outcomes (grading criteria) of Unit 1.
- A number of tasks (about four) which you have to do. The tasks will use several skills – skills such as: reading instructions, listening to speakers from the public services, writing lists and reports, etc, speaking (e.g. giving a presentation), and using charts, graphs and pictures.

You will have a large part of the term in which to do your IVA. Your college will probably arrange for you to do it in stages, as follows:

1 **Set-up phase**. The assignment is given out, and the college makes sure you have access to the information you need, and the facilities, such as a library or computers, for doing the assignment.
2 **Initial phase**. This is where you work on the IVA. You do your rough notes and write them up as a first draft. The college will continue organising and providing resources, and may plan activities, such as visits, which will help you to collect your own information and ask any questions you need to ask.
3 **Review and support**. Tutors will look at your first drafts and give you the same kind of help and guidance that they would give you for any other assignments. They will ensure that it is your own work (i.e. that it wasn't done by your mother, brother, girlfriend, boyfriend or classmate) and that it wasn't ripped off the internet. Tutors are not allowed to fully mark ('pre-mark') your work at this stage. When your work has been reviewed you can write your final drafts, give your final presentations – and so on.
4 **Finalisation and hand-in**. Here you organise your file, make sure your cover sheet is filled in and signed, and hand it in to your tutors. It must be in by the college deadline. You may want to get a receipt for it.
5 **Centre marking**. Your tutors mark your assignments following the official marking scheme.
6 **Send-off**. The assignments, having been graded by the college, are sent off to the external marker for re-marking and checking. They must reach the external marker by the official BTEC Deadline, which will be around the end of April.
7 **Re-marking by Edexcel**.

Your results for the IVA should arrive sometime in June.

Extensions

There are some (rare!) circumstances in which you can have an extension for your IVA, e.g. serious illness. Contact your tutor (or get someone else to contact your tutor) at the earliest possible opportunity if you think this might be necessary. Extensions cannot be given without the official permission of Edexcel BTEC.

Appeals

Appeals or requests for 'special consideration' can only be made to BTEC in exceptional circumstances.

General advice for students doing the BTEC First Diploma in Public Services

You are most likely doing your BTEC First Diploma after leaving school. You will find that you have more freedom than you had at school, but you will still have some structure and discipline from the 'centre' (college) where you are studying.

You have three aims on this course:
- to pass the course
- to enjoy the course
- to improve your employability.

Passing the course

1 Do all your assignments.
2 Meet all deadlines.
3 Tell tutors if you have any problems (personal, financial or study) that might harm your success on the course.
4 Ask for special help from the college if you think your writing, spelling, arithmetic, etc are letting you down.
5 Go on all days out, trips, residentials, visits or expeditions organised as part of the course.
6 Always ask if you think you don't understand an assignment, or if you are not sure whether you are on the right track.
7 Take every opportunity you can to meet and talk to people who work in the public services.

8 Make collections of leaflets and handouts and try to keep them in a well-organised system, e.g. files.

Enjoying the course

You are the best judge of how to do this!

But – generally speaking – people who are prepared to go half-way to be friendly and considerate have little difficulty in getting on with people on a public services course. Public service students and teachers tend to be sociable people who like a laugh – even if they like to work hard as well! Likewise, students who are active, positive about life and willing to have a go at new activities and challenges usually get a lot out of a public service course.

If you feel you have any difficulties – with the work, the people on your course, your career plans, or with a tutor – it is best to talk to someone you like and trust about it, and get the problem sorted out. Although some tutors may seem too busy, others will be happy to do what they can to help – or direct you towards somebody who can help.

Improving your employability

The number of public service jobs is likely to go up, not down, in the foreseeable future. Even so, there is plenty of competition, and you are now at a stage where you can start building a strong foundation for getting the career you want. You can do this by:

- increasing your physical fitness and strength. Get involved with sports, get a training schedule – and get out there! Taking fitness seriously now means that in later life you will have the edge on other people when it comes to strength, fitness and health.
- improving your skills. Teamwork, communication, numeracy, motivation, study skills and organisation are important. If you are doing Key Skills you will be able to improve your skills *and* get nationally recognised certificates for doing it! Can't be bad, can it?
- meeting and talking to people who work in the public services. You should do all you reasonably

can, short of stalking or 'doorstepping', to talk to or get to know people who work in the public services – especially the public service you want to join. This will teach you to think in the way public service workers think, and will be an enormous help when it comes to applications and interviews. Read the Skillpower box below.

---

skillPOWER — How to get in with the public services

Being able to meet and talk with people who work in the public services – whatever the service – will be a great help to you in your BTEC course and in your career. You can get a lot from tutors, instructors, textbooks and the internet, but the real low-down comes from the public services themselves. Here is some advice on how to get the best out of them:

1 Encourage your tutors to get visiting speakers in to tell you about as many aspects of public service work as possible. Listen to them carefully, make as many notes as you can, and *ask questions* at the end. If you get a chance to talk to them personally after the lecture, go and talk to them. Don't be shy. Many a public service student has started their career this way!

2 Go on any visits or residentials that your tutors arrange to police stations, army camps or anywhere else. If you are on a police station visit be there on time, dress smartly, listen to what you are being told, and don't chat among yourselves. You want to give a good image of your college and your course, and most of all you want to give a good image of yourselves. You might get a job out of it later on.

3 Visit places like armed forces recruitment offices, and chat to the people who work there.

4 You can sometimes arrange visits, or interviews with people who work in public services, e.g. police, fire or Customs and Excise, without getting a tutor involved. The best way is probably to ring them up first, or write to them, explaining why you want to meet them, and what you want to talk to them about. (It may well be something to do with an assignment.) Your aim at this stage is to make an appointment.

When you have made an appointment, prepare for it by noting down and deciding what you really want to know. Then:

- Keep the appointment! Arrive on time, looking smart and interested.
- Take as many notes as you can.
- Don't rush off too soon, but don't hang on when it becomes clear that the person you are talking to has to go off and do something else.
- Never forget to thank the person for what they have done (even if you don't think it's been very useful!)

5 Consider arranging a work placement. This may be done by your college. But if it isn't, and you would like a placement, this is what you should do:

- Mention it to your tutor, so that you don't arrange a placement which clashes with your residential, or one which eats into the time you need for your IVA.

- Telephone the public service and find out who you should contact for a work placement. It may, for example, be a personnel officer, but the titles differ from place to place.
- Write to the person in charge of work placements. There is a specimen letter on page 12. Show that you are enthusiastic, that you want to learn, and that you are genuinely interested in that public service. The letter must be neat and properly laid out. If your handwriting is good, and your English accurate, use your own handwriting – but otherwise, do the letter on a computer. Do a rough draft of your letter and get someone to check it before you rewrite it as well as you can. Getting a work placement is not easy and there can be a lot of competition.
- Be prepared to wait for a reply, but after a couple of weeks you can ring up and ask how your application is going, if you haven't heard anything by then.
- If they want to interview you (which they probably will) get ready for the interview properly. There is advice on interviews in this book (page 15) – but ask your tutors or your careers service about it too. They will give you lots of useful guidance on interviews. Think about questions you could be asked, write them down, *then* write down the answers you would give. Get a tutor to give you a practice interview if you can.

- Get a good night's sleep before the interview.
- For the interview, arrive 20 minutes early, and believe in yourself. Be confident and polite. If you have got this far, they will almost certainly accept you for the placement. And if they don't – it's their loss!

Key skills

The new *Guidance and Units for the Edexcel Level 2 BTEC First Diploma in Public Services – issue 1 – May 2002* – otherwise known as the 'new specifications' or 'the syllabus' contains sections showing how key skills might be covered in each unit.

This means that key skills may be built into your assignments, and that when you get your BTEC First Diploma you will also get a range of key skills qualifications.

There is no room in this textbook to deal with key skills, but that doesn't mean they're not important. All the key skills are highly relevant for public service work, and you will use them – and improve on them – throughout your working life.

Key skills are therefore not a waste of time. But they are not part of the BTEC First Diploma. You can get your First Diploma without getting your Key Skills, and you can get your Key Skills without getting your First Diploma.

Acknowledgements

The author and publishers would like to thank the following for permission to reproduce material:

BBC Look North, Broad Oak Nature Reserve, BSES Expeditions at The Royal Geographical Society, Childline, Cockermouth Mountain Rescue Team, Crimestoppers Trust, The Department for Transport, DVLA, Geographer's A–Z Map Co. Ltd., Gloucestershire Fire and Rescue Service, Gloucestershire Youth and Community Service, The Greater Manchester Police, The Guardian, Hereford and Worcester Combined Fire Authority, The Home Office, HSE, National Probation Directorate, NHS Careers, RoSPA, Social Exclusion Unit, Solihull Metropolitan Borough Council, West Midlands Police, Victim Support, 2002.

Corbis GS(NT) (page 212), Corel 170(NT) (page 27), Corel 262(NT) (pages 24 and 204), Corel 343 (NT) (page 251), Corel 453(NT) (page 35), Corel 550(NT) (page 288), Corel 760(NT) (page 194), Digital Vision 15(NT) (page 265), Digital Vision SC(NT) (page 167), Digital Vision XA (NT) (page 145), Photodisc 16(NT) (page 35), Photodisc 22(NT) (page 221), Photodisc 33(NT) (page 35), Photodisc 45(NT) (page 226), Photofusion (pages 66, 88, 259, 293) Tom Le Goff/Digital Vision HU(NT) (page 35)

Crown copyright/MoD material is reproduced with the permission of the Controller of Her Majesty's Stationery Office. This product includes mapping data licensed from Ordnance Survey® with the permission of the Controller of Her Majesty's Stationery Office, © Crown copyright. All rights reserved. Licence no.100000230

Every effort has been made to contact copyright holders, and we apologise if any have been overlooked.

Many people have helped me in the preparation of this book. I would particularly like to thank Carolyn Lee for the invaluable encouragement and guidance she has given me. I should also like to thank those who reviewed this book in its early stages and made many helpful comments and criticisms. In addition, I should like to thank the editorial team at Nelson Thornes for their hard work in ironing out inaccuracies and inconsistencies. Most of all I should like to thank Loretta – for everything.

Nick Cullingworth, 2003

Unit 1 — The Public Services

Grading criteria

PASSGRADE	SUPERGRADE! Merit	SUPERGRADE! Distinction
To achieve a pass grade the evidence must show that the learner is able to:	To achieve a merit grade the evidence must show that the learner is able to:	To achieve a distinction grade the evidence must show that the learner is able to:
● identify and explain the primary role, purpose and responsibilities of at least two public services **3**	● show in-depth primary and secondary research for chosen public service roles and jobs **4**	● provide a detailed analysis of the roles, jobs and selection process of a given public service **5, 16**
● describe the type of work done by at least three different personnel from within a public service **5**	● complete a simulated application and selection process accurately and within given timescales **15**	● evaluate both the potential and the limitations for their own career development within their chosen public service **21**
● explain in detail the conditions of service of a given job within a public service **6**	● make considered comments about their own suitability to complete basic training for their career development **19**	
● accurately describe the current entry and selection stages for a given public service **7**		
● complete an application form, letter of application and curriculum vitae for a job in a given public service **8**		
● describe in detail the initial training programme for a given public service **18**		
● produce an action plan for career development **20**		

Many of the biggest and most powerful organisations in Britain are public services. They do an amazing range of essential jobs. And they offer a great choice of interesting, satisfying, secure and reasonably well-paid careers. Anything from spying and soldiering to teaching and mountain rescue – you have it in the public services.

In this unit we're going to look at the work the public services do, and what you have to do to get into them.

Note

This unit is the big one. It carries twice as many marks as any other unit. And it's the only unit which is assessed using an Integrated Vocational Assignment, set by Edexcel/BTEC.

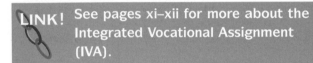

LINK! See pages xi–xii for more about the Integrated Vocational Assignment (IVA).

What is a public service?

A public service is any organisation which aims to protect or help people in a professional and caring way.

These are the different types of public service organisation in Britain.

Uniformed public services – wear special, clearly recognisable clothes when on duty
• The Police   • The Fire Service   • The Royal Navy   • The Royal Air Force
Non-uniformed public services – wear ordinary clothes when on duty
• Teachers   • Social workers   • Civil servants   • Doctors

Professional – these are paid a monthly salary
• Police   • Armed forces   • Teachers   • Nurses
Voluntary public services – these do unpaid or charity work
• Mountain Rescue   • Red Cross   • Special constables   • Prison visitors
Statutory public services – these have to exist by law
• Police   • Fire service   • Ambulance service   • Army
Non-statutory public services – not required by law
• NSPCC   • Trade unions   • Community groups   • Salvation Army
State-run public services – paid for by the taxpayer
• Police   • Fire   • Ambulance   • Armed forces
Privately run public services – paid for by customers
• Security guards   • Private prisons   • Window cleaners   • Banks

! CHECKPOINT …

(a) Find more examples of each of these types of public service.

(b) How many services come under more than one of the above headings? Why?

Who pays for the public services?

1 *Central government*. All the money for the armed forces, and about 51 per cent of the money for the police, fire and other main services comes from central government (e.g. the Home Office). This money comes from national taxes, such as income tax.

2 *Local government*. Local government (local authorities) pays 49 per cent of the police and fire services. They also pay for many local and community services – libraries, parks, community organisations, local refuse collection, etc. This money comes from local taxes, such as the council tax.

3 *Customers*. For example, if you go to a night club, some of the money you pay goes to pay the door staff.

Central government is responsible for the smooth running of the uniformed public services, though for the police, fire and ambulance services local government has a part to play as well.

Central government has overall control of the civil service and other non-uniformed public services (e.g. nursing or teaching). But most civil servants, nurses and teachers are employed by local authorities.

PASSGRADE

> Identify and explain the primary role, purpose and responsibilities of at least two public services.

FOCUS

If we ask: '*Why* do we have a police force?' we are asking about the **purpose** of the police.

If we ask: '*What* do the police do?' we are asking about the **role** of the police.

If we ask, 'What *should* the police be doing?' we are asking about their **responsibilities**.

The police

Each of the forty-three police forces in England and Wales has to produce a statement of its role, purpose and responsibilities. Here is an example:

FOCUS

Our purpose

- To protect life and property.

- To provide high quality police service, 24 hours a day.

- To work within the community and other agencies to improve safety, security and quality of life.

- To maintain the public's respect for our role in upholding the rule of law.

Our people

Our people are our greatest asset in achieving our purpose. Our people should be open, honest, fair and courteous, both to the public and each other. Our people's hard work, creativity and unique contribution are valued. Our people are required to act with integrity and loyalty to our purpose, but allowances will be made for honest mistakes. Our people can expect training for their role and the opportunity to develop their skills.

Our priorities

- To make effective use of our police officers and support staff.

- To prevent and detect crime.

- To protect and reassure the community.

- To provide the best possible response to calls from the public.

- To develop and maintain partnerships and improve community safety.

- To care for victims and witnesses.

- To undertake uniform patrol that is focused and tasked by proper briefing.

Source: West Midlands Police (2002)

If you find a statement like this, then you have identified 'the primary role, purpose and responsibilities' of a public service.

To *explain* them, you have to say *why* they have that role, that purpose, and those responsibilities.

Profile

The West Midlands Police work 'to protect life and property' because these are the things at risk from crime. They put 'life' first because life is more important than property, and crimes such as murder and rape are more serious than theft or criminal damage. This is their

primary role because it is the most important one. It is also their **primary purpose**.

They list a number of responsibilities. These include: 'To make effective use of our police officers and support staff. To prevent and detect crime. To protect and reassure the community.' These are **primary responsibilities** because they are very important duties. The first phrase means they should work efficiently and professionally. The second says they must stop crime happening, or find out who has done it. And the last phrase means that they must look after ordinary people.

The Fire Service

Here is a fire service mission statement:

'West Yorkshire Fire and Civil Defence Authority will: reduce death, injury and property loss due to fire, provide humanitarian services and protect the people and environment of West Yorkshire.'

Source: West Yorkshire Fire Service

This statement identifies the primary role, purpose and responsibilities of the West Yorkshire Fire Service. The **primary role and purpose** is to 'reduce death, injury and property loss due to fire'. They use the word 'reduce' because they cannot prevent death, injury and property loss completely. There will always be some fires which kill or injure people, or destroy their property. The West Yorkshire Fire Service put 'death' first, because saving lives is more important than saving property.

Their **primary responsibilities** are to 'provide humanitarian services and protect the people and environment of West Yorkshire'. 'Humanitarian services' reduce suffering, and 'protecting people and the environment' means preventing fires and accidents and dealing with events such as chemical spills which can destroy landscape and wildlife.

 *Merit*

> Show in-depth primary and secondary research for chosen public service roles and jobs.

In-depth means getting more information than just the basics.

Primary research means:
- talking to people who work in the public services (either in person or on the phone)
- listening to visiting speakers from the public services
- writing to recruitment offices and public relations departments

and making **full notes** of what you are told about public service roles and jobs.

---

skill POWER **How to make notes**

(a) From a speaker
- Write down main ideas and facts.
- Don't write down examples unless you need them.
- Write as fast as you can.
- Don't try to use sentences.
- When you have finished, put a title on your notes and keep them in a file.

(b) From a book, newspaper, etc
- Write down names, facts, figures, etc, and main ideas.
- Don't use sentences.
- Don't write down any examples or 'waffle' unless you need to.
- Put a title on your notes and keep them in a file.

Secondary research means:
- collecting leaflets
- visiting websites
- getting information from magazines, newspapers and books.

When you write about public service roles and jobs, put down where you got the information from (e.g. 'PC George Dixon, Youth Divert Officer, Kettering' or 'Essex Police Website – http://www.essex.police.uk/pages/setup/wel.htm').

References like this can be checked by your tutor or by the Edexcel marker of your Integrated Vocational Assignment, and give evidence that you have done primary or secondary research.

 *Distinction*

> Provide a detailed analysis of the roles, jobs and selection process of a given public service.

FOCUS

THE NATIONAL PROBATION SERVICE

The aims of the NPS are:

- to protect the public
- to reduce re-offending
- to provide for the proper punishment of offenders
- to ensure that offenders are aware of the effects of their crimes on their victims and on the public, and
- to rehabilitate offenders.

Source: NPS website

This means showing that you really understand the roles, purposes and responsibilities of your two public services, and can give reasons and explanations of them.

Profile

The National Probation Service has a very complex job, working with very difficult people. Their chief aim is rehabilitation of offenders, which means trying to prevent them from breaking the law again. This is not an easy job, roughly 70% of criminals re-offend.

Probation officers have to be skilled at counselling (a mixture of listening, role play, group therapy and advice) and this takes a lot of training and practice. They are busy people, and have to work with large numbers of offenders. They also have to work with police, lawyers, social workers and the prison service, so that they can get all the information and support they need for dealing with the offenders on their caseload.

The work of probation officers is demanding partly because they are dealing with people who could become aggressive or dangerous. They sometimes have to work with sex offenders and others who are a threat to society. It is often hard for them to keep a professional attitude towards people who have done such crimes, but they have to keep cool and try to help the offender. If they reform offenders so that they do not offend again, they have also protected the public.

LINK! 'Detailed analysis of a selection process' is dealt with on pages 16–18.

Probation officers have to be skilled at counselling

PASSGRADE

> Describe the type of work done by at least three different personnel from within a public service.

To meet this outcome you must choose one public service (either uniformed or non-uniformed) and find out the main work done by three or more people who do different jobs within the same organisation. They can be in civilian as well as uniformed roles.

Profile

HM Customs and Excise

1 Anti-smuggling officer

Anti-smuggling officers search freight vehicles coming into the UK for illegal drugs, obscene material (videos, magazines, child pornography, etc), firearms and endangered species (rare animals or plants). They also look for excise products – legal goods like tobacco, alcoholic drinks and petrol – which are taxed by the government.

These officers usually work at ports or airports, where goods come into the United Kingdom. But they don't just search vehicles. They also arrest and caution suspects, and search them. Sometimes they have to list and remove suspect goods from vehicles for forensic examination. They work closely with the police and with the security services such as MI5.

2 Administrative officer in Personnel

An administrative officer works in an office, keeping the organisation of Customs and Excise running smoothly. Officers in Personnel look after other staff working in Customs and Excise. They answer questions – about things like pay and holidays – from other members of staff. They also keep records up to date. These records are about staff promotions, training, sickness, and so on.

As well as all this, administrative officers in personnel have to arrange interviews for new staff, or staff already working in Customs and Excise who are being interviewed for promotion or for some other reason.

Some of their time is spent at a computer, writing letters, some of it is spent filing and organising paperwork, and the rest is spent dealing with people's questions.

3 VAT Insolvency Team Manager

This job involves the 'Excise' part of Customs and Excise and is concerned with collecting unpaid tax from VAT registered traders who have gone bankrupt. The team manager has to look after four insolvency caseworkers – people who investigate the affairs of firms that have gone bankrupt and owe people a lot of money. The

manager organises the workload of the caseworkers and decides what will happen to each bankrupt firm.

The team manager makes sure the team is dealing with its cases quickly and efficiently and that the team spirit is maintained at all times.

Adapted from HM Customs & Excise website

! CHECKPOINT …

The best way to cover this outcome is to talk to people working in a local public service. Visit them yourself, or ask your tutor to arrange something!

PASSGRADE

Explain in detail the conditions of service of a given job within a public service.

Conditions of service include:
- the hours people work
- the pay they get
- their holidays
- the arrangements for sickness
- the rules about trade union membership
- their pensions.

The Prison Service

The Focus on the facing page shows the conditions of service for prison officers in October 2002. Salaries and some other details will change from time to time.

Other points

(a) The prison service is an equal opportunities employer. This means it cannot discriminate against officers because of their sex, race, etc.

(b) Prison officers are not allowed to belong to a trade union, or to go on strike. They can, however, belong to the Prison Officers' Association, which tries to improve their pay and conditions.

(c) The rates of pay increase steeply from grade to grade. This is to encourage prison officers to stay in the service and seek promotion.

FOCUS

CONDITIONS OF THE PRISON SERVICE

Salary

The salary range is £16,725 to £23,065; in addition, a local pay allowance of £1,000 to £3,500 may be paid for some establishments.

Pension

Pension benefits are provided under the Principal Civil Service Pension Scheme (PCSPS), which is contracted out of the state scheme. It is non-contributory, apart from $1\frac{1}{2}$% of salary for widow's/widower's benefits.

Hours

Weekly hours are an average 39 hours over the shift cycle, net of meal breaks. Meal breaks are unpaid. Additional hours worked are recompensed by time off in lieu.

As a Prison Officer you will be expected to work a variety of shifts including nights, weekends and some long days.

Part-time working

There are opportunities for part-time working and job-sharing.

Leave

The annual leave allowance is 22 days on entry, rising to 25 days after one year's service and 30 days after 18 years' service.

In addition, Prison Officers are entitled to 11 days in recognition of Bank, Public and Privilege holidays. These are added to the annual leave allowance.

Posting

You should be aware that once employed as a Prison Officer you can be required to work anywhere in England and Wales.

EQUAL OPPORTUNITIES

The Prison Service is an equal opportunities employer. We welcome applications from candidates regardless of ethnic origin, religious belief, gender, sexual orientation, disability or any other irrelevant factor.

Source: H M Prison Service website

! CHECKPOINT ...

Find out about the pay and conditions for other public services.

Applying for a job in the public services

PASSGRADE

Accurately describe the current entry and selection stages for a given public service.

Now we are going to look at how to get into the public services. This is something you need to know long before you actually apply.

If you know what to expect you can practise the various tests in the selection procedure, and build up your fitness. Then, when the time comes, you stand a better chance of getting in!

For this outcome you need to be accurate. This means being up to date, and giving the correct information.

Information about entry tests and selection procedures can be obtained from most public services, by writing to them, telephoning them, or looking up their websites on the Internet.

FOCUS

Entry to the Royal Navy as an Ordinary Seaman (rating)

First you have to go to the local Armed Forces Recruiting Office (see local telephone directory) and tell the officer there that you would like to join the Royal Navy.

If you seem to be the right kind of person the Royal Navy will invite you to go through the selection process. The selection process takes place at the local Armed Forces Careers Office. It has five stages:

Stage 1
General conversation with recruiting officer to ensure that you satisfy the nationality requirements.

Stage 2
A five-part questionnaire covering family details, school and education, work, hobbies and pastimes and why you want to join the Navy.

Stage 3

An academic test in four parts (reasoning, English Language, numeracy and mechanical comprehension) with multiple-choice questions.

Successful Artificer Apprentice candidates then take a further test of mental arithmetic. (This is if you wish to work with weapons.)

Stage 4

An interview lasting about 30–40 minutes. This usually takes place within 10 working days of successful completion of the first stage.

Stage 5

A medical examination.

All successful candidates must complete a security questionnaire. This includes a check against the National Criminal Records and a Credit Reference Check.

After successfully completing all stages, your application is forwarded to the Ministry of Defence. All applications are subject to Ministry of Defence approval.

Once a decision has been made, you will receive a letter telling you whether or not you have been selected to enter the Naval Service.

Source: © Crown Copyright/MoD

Complete an application form, letter of application and curriculum vitae for a job in a given public service.

The purpose of an application form for a public service is to show that you fulfil the entry requirements. Entry requirements for a public service are the qualifications, fitness, medical, nationality and character requirements that they want in their applicants.

FOCUS

ENTRY REQUIREMENTS FOR GLOUCESTERSHIRE CONSTABULARY

Age

You have to be at least 18 to apply to Gloucestershire Constabulary and $18\frac{1}{2}$ years old to join. There is no specific upper age limit.

Character

Only people of good character will be accepted as police officers.

Education

You should have a good education, preferably educated to GCSE/GCE, 'O' level, but formal qualifications are not essential. Regardless of qualifications, all applicants will need to pass the standard Police Initial Recruitment Test.

Eyesight

You must have unaided vision of at least 6/24 in each eye, which must be correctable with approved aids to 6/6 binocularly, each eye aided reaching a standard of at least 6/12.

Health

A good standard of health is needed and all applicants must undertake and pass a medical and fitness test that really tells us what shape you are in.

Height

There is no height restriction to join the Constabulary.

Nationality

Applicants must be British, Commonwealth or Irish Republic citizens.

Most applicants to public services are rejected because of the way they fill in their application forms. The aim of this outcome is to show you how it should be done.

Public service application forms are often long and complicated. Applicants to the police have to fill in several forms – they are given a month to do it.

Police application forms

1 Preliminary form

The purpose of this form is to obtain basic information about you. It has the following sections:

1 Details of candidate – your name, address, phone numbers, age, nationality.
2 Education – names of schools and colleges, and all examination results.
3 Any other applications being made to the police (you are not allowed to apply to more than one police force at a time).
4 Employment history – past jobs: addresses, nature of job, starting and finishing dates, reason for leaving. Your present job and employer.
5 Voluntary and community work.
6 Achievements – anything you feel proud of, and which could help you in your application.
7 Why you wish to join the police service and, in particular, the force to which you are applying.
8 Health – medical conditions that might affect your performance as a police officer.
9 Eyesight.
10 Convictions and cautions – in other words, your police record, if any.
11 Equal opportunity statement; gender and ethnic monitoring questions.
12 Declaration – that what you have said in the form is true.

2 Supplementary form

This asks for:

1 Previous addresses of applicant.
2 Two referees – not police officers, and not related to you.
3 Additional skills, e.g. driving licence, other language, swimming, first aid certificates.
4 Financial position. Are you in debt, and have you ever been in court because of debt?
5 Family details – parents' names at birth, date of birth, nationality at birth, nationality now, address, occupation. Similar questions are asked for brothers, sisters, husbands, wives, cohabitees, children and stepchildren.

3 Self-appraisal form

This asks questions like those you might get in the interview.

For example:

1 What do you think will be the most interesting and challenging aspects of police work?
2 What personal qualities do you possess that will make you a successful police officer?
3 What difficulties do you think you will have to overcome in adjusting to life in the police service?
4 What characteristics in yourself do you think other people find unattractive?
5 What qualities in yourself do you think are admired by people you know?
6 What, so far, has been the high spot or low spot in your life?
7 List any qualifications or awards you hold relating to spare-time activities, including details of any voluntary work carried out. Please give some details of not just 'reading' but the kind of books you read, not just 'sport' but the actual games you play and the extent of your involvement.
8 A police officer needs to be sensitive to the needs of others, being unselfish and willing to help any member of the general public. Give examples of where you have shown understanding and helped others.
9 A police officer needs to be punctual, reliable and to have high standards of honesty and integrity. Give an example of how you have displayed each of the above, in either a work situation, or a position of responsibility.
10 The majority of police officers work a rota of 10-hour shifts. (This obviously disrupts normal social activities.) How do you think this will affect you?
11 If you have a partner, have you discussed this application with him or her, considering the possible effects? How will you deal with this?
12 Once accepted to be a police officer you can be posted anywhere in the area, and this may mean moving house or leaving home. Do you have any experience of this?
13 In the course of your work you will be called upon to talk to an extremely wide range of

people. Obviously some situations will be easier to deal with than others. Below we have twelve types of people you may come across. Rate them on a scale of 1–10, 1 being easy to deal with and 10 being hard.

- prostitutes
- bereaved families
- juveniles
- drug addicts
- sexually abused
- the elderly
- the mentally ill
- physically abused
- civilian staff
- flea-ridden tramps
- sex offenders
- superior ranks

14 During your service how often do you think you will be assaulted each year? Twice; three times; more; no idea.

15 What are your long-term career plans? Do you want promotion? If you were still a constable at the end of your service would you feel that your career had been a success?

CHECKPOINT ...

What is the aim of an application form:
- (a) for the employer
- (b) for the applicant?

FOCUS

Advice on completing the application form (from the West Midlands Police)

It is in your own interest to complete this application form as accurately as possible. The information you supply will help us determine your suitability for appointment.

If any portion of this form is not completed, it may result in either the whole form being returned, a delay in your application or the possibility of your application not being considered. All forms must be returned within 28 days of receipt.

Please remember to:

- Complete the form clearly, using black ink.

- Use normal handwriting for all sections.

- Answer *all* questions by providing the required information or ticking the appropriate box. If any question or part of a question does not apply to you write 'NOT APPLICABLE'. Do not submit a

curriculum vitae as an alternative to completing sections of this form.

- Where possible please try to contain your answers within the space allocated. If you require more space continue on a separate sheet, indicating the question number it refers to.

- Ensure that you have signed the declaration on page 3.

Please return the Application Form to the address provided on the front page.

Here is some more advice.

Preliminary form

There are 12 sections on this form. The following points refer to each section in turn.

1 Write this clearly and carefully. It is surprising how many people misspell their own address!

2 Start with your secondary or high school. Put in all exam results, however bad the grades were!

3 As a student on a BTEC First Diploma you can write 'not applicable' for this section.

4 Put in work placement, part-time jobs and full-time jobs. Include the name of your employer and the kind of work you did, e.g. 'stacking shelves'. If you can't remember the exact dates, the month will do. Be honest about your reason for leaving.

5 This is unpaid work. Even if you regularly helped your neighbour with her shopping, or taught your friends how to play cricket, you could put these in. Youth club and charitable work would look good here.

6 Think hard about this section. Choose something that shows you made an effort and/or have a good character. You might have captained a team, organised a charity fundraising, helped at a road accident or even saved somebody's life. But it could be something like learning to drive, passing an exam or caring for someone.

7 This section is like the last one. You need to give it a lot of thought. Try to write up to 200 words on why you want to join the police force you are applying to. (They actually give you two-and-a-half pages to answer this one question!)

skill POWER

Here are things you could put in this section:

- You want an interesting and varied job which makes the most of your abilities.

- You want to do something useful with your life – something that will help other people.

- You enjoy working with people and feel you can be a good influence on them.

- You are a good team player.

- You also enjoy working on your own, and using your initiative.

- You are interested in people and how they behave.

- You want an active job which is not tied to a desk.

- You enjoy solving problems.

- You want to do a job that will make the world a better place.

- You enjoy meeting people from all backgrounds, cultures and age groups.

- You have always wanted to be a police officer.

- You want a career with good prospects and adequate pay.

- You have friends or relatives whom you admire, who are in the police.

- You are interested in preventing and fighting crime.

Remember to give evidence or examples to support some or all of these points.

You also need to say why you are applying to a particular force (say, the Metropolitan Police, Avon and Somerset Police – or whatever).

The smart thing to do is to study any booklets put out by that police force – especially annual reports or policing plans showing what their priorities (main aims) are. If they want to cut down on car crime, or racial hatred, then mention these things in this section, and show an interest in them.

Possible points you can add might be:

- You believe the force you are applying to is a good, progressive force, which will give you an excellent grounding in the skills and knowledge of policing.

- The area is diverse socially and ethnically, and will be an interesting place in which to work.

- You have read about the force in their annual report, *Police Review*, etc, and were impressed with what it said.

8 Health problems that might stop you getting into the police include asthma, diabetes, eyesight defects, epilepsy, cartilage removal, organ transplant, and poor hearing.

9 Eyesight

10 The police want to know if you have any present or past convictions. This means all convictions even if they were very minor, or if they happened a long time ago and have 'expired'.

11 You have to sign that you understand and agree with the police's equal opportunities policy, and answer questions about your gender and nationality.

12 You sign that what you have written on the form is true.

Supplementary form

This form is straightforward since it asks for facts which you either know, or can ask your family about.

If your parent is retired, say what he or she used to be, e.g. 'retired textile worker'.

Self-appraisal form

This form is very difficult to complete, because you have to (a) think about yourself in a mature and honest way and (b) express your ideas in a clear and thoughtful manner. It is important because the questions – and your answers – will probably be used in your interview.

You should try to show that you are:
- intelligent
- honest
- caring
- streetwise
- compassionate
- firm
- unselfish
- culturally aware
- not racist or sexist.

> **! CHECKPOINT ...**
>
> With a friend, decide how you would answer the questions on the self-appraisal form.

Letter of application

For most public service jobs you do not have to write a letter of application. The only letter you normally have to write is like this:

> 11 High Street
> Lowborough
> Anytown
> AN12 9GH
> South Yorkshire
>
> 12 October 2003
>
> Recruitment
> East Loamshire Police
> PO Box 666
> Letsby Avenue
> Loamtown LO1 4DJ
>
> Dear Sir or Madam
>
> Could you please send me application forms and information for the post of Police Constable, as currently advertised on your website.
>
> Yours faithfully
>
> M Akram

However, a full letter of application can be useful for some jobs, or if you want to arrange a work placement with a public service which interests you.

> 32 Fleet Street
> Weston on Sea
> Suffolk
> WS23 4WH
> 23 October 2003
>
> HM Customs and Excise
> Colne Docks
> Watergate
> Essex
> WG1 2PS
>
> Dear Sir or Madam
>
> **Application for work placement**
>
> Recently I was looking at the Careers Service website, and I found a section on careers in HM Customs and Excise. They seemed very interesting and I am therefore writing to you in the hope that you might offer me a work placement.
>
> I am 16 years old and a student on the BTEC First Diploma in Public Services course at Bagthorpe College. I have always been interested in doing some kind of public service work, and I now feel that working in HM Customs and Excise would suit me best of all.
>
> I went to school at Weston High School where I obtained a B in PE and Ds in GCSE English, Maths, French and Combined Sciences. I am now working hard to build on these grades on my Public Service course, which I find very interesting. I have gained merits and distinctions for the assignments I have finished so far, and I am up to date on all the others.
>
> While at Weston High School I also successfully completed my Duke of Edinburgh Silver Award and I have started now on the Gold.
>
> My main interests are horse-riding and athletics, and last year I came fourth in a regional show-jumping competition at Colchester. But in my career I would rather work with people than animals.
>
> I have done work experience with the Weston Fire Service, based at the regional headquarters for a week in March 2003. I practised hose-running and

took part in an exercise where we had to lower an injured person from a window on a stretcher. After the work experience they gave me a certificate of merit, and I am enclosing a photocopy of it with this letter.

I also have a weekend job at Patel's Newsagents, where I fill shelves, serve the public, help with the stocktaking and organise the paper rounds on Sunday mornings. I have been doing this job since November 2002.

Having read about Customs and Excise I know that some of the work you do involves combating smuggling at ports, and ensuring that people who import things like drinks and cigarettes are doing it legally and paying the necessary duties. I also know that you are involved in VAT collection and inspections. Both these aspects of your work would interest me very much, and I would really appreciate a work placement in one of these areas. I do not know how long the placements could be, but I would be able to do up to two weeks, and would be able to travel to the placement. The only time I would not be able to do it would be the week beginning 15 March 2004 – when the BTEC First Diploma students are going on a residential course in Wales.

Please find enclosed a copy of my CV, a copy of my Fire Service Certificate of Merit, and a testimonial from Mrs Patel. I also enclose a stamped, self-addressed envelope for your reply.

Yours faithfully

Mary Whitehouse

Encs.

FOCUS

Advice on letters of application

- They are best done in black ink, in your own handwriting. Failing that, they can be done on a computer, in Times New Roman or Arial font (size 12) – but don't forget to sign them!

- Use the layout shown in this book. There is no need to put commas in the addresses, or after 'Dear Sir or Madam' and 'Yours faithfully'.

- Always write them out in rough first. Get a tutor or some other reliable person to look them over, and suggest improvements.

- Try to show that you are (a) enthusiastic; (b) reliable; (c) capable of doing the kind of work you are interested in; and (d) able to work with others.

- Always say that you are enjoying your course (even if you're not).

- Put in one or two past achievements.

- Mention any work experience.

- Show that you are healthy and fit by mentioning a sport or physical activity.

- Always include a CV and a stamped, self-addressed envelope.

Curriculum Vitae (CV)

A curriculum vitae is an outline, in table form, of the information about you which would interest a future employer.

As most public services make you fill in application forms, you do not normally need to send a CV to them unless you are applying for a work placement (or a voluntary public service).

Profile

Curriculum Vitae

FAMILY NAME:	Whitehouse	**OTHER NAMES:**	Mary Louise
ADDRESS:	32 Fleet Street Weston on Sea Suffolk WS23 4WH	**TELEPHONE:**	01326 839625
DATE OF BIRTH:	16 November 1987	**NATIONALITY:**	British

EDUCATION:

Date	School/college	Qualifications with grades
09/1997 – 06/2003:	Weston High School	**GCSEs** English Language D English Literature E Mathematics D French D Geography E Combined Sciences D Craft, Design and Technology E PE B Religious Studies F
09/2003 – present:	Bagthorpe College	**BTEC First Diploma in Public Services** Result not yet available

EMPLOYMENT (most recent first)

Date	Employer	Responsibilities	Reason for leaving
March 2003 (for two weeks)	Weston Fire Service	Work placement: observation and piloting exercises	End of placement (after two weeks)
November 2002 – present	Patel's Newsagents, High Street, Upper Weston	Filling shelves, helping customers, working on till, stocktaking, supervising paper deliveries	Not applicable
November 2001	Patel's Newsagents	Paper girl – delivering Sunday papers	Became shop assistant in November 2002

OTHER ACTIVITIES/ INTERESTS

1997–2002: Member of Guides. Went on walking and canoeing activities.

2002: Successfully completed Duke of Edinburgh Silver Award and started on Gold Award.

1998 onwards: Voluntary work at Nevada Riding Stables, Weston (grooming, cleaning stables, helping new riders).

June 2002: Came fourth in Junior section of regional show-jumping competition at Colchester, Essex.

I have represented my school and college as a middle distance runner in athletics competitions.

REFEREES

The following people, who are not related to me, would be willing to act as referees:

1. Mrs Amina Patel
Patel's Newsagents
High Street
Upper Weston
WS23 5WH

2. Mr David Beckham
Course Tutor
BTEC First Diploma in Public Services
Bagthorpe College
East Road
Bagthorpe
BG3 8RG

Signed (Your signature): ....   Date: ....

SUPERGRADE! *Merit*

> Complete a simulated application and selection process accurately and within given timescales.

For this outcome you pretend to be a candidate for a public service and do all the mock tests to get into that service.

They will be arranged by your tutors – perhaps with the help of a friendly public service.

The word 'accurately' means you must do your best in each of the stages, and not miss bits out or make mistakes.

Now we are going to look at some of the things you will have to do for this outcome.

The selection process

Interviews

The secret of preparing for interviews is – preparing for interviews! So this is what you do …

Before the interview

1 Learn as much as you can about the job and the organisation you are applying for. If you are applying for the West Yorkshire police, find out about West Yorkshire and the West Yorkshire police. Where is West Yorkshire? How many people live there? What sorts of jobs do they do? What cultures and ethnic groups live there? What are the main types of crime in West Yorkshire? What does it say in the West Yorkshire Policing Plan? Who is the Chief Constable? How many police officers are there in West Yorkshire, and how many are women or from ethnic minority groups?

2 Think about yourself and what you have to offer. What are your strengths and weaknesses? Why do you want to join the police? Why is it important to fight crime? What special skills – e.g. driving, languages – do you have which would help you in the job? Do you get on with people? Are you physically fit? Have you done voluntary work? Have you done paid work that will help you with police work? How did you first become interested in joining the police?

3 Collect evidence of your good qualities. Make sure your Record of Achievement contains plenty of certificates, work placement reports, testimonials, exam results, and other things that give a fuller and more truthful picture of what you are really like. It isn't enough to say, 'I have good leadership qualities' unless you can back it up. For example, if you were captain of a football team, make sure you remember the team's name, and when you were its captain!

- Think of all the questions you might be asked, then write them down. When you have done that, write down the answers you would give. This may sound like hard work, but when it comes to the interview you will be really glad you did it, because your mind will be calm and focused, and you will express yourself well.
- Ensure you know when and where the interview is.
- Dress smartly.
- Arrive 20 minutes early.
- Get a good night's sleep before the interview.

In the interview

- Greet your interviewers with a handshake and a smile.

- Make frequent eye contact with your interviewers, but do not stare at them.
- Sit up straight and keep your hands away from your face.
- Speak clearly and loudly, and avoid slang.
- If you didn't hear or understand the question, ask the interviewer to repeat it.
- When you've said what you need to say, finish speaking and wait for the next question.
- Never lose your temper.
- Think of a question of your own to ask at the end of the interview. It could, for example, be about promotion, training, where you might be posted, or when you might hear the result of the interview.
- At the end, say 'thank you very much', and leave.

Fitness test

LINK! Read about fitness tests on pages 53–54.

Extended assessment

In real life this takes two or three days at a selection centre. On your course you are more likely to do a few exercises which test your ability to solve problems and work with others.

LINK! Problem-solving and teamwork are discussed on pages 26 and 36–37.

They may be like this one:

FOCUS

The 'Carousel'

The applicant goes from one room to the next, acting out a series of different situations. In the first room, the candidate might be a store detective, and the actor a mother who has lost her child in the store. The candidate has to get the information, calm the 'mother' and arrange for the child to be found. In the second, the candidate might 'find' a person lying on the floor in the bus station, and have to take appropriate action. And so on …

The aim is to test whether you are practical and caring, and can keep calm in an emergency.

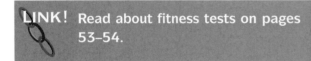
SUPERGRADE! *Distinction*

Provide a detailed analysis of the roles, jobs and selection process of a given public service.

LINK! Roles and jobs are dealt with on pages 3–6.

Selection process for Greater Manchester Police

The recruitment procedure for the Greater Manchester Police is shown in the figure on page 17.

For a detailed analysis you need to give full information about each stage, and explain what the purpose and importance of each stage is.

LINK! Detailed information about police application forms is given on pages 9–12.

Stage 1 – Application forms and paper sift

The purpose of the application form is to enable applicants to show that they are suitable for the police, and to give the police plenty of information about the applicant.

Police application forms are long and complex, and ask for a great deal of information. This:
- saves time and money that would be wasted by recruiting the wrong type of person
- cuts security risks
- ensures that applicants understand the nature and importance of the job.

It is vitally important for the applicant to fill in the application forms as fully, accurately and thoughtfully as possible.

In the paper sift the police sort through the forms to see what they like and don't like about each candidate. They get many more applications than there are vacancies, and most candidates are turned down. It would be a waste of money to try to interview every applicant.

Stage 2 – Basic physical tests, initial entrance tests and other questionnaires

There are now no official height restrictions for the police, but height and weight are measured because there must be a suitable relationship between the two. In other words, applicants must not be too thin or too fat. Eyesight tests are to ensure that police can function without spectacles or contact lenses. Colour vision tests ensure that they are less likely to make mistakes when observing or describing incidents (e.g. the clothes suspects are wearing).

The usual initial entrance test is the Police Initial Recruitment test (PIR) – though some forces are trying other tests.

The PIR is a multiple choice test divided into the following sections:

Verbal usage – 12 minutes
Checking test – 8 minutes
Working with number – 12 minutes
Verbal reasoning – 25 minutes
Observation – about 20 minutes.

For the first four parts applicants have to read the questions and answer them. For the last part they have to watch a short video of a crime scene and remember important details. The purpose of the test is to check levels of literacy, numeracy, speed of thinking and accuracy – since police work needs all these skills. The questionnaires give further information about the applicant's personality and character.

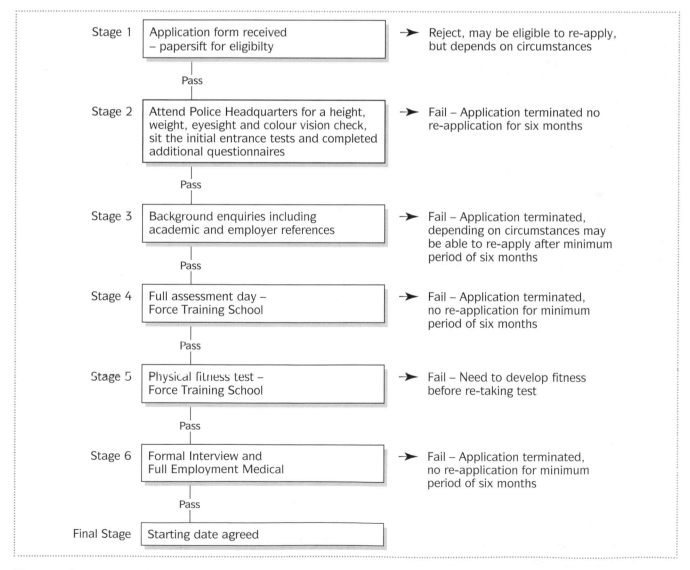

Stage 1	Application form received – papersift for eligibilty	→	Reject, may be eligible to re-apply, but depends on circumstances
	Pass		
Stage 2	Attend Police Headquarters for a height, weight, eyesight and colour vision check, sit the initial entrance tests and completed additional questionnaires	→	Fail – Application terminated no re-application for six months
	Pass		
Stage 3	Background enquiries including academic and employer references	→	Fail – Application terminated, depending on circumstances may be able to re-apply after minimum period of six months
	Pass		
Stage 4	Full assessment day – Force Training School	→	Fail – Application terminated, no re-application for minimum period of six months
	Pass		
Stage 5	Physical fitness test – Force Training School	→	Fail – Need to develop fitness before re-taking test
	Pass		
Stage 6	Formal Interview and Full Employment Medical	→	Fail – Application terminated, no re-application for minimum period of six months
	Pass		
Final Stage	Starting date agreed		

The recruitment procedure for the Greater Manchester Police

> ! ■ **CHECKPOINT ...**
> Contact a police force that is recruiting and ask them for their applicants' pack. They should send you all the forms, and practice questions for the PIRT.

Stage 3 – Background inquiries

The police now carefully check the backgrounds of their applicants. They want to know if:

- applicants have criminal records they have not declared on the form
- their families or friends are criminals
- they belong to political organisations such as the National Front, which do not always respect the law, or which disagree with the police's equal opportunities policy
- they do not fulfil the nationality requirements
- they have terrorist links.

The inquiries are done by (a) checking through police records, (b) studying references given by former teachers, employers, etc. They need to be done to protect the security of the police, and to ensure that police officers can be trusted by their colleagues and by the public.

Stage 4 – Full assessment day

Applicants who are still in the running spend a full day being observed and assessed while they carry out a range of activities and tests. The aim of these tasks is to see how the applicants relate to each other, and whether they show teamwork and leadership qualities. They want people who can listen as well as speak, who are confident yet open-minded and willing to learn.

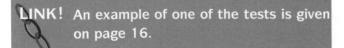
LINK! An example of one of the tests is given on page 16.

Stage 5 – Physical fitness test

This tests endurance, speed and agility, dynamic strength and grip strength. These fitness qualities are all needed in police work – for example when arresting somebody who is violent. Endurance is

also needed in the long shifts the police have to work. There are, however, no fixed pass standards for these tests. This may be because the police are not always looking for the same kinds of recruits, or because physical fitness is not necessarily the most important quality for a police officer.

Stage 6 – Formal interview and medical

The interview is by a panel of three police officers. It lasts about half an hour and they ask searching questions, based on what they have learned about the applicant from the forms they have filled in – especially the self-appraisal form. Some of the interviewers may be taking notes and recording impressions rather than asking questions. The interviewers are interested not only in what candidates say, but also in the way they say it. They study tone of voice and body language to help them make an assessment of the applicant's personality.

Medical examination

Police officers need to be in excellent health if they are to do their difficult and demanding job. Certain medical conditions, such as asthma, epilepsy, or serious past injuries, could prevent a police officer from doing the job properly. People who are rejected for health reasons might still be able to work for the police – but only as civilian employees, not police officers.

C**OO**L SITES:

www.west-midlands.police.uk/
recruitment/police_fitness.htm

www.gmp-recruitment.co.uk/uniform.html

PASSGRADE

> Describe in detail the initial training programme for a given public service.

Initial training is the first period of training that recruits are given after they have joined a public service. It is sometimes called basic training.

For this outcome you need to research the initial training programme for one public service.

FOCUS

Army basic training

Most soldiers attend basic training at any Army Training Regiment (ATR). This normally lasts 12 weeks. This basic course trains recruits in the skills common to all soldiers in the Army. After basic training, soldiers go on to complete specialist training with the arm or service they chose to join. Those aged between 16 and 17 years 1 month can go to the Army Foundation College (AFC) and follow the 42-week course. It covers the basic military skills and develops fitness, teamwork, self-discipline and leadership through challenging activities such as abseiling, canoeing and climbing. Qualifications are also gained in six key/core skills.

These are the main skills learned in army basic training for soldiers.

A: *Fieldcraft*: how to look after yourself and your equipment; how to live in the field, and how to observe, detect and report an enemy.

B: *Weapon training*: how to use and fire the SA80 rifle at distances of up to 300 metres.

C: *Map reading, first aid and defensive measures against NBC (Nuclear, Biological and Chemical) warfare.*

D: *Military education, military history, welfare and financial advice.*

E: *Recreation, adventurous and initiative training*: outdoor pursuits, including team sports and 'Outward Bound' activities aimed at character development.

F: *Physical fitness and endurance training*: as well as the organised sport in the training programme, there is time to enjoy the many facilities of the ATR. All have gymnasiums and squash courts, and there is plenty of opportunity to play team games.

G: *Drill:* foot and arms drill building up to the Passing Out Parade, which relatives and friends will be invited to attend.

H: *Administration*: throughout the ATR training, the aim is to build up your basic military knowledge and skills, step by step, to a point where you can undertake specialist training and then take your place as part of the Field Army. Your fitness training at the ATR is also progressive. It aims to build up fitness, stamina, strength and endurance. On successful completion of initial training, recruits go on to complete their military trade or employment training. This is known as Phase 2 Training.

Source: © Crown Copyright/MoD

CºOL SITES:

www.staffordshire.police.uk/ probation.htm

www.policecouldyou.co.uk/ careers_in_the_police/training.html

A police training exercise

! ## CHECKPOINT ...

(a) Contact any public service you are interested in, and ask them about their initial training.

(b) Talk to someone who has done initial training in a public service – and find out what it was really like!

SUPERGRADE! *Merit*

Make considered comments about their own suitability to complete basic training for their career development.

For this outcome you should do something which trainees in public services do all the time – carry out a self-appraisal. This means looking at yourself, honestly, and deciding how suitable you are to do the basic training in the public service of your choice.

You could do this in the form of a profile:

Profile

Name: Abdul Aziz
Subject: My suitability for army basic training.

Aspect of training	Comments on my suitability
Fieldcraft	I have enjoyed outdoor activities and the camping we did in Snowdonia. I was good at pitching tents but not very good at cooking. I don't mind bad weather and hard work, so I think I would enjoy this and be quite good at it.
Weapon training	I went on a 'Look at life' day with the army and did some target shooting. I thought it was great! That might be because I did very well and got some good scores.
Map reading, first aid and defensive measures against NBC (Nuclear, Biological and Chemical) warfare	At the moment I am not very good at map reading, so this is something I would have to work at to improve. I understand the symbols but I find grid references difficult. For first aid I should do OK, as I passed the First Aid certificate first time round at the beginning of the year. Defensive measures against NBC sounds a bit scary, but I am quite practical and good with my hands, so I should be able to manage with the gas masks, etc.
Military education, military history, welfare and financial advice	I don't really like listening to lectures so I might find this part a bit boring. I like history but I hope they don't look at it from just the British angle. I would like to know more about what happened in Afghanistan. Financial advice sounds useful – it might stop me from borrowing from my mates!
Recreation, adventurous and initiative training	I love abseiling and rock climbing, so I would really look forward to this part of the training.
Physical fitness and endurance training	Since I am keen on cricket and football, and play for some college teams, I am already fairly fit. But the army has really good equipment and I would enjoy this part of the training.
Drill	I have no experience of marching, so I don't know if I would enjoy this or not.
Administration	I'm not too sure what this is, but I would try my best.
General comments	My main worries would be: (a) I might get a bit homesick on basic training, because it would be the first time I had spent as much as 12 weeks away from home. (b) As I am a Muslim I am not sure if I would be able to get halal food.

PASSGRADE

Produce an action plan for career development.

Let us imagine a 16-year-old BTEC Public Service student. Her name is Emma Bovary. She wants to join the police when she is about 20, and to be promoted to at least the rank of inspector. What sort of plan should Emma make?

Here is a suggestion.

- She should start off by considering her present position, using a SWOT analysis. This means looking closely at her **S**trengths, **W**eaknesses, **O**pportunities and **T**hreats.

Profile

Emma Bovary
Date: 12 Dec. 03
SWOT analysis for career

STRENGTHS
- Determined to join police.
- Am studying a police-orientated public service course.
- Am physically healthy and fit and like sport.
- Am quite good at English, interested in psychology.
- I can make friends, and people like telling me their secrets.
- Have no criminal record.

WEAKNESSES
- Too keen on dancing, raving, etc.
- Smoking.
- I get impatient with teachers who go on a lot.
- I only got a D in GCSE Maths.
- I'm a bit overweight, despite being so active.

OPPORTUNITIES
- It's the right time of year to contact the police for a work placement.
- They're looking for a part-time youth leader down at the club.
- I could volunteer to train a girls' football team at Brierley Middle School (my cousin teaches there).
- There's a new gym opened at Oldthorpe: I could go there and get properly fit.

THREATS
- I might want to take a year out and travel round the world as soon as I've finished my BTEC.
- I could start getting slack about assignments and deadlines: they seem to be piling them on at the moment, and people who hand them in late are still getting graded.

Emma can use her SWOT analysis as a starting point for her action plan for career development. She then needs to write herself a timetable.

To be realistic, her timetable should not stretch too far into the future, nor should it pretend that she can do things which she cannot. A realistic action plan is one which the planner believes in.

But being realistic needn't mean being limited and unambitious. If you want something, you should believe in yourself and go for it!

Emma's action plan is shown on the next page.

The main thing to note is that, on the whole, Emma chooses activities which will help her to get into the police. They will either help her to pass the entrance procedures, or they will look good on her CV.

This outcome asks you to look at your strengths and weaknesses, and work out how they may influence your future public service career.

> ## ! CHECKPOINT ...
> Make your own action plan for career development – then discuss it with a friend and/or your tutor.

SUPERGRADE! *Distinction*

Evaluate both the potential and the limitations for their own career development within their chosen public service.

skill POWER

For this outcome you need to:
- examine your own strengths and weaknesses
- know the career (or rank) structure of your chosen public service
- understand the qualities needed for promotion
- outline how job specifications change as you get promoted up the rank structure
- say how your strengths and weaknesses might affect your career development
- indicate the possible limits to your ability or your ambition.

By age	Action/target	Outcome
17	(a) Apply for work placement with police.	(a) If successful, make good use of placement. If not, reapply, or try another public service.
	(b) Stop smoking.	(b) Good for health and pocket.
	(c) Start fitness training at gym.	(c) Good for health.
	(d) Start training football team.	(d) Will look good on CV.
	(e) Aim for distinctions on my course.	(e) Good for CV.
	(f) Start learning to drive.	(f) Has to be done.
18	(a) Apply to work in special constabulary.	(a) Increase chances of getting in to police.
	(b) Retake GCSE maths.	(b) Pass – I hope!
	(c) Will complete BTEC National in Public Service. Keep working for distinctions.	(c) Uni? I don't think I'll want to go, but would it help me to get into the police?
	(d) Pass driving test.	(d) Or retake? I mustn't give up, whatever happens.
19	(a) Apply for the police. There are some people who get in at 19.	(a) This is what I would like – but will I be too young? They might think I'm not mature enough.
	(b) If I don't apply, I'll get a full-time job. I feel I need more experience of life. What kind of job? Retail?	(b) This idea is a poor second best. Needs more thought.
	(c) If I don't get a job, should I go round the world?	(c) NO – seems like running away. I shouldn't do this, and I probably won't want to when the time comes.

FOCUS
EXAMPLES OF RANK STRUCTURES IN UNIFORMED PUBLIC SERVICES
– HIGHEST RANKS AT THE BOTTOM

Metropolitan Police
- Constable
- Sergeant
- Inspector
- Chief Inspector
- Superintendent
- Chief Superintendent
- Commander
- Deputy Assistant Commissioner
- Assistant Commissioner
- Deputy Commissioner
- Commissioner

Other police
- Constable
- Sergeant
- Inspector
- Chief Inspector
- Superintendent
- Chief Superintendent
- Assistant Chief Constable
- Chief Constable

Army (soldiers)
- Private
- Lance Corporal
- Corporal
- Sergeant
- Staff Sergeant
- Warrant Officer

Fire Service
- Firefighter
- Leading Firefighter
- Sub-Officer
- Station Officer
- Assistant Divisional Officer
- Divisional Officer Grade III
- Divisional Officer Grade II
- Divisional Officer Grade I
- Senior Divisional Officer
- Assistant Chief Officer/Assistant Firemaster
- Chief Officer/Firemaster

22

Here is an example:

Profile

Name: Silas Onyango
Preferred Career: Fire Service

1 Analysis of my present strengths and weaknesses

Strengths:	Weaknesses:
November 2003	November 2003
• Good at sports, especially football and middle-distance running.	• Not as good as I should be at spelling.
• Very interested in the fire service after a successful work placement, and the promise of help from them with my Duke of Edinburgh's Gold Award.	• Need to increase speed and confidence in mental arithmetic. • Handwriting scruffy. • Sometimes prefer socialising to getting down to work!
• Good at English; have gained merits and distinctions in some assignments.	• Tend to waste money on smart clothes. • I can be too keen on the sound of my own voice.
• Good mechanic; have reconditioned a motorbike.	• I lend too much money to my friends, and don't get enough of it back.
• Enjoy teamwork, and was elected as student representative for Course Team meetings.	
• Prepared to work anywhere.	

2 The career structure of the fire service

(see opposite page)

3 My potential and limitations for career development in the fire service

I know that it is extremely difficult to get into the fire service, because they only recruit every two years and there are a huge number of applications for every vacancy. ▮▮▮▶

Nevertheless I believe I have the potential to get into the fire service because I am extremely highly motivated, and am physically fitter than the average. After my work placement at Anytown Fire Station I was told by Mr S. Parks, the Station Officer, that I was one of the best work placement trainees they had ever had from Anytown FE College. Of course, I do not know what the others were like!

I enjoy teamwork, and firefighting is a job in which teamwork is of vital importance. You have to be able to trust your colleagues, and they have to be able to trust you. I liked the people I met at the fire station, and if all firefighters are like them, I will be very happy.

You have to have some mechanical ability to work in the fire service, and you need to understand such things as electricity, and building methods. I helped my dad to re-wire the house. I think this adds to my potential for becoming a firefighter.

My weaknesses include scruffy handwriting and lack of confidence in mental arithmetic: these are both things that I will have to improve if I get into the fire service, since people's lives can be lost through stupid arithmetical errors, or because somebody can't read something you have written. But though my spelling is not perfect I am certainly not dyslexic, and I'm sure I can improve it.

I think the fact that I belong to an ethnic minority may help me to get into the fire service, but I would certainly not want or expect them to lower their standards for me.

After I get into the fire service I would like to be considered for promotion after a few years – if I show the ability. But I do not want to get promoted so far that I end up doing a desk job – at least, not until I am over forty. In fact I would consider my career to be successful if I became a leading firefighter. I would like to be expert at dealing with major incidents or road traffic accidents, and be trusted by my fellow firefighters.

23

Some firefighters don't want promotion – they like to be where the action is!

! CHECKPOINT ...

■ Self-assessment – sometimes called 'self-appraisal' – is used a great deal in public service training. Try looking at your own potential, as Silas has done, in relation to the public service career of your choice.

Unit 2 Public Service Skills

Grading criteria

PASSGRADE	SUPERGRADE! *Merit*	SUPERGRADE! *Distinction*
To achieve a pass grade the evidence must show that the learner is able to:	To achieve a merit grade the evidence must show that the learner is able to:	To achieve a distinction grade the evidence must show that the learner is able to:
● explain the importance of teamwork in at least two different public services **26**	● present considered comments and explanations on the five qualities of effective teamwork **29**	● evaluate the use of teamwork and communication skills in public services **29**
● describe at least five qualities of effective teamwork in the two different public services **27**	● demonstrate responsibility within roles during team activities **40**	● demonstrate exceptional teamwork, interpersonal, personal effectiveness and communication skills **40**
● actively participate in at least five different team activities **32**	● explain the importance of effective communication skills in the public services **44**	● critically analyse the importance of effective communication skills in the public services **45**
● describe the importance of interpersonal skills and personal effectiveness for public service work **32**		
● describe the importance of effective communication skills in the public services **41**		
● demonstrate a range of communication skills used in the public services **46**		

This unit shows you how to work effectively with other people.

Teams

A team is a small group of people who work together.

The way they work together – helping, supporting, motivating and disciplining each other – is called teamwork.

The aims of teamwork are:

(a) to achieve the best possible results
(b) in the quickest possible time
(c) with the least effort and expense
(d) without cheating or breaking the rules
(e) and without destroying the team.

PASSGRADE

> Explain the importance of teamwork in at least two different public services.

Teamwork

All public services make use of teamwork in order to achieve their aims and carry out tasks. This is because people work faster and better in teams. Most people also prefer to work in a team, rather than as isolated individuals.

Teams come in many shapes and sizes in the public services. Large teams may consist of several smaller teams working together. Teams can be defined according to the kind of job they do, the public service they work in, the kind of leadership they have and the length of time they last. Types of teams which exist in the public services include:

- Crews. A crew is usually all the people who work on board a ship. It consists of officers and ratings. The officers provide leadership and management, and the ratings carry out their commands. The crew remains a team as long as it remains together – and at least for as long as one voyage or operation. The word 'crew' is also used on aircraft, and for rescue teams – especially those which operate in helicopters.

- Shift work. A shift is a group of people who work for a certain number of set hours in the day. It might be from 9 to 5, but it might be between other hours of the day, or at night. In the public services shifts often change from week to week, so the team that works on a night shift one week will work on a day shift another week. People working the same shift work together as teams. The police and ambulance services use shift systems.

- Watches. A watch is a shift in the fire service. The same people always work together. Fire service watches are named after colours, e.g. 'blue watch'.

- Regiments. A regiment is a large group of teams in the army. 'The Regiment is often considered to be the most important unit in the British Army. It carries the spirit of the people who have gone before and would usually contain approximately 650 soldiers depending on its cap badge and role.' (See www.army.mod.uk/unitsandorgs/subsections/index.htm)

- Multi-agency teams. These are teams consisting of members of more than one public service. For example, teams dealing with young offenders may consist of the police, probation workers, social workers and youth workers who all work together to help young people who have offended or are at risk of offending.

- Specialist teams. These have tasks which need special knowledge and skills. 'The Art & Antiques Unit was set up in 1984 and is based at New Scotland Yard. The officers in the unit are trained to investigate offences involving art, antiques, collectibles and cultural property. The team works closely with similar units throughout the world to combat the illicit trade in stolen art and cultural property. Databases are maintained to gather intelligence on suspected art thieves and handlers, and also a stolen art database (ACIS).' (Metropolitan Police; www.met.police.uk/so/so6.htm)

The Army

Teamwork is essential:

(a) for the success of the army
(b) for the well-being of the people who work in it.

Teamwork benefits the army because it:

1 **achieves organisational objectives**. The work of the army – training, peacekeeping, relief work and operations – is done by teams who work closely together, and get the maximum results for the effort they put in. Using teamwork, more work is done by fewer people so the work gets done faster and lives and money are saved.

2 **is good for camaraderie, morale and discipline**. Camaraderie is 'team spirit' – the pleasure of working with people who you like and respect. Morale is a mixture of enthusiasm, courage, confidence and determination, and an army which has good morale will always fight better than one which has poor morale. Discipline is good organisation, high standards and a willingness to follow orders. It is based on the respect which team workers have for each other and for their leaders.

3 **is good for command and control**. Teams have leaders who communicate with the leaders of other teams, and with officers higher up the rank structure. An effective team is good at carrying out orders, but it is also good at feeding information up the organisation to the officers in charge. This means that decisions are based on knowledge, not ignorance. Within the team there should be good communication between the leader and the team members, and between the team members themselves. People therefore know what they should be doing, and an organisation made of effective teams can react quickly and firmly to any challenge.

4 **is good for problem solving**. Good teamwork encourages people to share their knowledge and ideas. It often happens that different team members have different strengths and skills. They can pool their knowledge and ideas to solve problems. This is sometimes called 'combing individual skills'.

5 **enables team members to support each other**. Members look out for each other, because they know them personally. This is important in dangerous situations – above all when the army is fighting. Team members can help each other at times of stress, giving encouragement and comfort – since, at times, a team can work a bit like a family. Teamwork also supports people by allowing them to develop skills, such as leadership skills, in a real-life setting. Belonging to a team also helps to get rid of ethnic, cultural and class differences, and tends to stop bullying and discrimination.

> **! ■ CHECKPOINT …**
>
> For this outcome you have to look at two public services.
>
> Using similar key points to those given above, make notes on the importance of teamwork in another public service.

Teamwork is essential in the armed forces

PASSGRADE

> Describe at least five qualities of effective teamwork in the two different public services.

Effective teamwork is teamwork that brings good results. In the public services, it also benefits the public.

The aim of this outcome is to help you recognise effective teamwork when you see it.

Seven qualities of effective teamwork in the fire service

1 Good leadership

A fire service team is called a 'watch' and is led by a leading firefighter. The role of the leading firefighter is to direct, organise and motivate the team, and communicate with the 'bosses' higher up the organisation. The leading firefighter has to:

- know the team
- share their aims
- have knowledge, expertise and experience which the team can use
- have a character which the team can respect and admire
- have the ability to listen to the team
- be able to make good decisions
- be steady and trustworthy
- be caring and helpful towards team members
- encourage high professional standards
- be a good communicator
- have good management skills – motivating, disciplining and rewarding the team as appropriate.

2 Commitment

Commitment is determination – sticking at a task until it is finished. This is very important in the fire service where, if a fire is not properly put out, it starts again. In major fires, explosions and chemical leaks, firefighters have to work for long periods of time in hard conditions (sometimes taking numerous short breaks to recover from heat, dehydration or exhaustion before going back to work).

3 Loyalty/Trust

These are similar to camaraderie. Loyalty means sticking up for your colleagues and for the organisation you work for. Where a team is loyal, the members can trust each other. Trust means

knowing that other team members will behave and respond to challenges by always giving of their best, and not letting anybody down.

4 Cooperation

A team – such as watch in the fire service – needs people who work together, not individualists who are just looking for a chance to show off. Cooperation means 'working together'. Sometimes this means physical work, because there are many jobs in the fire service which cannot be done by one person alone – one person wouldn't be strong enough (carrying a stretcher is a simple example). Cooperation is also needed to get a fast response – everyone in the watch has to know their job and do it, in order to save time in those vital first minutes.

5 Identity

A watch has an identity – its colour – and members of the watch share a loyalty to each other as well as the fire service. This identity is a 'team spirit' which shows itself in a determination to be better than other teams. This is why watches in the fire service often compete in a friendly manner – for example in sport, but also in their speed and standard of work.

6 Norms

Norms are types of behaviour that people in a team often share. If the team works well these norms are good qualities – such as efficiency and determination. But it is possible for teams to work less well (for example, if the leadership is poor). Standards of behaviour and achievement drop – and it may be that laziness and sloppiness become norms. But this rarely happens in the fire service.

7 Good communication

This means giving and receiving information quickly, clearly and accurately. In the fire service most communication takes the form of listening and speaking. Good communication in a watch must be:

(a) between all the members of the watch. They must understand each other well and quickly when working together in an emergency, and be able to learn from each other during training.

(b) between the watch and the public. They must listen to complaints, questions, appeals for help, etc, and give clear instructions and advice.

(c) between the watch and other people in the fire service – e.g. divisional.

(d) between firefighters and other public services such as the police and ambulance services headquarters, firefighters from other divisions and retained (volunteer) firefighters.

> ## ! ■ CHECKPOINT ...
> Take five of the teamwork qualities described above, and show how they are used in a public service other than the fire service.

SUPERGRADE! Merit

> Present considered comments and explanations on the five qualities of effective teamwork.

A 'considered comment' can be:

- an example
- a clarification (e.g. of a difficult word or idea)
- a reason
- an explanation
- anything which shows that you have 'considered' (thought carefully about) the qualities of effective teamwork.

> ## ! ■ CHECKPOINT ...
> There are already some considered comments in the descriptions of qualities of effective teamwork given above.
> (a) Identify these.
> (b) Add others of your own.

SUPERGRADE! Distinction

> Evaluate the use of teamwork and communication skills in public services.

> **LINK!** Communication skills come under 'Describe the importance of effective communication skills in the public services', page 41.

SKILL POWER

'Evaluate' means 'judge', 'assess' or 'work out the value of'. If you evaluate the use of teamwork skills you:

- say whether you think it is good, bad (or a bit of both)
- give reasons for your opinion
- support your opinion with quotations or examples if you can.

Evaluations usually give both good and bad points. No public service is perfect, and none are all bad.

It is hard to evaluate the use of teamwork and communication skills in public services:

(a) because it is hard to get a true picture of a team unless you belong to it

(b) because, especially in the armed forces, the real work of many teams is kept secret

(c) most of us lack the experience and knowledge to evaluate teamwork and communication skills.

You will therefore have to depend on other people's evaluations for this outcome. The best methods are to:

(a) ask someone who works in a public service to evaluate the service's use of teamwork and communication skills for you. (Your job is to take good notes!)

(b) use a news story about failures of teamwork and communication in the public services. One – the tragic story of Victoria Climbié – is outlined below.

FOCUS

On 24 July 1999 Victoria Climbié first came to the attention of an agency in Haringey when she was brought to the Accident and Emergency Department of North Middlesex Hospital by Marie-Therese Kouao. Ms Kouao said that Victoria had poured boiling water over her head to relieve the itching from a scabies infection. Subsequently, Victoria came to the attention of a number of agencies within Haringey. She died of multiple organ failure on 25 February 2000. Marie-Therese Kouao and Carl Manning (her boyfriend) were found guilty of her murder at the Central Criminal Court.

THE KEY ISSUES ARISING FROM THE CASE

- The need for a Case Review Sub-Committee to oversee all case reviews.
- Failure of all agencies to carry out a proper and comprehensive assessment or investigation of the child's needs.
- Failure of all agencies to implement fully the child protection procedures.
- The adequacy of record keeping practices.
- Communications between professionals and between agencies.
- The need for clarity about each agency's responsibilities.
- The standard of interviewing of children.
- The adequacy of management oversight of child protection enquiries.

Source: Haringey Area Child Protection Committee
February 2002

This is a case where it appears that teamwork in more than one public service broke down. The need for a Case Review Sub-Committee was not recognised – and it seems that there was therefore a lack of teams to deal with the case.

There was 'a failure of all agencies to carry out a proper and comprehensive assessment or investigation of the child's needs'. It may be that this is because teams were overworked, and did not have the time or staff to assess Victoria Climbié's needs. Teamwork needs people and resources to work properly, and it may be that the government, the local authority, or someone else did not recognise this fact. On the other hand, the problem could be that the teams did not work effectively because they had not been well-trained, or the members didn't communicate well.

'The adequacy of record keeping practices' was apparently poor. This suggests that team leadership may have been poor, or again, that there was neither the time nor the staff to do work which might not have seemed urgent at the time.

In the last paragraph the management of teams is criticised, suggesting poor communication or some other failure of teamwork.

This tragic case is not typical of the public services, which, most of the time, do an excellent job in difficult conditions. It shows how difficult public service work can be, and how necessary effective teamwork is. The case also shows how breakdowns in communication can cost a child her life.

There are many cases in public service work where outstanding teamwork brings success. One case, on an international scale, was the involvement of different countries and NATO in resolving the Kosovo crisis in 1999.

Another case, closer to home, was the foiling by the Metropolitan Police of the Millennium Dome robbery.

FOCUS

The date of the robbery, 7 November 2000, marked the climax of months of planning in two separate schemes.

The first was the attempt to snatch the millennium jewels by a gang of south London villains.

The second was the police surveillance operation. Officers disguised as tourists, dome workers and passers-by had monitored the gang for months. Hundreds were posted at the dome throughout October and November as Scotland Yard waited for the men to strike.

Without the Flying Squad's intervention, the raid would have been the world's biggest ever – "the robbery of the millennium", the prosecution said.

Source: © *The Guardian*, 'Dome's day of drama', Tania Branigan and Nick Hopkins (Monday 18 February 2002)

Teamwork and communication skills are of vital importance in the public services. This is where many of their successes come from, and they are normally of a consistently high standard. But when the public services fail, it is usually the result of a failure of teamwork and communication.

! CHECKPOINT ...

(a) Search through prison service inspection reports and the website of the Police Complaints Authority to find examples of areas in which teamwork or communication in the public services has sometimes broken down.

(b) Talk to someone who works in a uniformed or non-uniformed public service, and ask them to tell you about the good and bad points of teamwork and communication in their service. Teaching is a non-uniformed public service, so try asking your tutor!

(c) Do you know of any cases, perhaps within your own college, at work, or within a sports team that you play for or support, where teamwork has been very good – or has gone wrong?

PASSGRADE

Actively participate in at least five different team activities.

You will be surprised at how many team activities you will be asked to take part in, during your First Diploma year. Here are some of them:

- **Classroom exercises and groupwork**. These include role-plays, meetings or group assignments. Group assignments may last weeks or even months – and involve things such as writing a careers booklet or advice leaflets, or carrying out mock arrests and trials.
- **Team sports**. If you play football, cricket, basketball, rugby or any other team game, then you are actively participating in a team activity. You are also actively participating if you referee or officiate at such games, or if you help to organise them.
- **Outdoor activities**. Camping, going on group expeditions, potholing, rock-climbing and canoeing are team activities. So are tasks such as building rope bridges or rafts, finding 'bodies' and doing group (not individual) orienteering exercises.
- **Work**. If you do part-time or holiday work, for example at a restaurant, a football ground, on a building site or in a nursing care home, you will be part of a team. The same is true on work placement if you are working, but not if you are observing or shadowing.

PASSGRADE

Describe the importance of interpersonal skills and personal effectiveness for public service work.

skill POWER — Providing evidence

For this outcome you need *evidence* of active participation in five different team activities. Just doing it is not enough.

The evidence can be:

- Written assignment feedback ('cover sheets', 'feedback sheets', etc) from your tutors, proving you have met the outcome and giving you a grade. These must be for team assignments, outdoor or sporting activities in which this outcome (grading criterion) is clearly covered.
- Photographs.
- Video, or perhaps tape recordings, of a team activity. These should be backed up by written witness statements or feedback from your tutor.
- Authentic (genuine) letters or written feedback from work placement supervisors, employers or voluntary work supervisors – such as youth leaders. These are sometimes called 'witness statements'. They must show that you have actively participated in team activities. They should not come from family members.

Your evidence must show that you participated *actively*, that there were *at least five* activities, and that they were *team activities*. The activities must be of different kinds. For example, they should not all be team sports.

If in doubt about the evidence you need to provide, ask a tutor!

Interpersonal and personal effectiveness skills

Interpersonal skills help you to get on with other people. They include:

- assertiveness (getting what you want without being nasty)
- dealing with conflict (i.e. disagreement and aggression)
- using body language
- communication skills (listening, speaking, reading, writing and non-verbal communication).

Personal effectiveness skills help you to get the best out of yourself. They include:

- problem-solving techniques
- decision-making
- goal-setting
- stress management
- time management.

Interpersonal skills

Assertiveness

This means sticking up for yourself in a straightforward way, so that you get what you want from a situation, without hassle or aggression.

The three main rules of assertiveness are:

- State what you want, clearly, without exaggeration and without understatement (i.e. be straightforward and honest).
- Give one good reason why you want it (giving lots of reasons makes you sound unsure of yourself and weakens your position).
- State what you will do if you don't get what you want. This must be something that you are prepared to do. Don't make empty threats (or threats of violence).

Importance for public service work

Assertiveness is necessary for all work with people, and that means all public service work. Why?

- It is the most effective way of getting other people to do what you want. For example, if you are a firefighter at a road accident, and you use techniques of assertiveness to keep bystanders out of the way, they are more likely to obey you.
- Assertiveness shows confidence and gives confidence to others. Victims of crime, injured people, and others who are suffering gain confidence if the public service worker dealing with their case is assertive.
- Assertiveness gets respect. For example, if prison officers are passive (too soft) the prisoners may give them a hard time. If, on the other hand, officers are aggressive, the prisoners may not cooperate. But an assertive prison officer will be seen as firm but fair.
- Assertiveness saves time. You say what you mean, people understand you, and the job gets done faster.
- It makes the job less stressful, since it cuts down conflict and gets results.

Dealing with conflict

Conflict means aggression, disagreement and violence. There is plenty of it about. We have all heard of people getting aggressive at places like benefit offices, job-centres, hospitals and prisons.

Often, it's somebody in the public services who has to sort it out.

There are six main ways of dealing with conflict. Here they are, together with their importance in public service work.

1 Running away

This is the right thing to do in some situations. If an army unit faces death from a more powerful enemy, it's better to run away, and come back later with reinforcements. Police or others who try to 'go it alone' can get hurt – or killed. But running away from a conflict does not really 'deal with' it – it leaves it for another day.

2 Ignoring the conflict

A trivial disagreement in an office is still a conflict. But some conflicts are too small to bother with. In the public services minor conflicts with, say, workmates, might be best ignored. But if the conflict starts causing unhappiness, something has to be done about it.

3 Fighting

Everybody, including people working in the public services, has the right to use 'necessary force' in self-defence. But starting a fight creates a conflict – it doesn't solve it.

4 Control and restraint

This is a skilled way of dealing with physical conflict. It is used in the prison service and the police as a way of dealing with violent people without injuring them. It involves holds like those used in judo and other martial arts. Occasionally it still leads to injuries and deaths, and it doesn't deal with the cause of the conflict (which is usually inside someone's mind).

5 Talking your way out of trouble

A police officer once said that his way of dealing with conflict was 'getting people to do what you want them to do, while letting them think that they are doing what they want to do.' This is an interpersonal skill which comes from understanding human nature, understanding what you want, and trying to solve the problem by using your brains, rather than your muscles. This doesn't just deal with conflict; it deals with the *causes* of conflict.

6 Listening

Talking is no good without listening. Listening is the interpersonal skill which enables you to understand the cause of conflict. When a police officer has to mediate between people who are in conflict (it might be neighbours who hate each other, or communities in Northern Ireland) he or she has to listen before they can act to deal with the conflict. And if the conflict is personal – whether it is a disagreement with a workmate, or somebody is threatening to kill you – it pays to listen!

> **! CHECKPOINT …**
> Which of these skills for dealing with conflict is most useful in the public service you want to join. Why?

Use of body language

Body language means things like facial expressions, eye-contact, the way you stand or sit, the way you move your arms, and the amount of space you choose to have between yourself and another person.

Psychologists believe that each bit of body language means something. Here are some examples.

Gesture, expression, etc	Meaning
Raised eyebrows	Surprise; an unspoken question; recognising someone who is coming towards you
Narrowed eyes	Doubt; aggression (in some cultures)
Nodding head	Yes (in British culture) No (in Saudi Arabia)
Frowning	Pretending to think Anger (in some cultures)
Standing close to someone	Intimacy Aggression Possessiveness Belonging to certain cultures
Touching cheeks	Flirting
Touching lips or lower part of face	Dishonesty; the person has something to hide

Gesture, expression, etc	Meaning
Touching ears	The person wants to get away from you
Staring	Aggression Surprise Childishness
Avoiding eye contact	Shyness Immaturity Anger/strong dislike
Twitching legs	Impatience Aggression
Hunching shoulders	Lack of confidence

What does each of these expressions mean to you?

Importance of body language for public service work

Understanding people

You can – to some extent – 'read' other people's minds by watching their non-verbal communication. For example, if somebody is angry, their face might go red and they might start waving their arms about. The police, prison officers, social workers and nurses can see the signs and then decide how to react.

Influencing people

Public service workers can also use their own body language to influence people. By standing closer they can put pressure on someone, or suggest friendliness, either of which might make the person more cooperative.

Getting on with people

Public service workers can get on better with their colleagues if they can read their moods through their body language, and use body language to show their own liking or respect for them (e.g. smiles suggesting friendliness).

Communication skills

 LINK! You'll find out about these, and how they are used in the public services, under 'Describe the importance of effective communication skills in the public services', page 41.

Personal effectiveness skills

These skills help you to work fast and effectively – without putting in too much effort!

Problem-solving strategies

Public service work is about solving other people's problems. These problems come in all shapes and sizes. Some have to be solved at once (for example if a terrorist bomb has gone off). Others take time.

Strategies are methods of solving problems. The aim is usually to break the problem down into its parts, then tackle these parts in the easiest and most effective way. So problems are often solved in stages, as follows:

Getting information

1 Ask and answer these questions:

What is the problem?
How urgent is it?
Who should solve it?
What resources are needed to solve it?
What is the result you really want?

2 Ask advice. This may mean getting someone else to solve the problem for you, but it could be the easiest and most effective solution.

3 Find out what was done about similar problems in the past. Are there any laws or rules which must be followed? This may be better than trying to 'reinvent the wheel'! If the problem is a new problem and needs fresh thinking, go on to the next stage.

Thinking of solutions

4 Generate ideas. This can be done by individuals or teams. You note down as many ideas for solving the problem as possible, without worrying whether they are good or bad.

5 Make a choice. When you have a note of all possible solutions, pick the best one. If you are working in a team get others to agree to it.

Doing the work

6 Tackle the problem. If there is time, draw up an action plan showing who has to do what, and when. Get it approved by someone in authority, if this is necessary. Think about people, resources, time, and possible difficulties, including opposition from other people.

7 If necessary, draw up contingency plans (things to do if the problem isn't getting solved).

Making sure it's solved

8 Review what you have done. Ask yourself and your team: Is the problem really solved? If not, what next?

The importance of problem-solving in the public services

Every public service solves problems all the time. If car crime is going up, the police are expected to do something about it. The problem is, what? If an ambulance arrives at the scene of a car accident, and they find an unconscious man in the car, the paramedics have a number of problems to solve. Is he dead? If not, what immediate treatment can they give? Should they try to stabilise his condition on the spot, or get him to hospital as fast as possible?

Non-uniformed public services also solve problems. They have a budget (a supply of money) and they have to decide how to spend it. Housing departments have to house homeless people. Hospitals have to heal the sick. And in the library service, some people have to decide what books to buy, others have to stop people from stealing the books, and others still have to think of ways of getting more people interested in reading.

Decision making

This can be defined as making a reasoned choice between two or more possible actions, with the aim of getting the best possible result.

It is like problem solving, since you cannot solve a problem without making decisions.

FOCUS

An outline of the decision-making process

Imagine you are a police superintendent. The lecturers in a local college have gone on strike and have asked you whether they can hold a march through the centre of your town. It is likely that large numbers of students will join them. The decision you have to make is: Will you allow the march to go ahead or not?

This is the decision-making process you might follow:

1 Understand the situation. This means getting as much accurate information as possible – about the march, how long it will take, how many people will take part, and where it will go. What is the real reason for the protest? Who will be in control? Is there a risk of violence? Who will be inconvenienced or threatened by the march? What will the effect be on traffic, and business? What does the law have to say about such marches?

2 Decide what matters. Which is more important: that ordinary townspeople can go about their daily business without interference, or that teachers and students can have freedom of speech and make a protest?

3 Outline options. You could:

- ban the march because it will stop traffic and cause chaos
- allow the march but limit it to lecturers only
- allow everybody to march who wants to
- change the proposed route of the march
- suggest another day so it doesn't clash with the market
- close shops along the route of the march
- use only your own officers to police the march
- draft in other officers from neighbouring forces.

4 Assess the options. Decide which of the above choices you will go for, and which you will reject.

5 Carry out the decision.

6 Review the outcome after the march.

Notice that decisions have to be based on such questions as:

- Is the *aim* of the decision morally right?
- Is the *method* of carrying out the decision morally right?
- Will most people *agree* with it?
- Is it *possible* to carry it out?
- How much will it *cost*?

! CHECKPOINT ...

What would you decide in the situation above?

The importance of decision-making in the public services

Quick decisions can save lives. For example, RAF helicopter crews winching seamen up from a wrecked ship need to decide within minutes how to position themselves, and whether to carry on trying to rescue people in stormy weather when their own lives are at risk.

Quick decisions save time and money. For example, if a police crime prevention team spent weeks deciding a strategy, nothing else can get done in the meantime and money (spent on salaries) is being wasted.

Decisions must be correct. If they are not, someone else has to pick up the pieces. Incorrect police decisions after the murder of Stephen Lawrence in 1993 led to the Metropolitan Police being branded in the press as racists.

Goal-setting

If you plan to do something and give yourself a deadline, you are setting a goal. It can be a big thing, like a career move, or a small thing, like clearing your desk before you go home. Either way, you decide it yourself.

A goal is personal. It is not the same as a target, which is set by an organisation such as the government or a police authority.

Examples of goals are: the police constable set herself the goal of becoming a sergeant by 2005; the Fire Authority set a target of five minutes as the average response time for a call-out.

Goal-setting is good because it helps you to:

- organise your life, and
- motivate yourself.

Effective goal-setting is ambitious, yet realistic. If you set yourself a goal which is too difficult, you won't reach it, and this will leave you with a sense of failure. If you set yourself a goal which is too easy, you are being lazy. The best goals are difficult to achieve, but not impossible.

The importance of goal-setting for public service work

In public service work you often have to make up your mind what to do and when to do it. A police officer on a beat, for example, has to decide what she thinks is important for that particular beat. She could set herself limited goals, such as stopping the children in Smith Street from throwing bottles, or longer-term goals such as lowering the rate of burglaries on Weston Estate.

Goal-setting enables you to make appointments with people and plan ahead, so that you don't waste other people's time.

Goal-setting motivates you and makes you learn new skills. It also enables you to plan your career within a public service. For example, if you joined the RAF as an airman in 2004 you might want to ensure that you are a corporal by 2009.

Stress management

Stress management is the controlling and reducing of health and emotional problems caused by:

- pressure of work
- frightening or distressing events.

These health and emotional problems are known as stress. They are very common, and in both the public services and private industry, about 30 per cent of people suffer from depression and anxiety (forms of stress) each year (according to the Health and Safety Executive in 2000).

Stress weakens the immune system and makes people more likely to get illnesses like flu and bronchitis. Some forms of heart disease, high blood pressure and cancer are also stress related.

There are two kinds of stress management:

1. By the employer. Employers can improve working conditions to reduce stress. This does not come directly into this syllabus.
2. By the employee. Employees can change their work methods and lifestyle to reduce stress. This kind of stress management is a personal effectiveness skill.

Examples of personal stress management are:

(a) **At work**
- not working too many hours
- being assertive so that you don't get bullied or 'put upon'
- organising your work and setting realistic goals
- making the effort to get on well with your colleagues
- asking for help if work gets too difficult, or you have too much to do.

(b) **Outside work**

- taking up interests such as sport, or a creative activity
- making time to see friends
- getting enough sleep
- avoiding alcohol and drug abuse
- eating a balanced, healthy diet
- staying out of debt.

The importance of stress management for public service work

For the organisation

Levels of sickness and absenteeism drop. This saves money spent on sick pay and cover, and lessens the stress of employees who have to pick up the sick person's workload.

Fewer people leave the job or take early retirement because of stress. Their skills and experience are not lost. And the cost of replacing them is saved.

For the individual employee

Stress management improves their health, efficiency and job satisfaction. It makes life outside work more enjoyable, and benefits their families and friends.

Time management techniques

These are simply ways of making better use of your time. Time management does not mean working harder: it means working more intelligently.

Everybody is different, so it is hard to lay down rules about good time management. But here are some ideas.

1 Identify your timewasters; for example:

- telephone interruptions
- visitors
- meetings
- unclear communication
- indecision
- putting off work
- talking to friends
- lack of planning
- inability to say no
- messy desk and files.

2 Deal with the timewasters; for example:

- get an answering machine
- arrange an appointments system for visitors
- do not attend meetings unless you are sure they are relevant
- ignore unclear communications (memos, e-mails, etc) unless they seem to be matters of life and death.

> **! CHECKPOINT ...**
>
> ■ What would you do about the other timewasters? Discuss it with a friend.
>
> Making lists and action plans, though it takes time, can sometimes save time in the long run. Another way of managing your time, if you are too busy, is to persuade someone else to do the work!

The importance of time management techniques for public service work

For the public service

Time management is efficient. People get on with the job. This means that the public service itself can

39

be more 'productive', in the sense that it does more work for the same amount of public money. The police, for example, can make more arrests; the fire service can issue more fire certificates and teachers can mark more assignments!

For public service workers

Good time management reduces stress. Workers can think more clearly and act more effectively. They get more job satisfaction because they feel they are well organised and working to higher standards.

> ! CHECKPOINT ...
> ■ What disadvantages are there (if any) in using time management techniques?

 *Merit*

> Demonstrate responsibility within roles during team activities.

This means:

- taking your teamwork seriously and carrying out your part of the job to the best of your ability
- showing willingness and enthusiasm to get the best out of yourself and other team members
- showing a range of interpersonal skills
- showing awareness of safety
- treating other team members with respect and consideration
- being punctual, attending well (if the activity has gone on over a period of time) and notifying the team if you have been unable to attend.

 *Distinction*

> Demonstrate exceptional teamwork, interpersonal, personal effectiveness and communication skills.

This means doing everything you have to do to get a merit – and then some! In fact, your teamwork should be of a standard that would impress a professional working in the public services.

'Exceptional' means 'unusually good', and to get a distinction for this outcome you have to do very well in teamwork, interpersonal, personal effectiveness and communication skills.

And you must provide evidence. This means getting a written statement, such as an assignment feedback sheet from a tutor, or a letter or witness statement from an employer. It must show beyond doubt that you excelled in the teamwork, interpersonal, personal effectiveness and communicative aspects of at least one of the following:

- interactive assignments such as role plays
- a work placement
- a residential
- outdoor activities
- team sports
- a job involving teamwork
- a voluntary or charitable activity.

> ! CHECKPOINT ...
> ■ Critically examine your own performance in a team activity. Note down
> (a) what you think was good about your teamwork
> (b) areas where you could do better.
> Then compare your self-appraisal with that of another team member. Have you been fair to yourselves?

> LINK! Interpersonal skills and personal effectiveness, mentioned under 'Distinction' above, are covered above on pages 33–37 and in the Focus, to follow.

FOCUS

Checklist for 'exceptional teamwork, interpersonal, personal effectiveness and communication skills'

Teamwork skills

- Effectively motivating the team (without undermining the leader if you are not the leader), and contributing actively to the good team spirit
- Encouraging other team members
- Carefully following good health and safety practice
- Leading when necessary but also delegating
- Contributing actively and constructively to decision-making

Interpersonal skills

- Avoiding sarcasm, unpleasant remarks and bad language
- Never showing discrimination against others
- Mixing easily with all members of your team, and group, whatever their gender, ethnic background, etc
- Acting calmly and responsibly if your team-mates are annoying you
- Not trying to do everything yourself
- Keeping your tutor informed of serious problems

Personal effectiveness skills

- Active and enthusiastic participation in activities
- Showing organising skills without being bossy or bullying
- Concentrating on the task and not letting yourself be distracted by less motivated classmates
- Excellent time management, including punctuality, attendance and meeting deadlines
- Showing self-discipline in conduct, and setting a very good example to others
- Helping to plan activities, setting targets
- Being able to carry out a reasoned self-appraisal of the role you played in the team activity, and to suggest possible improvements or alterations in the way you did it

Communication skills

- A range of reading skills – skim, scan and detailed reading
- Clear and appropriate verbal communication (speaking)
- Good writing skills – notes, letters, reports, etc as needed
- Good listening skills – including note-making and body language
- Good technical skills – ICT use, etc, and research skills

! CHECKPOINT ...

Write an action plan for improving your own communication skills.

PASSGRADE

Describe the importance of effective communication skills in the public services.

Communication means giving and receiving information.

Communication skills

There are five basic communication skills:

1 Reading – used for receiving information
2 Writing – used for giving information
3 Verbal communication – used for giving information
4 Listening – used for receiving information
5 Technical skills – for giving and receiving information.

1 Reading

There are different kinds of reading skills:

- Skimming – looking quickly at a document (e.g. a newspaper or book) to see what it's about. You are not looking for anything specific.
- Scanning – reading quickly to pick out specific information (e.g. looking up a telephone number; picking out the main points in a notebook entry about a crime; looking up a law in a police law book).
- Detailed reading – the kind of careful reading a police constable might do if taking the sergeants' exam (OSPRE). Careful reading of a battle plan to make sure it was fully understood.

Grading criteria

PASSGRADE	SUPERGRADE! Merit	SUPERGRADE! Distinction
To achieve a pass grade the evidence must show that the learner is able to:	To achieve a merit grade the evidence must show that the learner is able to:	To achieve a distinction grade the evidence must show that the learner is able to:
● plan and implement a personal fitness programme demonstrating a knowledge of training methods and health and safety 49	● analyse the personal fitness results from the appropriate public service fitness test used 54	● evaluate personal fitness results, comparing them to relevant fitness data 55
● undertake one appropriate fitness test used by one of the public services highlighting the key points of fitness testing protocol 53	● analyse the operation of the major body systems in relation to health and fitness 64	● evaluate the main components of fitness and their importance in public service activity 67
● explain the use of repeat fitness tests used by one of the public services 56	● analyse the impact of good nutrition and diet on health and fitness 70	● evaluate the impact of good nutrition on the human body and from the planning of a dietary programme make clear recommendations explaining briefly the nutritional value of food 73
● describe the major body systems and the principles of health and fitness 58		
● explain the importance of good nutrition and its impact on health and fitness 68		
● plan a dietary programme including an explanation of Recommended Nutrient Intake and the food group system 71		

To most people fitness is being able to run upstairs without getting tired. To the uniformed public services it is this and a lot more. In this chapter you will learn about how to get fit, how to stay fit, and how to eat for health.

You'll also learn about public service fitness tests, and what level of fitness the public services are looking for.

PASSGRADE

> Plan and implement a personal fitness programme demonstrating a knowledge of training methods and health and safety.

Finding out your present fitness level

You may think you know already whether you are fit or not. But the best way to find out your fitness level is to have it checked by your fitness instructor or at a gym. By measuring your blood pressure and heart rate while you are on an exercise bike, or by recording your performance on activities such as sit-ups, press-ups or the bleep test, your instructor will be able to tell you whether you are fit, unfit or about average – for your age and body type.

Deciding why you want to be fitter

There are three main reasons for getting fit:

1 **Personal**. Being fit adds to your confidence. You feel good and you look good. You can take part in sports and social activities with more enjoyment.
2 **Health**. Fit people live longer and have a better quality of life. They have less risk of cancer, heart disease and diabetes.

! CHECKPOINT ...

Which is more important – improving the areas in which you are unfit, or getting even fitter in the areas you are already good at? Note down reasons for your point of view.

---

3 **Professional**. Fitness is needed for public service work.

Your personal fitness plan should begin by stating how fit you are now, your future plan(s), and your fitness need(s). Here is an example.

Situation now
Female, age 17; good at running, light weight for my height

Future plan
Want to join the army

Fitness need
Develop all-round strength, probably concentrating on upper body

Your personal fitness plan could look like this:

Name: Steven Hampshire

Age: 17 years 9 months

Situation now: Height 184 cm; weight 80 kg. I consider I am fit and play rugby and ice hockey fairly regularly.

Future plan: Join the fire service

Fitness need: Develop all-round fitness

Planning a fitness programme means writing a timetable for exercises which will go on until you are as fit as you want to be.

Implementing the programme means doing it.

For this outcome it has to be a *personal* fitness programme: one for you and you only, designed for *your* fitness needs.

You have to 'demonstrate a knowledge of training methods'. This means using the training methods:

- which experts use
- which do not damage your health
- which you can describe and explain where necessary.

'Health and safety' means avoiding accident, illness and injury.

When planning a personal fitness programme you first need to know:

(a) your present fitness level

(b) your reasons for wanting to become fitter

(c) the level of fitness you want to achieve.

Your fitness programme should mention:

- **Frequency** – how often you train. Three times a week is a good frequency for serious training, though twice a week will still do you good. Frequency also refers to repetitions ('reps') – how often you do a given exercise in one exercise session. For example if you do ten press-ups it is ten reps.

- **Intensity** – this is to do with the amount of strength you use in an exercise. If you are running, you raise intensity by running faster. If you are weightlifting you raise intensity by using heavier weights.

- **Time** – this is the amount of time you spend training, either in a session or in a week. Three one-hour training sessions would be enough.

- **Type** – this is the kind of training you do. Training for fitness usually means increasing repetitions. Training for strength means increasing intensity.

- **Instituting and following your programme**. Instituting is starting the programme and making arrangements about where, when and how you will do it. It also includes the equipment you'll need, and any medical or fitness checks before you start.

- **Rest periods**. You need short breaks during each session, and at least a day between each session, to protect your body against injury, and your mind against boredom!

- **Routines and variations**. Routines are things you do regularly. Training should be fairly regular so that you can measure your progress, but if it gets too regular it might strain certain muscle groups, or become boring. Varying activities between – say – running and weight-lifting can help both fitness and strength, in a balanced way.

Introduction

The purpose of this fitness programme is to increase my general fitness in preparation for the Fire Service fitness test, which I hope to take as soon as possible after my eighteenth birthday.

This personal fitness plan is divided into three sections:

Section 1 describes the activities I will be doing in my fitness programme.

Section 2 shows the circuits and progression. It outlines the order in which the activities should be done, and shows how they increase in frequency as the weeks pass.

Section 3 is the plan itself, showing the training activities I will be doing each week over a period of twelve weeks. The circuit training, which involves all the activities listed in Section 1, is done twice a week and the repetitions for each circuit increase as the training progresses. In the first week I will be doing progression 1, but by the last week I will be doing the progression with the most reps – progression 6.

In between circuit training there will be two rest days and one day in which I do a training session of walking and running. So the sequence is: Circuit ... Rest day ... Walk/run ... Rest day ... Circuit.

The training schedule, or timetable, has spaces in it where I can keep a record of my progress and note down any problems I might have.

Advantages of this plan

The rest days will prevent me from over-training, which would risk injury and bring no real benefit. The walking and running will help to prepare me for the shuttle run, and other items in the fire service fitness test for applicants. The circuit training will increase my upper body strength, so I can do hose-running, ladder raising, and carrying heavy equipment.

The plan lasts twelve weeks, by which time I hope to be applying for the Loamshire Fire Service.

The plan

SECTION 1

Activities to be used in fitness programme:

Press Ups	Half Press Ups
Lunge	Triceps Press
Sit Ups	Squat
Dorsal Raise	Stair Running
Chester Step Test	

COOL SITE:

Explains what each of these activities is:
www.hantsfire.gov.uk/

SECTION 2

Circuits and progression. The circuit is the activity; the progression is the number of repetitions or – in the case of jogging on the spot – the number of seconds or minutes.

Circuit	Progression 1	Progression 2	Progression 3	Progression 4	Progression 5	Progression 6
Press-ups	10 reps	15	20	25	30	35
Standing squats	10 reps	15	20	25	30	35
Lunges	10 reps	15	20	25	30	35
Triceps press	10 reps	15	20	25	30	35
Jog on spot	30 secs	40	50	1 min	1 min	1 min
Dorsal raise	10 reps	15	20	25	30	35
Stair run	5 reps	6	7	8	9	10
('reps' = repetitions)						

Training Schedule and Record Sheet

Running pace: approx. 8–8½ min/mile for Steady (S); 7–7½ min/mile for Fast (F)

Week	Monday		Tuesday		Wednesday		Thursday		Friday		Saturday		Sunday	
	Aim	Actual	Aim	Actual	Aim	Actual	Aim	Actual	Aim	Actual	Aim	Actual	Aim	Actual
1	10 min walk/run		Rest		Circ. prog. 1		Rest		15 min walk/run		Rest		Circ. prog 1	
2	Rest		15 min run (S)		Rest		Circ. prog. 2		Rest		20 min run (S)		Circ. prog. 2	
3	Rest		20 min run (F)		Circ. prog 2		Rest		20 min run (S)		Circ. prog 2		Rest	
4	20 min run (S)		Circ. prog 2		Rest		20 min run (F)		Rest		Circ. prog 3		20 min run (F)	
5	Rest		Circ. prog 3		25 min run (S)		Rest		Circ. prog 3		Rest		30 min run (S)	
6	Rest		Circ. prog 4		Rest		30 min run (F)		Circ. prog 4		Rest		30 min run (S)	
7	Circ. prog 4		Rest		20 min run (S)		Circ. prog 4		Rest		30 min run (F)		Circ. prog 4	
8	Rest		Circ. prog 5		Circ. prog 2		Circ. prog 5		Rest		20 min run (S)		Circ. prog 5	
9	30 min run (S)		Rest		Circ. prog 5		Rest		40 min run (S)		Circ. prog 5		Rest	
10	40 min run (S)		Circ. prog 5		30 min run (F)		Rest		20 min run (S)		Circ. prog 6		Rest	
11	40 min run (S)		Circ. prog 6		20 min run (F)		Circ. prog 6		Rest		40 min run (S)		Circ. prog 6	
12	Rest		40 min run (S)		Circ. prog 6		30 min run (F)		Circ. prog 6		Rest		20 min run (S)	

1 Medical check

I have arranged to visit my doctor, Dr Kapoor, for a full medical check. He knows that I intend to start training, and that I plan to apply for the fire service.

2 Equipment and venue

I have bought trainers suitable for running, and shorts and a T-shirt for exercising in the gym. I have jogging bottoms and sweater to keep me warm when not training. I also have a first aid kit containing a range of bandages, crepe dressings, elastoplast, scissors, soap, tissues, antiseptic solution and cotton wool. These are to deal with cuts and grazes that I might get if I fall while running. I have been on a first aid course so I understand the basics of first aid.

The running will be done on Clayton Fields running track. It is a cinder track but reasonably quiet and safe, though there are sometimes dogs running loose in the area.

I will use the college gym, which is staffed by an instructor, for my circuit training.

3 Warm-ups

I will do a five-minute warm-up before each circuit training session. This will:

- make me more mentally alert
- increase my pulse rate in preparation for more serious exercise
- loosen my joints and muscles
- exercise the main muscle groups.

These groups are:

- **Arms and Shoulders** – Warm-up can include arm circling, shoulder shrugging, arm swinging (outwards), arm shaking, and crawl strokes (as in swimming).
- **Trunk and Back** – Warm-up can include trunk rotation, side bending, dorsal raises and sit-ups.
- **Legs** – Warm-up can include knee bends (squats), side jumps and lunges. Finish with some gentle jogging on the spot – this uses the lower leg muscles and raises the pulse.

I will avoid stretching until the warm-up is over.

4 Checking my plan

I will check my training plan with my tutor or instructor before I start implementing the programme.

Implementing your personal fitness programme

Carry out your plan as well as you can. Keep a careful record of your progress. Make sure you get evidence that you really are carrying out your programme. If you injure yourself or feel ill, get advice before continuing.

PASSGRADE

> Undertake one appropriate fitness test used by one of the public services highlighting the key points of fitness testing protocol.

For this outcome you must do a fitness test.

Fitness test

The test should be appropriate. So:

- it should be an entrance test
- it should be for a service which you are interested in joining
- it should test fitness rather than strength (but see below)
- there should be facilities and staff available so that the test can be done realistically and safely
- it should not be too hard for you.

Fitness testing *protocol* is the organisation and rules of the fitness test (see Focus box below).

FOCUS

Hereford and Worcester Combined Fire Authority

Strength and Fitness Tests

- Hand Grip Test.
- Lower Back Test.
- Multistage shuttle run – you will need to run between two lines, 20 metres apart, to a bleep that gets progressively faster. If you fail to complete a shuttle on 3 consecutive occasions before the bleep sounds, or if you are physically unable to complete the test, you will be unsuccessful. You will need to reach level 9.6, which means that you will have been running for almost 10 minutes.

Practical Tests

- Hose Running (unrolling fire hoses, laying them straight on the ground, then rolling them up again neatly).
- Breathing Apparatus Wear (this is sometimes done in a confined space, to test claustrophobia).
- Ladder Ascent (tests speed of climbing and fear of heights).

These test:

- endurance – in the shuttle run and the hose running
- strength – in the dead lift, the ladder extension simulator and the grip test
- flexibility – in the hose running, where you have to keep bending your back
- coordination – in the practical tests, where you have to do a series of difficult and unfamiliar movements.

The key points of fitness testing protocol

The protocol, or rules, for fitness tests vary depending on the service you are applying for.

The following points are worth noting:

1 The tests are usually conducted at a training centre.

2 Correct kit must be worn.

3 The tests are the same for men and women.

4 The tests are conducted by qualified instructors, with occupational health nurses present in case anything goes wrong.

5 Almost all tests are timed. One minute is usual for sit-ups, press-ups, etc.

6 Different forces or areas can make alterations to their fitness tests, or add extra elements. For example, some police forces require a standing long jump.

7 A 'skinfold test' is sometimes done. A nurse pinches the skin and surface fat on various parts of the body with a pair of callipers, and measures the thickness. Using tables they then work out the 'body percentage fat measurement'.

8 All the public service tests contain shuttle runs, but other items depend on the service, and what kind of fitness they are looking for.

9 Some public services, such as the police, do not have fixed passmarks for their fitness tests. Others, such as the Royal Navy do.

10 Some tests, such as the fire service tests above, are divided into fitness tests and practical tests.

11 It is your responsibility to ensure that you are fit and well enough to take the test.

Fitness tests change from time to time. Your tutor or instructor should be able to give you further information about test protocols.

! ■ **CHECKPOINT ...**

(a) When you take a fitness test, make a note of the activities you do and the time it takes to do each one. Also note down the passmarks (if any). All these details will help you to pass this outcome.

(b) Contact your favourite public service and ask them about their fitness tests.

Armed Forces Careers Offices have leaflets about all their fitness tests.

Disability

If you are disabled you should still be able to work for the public services, but as a civilian employee.

Disability need not stop you from being fit, or wanting to be fit. For this outcome you should consult your tutors about fitness training, and fitness issues.

SUPERGRADE! *Merit*

Analyse the personal fitness results from the appropriate public service fitness test used.

skill POWER

This means you have to:

(a) record your fitness results

(b) say whether they are better or worse than they should be

(c) explain why they are good, bad or what you expected

(d) relate them to the training (if any) that you have done beforehand

(e) suggest how you could improve them.

Here is an example of an analysis of personal fitness results from a public service fitness test.

Profile

Male aged 17 (height 5 ft 9 in)

Bleep test	13.1 VO_2
Dynamometer (best of two attempts)	right hand 56; left hand 58
Sit-ups (maximum in 1 minute)	62
Press-ups (maximum in 1 minute)	65
Sit and reach (1 minute)	32
Standing long jump	2.50 m

Male 17

I took the Loamshire police fitness test on 25 November 2003. My results are given above.

I am quite pleased with how I did, and I think I am a good deal fitter than average. I found the bleep test quite easy except towards the end. This is probably because I play rugby and belong to the Territorial Army, where we do a lot of fitness training. I do running and weight lifting twice a week.

I was surprised that my left hand is stronger than my right, since I am right handed, but I think my scores for both hands were good. I was very pleased with my sit-ups and press-ups (in fact I broke my personal record for press-ups), but I did not do so well on the sit and reach exercise. I seemed to be stiffer than some of the other students who were taking the test, and I think perhaps I ought to start doing some flexibility training.

I was very pleased with my standing long-jump score. Police entrants are supposed to be able to jump their own height. My height in metres is 1.76, and I actually jumped 2.50 m.

The tests showed that I have a good all-round level of fitness, and I believe I could already pass the fitness tests for entry into most public services. However, fitness is not something I take for granted, so I plan to continue training through the personal programme I have written for this course. But I do intend to change it to include some flexibility training.

An evaluation goes deeper than an analysis. You give more detail and you compare your results carefully with other relevant results ('fitness data'). For a public service fitness test there are four sets of data which might be relevant:

(a) your fitness scores on your own personal fitness programme
(b) average scores for your age group
(c) the scores of other members of your class, in the same fitness test
(d) standard or pass scores issued by the public services.

FOCUS

Fitness test standards
Minimum standards for an officer in the Royal Navy

Swimming Test
Swim 40 metres and tread water for 3 minutes in overalls, retrieve a brick from the deep end.

One and a half mile run (men under 25)
– 11 mins 13 sec

Press-ups – 23–26

Sit-ups – 39–53
Burpees – 23–26

300 metre shuttle run – 53–59 sec

SUPERGRADE! *Distinction*

Evaluate personal fitness results, comparing them to relevant fitness data.

How come the swimming-pool's empty?

The last applicant was told to fetch a brick off the bottom and got the wrong one!

Profile

An evaluation of personal fitness results

Name: Martin Cudjoe

Age: 17

Target Fitness Test
Royal Navy Officer

My results:

Swimming test

I succeeded in swimming 40 metres and treading water for 3 minutes (in pyjamas) before retrieving a brick wrapped in a polythene bag from the deep end (7 feet).

I did a one-and-a-half mile run in 11 minutes 10 seconds.

I did 45 press-ups in one minute and 45 sit-ups – each in one minute.

I did a 300 metre shuttle run in 60 seconds.

Profile

On 16 November I took a series of fitness tests intended to simulate the fitness entry test for Royal Navy officers. I chose these tests because it is my ambition to apply to become an officer in the Royal Navy after I have completed my BTEC First and National Diplomas in Public Services.

Here is my evaluation of my results, comparing them to the standards published in the current Royal Navy recruitment website.

I succeeded in meeting the Royal Navy standard in the swimming test, which did not surprise me as I swim for the college. I was not required to swim quickly. Treading water involves swimming on the spot. I was wearing pyjamas rather than overalls because I do not possess any overalls, but though I found them 'clingy' I did not feel I was in any danger. I picked up the brick successfully.

I was disappointed in my performance in the one-and-a-half mile run. With a time of 11 minutes 10 seconds I only beat the Navy minimum by three seconds. I was tired on my run and I realise I need more training in running.

For the press-ups and sit-ups I got the same score – 45 in a minute. Compared to the Navy standards this was very good in the press-ups but only 'reasonable' for the sit-ups, where the Navy range is between 39 and 53.

I did not do burpees because our instructor says they are dangerous and risk injuries.

I did the shuttle run in 60 seconds, while the limit in the Navy standards is 59 seconds. This again suggests that I have a problem with endurance running, especially as I felt tired at the end of it. I intend to go for a medical check and, if that is all right, start a suitable programme of fitness training.

Points to notice:

- The writer did a detailed and honest evaluation of his own performance.
- He compared his performance with the official standards laid down for the Royal Navy Officers' fitness test.
- He gave reasons and explanations for both his good and bad performances.
- He made realistic suggestions about what he ought to do to improve his future fitness.
- He related his scores to the personal fitness programme discussed on pages 50–52 above.
- His comments were relevant to his own aim of getting into the public services.
- He is aware of the health and safety implications of his test.

PASSGRADE

> Explain the use of repeat fitness tests used by one of the public services.

Some public services use repeat fitness tests. These are tests taken by people who have joined the service, and they are retaken either every six months or every year.

Repeat fitness tests are compulsory in the:

- armed forces
- prison service
- some fire services (e.g. Hampshire, Dorset)
- for certain grades – e.g. firefighter, prison officer, ordinary soldier, naval rating.

Repeat fitness tests in the prison service

The fitness test which is taken annually by prison officers is the same as the fitness test they take when they are applying for the service (see Focus box).

CHECKPOINT …

(a) Ask somebody who works in a public service what they think about repeat fitness testing.

(b) Find out what happens to someone who 'fails' a repeat fitness test.

Though no passmarks are given, this test is easier than some public service fitness tests. This is because prison work is less energetic than army work, and prison service applicants are – on average – older than army applicants. Even so, prison officers have to retake this fitness test every year of their working lives.

The reasons for this are:

1 Being a prison officer is tiring work in which you have to keep alert at all times. Fit people have more stamina and work more effectively.

2 Prisoners can be violent. In these cases prison officers have to be fit enough to control and restrain them.

3 Prisoners might run away, and need to be chased.

4 Fit officers get more respect from the prisoners, and are better role models.

5 Fitness is good for the morale of prison officers – and reduces stress.

6 Fitness equals health, and fit prison officers are less likely to take time off work.

7 Fitness training is enjoyable in itself.

This outcome looks at the basic workings of the human body – and how these relate to health and fitness.

The body is divided into organs and systems.

Organs are particular parts of the body which do a special job. The heart, brain, lungs and glands are all organs, each with a different function.

Systems are groups of organs which act together in the body (see table below).

Name of system	Main organs	Main functions
Cardiovascular system	Heart, blood, blood vessels	Supplies oxygen, nutrients and water to the body
Respiratory system	Nose, windpipe, lungs	Breathing and absorbing oxygen
Digestive system	Mouth, oesophagus, stomach, small intestine, large intestine, rectum	Processes food into nutrients the body can use, then gets rid of waste
Nervous system	Brain, spinal column, nerves	Gathers information; decides and controls actions
Skeleton	Bones, marrow, cartilage, ligaments	Supports and protects the body and its organs
Muscles	Muscles, tendons	Provide movement and strength
Endocrine system	Glands – pituitary, thyroid, thymus, adrenals, ovaries/testes	Enables the body to grow, develop, reproduce, protect, and defend itself
Urinary system	Kidneys, ureters, bladder, urethra	Purification and waste disposal
Skin	Epidermis, dermis	Provides protection

PASSGRADE

Describe the major body systems and the principles of health and fitness.

Description of the major body systems

1 The cardiovascular system

This consists of the heart, blood, arteries, veins and capillaries.

The heart is a pump made of muscle which moves 9,000 litres of blood round the body every day. It beats about 70 times a minute, speeding up when we are active – or stressed – and slowing down when we relax.

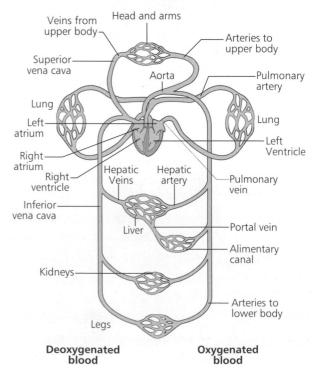

Blood is made of a liquid called plasma, which carries red blood cells, white blood cells and platelets. The red blood cells carry food and oxygen, the white blood cells catch viruses and bacteria and the platelets make the blood clot.

There are three kinds of blood vessel – arteries, veins and capillaries. Arteries carry blood out of the heart; veins carry blood back to the heart. Capillaries are tiny blood vessels which supply the muscles and organs with nutrients and oxygen.

2 The respiratory system

This supplies oxygen to the blood. Fresh air goes down the windpipe or trachea, splits to go down the bronchi and enters the lungs. Here the oxygen is absorbed into millions of capillaries.

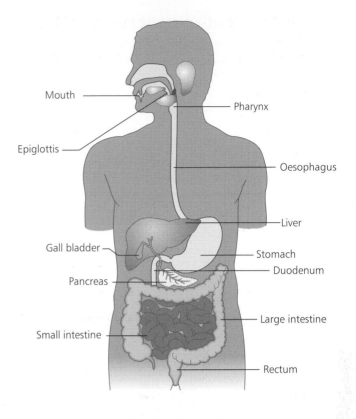

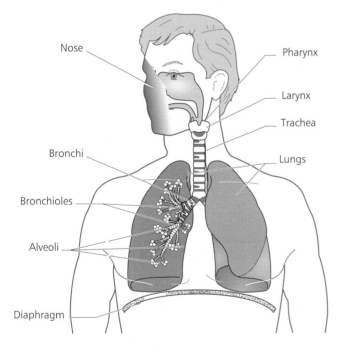

3 The digestive system

This begins at the mouth, goes down through the oesophagus (gullet) to the stomach, then through the small intestine and large intestine to the rectum and anus. It changes the fats, proteins and carbohydrates in our food to simpler chemicals, such as amino-acids, which can be absorbed and used by the body.

Digestion is a chemical change caused by fluids called enzymes. These come from the salivary glands near the mouth, the stomach, the pancreas gland and the liver, and do most of their work in the small intestine.

Digestion is followed by absorption. In this stage the nutrients in the intestine pass through the walls of the intestine into the bloodstream. Water is absorbed in the large intestine.

Elimination is the last stage of digestion, in which waste matter – fibre and dead bacteria – is removed from the body through the rectum and anus.

4 The nervous system

This has three parts to it: the brain, the spinal column (the main nerve running down the middle of the spine) and then the rest of the nerves in the body.

The brain weighs about 1,100 grams and has two main parts: the cerebrum, which is the larger, outside part, and the cerebellum which is the inner part. Thinking, seeing, hearing and speaking are controlled by the cerebrum; balance, heart-rate, digestion and body temperature are controlled by the cerebellum.

Nerves are a network of tubular fibres that carry information from the body to the brain, and commands back from the brain to the body.

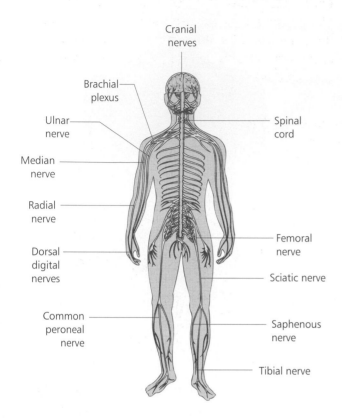

hinged so that they will only move in one direction, while shoulder-joints (for example) are ball-and-socket joints which will move in any direction. Moving joints are lubricated by cartilage (a sort of gristle) and synovial fluid.

6 Muscles

There are three kinds of muscle: smooth muscle, which makes up veins, arteries and the intestines; heart muscle, only found in the heart; and ordinary muscle which makes up about 40 per cent of our body weight. Muscles are made of long thin cells which contract (bunch up) when we want to move. There are two types of cells: 'fast twitch' which give us strength and are used in sprinting and weight-lifting, and 'slow twitch', which give us stamina and are used in walking or long-distance running.

Muscles are fastened to bones by natural cables called tendons. When the muscle contracts and pulls the tendon, the bone moves.

5 The skeleton

This has 206 separate bones. These contain minerals and calcium, but are alive and can grow and mend themselves. Some contain marrow, a kind of jelly which makes blood cells.

Bones are linked by joints. Some joints, such as those which connect different parts of the skull, won't move at all. Others, such as finger-joints, are

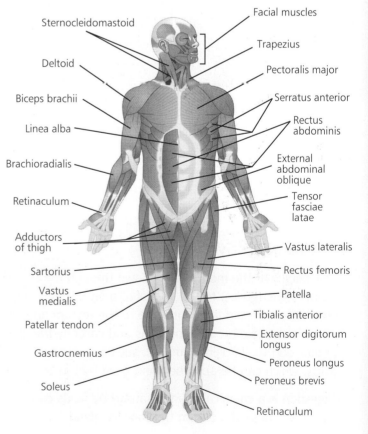

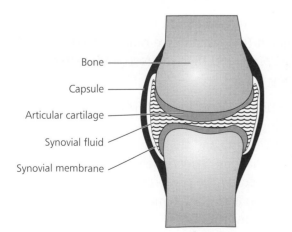

7 The endocrine system

This is the name for our glands and the hormones they produce. These hormones, which are powerful chemicals, go into our bloodstream and affect our health and behaviour.

The jobs of the main glands are as follows:

1 adrenal glands – raise blood sugar, and protect us against stress
2 hypothalamus – controls sleeping and eating
3 ovaries; testes – make 'eggs' and sperm; develop female characteristics in women and male characteristics in men
4 pancreas – controls the body's use of sugar (glucose)
5 parathyroids – keep calcium levels up in the blood
6 pituitary – controls growth and the other glands
7 thymus – strengthens the immune system, to protect against illness
8 thyroid – helps to produce body heat.

8 Urinary system

The urinary system starts in the two kidneys, goes down tubes called the ureter, and includes the bladder, and a tube called the urethra. Its main purposes are (a) to balance the water and the chemicals in our body and (b) eliminate wastes – such as urea.

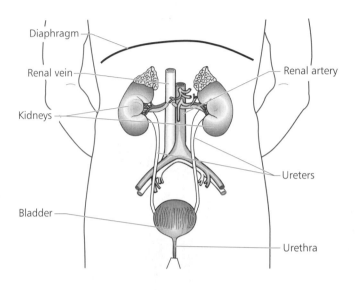

Diaphragm

Renal vein

Renal artery

Kidneys

Ureters

Bladder

Urethra

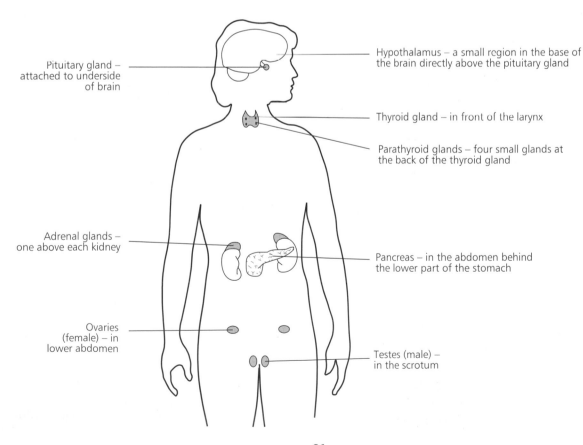

Pituitary gland – attached to underside of brain

Hypothalamus – a small region in the base of the brain directly above the pituitary gland

Thyroid gland – in front of the larynx

Parathyroid glands – four small glands at the back of the thyroid gland

Adrenal glands – one above each kidney

Pancreas – in the abdomen behind the lower part of the stomach

Ovaries (female) – in lower abdomen

Testes (male) – in the scrotum

9 The skin

The skin is a body system because it consists of different layers which interact with each other and with the body underneath.

The two main layers are:

- the epidermis. This is the surface of the skin. The top layer is made of dead cells which are strong and tough enough to protect us against many injuries. Below it is a layer of cells containing melanin, the colouring matter which protects us against the ultraviolet rays of the sun. This layer of the skin also produces vitamin D, which is needed for good health.

- the dermis. This is the thicker underlying layer of the skin. It contains blood vessels, lymph vessels and nerves, as well as hair roots (follicles), and sweat glands. The sweat glands cool the body by producing sweat when we are too hot. Sweat also helps to rid the body of urea and other waste products.

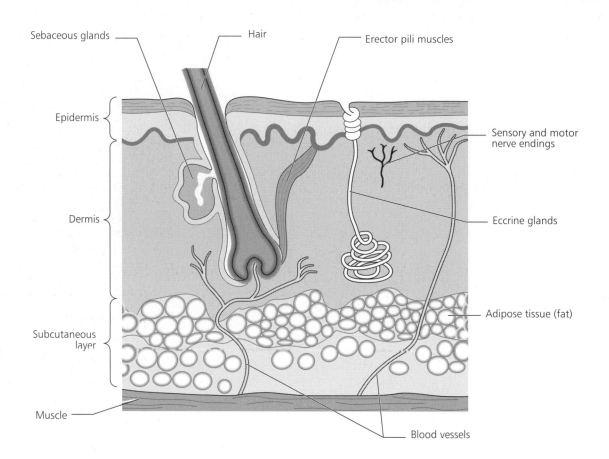

Sebaceous glands — Hair — Erector pili muscles

Epidermis

Sensory and motor nerve endings

Dermis

Eccrine glands

Subcutaneous layer

Adipose tissue (fat)

Muscle

Blood vessels

Operations of systems at rest and during exercise

At rest

When we are at rest some systems, such as muscles and joints, do very little. Parts of the brain and nervous system are less active. The heart beats at (on average) 70 times a minute. Blood travels evenly to different parts of the body. Breathing is slow and regular, bringing a steady intake of oxygen. Digestion is more rapid when we are resting, and so is the urinary system. Some parts of the endocrine system, such as the pituitary and thyroid glands, are relatively active when we are at rest and produce more hormones – for example for growth and general protection of the body.

During exercise

During exercise the systems operate differently:

Name of system	Changes caused by exercise	Reasons
Cardiovascular system	This becomes much more active. The heart beats much faster – up to 160 beats a minute. Blood vessels supplying muscles get wider. Blood is diverted away from digestion and the urinary system, and goes to the muscles, lungs and skin instead.	The muscles need extra oxygen and nutrient to convert into energy so that they can work harder. Other less urgent needs of the body are set aside. The skin gets more blood so that the body can keep cool, since muscle movement generates a lot of heat.
Respiratory system	Breathing gets faster and deeper.	More air gets into the lungs to give more oxygen to the blood. Blood from the lungs goes to the heart, then out to the muscles.
Digestive system	This becomes inactive, but some nutrients are supplied to the blood by the body's fat stores.	The blood normally used for absorbing nutrients from the digestive system goes to the muscles instead. The breaking down of fat gives extra energy to the muscles.
Nervous system	The cerebellum controls balance, the cerebrum controls movement – both are active, but divert attention away from other body functions.	The brain and nerves are occupied by controlling the body's movements, and processing feedback resulting from those movements (e.g. pain).
Skeleton	This moves during exercise. Fluid lubricates the joints, and the bones are strengthened by repeated impact.	These changes protect the bones against breakage and the joints against damage, and enable the muscles to have a greater effect.
Muscles	These are highly active during exercise.	In prolonged exercise the 'slow-twitch' cells are most active; in sudden bursts of intense exercise the 'fast-twitch' cells are most active.
Endocrine system	The adrenal glands produce extra adrenalin. More testosterone is produced. Some other glands may temporarily get less active.	These hormones raise blood sugar levels and increase energy and aggression.
Urinary system	This is less active during exercise.	The blood it needs is diverted elsewhere.
Skin	This receives more blood and heats up.	This allows sweat glands to function – to cool the body down and eliminate wastes from the blood.

The principles of health and fitness

These are the key points of health and fitness – and they are explained below.

Health

A state of complete physical, mental and social well-being (World Health Organisation).

Fitness

Cardio-respiratory or aerobic endurance; muscular strength; muscular endurance; flexibility; and body composition, or the ratio of fat-to-lean body mass (The President's Council on Physical Fitness – USA 1992).

General fitness

A combination of aerobic endurance, flexibility and muscular strength.

Specific fitness

The ability to do job-related actions – such as climbing ladders or handling shields – which require aerobic endurance, flexibility, coordination and muscular strength.

Components of fitness

Fitness is divided into 'components' or parts. Some are 'health components' and others are 'performance components'. They are as follows.

1 Health components

These are linked to general health.

- **Cardiovascular fitness** – a healthy heart, healthy blood vessels and healthy lungs. If you have good endurance, don't get tired easily, and are rarely short of breath, you have a good standard of cardiovascular fitness.
- **Body composition** – the relationship between the amount of fat in your body, and everything else in your body, given as a percentage. Fit people have about 15 per cent body fat.

C⊙⊙L SITE:

www.healthchecksystems.com/bodyfat.htm

- **Flexibility** – being able to bend easily at the joints. It depends on the condition of tendons, ligaments, muscles and bones.
- **Muscular strength** – the ability of muscles to act strongly in a short period of time (e.g. when lifting heavy weights).
- **Muscular endurance** – the ability of muscles to continue working for long periods of time without resting.

2 Performance-related components

These abilities allow us to make the best use of our general fitness.

- **Agility** – the ability to change direction rapidly when running.
- **Balance** – the ability to avoid falling over.
- **Coordination** – the ability to do several movements at the same time.
- **Speed** – being able to move or react quickly.
- **Power** – the ability to make sudden, forceful movements.

SUPERGRADE! *Merit*

Analyse the operation of the major body systems in relation to health and fitness.

We cannot have fitness without health, or health without fitness. If any of the major body systems is not working well, poor health and reduced fitness will follow. But fitness training improves health by improving the working of the major body systems.

Let us look at this relationship in more detail.

The major body systems

The cardio-vascular system

A healthy heart benefits fitness by pumping blood strongly round the body. The fresh blood supplies food and oxygen to the muscles, so that the muscles have more strength and endurance. People with weak hearts are often short of breath because their muscles need oxygen but the heart is not strong enough to supply the necessary blood.

Healthy blood contains all the oxygen and nutrients that the muscles need. But diseases such as anaemia and leukaemia, and poor diet, lower the quality of the blood and reduce a person's fitness.

Healthy blood vessels are wide and supple, and allow all the blood to get to the muscles. But if blood vessels are 'hardened', as a result of age or alcohol abuse, or blocked with cholesterol, the muscles are starved of blood and fitness goes down.

Fitness training exercises the heart and makes it stronger. Fit people have lower blood pressure, slower resting heart rates, and can expect to live longer.

Fitness training also exercises arteries and veins. With exercise they open and close better, so they can supply the right amount of blood to the body.

The respiratory system

Healthy lungs get more oxygen into the bloodstream. They have large capacity and can fill and empty properly. The tiny blood vessels in the lungs take in plenty of oxygen. Where there is lung disease or damage from smoking the lungs cannot take in the amount of oxygen a person needs. Fitness declines and the person becomes short of breath if they try to exercise.

Exercise strengthens the diaphragm (the muscle that operates the lungs) and increases lung capacity.

The digestive system

A good diet, properly digested, is essential for a high level of fitness. If the digestive system is working badly, food will not be digested or absorbed well into the body. In addition, there is discomfort which makes it impossible to exercise well. If you have ever tried playing sport with indigestion or a hangover you will know what the problem is!

Exercise means movement, and this helps food to progress through the stomach and intestines and be digested.

LINK! There is more on diet and health starting on page 69.

The nervous system

The brain enables us to understand and feel fitness, and motivates us towards improved fitness. Some components of fitness, such as coordination, are learnt (by the brain). Planning for fitness takes place in the brain. A healthy brain is essential for all other kinds of health, and for full fitness. Brain damage (e.g. from strokes), and nervous illnesses (such as multiple sclerosis) can have a devastating effect on fitness, but even people suffering from these serious conditions can be helped (to some extent) by exercise.

Fitness improves the effectiveness of the brain by making our mind, our mental state, better. It does this by increasing the brain's blood supply, and producing hormones called enkephalins and endorphins which make us feel good. When we are fit we can think more clearly and creatively, and are less likely to feel tired and bored.

The skeletal system

Broken bones, or weak bones, such as those damaged by rickets or osteoporosis, are bad for fitness because they prevent exercise. Joint injuries such as torn ligaments or damaged cartilage interrupt sport and training and reduce fitness. Without a healthy skeleton it is hard to lead an active life and impossible to exercise fully.

Our bones strengthen when pressure is put on them. People who lead active, physical lives have heavier, stronger bones than people who spend their lives pen-pushing. Strong, fit muscles support the joints and make joint injury less likely. Flexibility training can make joints more supple.

However, the skeleton can be damaged by excessive training. Weight-lifters, gymnasts and ballet dancers run more risk of arthritis in later life than most people because of the strain they put on their joints when training and rehearsing.

Muscles

Fitness shows itself in the strength, stamina and easy movement of our muscles. Muscles which are exercised frequently and are well supplied with blood have good tone. They are firm yet supple, and can easily work at full strength.

Fitness training is good for muscles. Jogging, for example, develops the 'slow-twitch' muscle cells and greatly increases endurance. It also removes excess fat which can build up round the muscles and between the muscle cells. Weightlifting can develop strength by making the 'fast-twitch' cells grow bigger.

Strong muscles are good for general health. But over-training can damage muscles and leave them permanently weakened.

The endocrine system

Hormones from the endocrine system do a great deal to make us what we are. They control our growth, make us male or female, and affect the way we think. If our hormones are balanced we feel well and active – and enjoy exercise.

It is hard to change our endocrine system, even by exercising, because many aspects of it are genetic, i.e. determined before birth. But exercise speeds up our general metabolism (the chemical changes such as 'burning off' of fat), which is linked to some hormones. And by reducing stress, exercise stops us producing too much adrenaline when resting, which can lead to high blood pressure.

Excessive training can damage the endocrine system, at least temporarily – as for example when female athletes suffer from amenorrhea (absence of periods) as a result of training too hard. Over-training can also weaken the immune system.

> **! CHECKPOINT …**
> ■ Some people try to 'improve' their endocrine system by taking anabolic steroids and human growth hormone. What are the effects of this?

The urinary system

Healthy kidneys are necessary for fitness. If the kidneys are not working properly, urea and other chemicals build up in the blood and can cause depression, illness and death. Infections of the bladder and urethra, sometimes related to venereal disease, cause discomfort, poison the blood and undermine fitness.

For fitness it is important to control the balance of water and other chemicals (especially salt) in the body and bloodstream. This is what the urinary system does.

Fitness training can cause dehydration, and it is important to drink enough water, so that the kidneys can keep the right balance of water and salts in the body.

The skin

The skin controls our temperature by sweating and so allowing us to cool off. It also protects us against the environment – sun, water, cold, heat, sharp or rough objects, and so on. Skin wounds, and diseases such as acne and eczema, though rarely fatal, reduce our fitness by causing pain and discomfort.

Exercise opens up the capillaries (tiny blood vessels in the skin). This is good for skin tone. Sweating clears the pores (holes) in the skin. Without exercise they get blocked up and this can lead to acne and spots.

Sweating is good for you – but dehydration isn't

SUPERGRADE! *Distinction*

> Evaluate the main components of fitness and their importance in public service activity.

This means deciding how important each type of fitness is – both in everyday life and in public service work. You need to back up your ideas with reasons and explanations.

Health components

Cardiovascular fitness

This leads to good endurance and generally good health. Cardiovascular fitness is a professional and social advantage, because it gives a person 'bags of energy' and makes them more physically attractive. People with this kind of fitness are usually the right weight for their height.

The importance of cardiovascular fitness in public service work is:

(a) for stamina. This is especially important in the armed forces. The exercises and route marches in the army and the marines require excellent cardiovascular fitness. Stamina is also needed for working the long shifts in any public service.

(b) for raising morale. Cardiovascular fitness is related to a general feeling of well-being, and this leads to good morale – a cheerful and positive feeling about life. High morale protects public service workers against stress and the risk of depression.

Body composition

This is an important issue in modern western society, where we judge people on their shape. And being overweight or underweight is bad for fitness.

The skinfold test given to public service applicants shows that public services such as the police consider the percentage of body fat to be important. Excess body fat can lead to mobility problems, e.g. when chasing a suspect. But it may be that the police share the 'lookist' attitudes of society, and worry about the image overweight officers would give the service.

Flexibility

The connection between flexibility and health has been recognised since ancient times, for example in yoga. It is also known that people get less flexible with age, so flexibility is linked with youth, or with feeling young. Flexibility raises your self-esteem – in other words, it makes you feel good about yourself. It is clearly important in sports such as football, tennis, gymnastics and athletics.

In the public services flexibility is important in the armed forces and the fire service, where people have to work hard in confined spaces. Some fitness tests, e.g. assault courses, test flexibility.

Muscular strength

Like other components of fitness, muscular strength is admired in society as a whole, especially in men. The popularity of Arnold Schwarzenegger and Sylvester Stallone shows this.

Muscular strength is needed in the ambulance service, the fire service and the armed forces, where heavy weights or equipment have to be handled.

Muscular endurance

This is related to cardiovascular fitness, but involves individual muscles and muscle groups. It is valuable in leisure activities like hiking, cycling, distance running and potholing.

It is needed in some of the public services, especially the armed forces. In the army the infantry, for example, have training in forced marches where a high level of muscular endurance is needed.

Performance-related components

These are related to how effectively – either in sport or work – we can use our fitness.

Agility

Agility is an important fitness component in sports such as football and rugby, where a lot of dodging and wrong-footing opponents is done. It's also useful for outdoor recreations such as hill-walking in rough country.

In public service work it is useful in emergencies such as arresting fleeing criminals, in mountain rescue, and in some fire service work. The police, among others, test this fitness component in their entry tests.

Balance

We use balance all the time, without thinking about it. It is developed by rock-climbers, horse-riders and cyclists who use balancing skills in their sports.

In the fire service it is used in ladder climbing; it is also used in special army training, such as skiing. It is tested in the fire service entry test – in the ladder climb – and in the army, where assault courses both test and train balancing skills.

Coordination

Coordination is needed for everything from breathing to brain surgery. Applicants for some mechanical jobs have to take aptitude tests to find out if their coordination is good enough. These tests involve fitting shapes into spaces, or pegs into holes, in a short period of time.

In the public services, typists, nurses, firefighters and many personnel in the armed forces, such as mechanics and pilots, need excellent coordination to carry out their jobs. Typing letters, giving injections, cutting people out of car wreckage and aiming a gun involve controlling many muscles, quickly and accurately, at the same time. Even routine tasks like driving, or writing memos, need a high level of coordination.

A good deal of public service training is training in coordination. Every day firefighters roll hoses and handle ladders, because in coordination only practice makes perfect.

Speed

Speed of action and reaction is rather like agility. We develop this fitness component through recreational sports.

Reaction time is related to speed; this is a trainable skill. The same is true of speed in running.

Speed of reaction is important in specialised aspects of public service work such as car chases and military activity in the armed forces.

Power

This, too, is a fitness component which is more important in sports than in most public service work. We now have machines which give us far more power than the unaided human body can supply.

In life-threatening situations power may be needed to rescue someone trapped in a burning vehicle. And again, power will help you to defend yourself from personal attack.

PASSGRADE

> Explain the importance of good nutrition and its impact on health and fitness.

Nutrition is the scientific study of food and how it is used by the body.

FOCUS

Food can be defined as something we eat – e.g. eggs, beans, hamburgers, apples – which the body can use.

Nutrients are the main chemicals in food – e.g. carbohydrates, fats, proteins, vitamins, minerals. These are absorbed and processed in the digestive system.

Water and fibre are not nutrients, because though the body needs them it cannot change them into anything else.

Oxygen is not called a nutrient because it enters the body through the lungs.

In this outcome 'good nutrition' means getting the right amounts of the right kinds of food for our bodies' needs.

Good nutrition is essential for good health. It helps children to grow, and old people to live longer. Poor nutrition has all sorts of bad effects, and is the cause of huge amounts of illness and suffering in the world.

Nutritionists have identified five groups of food which we all need.

If we eat the right amount of each group, each day, then we have a balanced diet. And a balanced diet makes us healthy and fit, if we take the right kind of exercise as well.

The five food groups and their impact on health and fitness

Group 1 foods

These include bread, cereals, rice, potatoes, etc. These starchy foods are rich in chemicals called carbohydrates. They give us energy without making us fat.

The carbohydrates these foods contain are unrefined, and it takes the body some time to break them down. This is good, because it means the energy they contain is released over a long period of time. Athletes eat large amounts of Group 1 foods to give them the energy they need in training.

Group 1 foods also aid digestion of other foods, thanks to the large amount of fibre they contain.

Group 2 foods

Fruit and vegetables. These are healthy foods because they contain vitamins, minerals and fibre. They are good for the eyes, bones, hair, skin, muscle tone and general health. They strengthen the immune system and protect against illnesses, including heart disease and cancer.

Group 3 foods

Milk and dairy foods, such as cheese and yogurt, are full of proteins, vitamins and minerals. They are good for children because they contain calcium, which is needed for healthy bone growth.

The problem with dairy foods is that some – such as cream and butter – contain a lot of fat. This fat is 'saturated' fat which is bad for the heart and can block the blood vessels.

Group 4 foods

These include meat, fish, chicken, eggs, etc. These foods are rich in protein. They contain vitamins and minerals as well.

They are good for active young people as the protein builds muscles and the minerals strengthen bones. Athletes, especially those who do strength-orientated sports, such as rugby or weightlifting, eat plenty of these foods – but they usually trim the fat off first!

Vegetarians eat food based on beans and nuts to get most of their protein.

Group 5 foods

These foods contain large amounts of fat and sugar. They include butter, cream, cakes, pastry, sweets, chocolate, fish and chips, some hamburgers and some types of cheese.

Fats and oils are related, and both are needed by the body to some extent – for example, for the digestion of protein. But most of us eat too much of them.

Fats come in two kinds: saturated and unsaturated. Saturated fats come from butter, cream, egg-yolks and fatty meat. They are high in cholesterol, a chemical we need in small amounts, but not in large. Too much cholesterol can cause heart disease.

Unsaturated fats, which include uncooked olive oil, sunflower oil, and oil from fish such as sardines, herring and mackerel, are good for us. But they change into saturated fats if they are used in frying.

Sugar is also a Group 5 food. It comes from plants like sugar cane and beet. Chocolate, sweets, soft drinks, jam, cakes, fruit pies, puddings and biscuits are rich in sugar. Sugar is a refined carbohydrate and gives quick energy, especially in the form called glucose.

Natural sugars such as those found in fruit and vegetables are not harmful. But refined sugar contributes to obesity and causes tooth decay, which is still a serious problem in Britain.

The amount of sugar in the blood is controlled by the hormone insulin, released from the pancreas gland. People who do not produce enough insulin suffer from diabetes. This dangerous condition can sometimes be controlled by low-sugar diets.

Water

Water is not a food, but all the body systems need it. If you don't drink enough water for fitness training you can die of dehydration!

Salt

It's an essential mineral, but if you eat too much it can raise blood pressure and increase the risk of heart disease.

C👓L SITES:

www.nutrition.org.uk/

www.foodstandards.gov.uk/

SUPERGRADE! *Merit*

> Analyse the impact of good nutrition and diet on health and fitness.

For this outcome you need to discuss the relationship between what we eat and our health and fitness in more depth. This means using some technical terms such as:

- **Calorie** – a measure of the amount of energy in a food.
- **Carbohydrates** – chemicals including starches and sugars which give energy when digested.
- **Protein** – complex chemicals found in meat and fish which the body uses to build its tissues.
- **Fats and oils** – chemicals which do not mix with water. They are rich in energy, used to digest protein, and can be stored in the body.

- **Vitamins** – chemicals which are found in food in small amounts, but which we need for healthy eyes, skin, hair, and protection against disease.
- **Minerals** – chemicals which contain no carbon. The main ones we need are salt, calcium and iron, but we need traces of others as well.
- **Fibre** – is found in vegetables, fruit, brown bread and most Group 1 foods except polished rice. It is needed for good digestion.
- **Digestion** – the breaking down of food in the digestive system, into a form which can be absorbed into the body.
- **Metabolism** – the use of nutrients by the body after they have been absorbed.

'Good diet' in this outcome is a range of foods which suit the body's needs.

If we want to be healthy and fit it is important to know something about nutrition, so that we can choose the kind of nutrition and diet which is best for our needs.

An analysis of the impact of good nutrition and diet on health and fitness could include the following points:

1. Good nutrition means eating the right amounts of all five food groups – i.e. plenty of 1 and 2; some 3 and 4; not much of 5. A balanced diet is vital for health and fitness. It should start in babyhood and continue through life.
2. Changing from bad nutrition to good nutrition will have far-reaching benefits on health and fitness, but these will not be noticed immediately.
3. Because we are all different, good nutrition varies from person to person. Age, lifestyle and body weight affect the kinds of food we should eat.
4. To get the best out of good nutrition, people must lead a healthy lifestyle with plenty of exercise.
5. There is no basic difference in the healthiness of food eaten by different ethnic groups – but any diet that regularly contains too much sugar or fat is harmful.
6. Nutrition includes what we drink as well as what we eat. Alcohol is an energy-rich food but with damaging health effects similar to oils and fats.

7 Overcooked vegetables are poor in vitamins, and undercooked meat can cause food poisoning.

8 Processed meats are more likely to carry food poisoning organisms than fresh meat that has been recently slaughtered or kept deep-frozen.

9 There are health worries about supermarket meat which might contain hormones, and fruit and vegetables with pesticide and herbicide residues. But it is better to eat these than not have a balanced diet.

10 It is essential to have some food from each of the five groups. None of them can be missed out completely.

Plan a dietary programme including an explanation of Recommended Nutrient Intake and the food group system.

Recommended Nutrient Intake

It is now compulsory to label the types and amounts of nutrients on tins, packets and jars of processed food. And in order to educate the public and improve public health, the governments of many developed countries have produced tables of recommended nutrient intakes.

In Britain the recommended nutrient intake is called the Reference Nutrient Intake (RNI). The RNI is defined as 'the amount of nutrient which is enough for at least 97% of the population'. Until 1991 it was known as the Recommended Daily Allowance (RDA).

The Reference Nutrient Intake covers vitamins and minerals. It does not include carbohydrates and proteins, because the need for these varies so much with age, body size and lifestyle.

The food group system

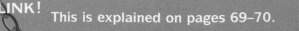

LINK! This is explained on pages 69–70.

Planning a dietary programme

A dietary programme is a plan showing what a person should eat, over a period of time. It should contain information about:

- the person the programme is planned for
- the dietary needs related to their age, sex, weight and lifestyle
- the food for each meal
- the main nutrients of each meal
- the number of calories per day
- any allergies or other food problems which might be relevant
- any relevant medical conditions, e.g. diabetes
- any relevant religious or cultural factors.

The outcome does not specify the number of days the programme should cover, and you should take advice from your tutor on this. One realistic way of doing it would be to plan the diet for a three-day residential at an outdoor centre.

Profile

Dietary Programme for John Heydon
Age: 17
Height: 183 cm
Weight: 80 kg
Lifestyle: Staying at Long Kin East Outdoor Centre; doing adventurous outdoor activities – caving, walking, rock climbing, mountain biking, etc.
Period: Wednesday 13 – Friday 15 March, 2004

Meal	Food	Food group	Nutritional information	Calorie totals
Wednesday				
Breakfast	Orange juice	2	141 kcal	
	Cornflakes	1	200 kcal	
	Bacon	4	350 kcal	
	Eggs	4	200 kcal	
	Toast	1	50 kcal	
	Butter	5	50 kcal	
	Marmalade	5	50 kcal	
	Coffee	5	20 kcal	1061
Packed lunch	Three chicken sandwiches	1 + 4	600	
	Apple	2	60	
	Two biscuits	5	300	
	Bar of chocolate	5	300	1260
Dinner	Chicken soup	4	150	
	Spaghetti bolognese	1 + 4	500	
	Tinned apricots	2	100	
	Cup of tea	–	17	767
Thursday				
Breakfast	Orange juice	2	140	
	Cornflakes	1	200	
	Bacon	4	350	
	Eggs	4	200	
	Toast	1	50	
	Butter	5	50	
	Marmalade	5	50	
	Coffee	5	17	1057
Packed lunch	Three chicken sandwiches	1 + 4	600	
	Two apples	2	120	
	Two biscuits	5	300	
	Bar of chocolate	5	300	1320
Dinner	Tomato soup	2	120	
	Three hamburgers	4	750	
	Mashed potatoes	1	200	
	Leeks and carrots	2	420	
	Apple pie	5	230	
	Hot chocolate	5	105	1825
Friday				
Breakfast	Orange juice	2	140	
	Cornflakes	1	200	
	Two boiled eggs	4	150	
	Toast	1	200	

Meal	Food	Food group	Nutritional information	Calorie totals
	Butter	5	50	
	Marmalade	5	50	
	Coffee	5	17	807
Packed lunch	Three cheese sandwiches	3 + 1	700	
	Apple	2	60	
	Two bars of chocolate	5	600	
	Two biscuits	5	300	1660
Dinner	Chicken soup	4	150	
	Three slices of bread	1	200	
	Sausage and vegetable casserole	4 + 2	500	
	Chips	1	450	
	Tinned apricots	2	90	
	Tea	–	17	1407

Daily calorie totals:

Wednesday 3088

Thursday 4202

Friday 3874

Comments

For these three days John's diet will contain more than the 2800 calories recommended for a young man of his age. The reason for this is that he will be doing strenuous, adventurous activities in cold and possibly wet conditions.

He will need a liquid intake equivalent to at least eight glasses of water per day to avoid the risk of dehydration.

The fruit and vegetables (Group 2 foods) are not enough for a long-term diet. They will be adequate for three days' residential, however. Fruit is heavy to carry on the mountain, and vegetables are hard to cook after a long day doing tiring activities.

Considering his age, John is slightly overweight for his height, and should therefore go back to 2800 calories, or even slightly less, after the residential is over – or he should follow an exercise programme.

SUPERGRADE! *Distinction*

Evaluate the impact of good nutrition on the human body and from the planning of a dietary programme make clear recommendations explaining briefly the nutritional value of food.

To evaluate the impact (effect) of good nutrition you have to make a reasoned judgement about how great that 'impact' is.

Your main points could be:

- Good nutrition is of vital importance in establishing health and fitness. Without good nutrition it is impossible to reach one's peak in either health or fitness.
- Children do not reach their full potential in either growth or strength if they do not have a good diet. Healthy eating also tends to increase intelligence. Some children's health is badly undermined by junk food and by artificial additives such as colourings and flavourings. These can affect the child's behaviour as well, and cause hyperactivity and attention deficit syndrome (inability to concentrate).
- Good nutrition is associated with long life. The country with the longest average life expectancy is Japan. The reasons for this may be partly

genetic, but the most likely reason is the Japanese diet. It traditionally contains raw fish, seaweed, plenty of vegetables, plenty of rice, and very little fat or sugar. The Japanese have low rates of both heart disease and cancer, though unfortunately these diseases are increasing there, as a result of copying western eating habits and the growing popularity of fast food.

- Good nutrition is important at all stages of life, from babyhood to old age. It is especially important for pregnant women, since the health of the baby depends on her eating properly. There is some evidence that malnutrition causes genetic defects, and that if there is a famine, a population takes more than one generation to recover from the bad effects.
- Fresh food is better than processed food, and gives some protection against most diseases.
- There is little evidence that it matters much when you eat, or how often you eat, though the general feeling is that it is better to eat little and often than to eat huge, widely spaced meals.
- Alcohol, with the possible exception of red wine in moderate amounts, is bad for health, and the same is true of recreational drugs – whether taken for enjoyment, or for bodybuilding and sports performance.

Recommendations explaining briefly the nutritional value of food

The nutritional value of food is based on the carbohydrates, proteins, fats, vitamins and minerals it contains.

LINK! See pages 69–70 for food groups and their nutritional value.

C👓L BOOK:

Manual of nutrition
10th edition MAFF Reference Book No. 342
HMSO (1995) 166pp tables
ISBN 0112429912

! CHECKPOINT ...

Examine your own diet and decide what changes should be made to help you achieve maximum health and fitness.

Unit 4 Citizenship

Grading criteria

PASSGRADE	SUPERGRADE! *Merit*	SUPERGRADE! *Distinction*
To achieve a pass grade the evidence must show that the learner is able to:	To achieve a merit grade the evidence must show that the learner is able to:	To achieve a distinction grade the evidence must show that the learner is able to:
● explain the term 'citizen(s)' as defined by at least two public services and the qualities of 'good' citizenship required for entry into at least two public services **76**	● explain how culturally diverse citizenship is affecting at least one public service **81**	● analyse the types and diversity of citizens and their effect on public services **82**
● identify the differing groups of citizens found within society and the origins and implications of diversity within the public services **78**	● analyse how two public services address the main issues associated with equal opportunities **87**	● evaluate and compare the approach used by two public services to the main issues of equal opportunities **88**
● name the legislative documents associated with human rights, individual rights and equal opportunities **85**	● differentiate between statutory and non-statutory public services, analysing the role the monarchy, and central and local government have in setting up or assisting each of these types of services **95**	● evaluate the role the monarchy, and central and local government play in the setting-up of, or assistance with, statutory and non-statutory public services **97**
● describe the principles of human rights and explain how two public services implement equal opportunities policies into their organisations **90**		
● describe the voting system employed in a democratic society and define the responsibility of central and local government towards citizens and citizenship issues **91**		
● explain the differences between statutory and non-statutory public services and how one statutory and one non-statutory service assists in the development of citizenship in the local community **93**		

Citizenship is a very old idea which is now coming into fashion again. It is about the rights and responsibilities which people have when they live together in a community or a country.

The word 'citizenship' comes from citizen, meaning the inhabitant of a city. Later it also came to mean the inhabitant of a country. These two meanings are still mixed up in the modern meaning of the word.

In this unit we are going to look at what citizenship really means, and its relevance to public service work.

PASSGRADE

Explain the term 'citizen(s)' as defined by at least two public services and the qualities of 'good' citizenship required for entry into at least two public services.

There are two ways of defining the word citizen:

- the nationality of a person
- someone with full adult rights and responsibilities.

Definitions linked to nationality

Home Office

The Home Office, the branch of government to which the police are attached, defines British citizens as follows: 'British citizens have the right to live here permanently and are free to leave and re-enter the United Kingdom at any time.'

This means that they can have British passports, vote in British elections (if they are old enough) and receive British benefits and medical care.

Police

The police have citizenship requirements linked to nationality when they are recruiting people.

FOCUS

Nationality
You must be a British, Irish or Commonwealth citizen with unrestricted right of residence in the UK.

A Commonwealth citizen comes from a country such as Australia, Canada, Nigeria, South Africa, Jamaica, India, etc. These are all countries that were governed by Britain at one time. But most Commonwealth citizens do not have unrestricted right of residence in the UK, and therefore could not join the police.

Ireland has closer links with Britain than any other country. For this reason Irish citizens can become British police officers provided they fulfil all other requirements.

Police nationality requirements come from the fact that the police are concerned with the security and protection of the country, e.g. against terrorists. The police use these citizenship requirements to help make sure that all recruits are loyal to Britain.

Civil Service

The job of the civil service is to work for the government, so the civil service is a public service. Services such as Her Majesty's Customs and Excise come under the civil service. Their citizenship requirements for applicants are as follows.

FOCUS

You can apply for any job in the Civil Service as long as you're a UK national or have dual nationality with one being British. As a European Economic Area national, EU national or Commonwealth citizen, you're eligible for about 75% of our jobs, but most Fast Stream candidates must be UK nationals. You'll be asked about your nationality at birth, whether you have ever possessed any other nationality or citizenship, whether you are subject to immigration control and whether there are any restrictions on your continued residence or employment in the UK.

The civil service, like the police and the army, expects a certain loyalty to Britain in its employees, and therefore has nationality requirements. These requirements are strictest for the top jobs, e.g. those done by 'Fast Stream candidates'. This is because they have to deal with more official secrets – information linked to the security of the country.

Definitions linked to rights and responsibilities

FOCUS

Definition of citizenship

'Citizenship involves three elements, civil, political and social. The civil element is composed of the rights necessary for individual freedom. The political element involves the right to participate in the exercise of political power. And the social element involves the range of rights to welfare, security and to live the life of a civilised being according to the standards prevailing in the society.'

Source: Adapted from T.H. Marshall, *Citizenship and Social Class* (Institute for Citizenship 2000 – an independent charitable trust)

This definition stresses rights. It says that citizenship is:

- freedom
- the right to vote
- the right to live a secure, civilised life.

Another definition is:

FOCUS

'Citizenship comprises three distinct but interrelated elements: social and moral responsibility, community involvement and political literacy.'

Source: *Education for citizenship and the teaching of democracy in schools*, the final report of the Advisory Group on Citizenship (Institute for Citizenship 2000)

This definition stresses responsibilities:

- upholding the law
- helping, protecting and respecting other people
- using your vote.

This definition is closer to what most people mean by 'good citizenship' because it links good citizenship with good behaviour.

The qualities of good citizenship required for entry into at least two public services

Public services like their employees to be good citizens. They don't want criminals, and they don't want people who are selfish and inconsiderate.

The following are two examples of the qualities of good citizenship that they are looking for.

1 Ambulance service

FOCUS

Ambulance personnel at all levels must be honest, show initiative, have good people skills and a caring personality and be prepared to work with all types of people. They must be responsible and take their work extremely seriously. They have to be well organised and enjoy working as part of a team, while being able to make their own decisions when necessary. They must stay calm when under pressure and possess good communication skills.

Source: www.nhscareers.nhs.uk/nhs-knowledge_base/data/5118.html

All the qualities here are good qualities, but three of them are closely linked to citizenship as defined above.

Honesty is a quality of good citizenship because it is linked to obeying the law. It is needed for public service work, because honest people can be trusted.

A caring personality is a quality of good citizenship. It shows responsibility towards other people, means you want to look after them and help them, and is linked to the caring nature of ambulance work.

Being prepared to work with all kinds of people is a sign of good citizenship. People who are snobbish, or who discriminate against others, are not good citizens, and would not be good for the ambulance service.

The aspect of citizenship linked to voting is not mentioned by the ambulance service. This is because good public service employees should be non-political. Public service employees who get involved in politics are likely to be accused of bias, prejudice or discrimination.

Public service employees who get involved in politics are likely to be accused of bias, prejudice or discrimination.

2 The fire service

The fire service expects qualities of good citizenship from its applicants. The example below is typical.

'Of good character' means almost the same as 'a good citizen'. It means 'honest and law-abiding'.

Many public services – even the fire service – will now accept people who have criminal convictions. But these must not go against the requirement of 'good character'. That is why the criminal convictions must be 'spent', i.e. more than three years old. A person who breaks the law is not of good character, but after three years have safely passed, their character may have become good. However, if the criminal offences were serious – e.g. theft, drug offences or rape – the fire service could refuse such applicants on the grounds that their character is still bad. They would also take it as a sign of bad character if an applicant failed to mention any previous conviction, however minor, because this would show dishonesty.

Identify the differing groups of citizens found within society and the origins and implications of diversity within the public services.

Society is a word we use a lot, but which is not easy to define. One dictionary definition is: 'The totality of social relationships among humans' (Webster's Dictionary). Another way of looking at society is to say that it is all the people around us – individuals, groups and organisations. So society includes just about anybody you can think of!

Here are just some of the groups of citizens that make up society.

FOCUS

What will I need to do to become a firefighter?

Entry criteria:

- At least 18 years old
- Good eyesight and colour perception
- Good medical background
- Of good character
- Have no unspent criminal convictions under the Rehabilitation of Offenders Act 1974

Source: Gloucestershire Fire and Rescue Service (2002)

Social influences

- Family
- Friends
- Schools
- Religions
- The law
- The media

Occupational groups

- Teachers
- Soldiers
- Non-uniformed public services
- Shopkeepers

Ethnic groups

- English
- Pakistani
- West African
- Chinese
- Irish
- European

Religious groups

- Hindu
- Jewish
- Christian
- Agnostic
- Muslim
- Atheist

Subculture and leisure

- Bikers
- Skinheads
- Travellers
- Football supporters
- Hippies

Socio-economic groups

- The middle classes
- The poor
- The unemployed
- Home owners
- Consumers
- Taxpayers

Political groups

- Labour Party
- Conservative Party
- Members of Parliament
- Local councillors

The media

- Radio
- Television
- Newspapers
- Advertising
- The Internet
- Music and art

Disadvantaged groups

- Bangladeshis
- Old people
- Young people
- Single parents
- Mentally ill
- Asylum seekers
- Women

Others

- Geordies
- Ufologists
- Readers of *The Times*
- Gays
- Cancer researchers
- Ourselves

All these people – and many other groups – live in Britain and are part of British society. Yet they are all different from each other. This difference is called diversity.

Origins and implications of diversity

1 Ethnic diversity

Ethnic diversity in Britain is thousands of years old. Celts, Romans, Saxons and Vikings invaded and then intermarried between a thousand and two thousand years ago. Their movements and where they settled can still be traced in regional accents and the distribution of different blood groups.

Though Britain was not invaded after 1066, many refugees came from Europe and Israel over the centuries between 1100 and 1800. From 1840 onwards over a million Irish people settled in Britain, first to escape the Potato Famine, then as labourers building canals, railways and roads.

In the 1930s and 1940s Jews, Poles and others came from central Europe to escape Nazism, Fascism and World War II. After them came refugees from communist Russia and countries like Hungary (1956) and Lithuania.

Our modern ethnic diversity began in the 1950s and 1960s, when British employers, keen to rebuild industry and wealth after World War II, advertised in India, Pakistan and the West Indies for labour. Each year, between 40,000 and 100,000 people came from these countries and got work. In the 1970s their families came and settled, as did thousands of Asians who were being thrown out of East Africa. In the 1980s, more immigrants arrived from Bangladesh and, in the 1990s, Hong Kong. All these people settled and had children and grandchildren who are British yet belong to their parents' ethnic minority group.

2 Other kinds of diversity

It isn't just ethnic diversity which has increased in the last fifty years. Other kinds of diversity that have changed society are:

- The break-up of the old class system. British society is no longer divided up into middle and working class people in the clear way that it once was.
- The kinds of work available are different, and more difficult to classify.
- Education goes on throughout life, so people keep changing and developing more than they used to.
- Lifestyles are different – marriage has changed and many couples live together without marrying.

In addition:

- Women now have equal pay (officially) and equal rights.
- We can have any religion we like, or none at all.

- We are no longer divided as rigidly into working classes and middle classes as we once were.
- Most children are taught at comprehensive schools, instead of the discriminatory grammar school/secondary modern system.
- People can be openly gay or lesbian if they want.
- Most of us no longer live and work where our parents lived or worked.
- Thanks to the pill, people can have sex without the risk of unwanted children.

The reasons for these lifestyle changes are complex. They are a development of a process which has been going on since the Industrial Revolution, in about 1800, when people first started living in towns and working in factories. Two world wars had a huge effect, especially on women who had to do men's work when men were away fighting. The media – films and books – have made people rethink the purpose of life and the kinds of life they want. The influence of America has given people a greater desire for personal freedom. And medical and technical advances such as birth control pills, easy transport and computers have given everybody more choice about how they live.

Implications of diversity on the public services

Public services are part of society, and diversity has affected them as much as it has affected everybody else. The main effects have been:

(a) on the way they work with the public
(b) on their recruiting.

Diversity and working with the public

1 The police, fire, ambulance and prison services have had to work with people from many different races and cultures. They have had to learn to understand those cultures in order to communicate with them and get their cooperation. For example, they have had to learn community languages and employ translators.

2 Laws have changed. The Race Relations Act of 1976 outlawed race discrimination. The public services have often been accused of racism and they have had to change their way of treating the public – especially the non-white public. The Police and Criminal Evidence Act (PACE) of 1984 gave strict guidelines to the police so they would be less likely to behave in a racist way.

3 Changes in everybody's lifestyles have changed public service work. The police are no longer allowed to hang about in public toilets trying to catch homosexuals – but they do have to get involved in domestic violence and child abuse cases, which used to be regarded as 'family matters'. The police are now also being asked to change their attitude to some drugs – especially cannabis – because they are becoming so widely accepted in society.

4 The police are having to deal with society's conflicts, e.g. between British citizens and asylum seekers. Their work is getting increasingly political, so they get a lot of criticism from the media.

Diversity and recruiting

1 One reason why the public services have so often been accused of racism is that they have not recruited from ethnic minorities. They are now trying as hard as they can to recruit people from ethnic minorities without bending the rules or reducing standards. Nevertheless, the average police force only has about 2% of its officers from ethnic minorities, yet the average percentage of people from ethnic minorities in society is 9% (2001 Census). The aim is for public services to have the same ethnic mix as the communities they serve.

2 The other side of this coin is that people from ethnic minority groups have often been unwilling to apply for public service jobs. Muslims of Pakistani or Indian background are unwilling to join the army because they may have to fight against Muslims in Afghanistan and Iraq. Afro-Caribbeans have often felt picked on by the police and fear they will be regarded as 'traitors' by their friends if they apply. Public services have to find ways of getting more people to apply from ethnic minority communities. They have tried to do this by removing height restrictions, and allowing Sikhs to wear turbans.

3 The public services ought to have about 50% women in their ranks if they are truly to reflect the society they serve. They are all well below this level. This is because of prejudice against women (e.g. in the fire service, where women have been traditionally seen as too weak for the job). In the army, women are still not allowed to join the infantry or fight in the front line.

 **SUPERGRADE!** *Merit*

> Explain how culturally diverse citizenship is affecting at least one public service.

The prison service is being changed considerably by diverse citizenship. This is because more and more prison inmates are coming from ethnic minority groups. Recent figures show that people from most ethnic minorities are more likely to be imprisoned than white people.

FOCUS

Prison population April 2002
Among male British nationals in the prison population 84% were white, 11% were black, 3% were South Asian (i.e. Indian, Pakistani or Bangladeshi) and 2% belonged to Chinese or other ethnic groups. For female British nationals in the prison population, 84% were white, 12% were black, 1% were south Asian and 4% belonged to Chinese or other ethnic groups.

This compares with the general population of England and Wales (British nationals aged 15–64) of whom 95% were white, 1% were black, 3% were South Asian and 1% belonged to other ethnic groups.

Source: Home Office

The figures in the Focus box refer to British nationals only. In fact there are also a large number of non-white foreign nationals in British prisons.

The prison service is making big efforts to satisfy the needs of these prisoners from ethnic minorities. This does not mean treating them better than British prisoners – but it means giving them the same level of consideration and respect.

Religious diversity

A recent survey showed that 26,000 out of the 65,000 prison inmates in the UK were classified as belonging to the Church of England, while only 4,355 inmates were Muslims. However, the prison service has appointed a Muslim adviser, Maqsood Ahmed, to ensure that Muslim prisoners and their religion and culture – are treated with respect.

Racial diversity

The prison service has suffered from racism over the years. The service now has an equal opportunities policy to attack racism and discrimination. One of the main aspects of this is to make sure that it recruits new prison officers from all sections of the population – until the percentage of prison officers from ethnic minorities is the same as that of the prisoners.

Gender diversity

In the past women prison officers worked only in women's prisons. Now women work in men's prisons as well. This is because of equal opportunities, and because women can sometimes deal with the kinds of problems met with in prison better than men, because they are less likely to take a 'macho' attitude to prisoners labelled as 'difficult'.

SUPERGRADE! *Distinction*

> Analyse the types and diversity of citizens and their effect on public services.

A citizen is an individual living in a society. So we are all citizens. The type of citizen we are depends on:

(a) what we are, e.g. male, female, young, old, our ethnic and cultural background
(b) what we do, e.g. consumer, family member, taxpayer, voter, worker, learner
(c) our lifestyle, e.g. religious, sporting, criminal, drug-taking, straight, gay
(d) our personality, e.g. sociable, aggressive, passive, cheerful, depressed.

The following table contains an analysis of the types of citizen listed in the 'Content' section of the new specifications, and their effect on the public services.

Type of citizen	Analysis of type	Effect on public services
Consumer	Consuming is buying, so we are all consumers. When we buy a hamburger, a holiday or a car, we are being consumers. When we buy goods we keep industry going, and we make the country richer – but we may also damage the environment.	Most crime is against property. In West Yorkshire in 1999 over 286,000 crimes were recorded, of which about 275,000 were against property. If we were not consumers, no one would have any property to steal, and this type of crime would cease to exist. So without consuming we wouldn't need many police officers, or prisons.
Family member	Everybody is, or has been, a family member. In Britain the traditional close family consists of mother, father and children. This is called the 'nuclear' family. A single-parent family is also a 'nuclear' family. In other cultures grandparents, uncles, aunts and cousins play a much more important role in each family. This kind of family is called an 'extended' family. In countries such as India, extended families often live together, but in Britain this is difficult because most houses are not big enough. Increasingly, though, people are living alone.	The family cuts down the work the public services have to do. Many old and long-term sick people are cared for by their families rather than the public services. However, changes in family structure in Britain mean that more care is carried out by professional public service workers such as doctors and nurses than used to be the case. Public services are increasingly involved in 'dysfunctional' families – where there is violence and abuse. The police have a good deal of 'domestic' work to do, and this means that they have had to develop new skills. New laws, such as the Children Act of 1989, have given the public services (including social workers) a bigger and clearer role in protecting children.

Type of citizen	Analysis of type	Effect on public services
Taxpayer	In Britain anybody who earns more than about £4,000 a year has to pay income tax. House-owners have to pay Council tax, and when we buy things, we often pay VAT. Taxes pay for public services such as roads, education, the National Health Service and defence.	Without taxpayers there would be little money to pay for public services. This would mean that, as in some African or Asian countries, most public service work in Britain would be done by volunteers. Some people try to evade (dodge) paying taxes. People who work in the Inland Revenue try to get them to pay. But if they still won't pay, the police, lawyers and Customs and Excise have to step in.
Voter	In Britain we can vote in elections if we are 18 or over. There are two main kinds of election: (a) local elections, where we vote for councillors who are there to help us with local problems – say to do with schooling or unsafe roads; (b) general elections, where we vote for Members of Parliament who sit in the House of Commons in London. Some of them serve in the government as ministers, etc. They make major decisions about the country, such as what kind of education system or public services we ought to have, and whether we need to go to war. We also have elections to choose Members of the European Parliament in Brussels. These are important for environmental and human rights issues, and for the long-term future of the country. The diversity of voters is reflected in the system of political parties we have in this country, e.g. Labour, Conservative and Liberal Democrat. Each of these parties sets out to represent a different range of beliefs about how the country should be run. As citizens we all have the right – and the duty – to vote in elections. If everybody votes, we get a better government, because they know what we really want.	The public services are controlled locally by councillors, and nationally by politicians (Members of Parliament). Councillors sit on Fire and Police Authorities and make decisions about the work of the local fire service and police. Members of Parliament vote on the police, new laws, prisons, the National Health Service – and so on. The police are linked to a government department called the Home Office; the armed forces are linked to the Ministry of Defence, and the Fire Service to the Department for Transport, Local Government and the Regions. The people in power in these departments are MPs chosen by the Prime Minister. European elections do not usually have a direct effect on our public services. But they have an effect on the way Customs and the police deal with asylum seekers and illegal immigrants. They also help us to deal with consumer issues such as the price of cars and fuel, and environmental issues such as pollution of the environment, and overfishing of the sea round Britain. The political party in power has a great effect on how public services are run. The present government, Labour, believes in spending as much as possible on the public services, and in having those services run (more or less) by the government. The Conservatives would like to see more privately run prisons and security, and less tax spent on public services. The Liberal Democrats are closer (at present) to Labour than they are to the Conservatives.

Type of citizen	Analysis of type	Effect on public services
Worker	It is good for individuals and for the country as a whole if everybody has a job. Most people feel bored and dissatisfied if they cannot work. There has always been diversity in work, because there are different needs for different kinds of work, and because some people are good at one kind of job, and others are good at another. There is also diversity in pay, because society seems to think some jobs are worth more than others. In general, jobs requiring more skill and training are paid better than jobs that most people could do. Many of society's problems stem from the fact that, due to inequality of pay, and due to the fact that some people are unemployed and can't get work, there are huge differences in wealth (the amount of money and property people have).	Public service employees are usually workers 'in the public sector'. This means that they are paid by the government (national or local) using money that comes from the taxpayer. Public services provide 'services', not goods. They help us, but they do not usually make or sell things. This means that they do not make money for the country in the way that car manufacturers or rock singers do. In fact they spend money. They also save money. Customs and Excise saves money by collecting unpaid taxes and catching smugglers. Teachers give children the skills they need to make money for the country when they grow up. The diversity of work is one of the reasons why we are all so different. The work we do to some extent determines our 'social class'. The police and the prison service have been accused of being 'middle class' and coming down harder on the 'working classes'. The diversity of work causes problems for the public services, which have to treat everybody the same – whether rich or poor.
Pupil/learner	Pupils, students, learners – whatever we want to call them – are just as diverse as the rest of society. Male and female, and of all ethnic groups, they reflect the beliefs and cultures of their families and friends. They differ greatly in the subjects they are good at, and the way they prefer to study. Learners often suffer from the diversity of schools and colleges, and the fact that some schools and colleges seem to be much better than others. And 'labelling' by examination results may push them towards crime, or lead them to waste their ability by 'turning off' at school.	Public services such as the police deliberately try to recruit as many different types of people as possible. They need people who are streetwise as well as people who can pass exams. Good communication skills are more important than the ability to understand $e = mc^2$. For this reason public services are less interested in what applicants have already learned at school than in the basic intelligence and knowledge that will enable them to be trained once they have joined their public service. The police and other public services such as the fire service and the armed forces set their own entrance tests because they feel these are more useful in dealing with the diversity of applicants than their exam results.

Type of citizen	Analysis of type	Effect on public services
Young, middle-aged, elder	Age is an important kind of diversity. Below the age of 18 people are not citizens in the fullest sense because they are not allowed to vote. But they can still show good citizenship by helping other people and treating them with respect. The age of a person affects their behaviour, rights and responsibilities. Behaviour changes with learning and with biological changes. Rights increase up to the age of 18 – the age of adulthood. Responsibilities increase with age, and with marriage or having children. They also increase as people are promoted in their jobs. People reach their maximum earnings, on average, around the ages of 40 or 45. Income then declines and becomes much lower after the age of retirement. In our society many old people suffer from poverty and insecurity.	The public services like to employ young adults, and some services prefer them to retire early. For example the fire service retirement age is 55. This because public service work is active and demanding, and often requires a level of physical fitness. The pensions of the police, etc, are good, and may allow them to start a business later in life; if not they can retire in some luxury. Public services are sometimes accused of being 'ageist', because they prefer young employees. It is because of this accusation that they are less fussy about the older age limits of applicants than they used to be. In 1990 you could not apply for the fire service over the age of 31. Now there is no upper age limit – except the age at which the fitness test becomes too difficult! Unfortunately it is at ages between 15 and 30, when people are most active, that they are also most likely to commit crimes. The 'clients' of the police and prison service tend to be in this age group.

Name the legislative documents associated with human rights, individual rights and equal opportunities.

Human rights are rights such as freedom of speech, freedom of movement, and freedom from racism and discrimination.

Individual rights are rather like human rights. But they are more to do with things like minimum wages, working conditions, maternity leave, etc.

Equal opportunities are to do with not being discriminated against – especially in education and at work.

Legislative documents are laws or guidelines written by governments and by international organisations. Here are the main ones:

Date/sponsor	Name and details of 'legislative document'	Main rights given
1948 **United Nations** **Organisation**	United Nations Universal Declaration of Human Rights Written after World War II to try to bring about a new attitude to human rights. It has no legal force in the UK, but is the basis of many human rights documents.	Freedom, equality, fair trials, freedom of movement, freedom from harassment, right to asylum, marriage, family, owning property, freedom of thought and religion, right to belong (or not) to associations, voting, social security, work, leisure, decent standard of living, education, culture.

Date/sponsor	Name and details of 'legislative document'	Main rights given
1970 UK Government	Equal Pay Act	Men and women must get equal pay when doing the same work.
1972 UK Government	European Communities Act	UK laws on human and individual rights should try, where possible, to be the same as those in the rest of the European Union.
1974 UK Government	Health and Safety at Work Act	Employers must make sure factories, schools and offices are safe for the people working in them.
1975 UK Government	Sex Discrimination Act	Men and women must be treated equally in employment, education, shops, and facilities (such as sports centres). Women must not be discriminated against because they are married or have children.
1976 UK Government	Race Relations Act	No one should be discriminated against because of their race or ethnic background. This applies to jobs, housing, education and services, such as hotels or shops.
1984 UK Government	Police and Criminal Evidence Act	This protects witnesses and people accused of crime from unfair treatment by the police.
1989 UK Government	Children Act	This protects children against abuse.
1995 UK Government	Disability Discrimination Act	This protects disabled people from (some) discrimination in employment, shops, other public buildings, education and public transport.
1996 UK Government	Employment Rights Act	This protects employees against unfair dismissal.
1997	Protection from Harassment Act	This protects against harassment from individuals, employers, etc.
1998 UK Government	Human Rights Act	This brings the UK into line with the rest of Europe in most aspects of human rights.
1998	National Minimum Wage Act	No one can be paid less than a certain wage per hour.
1998	Working time regulations	These limit working hours and give a right to four weeks' annual leave.
2000	Part-time workers regulations	These protect jobs of part-time workers and give them better conditions of service.

All citizens are equal ... but are some more equal than others?

SUPERGRADE! *Merit*

> Analyse how two public services address the main issues associated with equal opportunities.

Equal opportunities means equal recruitment, treatment and chances of promotion at work – for all of the different (diverse) groups in society.

1 The fire service

The fire service is, on paper, an equal opportunities employer. It aims to recruit from all sections of the community – men and women of all ethnic groups. It has abolished age and height restrictions, and it will not discriminate against gays and lesbians.

But the fact remains that very few women and members of ethnic minorities work for any of the fire services in the country. On 31 March 1998, there were only 513 people from black and ethnic minorities and 436 women employed in a service with a wholetime uniformed strength of 33,597 and a retained service of 14,483.

> **LINK!** See pages 90–91 for a detailed analysis and evaluation of how the fire service is addressing the main issues of equal opportunities.

2 The prison service

The prison service shares some of the issues faced by the fire service when it comes to equal opportunities. These issues involve recruitment, promotion and the treatment of prisoners.

Recruitment

The prison service is setting targets for higher recruitment from women and ethnic minority groups. The ethnic minority target for 2002 was 4 per cent. In 2002 22 per cent of prisoners were from ethnic minorities. The aim of having the same proportion among prison officers and the prison population is a long way from being met. Women are also under-represented.

The prison service is an equal opportunities employer and is trying to recruit more ethnic minority staff.

At one time the prison service only employed female officers at women's prisons. This is no longer the case. For example, at Cordingly there are eight female officers and 67 male officers.

Promotion

At higher ranks there are even higher proportions of white male staff. This is because recruitment was almost entirely of white males in years gone by, and it tends to be the older staff who are promoted. Efforts are being made to change this.

The prisoners

In prisons equal opportunities policies also apply to the prisoners, who live and work there. There is great diversity of prisoners, who come from every type of social and ethnic background. The officers aim to give prisoners enough freedom and respect to prepare them for release and rehabilitation (not offending again). There are many educational and training programmes to help improve prisoners' life chances when they get out.

There are also anti-bullying committees, race relations management teams, drug strategies and health care. This is important where many prisoners are thought to be mentally ill, or HIV positive.

> **LINK!** See more about this on page 91.

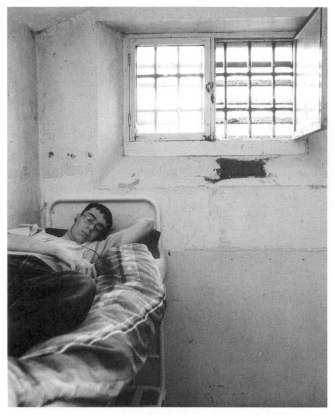

Prisoners have equal opportunities too

SUPERGRADE! *Distinction*

> Evaluate and compare the approach used by two public services to the main issues of equal opportunities.

The fire service and the prison service

Both the fire service and the prison service are committed to equal opportunities. Below is a table comparing the approach used by the fire and prison services to the main issues of equal opportunities.

Evaluation

Unfortunately, both the fire service and the prison service have a long way to go before they can truly be seen as equal opportunities employers. That is because both services are seriously under-represented as far as female and ethnic minority employees are concerned.

Issue	Fire Service	Prison Service
Recruitment	• Removing discriminatory entrance test procedures, such as fitness tests, that are too difficult for women. • Advertising in newspapers, magazines and radio stations, which are likely to reach more people from ethnic minorities. • Improving community links. • Doing audits (collecting statistics) about recruitment of women and minority groups.	• Has introduced educational requirements for applicants – 5 Cs at GCSE or the equivalent, including English and Maths. This tends to help female applicants who, on average, have slightly better GCSE grades than males. • The prison service stresses that it is an equal opportunities employer on all recruitment leaflets, etc.
Work practices	• Investigating the possibility of changing watches and duties so that they are more suitable for women, and can fit in with family responsibilities. • Thinking of getting rid of excessively long shifts. • Reviewing accommodation in fire stations. Strengthening systems against bullying. • Not sidelining women into 'soft' duties such as fire prevention.	• The main change is that women are now being employed at men's prisons – at one time women could only work at women's prisons. (Men were always able to work at both men's and women's prisons.) • Developing opportunities for part-time work which suits women with families. • The prison service is doing race relations monitoring – collecting statistics – and getting advice from race relations organisations such as the Commission for Racial Equality.

In the prison service 3.2 per cent of prison officers are non-white, and in the fire service only 1.7 per cent of firefighters are non-white. Approximately 12 per cent of prisoners are non-white, while 7 per cent of the British population as a whole is non-white.

Women constitute 15.8 per cent of prison officers but only 1.2 per cent of uniformed firefighters are women.

Recruitment

To improve recruitment from women and ethnic minorities, both organisations are trying hard to improve the situation, but it will not be easy. This is because:

- there is a low staff turnover, especially in the fire service
- it is illegal to discriminate in recruitment, so neither the fire nor the prison service can increase numbers of ethnic minority or women firefighters by accepting them because they belong to ethnic minorities or are women
- the entry standards are fixed nationally
- applications for these careers from women and members of ethnic minorities are low
- very few women or people from ethnic minorities were recruited in the past, so white men make up most of the older firefighters and prison officers.

Methods of improving recruitment are similar for both services. They are:

- advertising the fact that both are equal opportunities employers (see Focus box)
- advertising more widely so that people from ethnic minorities will know when the services are recruiting.

This is a problem for the fire service, since even with the small recruitment advertisements in local papers, which they have used in the past, fire services have had 160 applicants on average for every vacancy. They have, in fact, been snowed under with good applicants!

It should be stressed that there is now no discrimination in recruitment, and that both the fire and prison services now provide excellent careers for women and for people from ethnic minorities!

FOCUS

The Prison Service is an equal opportunities employer. We welcome applications from candidates regardless of ethnic origin, religious belief, gender, sexual orientation, disability or any other irrelevant factor.

Work practices

Changing work practices both in the prison service and the fire service in order to make the work more attractive to women and people from ethnic minorities is a priority.

In the prison service an organisation called RESPECT has been set up by the government to provide a focus for ethnic minority prison officers to express any difficulties they have with working practices or relationships with their white colleagues.

FOCUS

Aims of RESPECT

Equal access to regime opportunities and services.

Increased confidence of ethnic minority prisoners and support groups in fairness and justice.

Improved relationships with ethnic minority prisoners.

In the fire service the Fire Brigades Union has been active in trying to help ethnic minority firefighters, some of whom have experienced discrimination from their white colleagues in the past. Fire services are also setting up systems to combat bullying and harassment.

They are reorganising their fire stations to make them more suitable for women – especially in the accommodation areas.

Conclusion

The problems for both services are similar. Because they are behindhand with equal opportunities they are in danger of being out of step with the rest of society. An additional reason why an equal opportunities policy is important in the prison service is that it could help the service work more effectively with the large number of ethnic minority prisoners.

C**OO**L SITE:

www.hmprisonservice.gov.uk

Describe the principles of human rights and explain how two public services implement equal opportunities policies into their organisations.

Human rights principles

Human rights are rules which protect people from cruelty and exploitation of all kinds.

The idea in its modern form comes from the United Nations Universal Declaration of Human Rights of 1948. This was brought out at the end of World War II because six million Jews had been deliberately killed by the Nazis in Hitler's Germany. World leaders wanted to ensure that such crimes never happened again.

The European Convention on Human Rights is the list of human rights on which Britain's own Human Rights Act 1998 is based. Here are the main headings.

FOCUS

Article 1 – Obligation to respect human rights

Article 2 – Right to life

Article 3 – Prohibition of torture

Article 4 – Prohibition of slavery and forced labour

Article 5 – Right to liberty and security

Article 6 – Right to a fair trial

Article 7 – No punishment without law

Article 8 – Right to respect for private and family life

Article 9 – Freedom of thought, conscience and religion

Article 10 – Freedom of expression

Article 11 – Freedom of assembly and association

Article 12 – Right to marry

Article 14 – Prohibition of discrimination

Article 15 – Derogation in time of emergency

Article 16 – Restrictions on political activity of aliens

Article 17 – Prohibition of abuse of rights

Article 18 – Limitation on use of restrictions on rights

! CHECKPOINT ...

When is it (possibly) acceptable to infringe human rights?

How two public services implement equal opportunities policies into their organisations

1 The fire service

In 1999 a report commissioned by the Home Office – which was then still in charge of the fire service – *Equality and Fairness in the Fire Service*, drew attention to the problems of the fire service concerning equal opportunities. The report said that in the treatment of ethnic minority and women firefighters, in the general treatment of staff, and in recruitment, huge improvements were needed. These are now being implemented – see the government booklet: *Toward Diversity II*, December 2001.

Some of the main ways in which the fire service is implementing equal opportunities policies are:

- chief fire officers are making clear, full equal opportunities statements for each region
- new inspectors, who may be more aware of equal opportunities, are being used
- overall control of the fire service has been moved from the Home Office to the Department for Transport, Local Government and the Regions
- new organisations are being set up to support women and ethnic minority firefighters
- action plans for equal opportunities are being written
- attempts are being made to change the 'culture' of the fire service (the old-fashioned 'macho' way of thinking)
- they are considering changing the shift system of watches and 15-hour shifts to make it more suitable for women firefighters

- increasing the awareness of discriminatory language and how – and why – it should be avoided
- changing the uniform and various practices which seem militaristic (like the armed forces)
- reducing the emphasis on physical strength
- making selection tests less discriminatory
- eliminating bullying.

! CHECKPOINT ...

There are 40 applicants for every vacancy in the Fire Service. How would you explain this fact, considering the problems of equal opportunities which exist in the fire service?

2 The prison service

Prisoners do not have equal opportunities compared with the rest of us. But within the prison itself, equal opportunities must apply to prisoners as well as prison staff.

In a practical sense this includes things such as:

- helping foreign nationals or deporting them humanely
- giving treatment and counselling to drug addicts
- improving relationships between staff and prisoners
- trying to eliminate racism and homophobia among prisoners

- cutting down on the use of control and restraint procedures
- preparing prisoners for their release, so that they are able to find work, and are less likely to re-offend
- giving work training and education in the prison
- improving health care for prisoners
- ensuring that prisoners feel safe in the prison, and are not bullied either by staff or other inmates
- ensuring that health and safety risks are dealt with
- reducing the risk of suicide and self-harm
- allowing prisoners to make telephone calls to family and/or friends.

! CHECKPOINT ...

What are the differences between equal opportunities and human rights? What human rights do prisoners not have?

PASSGRADE

Describe the voting system employed in a democratic society and define the responsibility of central and local government towards citizens and citizenship issues.

We have already seen that citizenship consists of: obeying the law, helping and respecting other people and using your vote (see page 83). This last part, using your vote, will be new to you if you are under 18. But understanding the voting system is important if you want to be a full citizen. It is also important for the well-being of a democratic society that everybody – or as many people as possible – should vote.

What is a democratic society?

Democracy comes from an ancient Greek word which means 'rule by the people'. In a democratic society everybody can have a say in how they are governed.

In Britain we have a democratic system of government. It consists of:

- The Prime Minister
- The Cabinet
- Members of Parliament
- Local Government Councillors.

All these people belong to political parties, such as Labour and Conservative, and have to be voted for in elections.

The Prime Minister is the boss, and is elected for about five years.

The Cabinet is a group of about twenty-five heads of government departments, called Ministers.

Members of Parliament are elected by ordinary people in general elections. There are 659 of them and they sit in the House of Commons (Parliament) and debate (argue about) new laws.

Local government councillors are elected in local elections, and deal strictly with local issues and problems.

In a general election everybody aged 18 and over (except for prisoners and the mentally ill) is allowed to vote. When you vote you have to go to a polling station. You are given a piece of paper which has the names of all the candidates (people standing for election). There are usually between three and eight candidates, standing for different political parties. You put a cross next to the candidate – or party – you think is best, fold the paper, and put it in a big black box called a ballot box. At the end of the day all the votes for that particular area (called a constituency) are counted. The winner is the person with the most votes, and that person becomes the Member of Parliament for that constituency. In Britain each constituency has only one Member of Parliament.

This system is called 'First past the post'– because it is rather like a horse race which can only have one winner.

> **! CHECKPOINT ...**
>
> There are other democratic systems of voting – the 'single transferable vote' and 'the alternative vote'. Find out how they work, and where they are used.

The responsibility of central and local government towards citizens and citizenship issues

1 Central government

Central government is divided into departments called ministries. Each ministry does a part of the government's work.

You can find a list of ministries and the people in charge on:

 **SITE:**

www.parliament.uk/commons/lib/hmg.htm

The government is responsible for all the work in the country that is not done by individuals and private companies. It helps citizens:

(a) by setting up systems which help them to make money, e.g. transport, trade agreements, defence agreements and contracts, agricultural subsidies and so on

(b) by collecting taxes and spending the money on things we all need such as education, hospitals, the uniformed public services, the non-uniformed public services, social care, environmental care and some aspects of transport.

Of these two main functions (b) is more important. Without the government many, perhaps most, citizens would be uneducated, unhealthy, underfed and likely to die at a young age.

As regards citizenship issues, the government has a major role to play. The Home Office supervises the work of the police and prison service, who exist to protect good citizens and to limit the activities of bad citizens. The Department for Education and Skills oversees schools, colleges and universities. Citizenship has to be learnt, and it is in schools that we learn the basic aspects of citizenship – obeying rules and caring for others. The government is in the process of introducing citizenship as a compulsory school subject, in the hope not only of cutting crime, but also raising the quality of life by creating a more caring and trusting society.

2 Local government

Local government, run by town halls and civic centres up and down the country, is responsible for many aspects of our lives – including some public services. Indeed, local government is itself a public service. Like central government it collects taxes and provides services. Here is a list of the main responsibilities of one local authority: Kirklees Metropolitan Council.

1 Executive management – planning and strategy
2 Customer Services – general organisation
3 Education and Recreation – culture, education, leisure
4 Environment and Transportation – environment, transport, highways, refuse
5 Finance and Property – estates, property, revenues, benefits
6 Housing – building services, housing services
7 Policy and Health – health, hospitals, etc
8 Regeneration and Markets – licensing, controlling building, economic development, planning
9 Safer Communities and Human Resources – health, safety, equality, diversity
10 Social Services – social work, etc.

All these sections of Kirklees Council help its citizens in one way or another.

Local government varies from place to place, depending on how rich the area is, and the way people vote. In some places you pay lower council tax and get fewer services; in others you pay more council tax and get more services.

A good deal of the work of Kirklees Metropolitan Council has to do with citizenship. The area has an ethnically diverse population. The council works hard to encourage and celebrate diversity, but without breaking up the sense of community that exists in the area. It supports community projects such as youth clubs, which aim to turn young people into better citizens. Its police authority works with the local police to help them provide the service that local people want. It tries to make people more aware of environmental issues – an increasingly important aspect of citizenship.

Some public services are set up by law and operate all over the country. They are supervised by government departments, and billions of pounds are spent on them. These are statutory public services. (Statutory means: set up by law.)

Many other public services, such as clubs and charities, are started by individuals who see a need and want to help other people. As they develop they may get some help from local or central government, or from statutory public services. But they are still basically volunteer organisations. These are non-statutory public services.

We will now look at one of each, and see what they do to help encourage and develop citizenship among local people.

PASSGRADE

> Explain the differences between statutory and non-statutory public services and how one statutory and one non-statutory service assists in the development of citizenship in the local community.

1 The police (statutory public service)

The police are increasingly active in work designed to develop citizenship in local communities. In particular, they do a great deal of work with young people – helping youth clubs and, in some areas, arranging outings and residentials.

One good example of how the police develop citizenship and encourage diversity in a local community is the work they do at the Notting Hill Carnival, in west London, every August Bank Holiday.

The Notting Hill Carnival is a major cultural event, but there have been calls to ban it in the past, because of criminal activities by gangs of youths, and protests against the way the police handled the carnival. Now the police and local communities work closely together to produce one of the best celebrations of diversity in Europe.

The work the police do at the carnival is outlined below.

FOCUS

Close partnership work has been carried out with the Notting Hill Carnival Trust, British Transport Police, the Royal Borough of Kensington and Chelsea, Westminster City Council and the Greater London Authority, in order to make sure that all is done to ensure that revellers can enjoy themselves in safety. Carnival is a unique and vibrant occasion that attracts well over one and a half million people. The sheer scale of the event and the huge crowds may make some people feel uncomfortable. Overcrowding remains a serious concern for the MPS. The route has been altered this year with a view to help spread the crowds.

Crime was down at last year's Carnival, and the Met is working towards bringing about another drop this year. Enhanced tactics will be used and substantially more resources will be dedicated to dealing with crime both during and after the event. The whole Carnival area will be watched through 80 CCTV cameras, keeping an eye on crowd safety as well as crime prevention and detection.

Source: Metropolitan Police website

---

2 Neighbourhood Watch (non-statutory public service)

Neighbourhood watches are voluntary organisations designed to cut down small-scale crime and vandalism, mainly in residential areas such as suburbs and housing estates. They are helped and advised by the police, but not started by the police. They have to be started by a concerned member of the public.

FOCUS

Watching and caring – not snooping
That's what Neighbourhood Watch is all about – looking out for each other. Neighbours uniting and acting together means that dozens of eyes and ears are ready to pick up on anything happening in the neighbourhood that could cause worry or concern. It's not about being nosy or interfering, it's about being a good neighbour and caring about your community.

A better quality of life
And there is more to Neighbourhood Watch than protecting homes and property against burglary. By working together, neighbours can help reduce all sorts of local crimes. They can also take action to improve the environment by getting something done about things like vandalism, graffiti, poor lighting and a lack of local amenities.

Anyone can join a Neighbourhood Watch team and everyone can play a part in its activities. And any community or neighbourhood – however large or small – can set up a scheme. A scheme can be made up of just a few houses in a street, or a few households, the residents in a square or a whole estate. Each scheme can be different – you don't even have to use the title 'Neighbourhood Watch', or put a sticker in your window.

Source: www.met.police.uk/crimeprevention/neighbor.htm

Neighbourhood Watch schemes assist in the development of citizenship by encouraging people to:

- uphold the law
- help, protect and respect other people.

Further differences are that statutory public services are very big and expensive. The police, for example, cost over £6 billion a year. Most non-statutory public services (even most charities) have an annual turnover of less than £1 million a year. A Neighbourhood Watch organisation could – in theory – cost nothing at all.

"We've been burgled three times since that Neighbourhood Watch started up in the next street!"

Differentiate between statutory and non-statutory public services, analysing the role the monarchy, and central and local government have in setting up or assisting each of these types of services.

LINK! The essential difference between statutory and non-statutory public services is given on pages 93 and 94. Other examples of these services are given on page 2 (at the beginning of Unit 1).

The role of the monarchy, and central and local government in setting up or assisting these services

The monarchy

The monarchy is the Queen. She has no direct power over any statutory public service. Her role is ceremonial. She opens Parliament at the beginning of each session, and gives a speech (which she did not write) saying what the government plans to do. These plans are new laws – and many of these laws are to do with the public services.

The Queen also has to sign her approval of major new laws but she has no official influence over their content. She cannot say: 'We don't like this law and we are not going to sign it!'

The words 'Queen' and 'Royal' – and the titles of some other members of the royal family – are linked to some statutory public services – such as the Royal Mail and the Royal Navy. This may be a cause of pride but does not mean there is any influence.

The monarchy has a greater influence on non-statutory public services. Many members of the royal family give active support and publicity to charities.

C😎L SITE:

The Prince's Trust
www.princes-trust.org.uk/

Central government

Central government – i.e. Parliament (especially the House of Commons) – has two key roles in setting up and assisting statutory public services.

Passing laws

Parliament passes the laws which allow the statutory public services to exist, and defines their roles. For example, in 1999 the government set up two new organisations for fighting crime: the National Criminal Intelligence Service (NCIS) and the National Crime Squad.

'2–(1) The NCIS Service Authority shall maintain a body to be known as the National Criminal Intelligence Service (in this Part referred to as "NCIS").

(2) The functions of NCIS shall be–

(a) to gather, store and analyse information in order to provide criminal intelligence,

(b) to provide criminal intelligence to police forces in Great Britain, the Royal Ulster Constabulary, the National Crime Squad and other law enforcement agencies, and

(c) to act in support of such police forces, the Royal Ulster Constabulary, the National Crime Squad and other law enforcement agencies carrying out their criminal intelligence activities.'

The NCIS now has to exist – because the government has created it, and stated what its main job is. The NCIS cannot change its role unless the government says so – by changing the law again.

Paying for them

For example, central government pays 51 per cent of the cost of the police. The money comes mainly from the taxes we pay.

Role of central government in non-statutory services

Central government also has a very important role to play in non-statutory public services. It does not set them up, but it keeps a check on their activities – encouraging them in some cases, and making sure they do not break the law in others.

Many non-statutory public services are registered as charities. This means they pay less tax, but it also means they can be inspected or investigated by a body called the Charities Commission – set up by the government to make sure that charities aren't breaking the law (by running a scam, for example, and pocketing the donations). The Charities Commission, like the police, is linked to the Home Office.

If a non-statutory public service is seen as doing a good job, the government can give it extra money to do its work. The advantage of this is that the organisation has more money to do its good work. The disadvantage is that it loses some of its independence – and the government might try to make the organisation do things which it does not agree with.

Local government

Local government has three main roles in setting up and assisting public services.

(a) Building partnerships

Local government sets up groups of organisations which work together to help the public services and the community. These include the public services, businesses, charities and voluntary groups.

This kind of arrangement is called a partnership.

> **LINK!** See page 234 for crime and disorder partnerships.

Some partnerships exist in all local government areas – emergency planning, for example. The purpose of emergency planning is to deal with disasters such as large chemical leaks, floods, or huge fires. The local authority, the police, the fire service and the ambulance service draw up plans to rescue and protect citizens if disasters take place.

> **! CHECKPOINT ...**
> Ask your local authority head of emergency planning to talk to you – as a class.

Other partnerships (see Focus box) are started by a particular local government area.

> ### FOCUS
> **Example of a partnership**
> To help to tackle the under-reporting of racist and homophobic incidents, Kirklees Neighbourhood Housing has agreed that all its area housing offices will now act as hate incident reporting centres for victims of this type of harassment. They work in partnership with West Yorkshire Police and community/voluntary organisations. Victims can now visit any of the reporting centres to get advice from trained staff members in an informal and supportive setting.
>
> Source: Kirklees MC (2002)

(b) Allocating money

For example, 49 per cent of the annual income of the police comes from local government – and goes to the force that polices that area.

(c) Publicising small and community organisations

Local government will help publicise such organisations as long as they do not encourage bad citizenship or break the law.

Evaluate the role the monarchy, and central and local government play in the setting up of, or assistance with, statutory and non-statutory public services.

Remember that evaluation means giving reasoned opinions and judgements. Points that could be made for this outcome include the following.

The monarchy

The monarchy has no essential role to play. If there was no monarchy the statutory public services would not change – though some charities would.

Central government

Central government is itself a public service. It has more responsibility for statutory public services than anybody else.

This is not to say that central government has complete control over the public services – as happens in many other countries. If we were to draw a diagram it looks like the one at the bottom of the page.

The government ministries have to listen to the various chiefs of the services before making any decisions, and in most matters the chiefs have a great deal of power to decide how their particular service is run. That is one reason why crime figures are so different in different parts of the country – because chief constables decide what they want their particular services to concentrate on.

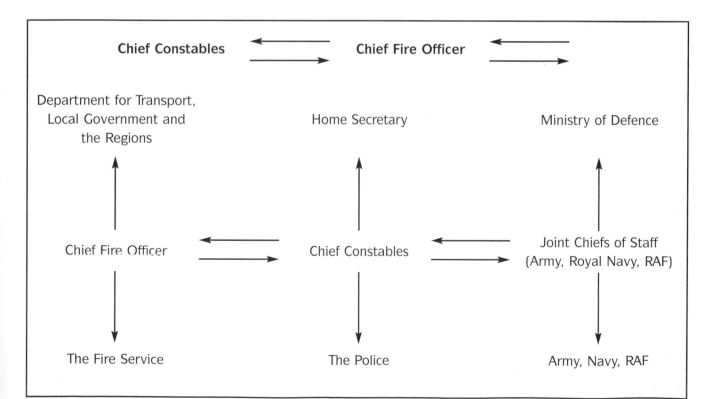

Although it might seem like the tail wagging the dog, this system makes sense because, although the government ministers have more power, they do not know nearly as much about policing, firefighting or defence as the various public service chiefs do.

If the government simply told the police what to do all the time, the country would become 'a police state', and the police would serve the government instead of the people.

The main responsibility of the government for non-statutory public services is to make sure they don't cheat – or break the law.

Local government

Local government, unlike central government, does not have much influence on or relationship with the armed forces, unless, for example, there happens to be an army camp or air force base in the local area. But local government has a very close relationship with the police, fire service and ambulance service. Committees of councillors, such as the Police Authority, have to be set up by law to supervise the work of the public service concerned, and make sure they carry out the wishes of local citizens.

As regards non-statutory public services, especially volunteer groups, and partnerships between business and the public services, local government is very active and does a great deal of good work. Much of this is to do with health care in the community, for example support groups for schizophrenics or the families of schizophrenics. They are also active with crime and disorder partnerships (see pages 234–235).

> ## ! CHECKPOINT …
> ■ Invite a member of your local police authority to explain the relationship between local government, local citizens and the police.

C👓L SITES:

Equal Opportunities Commission (equality for women)

www.eoc.org.uk/

Diversity, equal opportunities and the fire service

www.safety.odpm.gov.uk/fire/fepd/pdf/equalap.pdf

www.safety.odpm.gov.uk/fire/fepd/pdf/diversity.pdf

Equal opportunities in the army

www.mod.uk/issues/equal_opportunities/af_q-and-a.htm

http://news.bbc.co.uk/1/hi/uk/989713.stm

Grading criteria

PASSGRADE	SUPERGRADE! *Merit*	SUPERGRADE! *Distinction*
To achieve a pass grade the evidence must show that the learner is able to:	To achieve a merit grade the evidence must show that the learner is able to:	To achieve a distinction grade the evidence must show that the learner is able to:
● outline the various acts and regulations explaining the terminology used **100** ● explain the roles and responsibilities set out in the legislation and the practical implications to public service organisations and identify the possible outcome of failing to comply with legislation **102** ● explain the steps to be taken when discovering an incident and summarise emergency evacuation procedures **108** ● explain the requirements for the production of a risk assessment **112** ● outline the regulations concerning the provision of first aid at work, explaining the implications for public services **113** ● outline the term 'manual handling' and explain the training requirements **115**	● explain particular health and safety issues within a chosen public service and the consequences of failing to act **105** ● explain the regulations concerning emergency equipment and exits, demonstrating an understanding of emergency equipment and the circumstances when it would be most effective, i.e. fire extinguishers, fire blankets, first aid equipment, alarm systems **109** ● identify forms of protective equipment and clothing and explain their purpose in enhancing safety **111**	● analyse two cases where negligence relating to health and safety measures has been in question in a public service **106** ● assess the links between risk assessments and safe working practices in the emergency procedures of a public service **117**

There are two good things about the public services. One is the work; the other is the retirement package at the end of it.

With the police, for example, you can retire at the age of 50 with enough money to start a small business. But if you'd rather not bother, you should be able to afford to take the odd world cruise, and spend a good deal of time on the golf course.

The purpose of this unit is to make sure you enjoy your retirement …

PASSGRADE

> Outline the various acts and regulations explaining the terminology used.

People like to take risks. This is perhaps why you fancy a career in the public services.

The government doesn't like people to take risks. The lawsuits are expensive and the invalidity benefits cost the taxpayer a lot of money.

That's why we have Acts and Regulations designed to make us play safe and avoid risks.

The following are some of the main ones.

1 The Health and Safety at Work, etc. Act* 1974

This is the mother of all health and safety laws. Like most laws it is split into sections:

(a) Employers'* responsibilities

- Doing everything 'as far as is reasonably practicable'* to protect health and safety
- Setting up safe systems*
- Having a written safety policy*
- Having a safety officer* in charge of safety arrangements
- Having safety representatives* who can tell the safety officer about any problems
- Setting up a safety committee*
- Getting trade unions* involved
- Providing safety training to all employees

- Protecting not only workers but visitors and anyone else who uses the workplace
- Paying for workers' safety equipment.*

(b) Employees'* responsibilities

- To behave responsibly and take care of themselves and others
- To use the safety arrangements* or equipment provided by the employer
- Not to interfere with safety equipment (e.g. mess about with fire extinguishers).

(c) Other provisions

- Designers, manufacturers, importers and suppliers of any article or substance for use at work to ensure that it is safe and healthy for use
- Setting up the Health and Safety Commission (HSC)*
- Setting up the Health and Safety Executive (HSE).*

Explanation of terminology

The terms with an asterisk above are explained below.

- Act – an Act (often with a capital A) is a law.
- Employers – managers, bosses, senior officers in the public services.
- 'as far as is reasonably practicable' – sensible (e.g. it is sensible to have fire extinguishers in an ambulance station, but not sensible to have everybody wearing smoke masks all the time).
- Safe systems – safe ways of doing any given job (e.g. not sliding down a pole when you can walk down the stairs).
- Safety policy – a booklet or notice provided by the employers stating that they intend to have a safe workplace, showing how they will do it, and who is responsible for what.
- Safety officer – a senior and respected employee whose job is to check up regularly on all safety arrangements.
- Safety representatives – workpeople who carry out risk assessments, or get information about possible safety risks and tell the safety officer.
- Safety committee – meeting of safety officer and safety representatives, management and – where possible – union representatives to discuss safety.

- Trade unions – workers' organisations which campaign for better pay and working conditions and look after the welfare of their members. Some public services (police, prison officers and armed forces) have 'associations', instead, to look after welfare.
- Safety equipment – includes hard hats, machine guards, pepper sprays, batons, etc.
- Employees – workers; anybody who can be taken on or sacked.
- Safety arrangements – things like machine guards, instruments e.g. on diving equipment, fire drills, etc.
- HSC – this is a body set up by central government, and it oversees all the people concerned with putting health and safety law into practice in this country. It has to work with the cooperation of the government and the trade unions.
- HSE – these are teams of inspectors who go round workplaces and point out safety problems. They have strong powers to criticise or punish people who are not upholding safety laws.

Other Acts and Regulations

1 *Management of Health and Safety at Work Regulations 1999*: require employers to carry out risk assessments,* make the workplace safer, and improve health and safety training.
2 *Workplace (Health, Safety and Welfare) Regulations 1992*: cover a wide range of basic health, safety and welfare issues such as ventilation, heating, lighting, workstations,* seating and welfare facilities.
3 *Health and Safety (Display Screen Equipment) Regulations 1992*: set out requirements for work with Visual Display Units (VDUs).
4 *Personal Protective Equipment (PPE) Regulations 1992*: require employers to provide appropriate protective clothing and equipment for their employees.
5 *Provision and Use of Work Equipment Regulations (PUWER) 1992*: require that equipment provided for use at work, including machinery, is safe.
6 *Manual Handling Operations Regulations 1992*: cover the lifting and carrying of heavy objects by hand.

7 *Health and Safety (First Aid) Regulations 1981*: cover requirements for first aid.
8 *The Health and Safety Information for Employees Regulations 1989*: require employers to display a poster telling employees what they need to know about health and safety.
9 *Employers' Liability (Compulsory Insurance) Regulations 1998*: require employers to take out insurance against accidents and ill health to their employees.
10 *The Reporting of Injuries, Diseases and Dangerous Occurrences Regulations 1995*: improves systems for the recording and reporting of accidents.
11 *Noise at Work Regulations 1989*: require employers to take action to protect employees from hearing damage.
12 *Electricity at Work Regulations 1989*: require people in control of electrical systems to ensure they are safe to use and maintained in a safe condition.
13 *Environmental Pollution Act 1990*: connected with pollution of rivers, dumping of wastes, etc.
14 *Control of Substances Hazardous to Health Regulations 1999 (COSHH)*: require employers to assess the risks from hazardous substances and take appropriate precautions.

* Risk assessments – regular inspections of rooms and equipment to see if they might be dangerous
* Workstation – an area in a workplace assigned to a worker, especially a desk with a computer.

In addition, specific regulations cover particular areas, for example asbestos and lead, and:

15 *Chemicals (Hazard Information and Packaging for Supply) Regulations 1994*: require suppliers to classify, label and package dangerous chemicals and provide safety data sheets for them.
16 *Construction (Design and Management) Regulations 1994*: cover safe systems of work on construction sites.
17 *Gas Safety (Installation and Use) Regulations 1998*: cover safe installation, maintenance and use of gas systems and appliances in domestic and commercial premises.

18 *Fire Precautions (Workplace) (Amendment) Regulations 1999*: all workplaces should be inspected by the fire authority to check means of escape, firefighting equipment and warnings and a fire certificate issued. A breach of a fire certificate could lead to a prosecution of the employer or responsible manager or other staff member.

Explain the roles and responsibilities set out in the legislation and the practical implications to public service organisations and identify the possible outcome of failing to comply with legislation.

Safety is everybody's responsibility. But if you say that, people often think: 'Good, it's an SEP!' (someone else's problem). So health and safety laws try to make it as clear as possible who is responsible for what.

Roles and responsibilities

The Department for the Environment, Transport and the Regions

This government department is in overall charge of safety policy in the country. It prepares new laws, and decides future planning for safety in general.

The Health and Safety Commission

This small group of people is in charge of overseeing the general health and safety picture in the country, and suggesting what new policies or laws need to be put into practice.

The Health and Safety Executive

This is a team of several hundred highly qualified inspectors who go round factories, offices and public service buildings checking the standard of health and safety protection.

Employers and employees

See under 'Explanation of terminology' above.

The practical implications to public service organisations

All public service organisations are heavily involved in health and safety. This involvement is of two main kinds.

(a) As employers

As employers they have to follow the laws just the same as factories and shops have to. The only difference here is that because public service work can be dangerous, the phrase 'as far as is reasonably practicable' is understood differently. If you are loading and firing shells, it is reasonable to assume that it may be more dangerous than working in a library. Even so, the risks still have to be kept down as much as possible.

For this reason, public services, like businesses, have all the arrangements in place demanded by the Health and Safety at Work Act, and other safety laws. They have safety notice-boards, safety training, safety officers, safety policies, safety committees and safety representatives. This is true of both uniformed and non-uniformed public services, of army barracks and town halls. They have to take safety seriously because the law says so. What's more, being public services, if anything does go wrong on the health and safety front, it gets into the news, and gets them a lot of bad publicity.

(b) Public services

Public services often protect the public, and many have a special responsibility for health and safety issues. Traffic police are really looking after road safety, the United Kingdom Atomic Energy Authority police help to protect the security of nuclear power stations (so that terrorists don't sneak in and blow them up, or steal a few cans of plutonium), and crime and fire prevention officers try to make our homes safer. Meanwhile, HM Customs and Excise tries to keep illegal weapons and drugs out of the country, and Mountain Rescue, a volunteer organisation, works for safety on the hills.

However, some public services – both uniformed and non-uniformed – have a special involvement in the laws listed. Examples are as follows.

1 The ambulance service

This has to come and pick up the pieces, even after minor accidents. Its work would be greatly reduced if there were fewer accidents. It would then be able to respond even faster to emergencies than it does now.

2 Rail companies such as Railtrack

The Strategic Rail Authority (formerly known as Railtrack) owns Britain's railway lines. Train crashes spell big trouble for the SRA, as the following newspaper extract shows.

3 Environmental Health Officers (EHOs)

Local council Environmental Health Officers have, since 1974, been carrying out health and safety inspections – examining things such as food hygiene, noise, and air and water pollution. They are a non-uniformed public service. They operate in places such as shops, offices, churches, restaurants, zoos, cinemas, theatres and football stadiums. Each officer is responsible for around 806 premises.

FOCUS

Charges may follow Hatfield rail dossier

Rail executives could still face manslaughter charges over the Hatfield rail crash, in which four people died and 70 were injured, after a fresh dossier of evidence was submitted to the Crown Prosecution Service yesterday.

The file was compiled by the Health and Safety Commission, which published safety recommendations in the light of the crash that took place in October 2000. The HSC said that the accident happened because a train travelled over a rail "that had been identified as in poor condition and which should have either been replaced or a temporary speed restriction applied".

The high speed train, travelling from London to Leeds, was derailed on a stretch of track in Hertfordshire maintained by contractors Balfour Beatty. British Transport police are still investigating. Senior managers at both Balfour Beatty and Railtrack could face manslaughter charges if the CPS decides there is a prospect of conviction.

Source: Nicholas Pyke, © *The Guardian*, Friday, 23 August 2002

Why health and safety matters

4 The fire service

The fire service is actively involved in health and safety work, which is linked to its role in fire prevention. By law the fire service has to carry out safety checks on buildings, looking at what they are built of, the placing of fire doors and barriers to stop fire spread, the general layout for ease of access and escape, furniture and upholstery, and the use of fire extinguishers, sprinklers, etc. The latest law making them do this is the Fire Precautions (Workplace) (Amendment) Regulations 1999 (see page 102). If a building is safe for the use it is intended for, the fire service gives it a fire safety certificate. This has to be renewed from time to time, or if the building's use is changed.

Besides giving out fire safety certificates, the fire service educates the public on fire risks. It does this by:

- talking to people – especially young people
- distributing leaflets on fire safety
- holding community open days.

The fire service also carries out research to find safer building materials and methods.

The possible outcome of failing to comply with legislation

The law does not take kindly to people endangering health and safety and there are strict sentences. But many people think that even stricter sentences are needed. They also want to see higher levels of compensation for victims and the families of victims.

The law takes the view that companies which provide goods (e.g. hamburgers) or services (e.g. train journeys) owe the customer a 'duty of care'. The same, of course, is true of public services. If they don't take care of their customers, or of people who happen to be around, then there are penalties.

Rules about safety are often printed in booklets called ACoPs – Approved Codes of Practice.

Health and safety inspectors have more powers than the police to enter and search buildings. They don't even need a warrant. They can:

- enter and inspect premises at any time, if there is danger
- take a police officer, if they feel that they will be obstructed
- take along such people and equipment as will be necessary for the purpose of investigation
- require parts of the premises or equipment to be left undisturbed for as long as necessary
- take measurements, photographs and samples
- seize, render or destroy any items that may cause danger
- take possession of articles and examine them
- get information, ask questions and take statements (under caution if necessary)
- inspect relevant documents.

> ! **CHECKPOINT ...**
>
> Recently a man in America tried to sue McDonald's for millions of dollars for having ruined his health.
> (a) Is this a health and safety case?
> (b) What are the advantages and disadvantages of forcing companies to pay huge amounts in compensation in health and safety cases?

The possible outcomes of failing to comply with legislation (i.e. breaking safety laws) are:

- spoken and written advice
- spoken and written warning that the law is being broken
- improvement notices – clear written warnings that if a risk is not dealt within a certain period of time, prosecution may follow
- prohibition notices – the dangerous machine, etc, must be shut down until further notice
- withdrawal of licences
- formal caution (saying that the law has been broken and a prosecution will be brought unless full safety procedures are implemented)
- prosecution (of organisations or individuals, e.g. bosses).

Penalties

Maximum penalties for breaking health and safety laws are:

- in the magistrates' courts: £20,000 fine or six months' imprisonment
- in the Crown Court: unlimited fines or two years in prison
- if somebody dies there could be manslaughter charges, possibly resulting in life imprisonment.

SUPERGRADE! *Merit*

Explain particular health and safety issues within a chosen public service and the consequences of failing to act.

The prison service

Health and safety is a key issue in the prison service. This is for a number of reasons:

- A prison is a secure environment, and the layout, cells and locking arrangements mean it would be impossible to evacuate them quickly in the case of a fire.
- If the prisoners were evacuated, they would quite possibly escape.
- Many prisons are old buildings, put up in the nineteenth century, and their deteriorating condition poses health and safety risks.
- The nature of prisoners. It is estimated that 20 per cent of them have mental health problems. This means: (a) there is a high risk of suicide, or self-harm; (b) a high risk of violence; and (c) they cannot be trusted to behave safely.
- Many prisons have a drug problem, which affects the prisoners' behaviour.
- Prisons are overcrowded and understaffed.
- There are common, serious health problems such as hepatitis and HIV infection.

A report on Dartmoor Prison by the Chief Inspector of Prisons in 2001 showed up many health and safety issues. They are given in the table below, together with the possible consequences if the prison governor and his officers fail to act on them.

In addition to the consequences listed, the prison could be liable to prosecution by the HSE, or a private prosecution by a prisoner or relative (e.g. if a prisoner died as a result of the prison's negligence).

Issue	Consequence of failing to act
There was a risk of violence and an atmosphere of intimidation and bullying.	Prisoners or prison officers could be injured or killed. This could cause psychological damage to prisoners living in an atmosphere of fear – this may lead to suicide or self-harm.
Up to 500 prisoners at a time were allowed to gather in one exercise yard.	This could lead to violence and intimidation, which would not be visible to prison officers monitoring the exercise. It also increases the risk of a full-scale riot.
Control measures by staff were excessive and unnecessary. There had been excessive use of control and restraint techniques and special cells.	Prisoners could be injured – or even killed. Degrading treatment is bad for prisoners' mental health, and may lead to suicide or self-harm.

Issue	Consequence of failing to act
Leaking roofs in the gymnasium and some workshops created serious health and safety problems.	This could lead to physical injuries due to slipping, etc, or respiratory illness (such as bronchitis) following time spent in a damp, cold environment.
Prisoners are locked up for too long: '313 prisoners on the wings out of a population of 585'.	This leads to a build-up of frustration and anger among prisoners. It does not prepare them for release – therefore when they are let out they remain a risk to society.
There is a lack of education and training in prison.	This creates risks for society because prisoners will not be able to get jobs after release – so they will return to crime.
There is a lack of special treatment for special types of prisoner who need it, e.g. sex offenders.	When these prisoners are released they will re-offend.
There are poor 'lines of sight' on CCTV.	Officers cannot see what is really going on in the prison, which makes bullying possible.
Staff should carry scissors at night.	These are needed to cut down prisoners who might be trying to hang themselves.

Analyse two cases where negligence relating to health and safety measures has been in question in a public service.

Dartmoor prison inspection
http://193.195.1.174/cidart98.html

Analyse here means:

- give the main facts of the case
- show what is meant by negligence, and who was negligent – and how
- say if somebody tried to do the right thing, but failed
- finding out who is really to blame
- suggesting what should have been done.

Try to give reasons or examples to support what you say.

Public service work can be dangerous. But normally the public services go to great lengths to make sure that it is no more dangerous than it has to be. Sometimes, however, for one reason or another, things go wrong.

1 Gulf War Syndrome

In 1991 the Americans, the British and the French went to war against Iraq, because the Iraqi army – on the orders of the Iraqi leader, Saddam Hussein – had invaded Kuwait.

Iraq is not a powerful country compared with the USA, Britain or France. But Saddam Hussein had used chemical weapons (gas) against the Kurdish population in Iraq. He was also thought to be storing up biological weapons, such as anthrax spores (which cause a deadly disease), and possibly even nuclear weapons.

The USA and Britain decided to protect their soldiers from the possible use of these chemical and biological weapons by injecting them with drugs and antibodies which were supposed to offer protection. The French soldiers, however, received no injections.

Now many British and American soldiers who fought in the Gulf War, and took these medicines intended to protect them, have a disease called Gulf War Syndrome. But the British Ministry of Defence and the Pentagon (the US Department of Defense) have denied that the treatment given to their soldiers caused the illness – though they appear to admit that the soldiers are indeed ill.

FOCUS

French forces who served in the Gulf war were not given the vaccines and anti-biological warfare measures administered to UK and US veterans and are free from the illnesses that beset their allies, the US Congress has been told.

Evidence to the subcommittee on national security shows the effort made to protect service personnel from biological and chemical weapons is most likely to have damaged their health.

The French were issued with protective suits and not given the cocktail of drugs that British and US servicemen took. Only 140 of the 25,000 French Gulf veterans have reported illnesses related to Gulf war service, compared with more than 5,000 of the 52,000 British troops deployed, and 137,862 of the 697,000 US service personnel.

The most common symptoms and illnesses cited as Gulf War Syndrome include severe fatigue, nausea, fevers, muscle and joint complaints, memory loss, mood swings including severe aggression, insomnia, swollen glands and headaches.

Source: from 'French soldiers free of Gulf war illnesses' by Paul Brown, environment correspondent, © *The Guardian*, Tuesday, 12 February 2002

Although the Gulf War happened over ten years ago and many sufferers of Gulf War Syndrome have died, the case is still being argued, in the hope that the soldiers and their families will get what they believe is adequate compensation.

The British government and the Ministry of Defence do not want to admit that they injected British soldiers with poisons that had not been properly tested, in order to protect them from a danger which never materialised at the time. They also do not want to spend public money in paying compensation to the soldiers and their families.

It is in the interests of the soldiers and their lawyers to make the disease seem as bad as possible, in order to gain more compensation.

This is not to say that either side is lying, but it does show the scale of problems resulting from negligence relating to health and safety measures. In this case it might be said that it was not negligence, since the Ministry of Defence did at least try to protect its soldiers (whereas the French defence authorities did not). But it seems the Ministry of Defence failed to take proper precautions with hazardous substances, by injecting soldiers with medicines that had not been properly tested.

2 Drowning on school trip

It is not only the uniformed services which face danger. Sometimes the non-uniformed services have to face it as well.

The report below shows some of the results of an accident that took place on a school trip to North Yorkshire in 2000.

FOCUS

COUNCIL TO BE PROSECUTED OVER DEATHS

Leeds City Council is to be prosecuted following the deaths of two schoolgirls during a school trip to North Yorkshire.

Rochelle Cauvet, aged 14, and Hannah Black, 13, who were both pupils at Royds School at Oulton, took part in an outdoor adventure activity which involved a group of children and teachers walking upstream in Stainforth Beck in October 2000.

During the exercise both girls got into difficulty and were swept away and drowned.

Their bodies were later recovered from the River Ribble.

At a coroner's inquest lasting three weeks at Harrogate Magistrates Court in March 2002, a jury returned a verdict of accidental death on both girls.

This account gives some of the basic facts of the case, and of the way the authorities dealt with it afterwards. The two teachers with the girls attempted to save the girls but failed. The court hearings did not claim that the teachers themselves had been negligent. But they were not well informed about the dangers of river walks, or the regulations about taking children on such walks.

The coroner's inquiry gave a verdict of accidental death, but that doesn't mean that nobody was to blame. The Health and Safety Executive will be prosecuting Leeds Council because they failed to follow the Management of Health and Safety at Work Regulations 1999 – by not carrying out a risk assessment of the dangers of that particular river walk.

The case is complicated by the fact that the school is carrying out its own inquiry into the accident. This may mean that teachers or pupils could still be blamed. The fact that a teacher with 25 years' experience had never seen official government guidelines for such activities may mean that he was negligent, that the school was negligent, or that the government was negligent.

The stream itself is normally small, and you could cross it without getting wet feet. But safety awareness means imagining the worst, not simply taking a situation at face value. Outdoor activities are always more dangerous in bad weather, but people who are not experienced or trained would not know this.

CHECKPOINT ...

(a) From the facts as they are given, who (if anyone) would you blame in the above accident?

(b) Some people think that there should be no adventurous trips by young people because of the risk of accidents like these. What arguments can you think of for and against this idea?

PASSGRADE

Explain the steps to be taken when discovering an incident and summarise emergency evacuation procedures.

Fires

If you discover a fire:

1 Activate the fire alarm. Rescue or help anybody nearby – if you can. If not, tell the person in charge where they are. Close doors in the fire area (if possible).
2 Go out of the building to a safe place using the quickest route. Call 999. Say where the building is and where the fire is.
3 Wait for the fire brigade to arrive and tell them what you can.

If you hear the fire alarm:

1 Immediately leave the building. Always use the stairs – never use a lift. Close the door as you leave the room.
2 Crawl if the place is full of smoke.
3 Try to move any disabled person to the top of the nearest staircase – and tell firefighters or any safety official.
4 Never go back into the building (unless a firefighter or official says it is safe).
5 If a roll-call is being taken, give your name.

FOCUS

The continuous sounding (2-tone warble) of the fire alarm indicates that FULL EVACUATION should proceed immediately.

If you hear the continuous alarm:

1 Evacuate the building immediately using the nearest fire exit and report to the assembly point next to the lake (Vauxhall Parade) in a quiet and orderly manner
2 Do not stop to collect personal belongings
3 Do not use the lifts
4 Do not enter the building again unless authorised to do so by Security Staff.

Source: www.aston.ac.uk/hr/EmergProc.htm

As you can see, the main thing is to get out. This is much easier if you know the way, so you should always make sure you know the safety route in a building. In a college or factory you will probably have an assembly area where you and your colleagues or classmates should meet. At this point someone (a safety official or a teacher) will take your name. It is important to tell someone that you are out of the building, otherwise firefighters may go in and risk their lives looking for you.

For the public services there can be problems in evacuating people who refuse to go – especially if people are afraid that their property is going to be looted. But the police and others do have the right to remove people by force if necessary.

Evacuation of disabled people may have to be done by the fires service or some other qualified people.

Bomb threats

It is easier to make a telephone call than a bomb – so bomb threats are usually hoaxes. Nevertheless, they should always be taken seriously. You should leave the building as you would in a fire, but instead of assembling near the building, go at least 200 metres away.

Explain the regulations concerning emergency equipment and exits, demonstrating an understanding of emergency equipment and the circumstances when it would be most effective, i.e. fire extinguishers, fire blankets, first aid equipment, alarm systems.

Fire safety regulations

The fire safety laws which now apply to places where people work – such as factories, colleges and police stations – are the Workplace (Fire Precautions) Regulations 1997 and the Fire Precautions (Workplace) (Amendment) Regulations 1999. These two laws give the requirements for emergency equipment (such as fire extinguishers and smoke alarms) and for fire exits.

These laws say that a workplace must:

(a) have appropriate firefighting equipment with fire detectors and alarms;
(b) this equipment must be simple to use and indicated by signs.

An employer must:

(a) have equipment and methods for firefighting in the workplace;
(b) train employees to use the equipment;
(c) arrange any necessary contacts with the emergency services, for rescue work and firefighting.

Emergency routes and exits

Routes to emergency exits and the exits themselves must be kept clear at all times. Also:

(a) Emergency routes and exits must lead as quickly as possible to a place of safety.
(b) It must be possible for employees to evacuate the workplace quickly and safely.
(c) The emergency routes and exits must be enough for the size of the workplace and the maximum number of people who could be there at any one time.
(d) Emergency doors must open in the direction of escape.
(e) Sliding or revolving doors should not be specifically intended as emergency exits.
(f) Emergency doors must be easy to open.
(g) Emergency routes and exits must be shown by signs.
(h) There must be emergency lighting.

Maintenance

All fire safety equipment must be kept in efficient working order and in good repair.

Enforcement

It is the legal duty of the fire authority to ensure that this is done – by getting workplaces inspected. In practice this means the inspections are done by firefighters or HSE inspectors.

Emergency equipment

This can be:

(a) automatic, e.g. smoke alarms, sprinkler systems
(b) non-automatic, e.g. fire extinguishers and fire blankets
(c) built-in, e.g. fire doors and other barriers to fire spread.

It is the job of the safety officer, together with the fire service, to decide the types and amounts of emergency equipment needed for the workplace.

There is a great deal of emergency equipment available, but we are only going to look at the main types here.

1 Smoke alarms

These are battery-operated and should be fixed to ceilings in each level of a workplace. If they detect smoke they make a loud chirping noise. They should be checked every month, and the batteries should be replaced when necessary.

The two main types are described below.

FOCUS

There are two types of smoke alarm currently on the market – **ionisation** and **optical** (also described as **photoelectronic**).

Ionisation: These are the cheapest and can cost from under £5. They are very sensitive to small particles of smoke produced by flaming fires, such as chip pans, and will detect this type of fire before the smoke gets too thick. They are marginally less sensitive to slow-burning and smouldering fires which give off larger quantities of smoke before flaming occurs.

Optical: These are more expensive but more effective at detecting larger particles of smoke produced by slow-burning fires, such as smouldering foam-filled upholstery and overheated PVC wiring. They are marginally less sensitive to free-burning flaming fires.

Each type looks similar and is powered either by a battery, or mains electricity (or a combination of both).

Source: DTLR

Never try to deactivate a smoke alarm

2 Sprinkler systems

These are systems of pipes and nozzles supplied with water from a header tank. They are used in shops and warehouses to slow down the spread of fire. They are normally equipped with heat detectors so that they only sprinkle water on things which are actually burning. They work by cooling down the fire.

3 Fire extinguishers

There are various types of fire extinguishers used for different kinds of fire (see the diagram at the bottom of the page).

A fire extinguisher can only put out small fires. This is why it is always best to call the fire brigade.

If a fire extinguisher is used for the wrong kind of fire it can do more harm than good. For example if water is put on burning oil, the oil will float on the water and spread the fire.

Water cools and smothers fires; the other types of extinguisher smother the fire only.

4 Fire blankets, etc

These are made from non-flammable fabric and smother fires by preventing the air from getting at them.

LINK! First aid is discussed on pages 113–114.

SUPERGRADE! *Merit*

Identify forms of protective equipment and clothing and explain their purpose in enhancing safety.

Protective equipment and clothing is a complex and technical subject, involving a lot of physics and chemistry. For this outcome, however, you only need to recognise the different types of personal protective equipment (PPE) and say what they are used for.

PPE

1 Helmets

These are worn on the head:

- they protect the head against physical shocks (with, for example, a fibre-glass shell, inner strapping and foam inner lining)

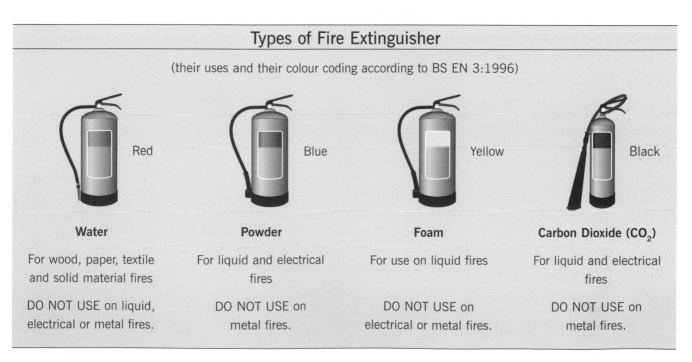

Types of Fire Extinguisher

(their uses and their colour coding according to BS EN 3:1996)

Red	Blue	Yellow	Black
Water	**Powder**	**Foam**	**Carbon Dioxide (CO_2)**
For wood, paper, textile and solid material fires	For liquid and electrical fires	For use on liquid fires	For liquid and electrical fires
DO NOT USE on liquid, electrical or metal fires.	DO NOT USE on metal fires.	DO NOT USE on electrical or metal fires.	DO NOT USE on metal fires.

- they protect the head against extreme heat (the foam also acts as an insulator)
- they normally have fireproof chinstraps.

They are used in firefighting and in industry.

Police helmets have less protective value, and are worn mainly because they are easily recognisable.

2 Suits

Protective suits are made of specialised material such as Dartex, PU Nylon, Nomex (III and delta-T), and treated wool and cotton fabrics. In the fire service they are either splashtight or gastight. They are designed to give protection against heat and flames, and also repel liquids. The heat protection comes from the two layers, and the space between which acts as insulation. Some suits have a jacket and trousers, while others are one-piece garments. They have Velcro and/or straps to protect legs and cuffs.

Chemical protection suits are one-piece with boots and gloves attached. They fit loosely and breathing apparatus can be worn inside the suit. These suits have pressure valves, airtight seals and zips.

3 Breathing apparatus

This is used by firefighters to protect against smoke and gases. It includes a cylinder of compressed air, a face-mask and a pressure gauge, together with a harness for carrying it on the back. The gauge warns the wearer when the air supply is getting low.

4 Protective boots

These are important for firefighters and other people working in dangerous industries. They protect against physical shocks, heat, cold, and dangerous chemicals such as acid. They have steel toecaps and steel or Kevlar protection in the soles, and sometimes up the shins as well. The soles have to be heat-proof and also skid-proof.

PASSGRADE

> Explain the requirements for the production of a risk assessment.

A risk assessment is a close look at a workplace, in order to identify any dangers to workers and other people who might go there. It can be done by an inspector, a firefighter, or an employee who knows something about health and safety.

The assessment is normally done using a form with five columns – as below.

The person doing the risk assessment goes round the workplace (it may be one room, a group of rooms or a whole building) noting down (a) the risks, (b) who they might affect and (c) what could be done about them. Sometimes column 3 can be written out as a proper action plan giving the action needed, who should do it, and when it should be done by.

There needs to be evidence that the actions required have really been done. That is the

Person doing assessment: ....

Signed: ....

Date(s): ....

1 Hazards	2 Who might be harmed	3 What needs to be done (with suggested deadline)	4 Details of action taken (with dates)	5 Review (with dates)
Loose mats above stairs	People going downstairs might trip and fall downstairs.	Mats fastened down or removed – to be done by 23.11.04.	*Mats glued down 23.11.04.*	*Mats coming loose again 12.03.05.*

1 Hazards	2 Who might be harmed	3 What needs to be done (with suggested deadline)	4 Details of action taken (with dates)	5 Review (with dates)
Photocopier with chemicals	People who don't know about chemicals.	Chemicals should be kept in secretary's cupboard – to be done by 23.11.04.	*Photocopier and chemicals now in secretary's office 25.11.04.*	*Secretary objected – too much disturbance. Copier and chemicals now in staffroom 12.03.05.*
Fire engines leaving station without warning	Visitors to fire station.	Warning notices must be put up, and all visitors accompanied by staff member – to be done by 23.11.04.	*Notices now up and staff members instructed about their duties 23.11.04.*	*No further problems – so far 12.03.05.*

purpose of the review column. If the review column shows that the necessary action is still not complete, and there is still a risk or problem, then more action and another review will have to be done.

Even when all the risks have been dealt with, risk assessments still have to be done from time to time, perhaps because new equipment has been installed, perhaps because parts of the building are being used for different purposes, or perhaps because of wear and tear on the building.

> **! CHECKPOINT ...**
> **■** Carry out your own risk assessment (first three columns) of part of your college, a local gym, or a workplace.

PASSGRADE

> Outline the regulations concerning the provision of first aid at work, explaining the implications for public services.

First aid regulations

The Health and Safety (First-Aid) Regulations 1981 require employers to provide adequate and appropriate equipment, facilities and personnel to enable first aid to be given to employees if they are injured or become ill at work.

This means there should be:

- a suitably stocked first aid box
- someone to take charge of first aid in the workplace
- first aid available at all times.

The amount and kind of first aid needed depends on several factors:

- the risks of injury and ill-health identified in the risk assessments carried out at the workplace; for example, there are radiation risks at a nuclear power station but not in a sweet shop
- specific risks, such as dangerous machinery
- the expected level of accidents and ill-health
- the number of people employed at the workplace
- people at special risk, such as new employees or disabled workers
- whether or not there is shiftwork
- the distance from doctors and hospitals
- the number of employees who travel or work alone
- whether the public visit the workplace.

If there are many employees, or the risks are great, first aiders should be employed.

This may mean:

- training people as first aiders
- getting extra first aid equipment
- having first aid available in many different parts of the workplace.

For a big workplace it is a good idea to:

- have links with local medical and emergency services
- give out personal first aid kits
- train as many employees as possible in first aid.

A typical first aid kit should contain:

- a leaflet giving general guidance on first aid (see 'Where can I get further information?')
- 20 individually wrapped sterile adhesive dressings (assorted sizes)
- two sterile eye pads
- four individually wrapped triangular bandages (preferably sterile)
- six safety pins
- six medium sized (approximately 12 cm x 12 cm) individually wrapped sterile unmedicated wound dressings
- two large (approximately 18 cm x 18 cm) sterile individually wrapped unmedicated wound dressings
- one pair of disposable gloves.

Tablets or medicines should not be kept in the first aid box.

A person must be chosen to:

(a) take charge when someone is injured or falls ill, e.g. calling an ambulance

---

FOCUS

Rules on first aiders

A first aider is someone who has undergone a training course in administering first aid at work and holds a current first aid at work certificate. **The training has to have been approved by the HSE.**

You have to inform your employees of the first aid arrangements. Putting up notices telling staff who and where the first aiders or appointed persons are and where the first aid box is will usually be sufficient.

Source: HSE:
First aid at work: your questions answered

(b) look after the first aid boxes and keep them stocked.

The implications to public services

The implications of having first aid at work are of great importance to public services. There are four reasons for this:

1 The public services employ large numbers of people, and their welfare matters.
2 Many public services do high-risk work.
3 Public service buildings are often in use '24/7'.
4 Sometimes the public need first aid.

In the uniformed public services as many people as possible should be trained in first aid. They also need large numbers of first aid boxes – in vehicles as well as in buildings. The first aid equipment available should be of a general type, because the work is often not very specialised.

In police work there is a limit to the amount of first aid that should be given to members of the public. Except in the most minor cases, the person they are dealing with should be taken straight to hospital, or given proper medical or paramedical care, even if they are under arrest.

First aid given to the public by the fire service is often *primary care*, since it is more specialised than ordinary first aid. It requires special equipment such as drips and painkillers including entonox. The aim is to stabilise car crash victims – people who may be suffering from shock or burns – before they are taken to hospital.

Firefighters themselves suffer many minor injuries such as cuts, grazes and bruises. First aid must be readily available for them.

The work done by ambulance crews and paramedics should not be called first aid, since it is very skilled and uses high-tech equipment and special medicines. First aid cannot save someone who is having a heart attack – but the primary care given by the ambulance service can.

In the non-uniformed public services, such as teaching, it is important that people even with slight injuries are taken to a qualified nurse, a doctor, or to hospital. This is because injuries and illnesses may be more serious than they appear.

> **! CHECKPOINT ...**
>
> Why should tablets not be kept in first aid boxes?

PASSGRADE

> Outline the term 'manual handling' and explain the training requirements.

Manual handling means lifting and carrying objects by hand. It becomes a health and safety issue if the objects are heavy, or if the actions are very repetitive.

A huge number of working hours are lost each year because people have hurt themselves carrying heavy loads at work. The government therefore brought out a law, the Manual Handling Operations Regulations 1992, to try to lessen the problem. The aim of the law is to make employers ensure that their workers do not carry heavy loads more than is necessary.

Manual handling

The duty of employers is:

(a) to avoid the need for workers to carry heavy weights as much as possible

(b) to assess the risk of heavy manual handling if it cannot be avoided

(c) to reduce the risk of injury to workers carrying heavy weights as much as possible ('reasonably practicable').

If employers don't do these they could be taken to court.

The duty of employees is:

(a) to use safe methods of working

(b) to use safety equipment

(c) to cooperate with their employer on health and safety

(d) to make sure they don't endanger other people.

Training requirements

To reduce the risks to workers from manual handling, employers have to train their workforce in:

1 recognising harmful manual handling
2 appropriate systems of work
3 use of mechanical aids
4 good handling techniques.

1 Training on harmful handling

Harmful manual handling is lifting and carrying which could cause injury. It includes:

- lifting weights which are too heavy
- awkward lifts where you have to twist or stoop
- carrying heavy weights too far
- repetitive actions
- lifting or carrying weights which are hard to hold
- lifting in narrow spaces or carrying over uneven floors, up and down steps, etc.

Employers should be trained so that they don't try to make their workers do dangerous manual handling.

Employees should be trained to recognise when lifting may harm them – so that they can avoid taking the risk in the first place.

2 Training on appropriate systems of work

Employers and supervisors should have training on how to organise the workplace so that it is not dangerous for people doing manual handling. They also need training on how to plan jobs so that workers do not have to do any more lifting and carrying than necessary.

Employees should be trained to recognise inappropriate systems – e.g. carrying things further than necessary, or having to stack them in high, awkward places – and either change them or avoid them.

3 Training in the use of mechanical aids

This means training workers to use fork-lift trucks, or other lifting machinery, so that they don't have to do the lifting by hand. They have to be trained to use the machinery, otherwise that too will be unsafe.

4 Training in good handling techniques

This is teaching people to hold and lift heavy objects in such a way that they do not injure themselves.

The Health and Safety Executive gives the following advice for lifting heavy weights:

1 Stop and think. Plan the lift. Use lifting aids, or get someone else to help, if the weight is too big or heavy.

2 Position the feet 30–40 cm apart. The leading leg should be forward, pointing the way you want to go.

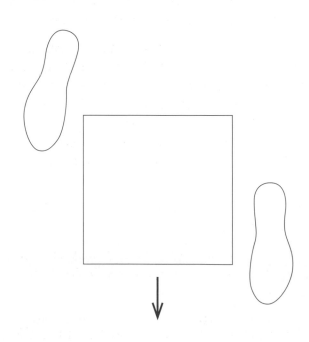

3 Get into a good posture. When lifting from a low level, bend the knees. Keep the back straight and the shoulders and hips facing forwards.

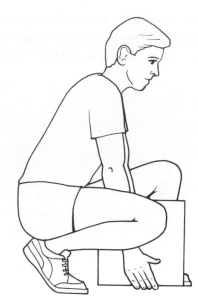

4 Get a firm grip. Make sure it is secure.
5 Keep close to the load, and keep the heaviest part of the load nearest to your body.
6 If you have to turn sideways, move your feet – don't twist your body.

SUPERGRADE! *Merit*

Explain particular health and safety issues within a chosen public service and the consequences of failing to act.

LINK! This outcome is discussed in relation to the prison service on pages 105–106.

The public services in which manual handling is most important are the armed forces, the ambulance service, the National Health Service and the fire service. If you wish to discuss the effects of poor manual handling, it could be done in connection with the work of one of these public services.

The main consequences of failure to act on the manual handling regulations would be injuries. Back injuries are a major cause of sick leave and early retirement.

Other consequences would be legal – the prosecution of the employers by the Health and Safety Executive, or suing by the injured employee (or family).

> **! ■ CHECKPOINT ...**
> Discuss manual handling and the results of failure to follow the right methods of lifting with someone who works in a relevant public service. Make notes on your discussion and keep them for future use.

> Assess the links between risk assessments and safe working practices in the emergency procedures of a public service.

Local authorities (non-uniformed public service)

Emergency procedures are the plans made to save people and property in the event of a disaster such as a fire, a terrorist attack or a flood.

The emergency procedures of local authorities have two aspects to them:

1 Dealing with an emergency within local authority buildings
2 Dealing with an emergency in the area controlled by the local authority.

1 Within local authority buildings

The emergency procedures within public buildings are much the same from building to building and from service to service. The aims are:

- to get people out as quickly and safely as possible
- to prevent the emergency from spreading

- to protect the building, the information stored in it, and the contents of the building.

So if a building is on fire, these are the priorities, whether the building belongs to the police, the army – or a local authority.

Emergency procedures are based on:

(a) an assessment of the risks in an emergency situation
(b) an emergency plan showing how to evacuate the building.

The link between risk assessments and safe working practices is that risk assessments force people to think about safety risks and do something about the dangers themselves *and* about the way they work. This is because some risks are caused by dangerous objects (e.g. exposed electric wires) while other risks are caused by dangerous methods of working (e.g. not wearing helmets on a building site). The definition of safe working practices is 'methods of working with a minimum of risk'.

You can never eliminate risk completely. For example, a local authority can employ security guards who will alert the authorities to suspicious packages left in corridors, and so on. But this would not eliminate the risk of a suicide bombing.

Even so, risk assessments can make a building much safer to work in, and much safer to get out of if there is a disaster. Emergency procedures, such as evacuation or firefighting, are far easier in a building that is reasonably safe than they are in a building that's unsafe to begin with. Access is easier, there are fewer flammable materials, and so on.

So the overall link where local authority buildings are concerned is:

Risk assessments = safe working practices = better emergency procedures = less loss of life in an emergency.

2 Emergencies in the area controlled by a local authority

Emergency planning for a local authority is compulsory by law, and all local authorities in the

UK have a disaster plan. Emergency planning for a local government area is the same as emergency planning for a building: it is based on the risks. For example, emergency planning in Kent, or Humberside, concentrates on flooding, because floods are the most likely emergencies in those areas. But emergency planning in the Sellafield area of Cumbria centres on the nuclear power station, because a risk assessment of the area identifies the power station as the biggest single risk.

Risk assessments for disasters carried out by local authorities are often based on the expertise of all the public services in the area. They ask the police, fire and ambulance services what the risks are from their point of view. They also get the opinions of local industry, local universities and central government. The Health and Safety Executive has a major role to play. So have the water, gas and electricity companies, since major emergencies often disrupt these essential services. If the emergency is agricultural in origin, as with Foot and Mouth disease, farmers, and the Department for the Environment, Food and Rural Affairs, also have to assess the risks. It is a complex business, made all the more difficult by the fact that disasters do not often happen.

Emergency procedures are coordinated by the local authority, but much of the work is done by the uniformed public services. Each public service is given a different role, so they can do the work they are best at. For example, the fire service deals with fire, floods and chemical spillages; the police look after transport problems, and make sure there are no problems of panic or looting. They too carry out risk assessments based on the kinds of work they do, and the hazards they have to deal with. By doing this they are less likely to be injured or killed themselves when dealing with emergencies. But it has to be remembered that emergencies are dangerous, and that some risk is always there.

COOL SITES:

Disaster management

www.hse.gov.uk/

www.hse.gov.uk/railway/rihome.htm

www.hse.gov.uk/pubns/indg143.pdf

www.homeoffice.gov.uk/epd/

http://society.guardian.co.uk/disasterresponse/story/0,1321,555881,00.html

www.hullcc.gov.uk/emergencyplanning/links.php

www.kirkleesmc.gov.uk/answers/emergency-plan/emergency-plan.shtml#whatis

www.keele.ac.uk/depts/por/disaster.htm

! CHECKPOINT ...

In groups, try drawing up an evacuation plan for part of your college. Include a list of the main hazards and difficulties, and make suggestions about the best way of overcoming them.

Unit 6 The Individual and Society

Grading criteria

PASSGRADE	SUPERGRADE! Merit	SUPERGRADE! Distinction
To achieve a pass grade the evidence must show that the learner is able to:	To achieve a merit grade the evidence must show that the learner is able to:	To achieve a distinction grade the evidence must show that the learner is able to:
● describe how public services, individuals and society work together **120**	● analyse the relationship between public services, individuals and society **121**	● evaluate the function and role of individuals and public services within society **123**
● define multi-cultural society and outline different groups found in a multi-cultural society **125**	● analyse equal opportunities issues in relation to current issues in the public services and society **130**	● evaluate the impact of equal opportunities legislation on current issues in the public services and society **132**
● explain the considerations taken into account by public services when dealing with ethnic minority groups **127**	● analyse changes in society in relation to the media, the family, communications and subcultures **137**	● evaluate the development, maintenance and influence of sub-cultures, media, communications and the family on society **139**
● explain the term 'equal opportunity' in relation to current issues in the public services and society **128**		
● outline the basic points of four named laws concerning equal opportunities **134**		
● outline changes in society identifying different influences which may bring about such change **135**		

The public services are constantly changing. These changes are brought about by two main factors – the advance of technology, and the changes in society and what people expect of the public services.

The use of new technology is learnable, but the changes in society – in the way everybody thinks and behaves – are more difficult to understand. Yet they need to be understood by people who work in the public services.

The success of a public service depends on how far it does the job that everybody wants it to do. If it fulfils society's wishes and expectations, it is a good public service. But if it is out of step with what people really want – there could be trouble ahead!

By studying this unit you will improve your understanding of yourself, of other people, and of where the public services really fit in.

PASSGRADE

Describe how public services, individuals and society work together.

CHECKPOINT ...

In pairs, and without looking at a dictionary, define the terms: 'individual' and 'society'. Make sure you reach agreement. Then look up the words in a good dictionary. Did the dictionary meanings agree with yours?

FOCUS

The individual

Each of us is an individual. And what this means is that each of us:

- is a single living human being
- is genetically different from everybody else (except an identical twin)
- is unique in looks, behaviour, character, abilities, etc

- has our own name
- has different thoughts, memories, knowledge, hopes and beliefs
- has a different set of friends, relatives and relationships.

Society is:

- a large community of people, e.g. everybody in a country
- the groups people form, e.g. families, clubs, teams, companies, organisations, etc
- the relationships between individuals, e.g. family members, lovers, friends, team-mates, workmates, etc
- the relationships between individuals and groups, e.g. employees, church members, people watching TV, attitudes of people to public services, etc
- the relationships between groups and other groups, e.g. team or business competition or cooperation
- the habits, beliefs, behaviour patterns and customs that people share.

Public services, individuals and society work together. Individuals need the public services, the public services need individuals – and society needs them both. Without individuals there could be no society, and without society there could be no public services. Each of them needs the others.

Here is a summary of how they work together – what each gains from the others, and what each gives to the others.

Individuals give, and society receives

1 Work that makes money or provides goods and services
2 Taxes which are paid to central or local government, then spent in protecting and helping society
3 Their time, energy and emotion – to groups such as family, clubs, workplaces, etc
4 Inventions, discoveries, ideas and culture (mainly from exceptional individuals such as scientists, writers, musicians and sportspeople).

Individuals give, and public services receive

1 Employees with special skills, qualities and commitment
2 Support and cooperation (from good citizens)
3 Problems or challenges (from criminals, victims of crime or accident, enemies of the country, or the physically or mentally ill).

Individuals receive, and society gives

1 Education and social training (e.g. from family, friends and school)
2 A full range of jobs and careers – which provide both money and status
3 A wide range of social roles, subcultures and cultures, e.g. recreation, groups of friends, the media, religions, interests and lifestyles of all kinds
4 Support for the needy
5 A framework within which we can all communicate and work together for the good of everyone.

Individuals receive, and public services give

1 Protection and help against a wide range of risks and dangers
2 A feeling of security
3 Role models of good behaviour, citizenship and heroism.

Society gives, and public services receive

1 A series of agreed roles and responsibilities
2 Taxpayers' money from central and local government
3 Support or partnership from other institutions (either other public services or private sector bodies such as firms).

Public services give, and society receives

1 Protection and help against crime, accident, disaster, sickness, enemies of society or enemies of the country
2 Education
3 Stability and confidence on which prosperity and culture can be built
4 Help in organising and regulating infrastructure (basic services such as water, power and transport).

SUPERGRADE! *Merit*

Analyse the relationship between public services, individuals and society.

skill POWER

For this outcome you need to put in more explanation – not only describing the relationships but also putting forward reasons for them.

Relationship between individuals, society and public services

To analyse the relationship between public services, individuals and society several points should be made.

Individuals are people made of flesh and blood, who are all different. As individuals we exist physically, and are aware of ourselves as people.

Society is really a collection of ideas. It does not exist except in the form of groups of individuals.

The groups of individuals that make up society are called 'institutions'. Any group is an institution.

Examples are:

- Families
- Schools
- Colleges
- Churches
- Youth clubs
- Your class at college

- Factories
- Public services
- Shops
- Pubs
- Duke of Wellington's Regiment

- Night clubs
- Governments
- Religions
- Angling clubs
- Neighbourhood Watch scheme

All public services are institutions in society. They have similar structures and organisation to other institutions, with leaders, teams, rank structures and so on – just as you might have in the government or in a large company.

There are three main kinds of relationship.

(a) Relationships based on money

These include:

- The relationship between employer and employee, where the employer pays the employee for work done. In manufacturing industry individuals are paid for making things. In the public services, individuals are paid for giving a service which makes people's lives better in some way. This is true whether the service provided is through working at a bank, in McDonald's, or in a public service such as the police.
- The relationship between buyer and seller. If we want something we have to pay for it. Sometimes this relationship is complex – like the relationship between people who grow coffee in Africa and the person who drinks a cup of African coffee in a café. The person growing or picking the coffee gets only a tiny fraction of the amount of money

that the coffee drinker pays. The rest of the money goes to firms which process the coffee, or 'middlemen' who distribute the coffee and sell it.

(b) Relationships based on power

Some people are able to tell others what to do. It may be because they are older, stronger, richer, more beautiful, more skilled or more knowledgeable than others. It may be because they traditionally have more power. Or it may be because they carry weapons and are ready to use them.

Power usually operates through the threat of punishment or the promise of reward. If your tutor says, 'If you miss your assignment deadline I will give you a verbal warning', he or she is using power based on the threat of punishment. If your tutor says, 'If you do a piece of very good work I will give you a distinction', the power is based on the promise of a reward.

(c) Relationships based on 'kinship'

This is the kind of relationship we have with family and friends, whom we know as individuals. These relationships do not depend on power or money (though power and money may sometimes affect them!). These relationships are only possible between individuals, not institutions.

Analysis of relationship

The relationship between public services, individuals and society is based on money and power. For example:

- The individual pays money in taxation and gets protection and security from the public services in return.
- Society has power over the public services because it can (through the government) tell them what is expected of them and can increase or decrease the amount of money they are given.
- Public services have power over the individual. The police can cause us to be punished if we break the law, and we take their advice on crime prevention because they are the experts.
- The individual has some power over the public services, for example by complaining to the Police Complaints Authority about the police.

Evaluate the function and role of individuals and public services within society.

POWER

For this outcome you should look at what individuals and public services set out to do in society, and decide how successful they are. You should back up any opinions you give with reasons and examples.

Function = the job done

Role = the part played

Individuals have many roles and functions, depending on their circumstances. If we have nothing, our role is simply to survive, and to find food and shelter. If we have these, we try to build relationships and start to have a social life. If both

our physical and social needs are satisfied, then we look for greater happiness by fulfilling ourselves as individuals – through education and doing the things we are best at.

> ! CHECKPOINT ...
> ■ Research the work of the psychologist Abraham Maslow (1954), who developed our modern ideas about the role of the individual.

Because every individual is different, you could say that each of us has an individual role – which no one else could play as well as we do. But here are some more general ones:

- belonging to families; starting new families; being children, parents, brothers, sisters, etc
- joining institutions such as schools, colleges, teams, clubs, etc
- working for institutions such as businesses and public services
- forming society, since without individuals there could be no society
- producing goods and providing services
- taking responsibilities: caring, leading, helping, being good citizens, organising and managing
- causing problems: being criminals of different sorts, troublemakers, rebels, complainers
- having rights: voting, being 'whistleblowers', taking part in politics
- expressing our characters: joking, having fun, accepting or rejecting challenges
- using our individual abilities: sport, music, art, languages, drama, craft
- extending society's knowledge: scientific research, philosophy, psychology, discovery and invention, engineering.

Obviously, not everything that individuals do is good. They can, for example, commit murder and rape. People may be criminals because (as some religions teach) they are in some way 'born evil'. Or they may (as some psychologists and sociologists might say) be criminals because society has failed: it is too unequal and cannot offer the right help to people with problems. Whatever the reason, criminals are still part of society – and it is the job of another part of society, the public services, to try to punish and reform them.

Function and role of society

If we didn't have society, life as we know it could not exist. All the advantages of modern 'civilisation' come from the fact that we are able to work together.

But if we evaluate modern society, as it exists in Britain at the start of the twenty-first century, how well does it carry out its functions and roles? In other words, what are its good and bad aspects?

Good aspects

1 It provides a wide range of institutions – factories, clubs, schools, public services, organisations … right down to the family. These satisfy most of our social and economic needs.
2 It teaches norms (accepted ways of behaving) and values (a range of beliefs) which tend to make us good citizens and help us to treat others with consideration and respect.
3 Because it is a plural society it allows us to behave differently and believe in different things. It tends to encourage diversity.
4 It has enabled British people to be, on average, more affluent (better off) than people are in most other parts of the world.
5 It is democratic, so people are fairly free to say and believe what they want.
6 There is a belief in human rights, a human rights law, and arrangements such as a court system to try to ensure that individuals' rights are respected and upheld.
7 There is not too much inequality, and, in theory, no one in Britain should be starving or homeless.
8 It encourages the public services to do a good job, and gives them some respect and reasonable funding (money) in return.

Not-so-good aspects

1 There is (in many people's view) too much inequality among individuals. Some people are very rich while others are very poor.

2 There is also inequality among institutions. The public services are uneven in standard. For example some schools, prisons and hospitals are much better than others, and the same seems to be true of fire services and police forces.
3 There is inequality between different parts of the country. The south (on the whole) is much richer than the north.
4 There is still discrimination against women, members of ethnic minority groups, and other disadvantaged groups. This shows in the average wages they get, in recruitment and promotion, and in their treatment by public services and politicians.
5 Public services are accused of discriminating against the poor, of being politically biased, and of being run mainly by white males.

FOCUS

Views of society

Society is a complex subject and the experts have different views on it. Some you may come across are:

Capitalists and functionalists. They believe that people should be free to get rich, that there should be less tax, fewer government controls and less money spent on the public services. They believe that if people want education or medical care they should pay for it themselves (perhaps through private insurance). Most Americans and many British have this view.

Marxists and socialists. These people believe that society is basically a battle zone between the rich and the poor. They say the aim of business leaders and industrial bosses is to get as much work out of their employees for as little pay as possible. They see the police and politicians as servants of the rich, working for the rich against the poor. Most socialists believe these problems can be sorted out peacefully, through negotiation or non-violent protest such as strikes. Marxists believe it will eventually come to an all-out class war.

Feminist viewpoints. These say that society discriminates against women at all levels. Families value boys and men more than girls and women, and education carries on this kind of discrimination. Most of the powerful people in society are men. Some public services appear to be almost a no-go area for women.

Religious viewpoints. People from various religions believe society should reflect the norms and values put forward by holy books such as the Bible and the Qu'ran. At present British society does not do this, but with the founding of more religious schools, and with more respect for diversity, religious views of society may gain more influence in the future.

Function and role of public services

If society is a machine, the public services are rather like the oil that is needed to make it run smoothly. Without the public services, the machine of society would soon overheat and seize up. Every country in the world, however poor, has public services of some sort.

All the public services produce mission statements saying what they think their functions or roles are. For example, the police give their role as: 'to protect life and property … To work within the community and other agencies to improve safety, security and quality of life. To maintain the public's respect for our role in upholding the rule of the law.'

> **! CHECKPOINT …**
>
> ■ Search the Internet and find other mission statements giving roles and functions.

To evaluate these roles we should ask ourselves:

(a) whether these roles are accurate statements of what these public services do (or try to do)
(b) whether these are the roles these public services should be doing
(c) whether the public services are successful in what they set out to do
(d) whether the real function and role of the public services is different from what they say it is.

> **! CHECKPOINT …**
>
> ■ Are functions and roles the same? Look in the dictionary, and discuss this with your tutor – or a friend.

An evaluation of the function and roles of public services within society might include these points:

1 The public services broadly carry out the roles they say they are carrying out. The police do try to uphold law and order, among other things, and the armed forces try to defend the country.

2 Public services are accused of discriminating against certain groups in society, such as women and ethnic minorities. How does this fit in with their mission statements?

3 Though the police work to prevent and fight crime, crime figures continue to rise. This may mean that the police are failing to stop crime, or it may mean that they are getting better at detecting offenders.

4 Roles change over the years. The fire service used to put most of its energy into rushing out and rescuing people. Now, while still rescuing people, its role is increasingly to do with fire prevention and public safety.

5 In Britain, the public services are generally liked, respected and admired. Does this mean they are generally doing a good job – or are we being influenced to like the police, army, etc by the government and the media?

6 It is extremely hard to be sure how successful public services are, because it is hard to measure their performance, in relation to the amount of money that is poured into them. Is a police service better simply because it arrests more people?

PASSGRADE

> Define multi-cultural society and outline different groups found in a multi-cultural society.

A multi-cultural society can be defined as 'a community of people from different ethnic groups who live freely together, according to their own customs and beliefs, without discrimination'.

> **! CHECKPOINT …**
>
> ■ What difference is there, if any, between 'multi-cultural' and 'diverse' – as a way of describing society?

Key points of this definition:

- 'Culture' includes way of life, language, dress, food, religion, beliefs, folklore, shared history, literature, art, music and customs.
- 'Community' means there is contact between one ethnic group and another.
- A multi-cultural society does not stop people from having their own language, lifestyle, beliefs, etc.
- A multi-cultural society aims to be non-racist.
- The ethnic groups do not have to be non-white, but most people are thinking mainly of non-white groups when they use the word.

The government wishes Britain to be a multi-cultural society, but it prefers not to use the word. See the Focus box.

> # FOCUS
>
> The government is committed to creating One Nation, a country
>
> - where every colour is a good colour
> - where every member of every part of society is able to fulfil their potential
> - where racism is unacceptable and counteracted
> - where everyone is treated according to their needs
> - where everyone recognises their responsibilities
>
>   and
>
> - where racial diversity is celebrated.
>
> Source: Race Equality,
> the Home Secretary's Employment Targets,
> published by the Home Office (2001)

Different groups found in a multi-cultural society

These are some of the ethnic groups living in Britain's multi-cultural society.

A proportion of the people from these ethnic groups are now born in Britain and have British passports.

Ethnic group	Main dates of arrival in Britain	Main reasons for arrival	Other information
Jewish	1933–45	Persecution in Nazi Germany	Mainly white; many follow the Jewish religion; no economic disadvantage in this country
Polish	Around 1947	Persecution by Nazis, then by communists	White, Catholic; no economic disadvantage
Afro-Caribbeans	1955–65	Poverty in Caribbean: invited to work in British industries to help rebuild after World War II	Black; Christian or Rastafarian; economically disadvantaged
Hungarians	1956	Failed Hungarian revolution; anti-communists driven out	White, Christian; no significant economic disadvantage
South Asians (India and Pakistan)	1960s onwards	Invited to Britain to help in post-war reconstruction (cheap labour in mills, etc)	South Asian; Muslim, Hindu or Sikh; those of Pakistani descent more disadvantaged than those of Indian descent
East African Asians from Uganda	1972	Driven out by dictator Idi Amin	South Asian descent; Muslim, Hindu or Sikh; no economic disadvantage

Ethnic group	Main dates of arrival in Britain	Main reasons for arrival	Other information
Black Africans	1960s onwards	Poverty in Africa; came to make a better life in Britain	Black; variety of religions; economically disadvantaged
Bangladeshis	1970s onwards	Poverty, floods, typhoons, etc drove them out; attracted by prospect of better life in Britain	South Asian; Muslim; economically disadvantaged
Chinese (mainly from Hong Kong)	1970s onwards	Came for better life, and from fear of what would happen after China took over Hong Kong in 1998	East Asian; variety of religions; not economically disadvantaged

! CHECKPOINT ...

Talk to someone from an ethnic minority group, and ask them about their family history.

PASSGRADE

Explain the considerations taken into account by public services when dealing with ethnic minority groups.

There are two aspects to this outcome:

(a) Considerations relating to people from ethnic minority groups working in or applying to the public services.

LINK! These are dealt with below on pages 128–129, under equal opportunities, and in Unit 4: Citizenship, page 79 onwards.

(b) Considerations relating to how the public services 'deal with' people from ethnic minorities. It is these that we are going to look at now. Considerations are 'things that have to be thought about', and there are three types.

1 Legal considerations

The way the public services deal with ethnic minority groups is controlled by laws.

(a) The Race Relations Act

The first version of this law came out in 1976, but it was updated and strengthened in the Race Relations (Amendment) Act of 2000. Now it is unlawful for the police, courts, prisons, etc to discriminate on racial grounds in any way.

(b) The Police and Criminal Evidence Act 1984

This law was introduced to control the ways the police stop, search, arrest, detain and question people. It was brought in because of the Brixton Riots in April 1981. The PACE Act said there had to be a proper reason for a stop or a search – and it could not be based on the person's appearance or colour.

! CHECKPOINT ...

Get a police officer to talk to you about the PACE Act and its importance.

2 Nationality considerations

Minority groups who are not British nationals are treated differently by the public services from those who are. This is because they do not have a right to live indefinitely in the UK. Their treatment is controlled by the Nationality, Immigration and Asylum Bill 2002 and the Immigration and Asylum Act 1999.

In the prison service foreign nationals are treated differently from British citizens and tend to be kept separate in prisons. They are liable to deportation – something which can never happen to a British citizen except when required by a foreign government to stand trial for a serious crime committed abroad. Recently (2002) Afghan asylum seekers have been offered a £2,500 flat payment to go back to Afghanistan.

The public services treat foreign nationals differently because British public opinion does not want them to stay in the country without good reason.

This is a problem area for the public services because it means denying asylum seekers and 'economic migrants' (people who try to get into Britain to find a better life) their basic human rights.

3 Cultural and racial considerations

In a diverse society the public services try to treat people from ethnic minorities in the way they would like to be treated. This includes:

- avoiding all kinds of discriminatory treatment
- being positive, friendly and helpful in their approach
- taking an interest in the culture of the ethnic minority communities, e.g. building links, attending festivals, melas, etc
- avoiding racist language and unnecessary reference to skin colour or physical characteristics
- avoiding rudeness, swearing, bad language, obvious impatience and displays of temper
- being careful and respectful on the subject of religion (e.g. taking shoes off before going into a mosque)
- not stereotyping people from ethnic minorities, e.g. thinking: 'All Asians are druggies', or 'All muggers are black' (because this type of thinking will influence their actions and make them worse at their job)
- treating women with respect
- using terms like 'ethnic' and 'ethnic minority' correctly
- learning community languages or employing properly qualified interpreters

- being aware of taboos and dislikes of certain cultures (e.g. Muslim and Jewish attitudes to pork) and not forcing people to eat food they don't like.

PASSGRADE

Explain the term 'equal opportunity' in relation to current issues in the public services and society.

Equal opportunity is the right of all members or employees of an institution to be treated in the same way, whatever their sex, ethnic origin, social background, sexual preferences, religion or political beliefs.

We will look first at equal opportunity in society as a whole, then at the situation in the public services.

Equal opportunity in society

This refers to an absence of discrimination against women, ethnic minority groups, people of different religions, people of different social classes and people of different sexual preferences.

Thanks to the various equal opportunity laws none of the above groups of people should be discriminated against in:

- employment – i.e. recruitment, promotion, pay, conditions of service, duties – or in the range of jobs available
- education – i.e. in applications to nurseries, schools, colleges and universities; in treatment at these places, in subjects studied, in exam results, in sports and other activities
- housing – i.e. when renting or buying a house in any area; in prices, lawyers' services, estate agents' services, etc
- goods and services – i.e. in shops, banks, leisure centres, night clubs, restaurants, transport, hospitals, pubs, etc
- public services – i.e. no discrimination in recruitment, etc, or in treatment by public services
- advertising and the media – these should be non-discriminatory.

There are some groups of people who are not treated equally in society but who are covered by some equal opportunities law:

- the disabled
- the very old and very young.

Then there are some people who do not have equal opportunities, but are still covered by human rights law. This means that even these people are protected, to some extent, against some types of discrimination:

- some foreign nationals, especially illegal immigrants
- asylum seekers
- convicted criminals
- some mentally ill people living in institutions.

Equal opportunity in the public services

This means that women, ethnic minority citizens, people of different social classes, people of different religious beliefs, people of different political beliefs and people of different sexual preferences should all have equal chances of working and succeeding in public service careers.

All British public services are 'equal opportunities employers'. They produce equal opportunities statements which they try to fulfil.

FOCUS

West Midlands Police has a positive equal opportunities policy to ensure that all applicants are treated fairly. We particularly welcome applications from members of minority ethnic communities and women who are under-represented in West Midlands Police.

This example is just a statement. A full equal opportunities policy is longer and more detailed.

! CHECKPOINT …

Ask your employer or your college for a copy of their equal opportunities policy. Then read it!

There is a major problem with equal opportunities in the public services. This is that though the public services are working hard to achieve equal opportunities, they still have a long way to go.

The equal opportunities problem has two sides to it.

1 Recruitment

Not enough women or people from minority groups are being recruited into any of the uniformed public services. Here are some figures:

Female employees	
Public service	% women
Police – all employees	28.4
Police officers (uniformed, full-time)	17.2
Fire Service	10.1
Firefighters – full-time	1.2
Probation Service	57

Source: Home Office (2001)

LINK! The bad situation with regard to recruitment to the fire service is discussed on pages 90–91.

Ethnic minority employees		
Public service	% of ethnic minority employees 2001	Target % for 2009
Prison Service	3.7	7.0
Police	3.1	7.0
Fire	1.6	7.0
Probation Service	9.8	8.6

Source: Home Office (2001)

These figures refer to all employees, including volunteers such as the special constabulary and retained firefighters. They are lower for uniformed officers.

The target of 7.0% is based on the percentage of people living in Britain who belong to ethnic minorities (1991 Census). The aim is for the percentage of employees from ethnic minorities to be equal to the percentage of ethnic minority citizens in the area they serve. This means that a police force working in an area with fewer than average ethnic minority citizens is allowed to set itself a lower target.

Notice that the probation service, a non-uniformed service, has a much higher proportion of ethnic minority employees than the others. The probation service also has plenty of women working for it (see below).

2 Treatment of people already working in public services

In some public services women and people from ethnic minorities find they have difficulty in getting the respect – and the promotion prospects – that they deserve. In the higher levels of the uniformed public services, almost everyone is a white middle-aged male.

Surveys suggest that women and ethnic minority recruits are more likely to be harassed or bullied than white male recruits.

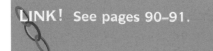

LINK! See pages 90–91.

SUPERGRADE! *Merit*

Analyse equal opportunities issues in relation to current issues in the public services and society.

Equal opportunities have had a huge effect on British society, and it would really need a whole book to cover this outcome. As a student you will have to take care not to get bogged down in this subject.

C**OO**L SITES:

Find out about the history of equal opportunities issues on the following websites:

Equal Opportunities Commission

www.eoc.org.uk

Commission for Racial Equality

www.cre.gov.uk

Gay rights

www.drc-gb.org/

www.lager.dircon.co.uk/

www.stonewall.org.uk/

Equal opportunities issues in society

Gender

Gender remains a major issue in society. It affects family life – especially the roles of men and women in the home, and the bringing up of children. Many people believe that gender stereotyping – the fixing of boys and girls in 'mannish' and 'womanish' behaviour from an early age – is a problem. It may affect the subjects boys and girls study at school, the careers they take up, and their ability to relate to each other. Problems faced by women, such as physical abuse, or anorexia, may have their roots in gender-stereotyping in the home, at school and in the media (TV, films, advertising, etc).

Also, even though women get the same pay for doing the same work as men, they find it more difficult to get good jobs, and the average woman is paid about 30 per cent less than the average man. Only 57 per cent of women drive, compared with over 90 per cent of men.

Race

Statistics show that most ethnic minority groups are more likely to be unemployed, and have lower rates of pay, on average, than white people. This is especially true of people of Bangladeshi, Pakistani, black African or African-Caribbean descent. The problems that these ethnic minorities suffer in the public services are discussed below.

Class

This idea has deep roots. Although officially it depends on people's jobs, it is linked in many people's minds to things such as the way people talk, the way they hold their knife and fork, the kind of music they like, the way they dress, and whether they prefer rugby union or rugby league.

Social class, and the social class of parents, has a major effect on the careers people take up. It can also affect the success they have, and whether they 'fit in'. Many famous people have hidden their social class by disguising their accent and making it 'posher' in order to get on in life.

Accepted ... but only up to a point

Sexual orientation

There is strong prejudice against gays and lesbians in some sections of society – though this is decreasing with time.

Religion

Religion is important (a) because many people think it is important and (b) because it influences people's behaviour. Recent events, such as the destruction of the World Trade Centre in 2001, have given religion a new importance in both politics and society, and may have increased the level of religious discrimination.

Age

This is an issue in society mainly because people are living longer, and it seems likely that the country will not be able to afford to keep the state 'old age pension' at its present level. There is some pressure to raise the age at which the pension starts, and to encourage older people to carry on working beyond 60 or 65. On the other hand, if this did happen, there would be a risk of more young people being unemployed – which is harmful for them and for society as a whole.

Disability

Unfortunately this is more an issue for the disabled themselves than it is for the rest of us, who just tend to take their problems for granted. Society has recognised their difficulties with the Disability Discrimination Act of 1995 – and there is some hope that more may be done in the future.

COOL SITE:

www.disability.gov.uk/

Nationality

This has become a hot political issue because of the problems of illegal immigration and asylum seekers. An asylum seeker is someone who comes to a safe country because they are being persecuted (usually by the government) in their own country. Britain is already densely populated and yet we (and other countries) have a duty to take genuine asylum seekers under a law called the Geneva Convention. The problem is very complex. Some asylum seekers have terrorist links; other people who say they are asylum seekers are actually 'economic migrants' who come to Britain in order to get work. Some of the economic migrants have useful skills which would benefit the country. The immigration service has to try to sort out the problem, which is difficult because the asylum laws are different at present in different European countries.

Equal opportunities issues in relation to the public services

> **LINK!** There is a detailed analysis of equal opportunities issues in the fire service and the prison service on pages 87–91.

Points to be made in relation to other public services are:

- Because the police are the most 'visible' public service, the one most people are most aware of,

they are under strong pressure to carry out their equal opportunities policies. This involves employing more people from ethnic minorities, more women, and more people from other minority groups, so that they can reflect as fully as possible the diversity of society. If not, many people will feel unwilling to cooperate with the police, and crime levels will rise.

- The ambulance service, as part of the NHS, has a better equal opportunities record than some other uniformed services.

- The issue of equal opportunities is a problem in the armed forces. Traditionally fighting has been done by men, and women are still not allowed to join the Infantry, the Marines, or fight in the front line. People from ethnic minorities have been bullied in the army in the past. The armed forces are making strong efforts to recruit from all parts of the population, but it is an uphill struggle. In 1999 the army even tried recruiting from prisons – a brave idea, but they were strongly criticised for it in the media.

- Non-uniformed public services, such as the civil service, the probation service, and local government, have much less difficulty recruiting women and people from ethnic minorities. Many have a very good equal opportunities record.

> **CHECKPOINT …**
> Find out what percentage of the staff in your college or workplace are (a) women and (b) from ethnic minorities. How do these percentages compare with those in the local community as a whole?

SUPERGRADE! *Distinction*

> Evaluate the impact of equal opportunities legislation on current issues in the public services and society.

This evaluation should decide:

- what forms the impact takes
- how great the impact is
- whether the impact is what was intended by the people who made the laws
- what problems (if any) are being caused by equal opportunities laws.

What forms the impact takes

Less discrimination

Equal opportunities laws such as those outlined on pages 134–135 below have had the effect of outlawing discrimination in many areas of life. The impact is greatest on those people who were being discriminated against before the laws were brought in. Women and people from ethnic minorities have benefited greatly from these laws, both in the public services, and in society as a whole. Men, especially white men, have not benefited as far as their careers or status is concerned; they now have more competition for jobs and promotion than they had before.

Impact on personal and family life

In their private lives, men and women have changed roles, to some extent. Men are more likely to help with housework and look after children than they were forty years ago. But it still seems as though most of the responsibility and work in the home falls on the woman – in most cases. And if a family has children it is usually the woman who has to cut down her outside commitments in order to look after them, rather than the man.

How great is the impact?

This is a matter of opinion. White men, especially those above a certain age, are more likely to feel that the changes brought about by equal opportunities law are bad. In some areas of society, including some parts of public service work, there has been stubborn resistance to change. An example of this has been in the fire service, where physical entry tests were made more difficult than the national standards – with the effect of making it more difficult for women to get in. Nevertheless, things are changing, and young people joining the public services now will find far more equal opportunities than those who joined in the past.

An impact that was not intended

In some cases the impact of equal opportunities laws has been to cause gloom, even panic, among the public services. New legislation against racial discrimination has been brought in following the 1999 Macpherson Report into the death of Stephen Lawrence, in which the Metropolitan Police were accused of 'institutionalised racism' in their failure to follow up Stephen Lawrence's death. When 10-year-old Damilola Taylor was killed in south London in November 2000 the police rushed to clear up the case, and there were accusations that one police officer had offered £50,000 to a 14-year-old 'star witness'. The case fell through, in that none of the accused were found guilty, and it seemed as though the Metropolitan Police had once again 'failed' in a race-related case. Yet, of all the police services in the country, the Metropolitan Police has the greatest number – and percentage – of ethnic minority officers.

Problems of equal opportunities law

For some people the problems are that the laws do not go far enough. In society as a whole women are not treated the same way as men, and ethnic minority communities remain poorer, and have higher unemployment rates, than the British average.

Other people think the laws go too far (especially in race) and that they are causing a 'white backlash'. The riots in Burnley, Bradford and Oldham in 2001

133

may be a sign of this. So, too, might the strong feeling against asylum seekers.

Conclusion

An evaluation must come to the conclusion that equal opportunities laws are basically a good thing. They tackle a difficult problem – discrimination – in a way that most people can understand. They may not be perfect laws, but they seem to be working, and if we want a fair society the equal opportunities laws seem to be helping us to get it.

PASSGRADE

> Outline the basic points of four named laws concerning equal opportunities.

1 Race Relations Act 1976 and the Race Relations (Amendment) Act 2000

These two laws can be taken together. They say that it is unlawful to discriminate against anyone on grounds of race, colour, nationality (including citizenship), or ethnic or national origin.

The Race Relations Act identifies three main types of racial discrimination:

- **Direct racial discrimination**: clear discrimination on the grounds of race or colour, e.g. if a black man and a white man apply for the same job, and the white man gets it simply because he is white. Also notices like: 'No blacks allowed.'
- **Indirect racial discrimination**: rules which effectively discriminate against ethnic minorities, e.g. 'all girls in the school must wear skirts'; 'all police officers must be above 5'8" in height'.
- **Victimisation**: picking on a white person who has stood up for non-white people who were being discriminated against.

The Race Relations Acts apply to jobs, training, housing, education, and the provision of goods, facilities and services.

- Public bodies (including the public services) cannot discriminate in any way.
- Public services must actively encourage equality of opportunity and good race relations.
- There must be no discrimination against ethnic minorities in schools or colleges, e.g. unfair exclusions.
- Positive discrimination – i.e. giving more jobs to black people so that the numbers go up to the recommended percentage (quota) – is illegal.
- Chief Officers of Police are liable for acts of discrimination by officers under their direction or control.

Exceptions

Discrimination is allowed:

- in private houses. For example, a white family can refuse to employ a black nanny
- in jobs where the employee will be working outside the UK most of the time
- where seamen are recruited outside Britain
- some civil service jobs, e.g. in embassies
- jobs with a genuine occupational qualification (e.g. waiters in Chinese restaurants)
- racial harassment and physical violence: these come under criminal law.

Cases involving this and other discrimination laws are usually heard at an employment tribunal. See the Cool Site below!

 COOL SITE:

www.employmenttribunals.gov.uk/ england/hearings.html

2 The Disability Discrimination Act (DDA) 1995

The Act defines a disabled person as someone with 'a physical or mental impairment which has a substantial and long-term adverse effect on his ability to carry out normal day-to-day activities.'

It aims to reduce discrimination against disabled people. It gives disabled people rights in:

- employment (making sure they are treated equally and given access to the workplace)
- access to goods, facilities and services (e.g. shops, banks and police stations)
- buying or renting land or property.

The Act also aims to make public transport easier for disabled people to use.

3 The Equal Pay Act 1970

The Equal Pay Act 1970 says that women must get the same pay and conditions if they are doing the same work as men.

This means making a comparison between men and women to see if they really are doing the same work. The comparison must be within the same workplace, or between workplaces which belong to the same company or group of companies.

Even if the jobs aren't exactly the same the woman can claim equal pay if it can be shown that the jobs are equal under such headings as effort, skill and decision-making.

4 The Sex Discrimination Act 1975

The Sex Discrimination Act 1975 applies to both males and females. Under this Act it is unlawful to discriminate:

- in employment (e.g. recruiting men and not women, or in job adverts, e.g. 'Man wanted as HGV driver')
- in job training (e.g. there should be no objection to women training as plumbers, or men training in cosmetics sales)
- in education (e.g. different subjects for girls and boys – though it is still allowable to have all-male or all-female schools)

- the provision and sale of goods, facilities and services and housing (discrimination in things such as bank accounts, sports facilities, selling cars, and selling or letting houses, flats, etc).

It is also unlawful to discriminate against someone because they are married (e.g. saying 'We can't employ you because you're married, which means you might have children and then take time off with maternity leave.')

There are two kinds of unlawful sex discrimination: direct and indirect.

Direct discrimination is where a person is treated less favourably than another on the grounds of his or her sex.

Indirect discrimination can occur when an employer demands something which would be much easier for one sex than another, and which cannot be justified by the demands of the job (e.g. in some fire service entrance tests where it helps to have a long reach).

Discrimination is allowed:

- for certain special jobs such as modelling or acting
- for jobs which for serious social or medical reasons have to be done by a woman (e.g. running a hostel for abused women)
- for certain training courses for careers in which there are not enough women.

As with the Race Relations Act, someone who considers that they have been discriminated against can make a claim to an employment tribunal.

PASSGRADE

Outline changes in society, identifying different influences which may bring about such change.

Society is changing fast, and some of these changes, especially those linked to diversity, are discussed in Unit 4: Citizenship.

Some of the major changes in society, together with their possible influences, are given in the table on the next page.

Influence	Brief explanation	Changes in society
1 Globalisation	This is the idea that fast communications, satellite links, big business, easy transport and the influence of the USA are affecting all our lives.	• Increased world poverty, global warming, serious environmental damage and political turmoil are all blamed on globalisation; the effects of these are limited in Britain at present. • Vast increase in consumerism – buying luxuries, tourism, etc. • Influence of other countries (mainly USA, but many others too) on British lifestyle, food, media and culture; changes in language and traditions; more diversity. • International crime such as drugs, illegal immigration, Al-Qaeda; internet crime has been made possible by easy, almost instant communication.
2 Birth control, easy abortion	These developments have changed attitudes to sex, childbearing and family structures.	• Over one-third of marriages in Britain now end in divorce, but the birth rate has dropped over the years; many more people live on their own or in one-parent families. • A big development in nursery education, but lone parents have suffered financially, and children may be more likely to suffer neglect, leading to a big increase in youth crime. • Much greater sexual freedom; far less guilt; gays and lesbians have been able to 'come out'.
3 Technology	Technology, the development of machines, computers, etc, is linked to globalisation.	• Computers now 'rule our lives', by dominating our workplaces; information is no longer private, so new laws such as the Data Protection Acts have been brought in; there are now different methods of banking, etc. • Too many vehicles for the roads, leading to great environmental damage and the threat of worse to come. • Greater inequality in society, between those who have technology and those who don't. • All countries are more interdependent since there is much more international travel and trade.
4 Politics	Politics means the way a country is governed. The type of government has a great effect on laws, public services and the way people live.	• In Britain many social changes depend on whether we have a Labour or Conservative government; Labour brings in more new laws – especially on human rights and equal opportunities; Conservatives try to keep taxes down. • Changes in education and in the public services are brought about by governments. • In Britain we have a democratic government, so each government tries to do what the people want.

Influence	Brief explanation	Changes in society
5 Economics	Economics is the study of how we trade and how we use money. Money has a lot to do with social changes.	<ul><li>Most people have a lot more spending money now than they used to have twenty or more years ago; we do more shopping, and what we buy or wear is socially important.</li><li>Industries in Britain have changed, and there are fewer big factories or heavy industries such as steel and shipbuilding; this means there are changes in the system of social class – the old working class is disappearing.</li><li>Unemployment comes and goes, and is linked to economics; crime rates vary according to how well business is doing.</li></ul>

 *Merit*

Analyse changes in society in relation to the media, the family, communications and subcultures.

The media

The media include television, radio, advertising, music, books, magazines, newspapers, films and the internet. What all these aspects of society have in common is that they communicate huge amounts of information to a wide audience.

The media affect society's 'norms' – the way people behave; and its 'values' – the things people believe. This means that people who control the media can influence society. During and after the attacks on the World Trade Center in September 2001, repeated film was shown of the collapse of the towers. This made people feel angry enough to support a war in Afghanistan. Without all that media input many people might have thought, 'Why bother to go to war in Afghanistan?'

The media also influence what we buy, by advertising products such as mobile phones or cars. They influence people's attitudes to family and social matters, through soap operas such as *EastEnders* or *Brookside*. They can even influence the way we vote.

Other media points

1 The media are thought to encourage crime by reporting it widely and 'glamorising' it in violent films such as *Reservoir Dogs*.
2 The internet is used by racists and pornographers to encourage violence and to sell pornography – including child pornography.
3 The treatment of crime in newspapers and on television is said to encourage copycat crimes.
4 The media has a mixed attitude to public services. It gives a good picture in popular programmes such as *London's Burning* or *The Bill*. Recruitment leaflets for public services promote a similar image.
5 Some newspapers, such as *The Guardian*, print articles which are very critical of the public services. This is good because it helps prevent public services from being racist or corrupt, but it also lowers people's respect for the public services, and ignores all the good work they do.

How society affects the media

1 Society provides the raw information which the media process into news, entertainment, propaganda or art.
2 The media have become much more diverse – partly because of new digital technology, and partly because the diversity of society has given them a more varied audience.

Changes in the family

The basic British family structure – since the nineteenth century – has been the nuclear family – mother, father and children.

Many other ethnic groups have an extended family system, where grandparents, aunts, uncles, cousins, children and grandchildren are all seen as part of the close family. Since the 1960s the extended family has become more common in British society, thanks to growing ethnic diversity.

Many more marriages (over one third) now end in divorce. This means there are more one-parent families, and more people living on their own.

Many couples now have families without getting married first. This may be partly due to the decline in religion.

Birth control means that people don't have to get married to have sex – so this has changed sexual habits. People have more sexual partners, on average, than they used to.

The roles of men and women in family life have changed to some extent – though women still seem to do more housework and have more responsibility for the children.

Communications

This can mean either easy travel, or electronic communications such as phones, satellites and the internet. Both have changed society.

Easy travel

This has made tourism into a vast industry, and has greatly increased international trade. It has also made illegal trade in drugs and illegal immigration into major criminal industries. It has made British people much more outward-looking, and less inclined to despise foreigners.

Electronic communications

The power and the influence of the media are increasing all the time. About 50 per cent of British households have computers, which has led to an explosion of communication through e-mail and the internet. Internet crime has become a serious policing problem – whether it's hacking, pornography or illegal arms deals. Most people have mobile phones – a good thing on the whole, but they are successfully used by criminals and rioters to outwit the police.

Lack of privacy

Almost all electronic communications are insecure – whether they're phone messages or e-mails. For many years *all* phone messages between Great Britain and Ireland have been electronically monitored! The Data Protection Acts have been passed to try to control the risk of electronic snooping, and the loss of privacy it brings.

Use by the public services

Public services now make major use of electronic communications to gather, share and store information. The services are much more efficient as a result, but a lot of jobs have been lost, as people have been replaced by computers.

Use by banks and businesses

Banks and other businesses carry out most of their transactions electronically, and vast amounts of money can be moved rapidly around the world using electronic methods – good news for business, but also good news for money-launderers!

Subcultures

These are groups of people who can be defined in relation to their lifestyle or their interests. They are not ethnic groups, but they have norms and values which identify them – and can often be recognised in the street!

LINK! Norms and values are discussed on page 240.

Examples of subcultures are: hippies, travellers, gays, football supporters, football hooligans, students, teenage gangs, the 'blue rinse brigade' of older people, and almost any other collection of people who share some norms and values (behaviour and beliefs) in common. Subcultures change more rapidly than 'cultures' (such as the cultures of ethnic groups).

Some subcultures are criminal, and these interest the police. Football hooligans, triad gangs, the mafia, drug-users, paedophiles and even teenage vandals are all subcultures. The police often have to infiltrate (secretly enter) subcultures in order to find out what they are really doing.

The public services themselves can be seen as subcultures, as the Thematic Review *Equality and Fairness in the Fire Service* (see page 90) made clear. They have norms and values, wear recognisable clothes, and are seen as being somehow different from everybody else.

Evaluate the development, maintenance and influence of subcultures, media, communications and the family on society.

Subcultures

Subcultures are groups of people who think and act alike, even though they may live in different places, or even different countries.

Development

They tend to come from the poorer levels of society. Criminal subcultures such as drug gangs have a background of unemployment, youth, and – often – belonging to an ethnic minority. The 'Yardies' who control drugs distribution in some inner cities have this background. In addition, like the Mafia or the gangs of Northern Ireland, the Yardies have a rural family background – coming from Kingston, Jamaica, they are usually the children of workers who have come into the town from the country.

Besides having a background of disadvantage, gangs of this sort are encouraged by prohibition.

The Mafia were encouraged by drink prohibition in the USA in the 1920s, and many present-day gangs in places like Moss Side, Manchester, have been encouraged by the possibility of trading in banned drugs.

Maintenance

The subculture is maintained by:

- the continued banning of drugs, which keeps the gangs outside the law
- the labelling of gang members as 'black', 'delinquent', etc
- unemployment or the lack of worthwhile jobs to do
- addiction to some drugs, which means that a life of crime is needed to pay for the drug
- a poor environment which lowers self-esteem and gives a feeling of failure
- a pool of young people who have not been successful in education, perhaps because the system is biased against them.

Influence

The influence of gangland subcultures is maintained:

- by fear, criminal activities, and the fact that, because they are armed, people are afraid to 'grass' on them to the police
- by the fact that they are a link in the chain of drug supply, and people who are dependent on drugs need them
- by the folk-hero qualities of media people such as 'gangsta rappers' who are admired by young, impressionable people in inner cities.

Media

Development

The media have been going since about 1700 when the first newspapers appeared. It was not until after World War I (1914–18) that newspapers became really important and began to gain political influence, both in Britain and America. Their influence increased with mass literacy (if everybody can read, newspapers have great power to influence the way people think, shop and vote).

Maintenance

Electronic media such as film, radio and television produce more vivid and effective images even than newspapers. Their political and social message is in tune with that of most newspapers. Such media always look for the biggest audience so that they can make as much money as possible, so they mainly put forward popular ideas and images. Minority interests (including ethnic minority cultures) tend to be ignored – unless it's something sensational such as forced marriages. The mass media maintain themselves by making money, developing their technology, and looking for new audiences.

Influence

The influence of the media is very great – on individuals, on society and on the public services. Most of what people know about the public services (and most other things) comes through the media. The public services want the media to give them a good image, to help them in their work.

Communications

Development

Modern communications started in 1912 with the first radio broadcast by Marconi. Their importance was discovered in the world wars – especially through the use of radar. The mass media used them to gain power over us all – and governments used them for propaganda.

Maintenance

Communications are now a vast industry in which huge fortunes have been made and lost. Methods of communication such as mobile phones and computers maintain themselves by bringing out new models with new capabilities, so that people want to buy them. Communications companies use much of the money they gain from their huge sales both to get rich, and to do more research and development so that they can keep ahead of the competition. This process maintains the industry

and ensures that most of us have easy access to cheap communications.

Influence

The influence of communications has been to increase the power of the media and to revolutionise the work of the public services – who now use electronic communications to gather, share, process and store information. All crimes are recorded electronically, and all data about motor vehicles and a good deal of information about each and every one of us is stored electronically, and could be communicated with great ease.

The family

The family has always existed in one form or another, and will continue to do so.

It is maintained by the need of people to bear and rear children. This is an inbuilt biological need, though the form it takes is strongly affected by the culture we are brought up in. The form of the family is influenced by education and the media as well. As we have seen earlier, family structures have been changed by social events, such as wars, which made one-parent families more 'normal', by the weakening of religion since the 1950s, and by technological developments – in particular the Pill.

Society influences the family as much as the family influences society. The media, especially advertising and TV soaps, have changed people's expectations of family life. The public services, especially the police and social workers, are expected to sort out the problems of violent families; in the past, what went on behind closed doors was seen as private.

Influence

The main influence of the family is on the individuals, especially the children, who belong to it. The way we think and act is affected more by our family and upbringing than any other single factor. As the influence of families on children is not always good, the government has greatly extended the amount of nursery education available in recent years – so that children can have a more equal start in life.

140

Conclusion

Under this outcome it is necessary to make reasoned comments about the good and bad sides of subcultures, media, communications and the family – and whether their effects on society are good or bad.

Evaluation is always difficult because sometimes a thing can be good, if you look at it from one angle, or bad, if you look at it from another. As an example, let's consider firefighters as a subculture.

> **! CHECKPOINT …**
>
> ■ With a friend, watch a television programme about the public services. Then discuss whether you think it gives a truthful picture of the service concerned – and if not, why not.

Unit 7 Outdoor Activities and the Public Services
Grading criteria

PASSGRADE	SUPERGRADE! Merit	SUPERGRADE! Distinction
To achieve a pass grade the evidence must show that the learner is able to:	To achieve a merit grade the evidence must show that the learner is able to:	To achieve a distinction grade the evidence must show that the learner is able to:
● explain the importance of a series of outdoor activities and their benefits to individuals **143**	● analyse the benefits of a series of outdoor activities, detailing the skills that individuals can develop **144**	● evaluate a series of outdoor activities for an individual's skills development **147**
● take part in, and record participation in at least two outdoor activities **149**	● take part in at least two outdoor activities and review their benefits **149**	● take part in and evaluate the benefits of at least two outdoor activities **150**
● explain how the public services can be involved in outdoor activities **152**	● compare and analyse a range of youth and community projects including their use of outdoor activities **156**	● evaluate a range of youth and community projects or groups including their use of outdoor activities **157**
● compare a range of youth and community projects or groups, including their use of outdoor activities **154**		
● examine the links one project has with the public services and explain the purpose of those links **157**		
● describe the benefits to individuals of participating in outdoor activity residentials **159**		

One of the good things about work in the uniformed public services is that much of it is done out of doors, away from the office. The police are out and about patrolling and visiting scenes of crime. When the fire service aren't fighting fires or rescuing people from accidents they're visiting schools or testing the hydrants; ambulance workers are always on the go. As for the armed forces, they can travel anywhere in the world – for training, disaster relief, peacekeeping or fighting.

This is only one reason why outdoor activities are so important for the public services, and for people who wish to work in them. There are many others. In this unit you will find out what outdoor activities are, and why they are so relevant for public service work.

PASSGRADE

> Explain the importance of a series of outdoor activities and their benefits to individuals.

An outdoor activity is anything that can be done in the open air. Gardening, fishing or hanging about in the park are outdoor activities. And these are all worth doing at various times. But the outdoor activities we are going to study in this unit are those which build character and give a mental and physical challenge. They are also like many activities carried out in the uniformed public services.

The importance of these activities is:

- They develop skills and character.
- They give people a love of the outdoors and the natural world.
- They provide a living for many people.

They have two main drawbacks:

- They are dangerous if not carried out correctly, or if the weather or the place is unsuitable.
- They damage the environment and can cause problems to farmers and others who use the countryside.

The table below briefly describes some of the activities and explains how they benefit individuals.

Activity (and where it can be done)	Description of activity	How it benefits individuals
1 Rock climbing – this can be done in sports centres, and in parts of Britain where there are suitable rocks, especially North Wales, the Peak District, the Lake District and the Scottish Highlands. The best rock is firm, dry and without too much vegetation!	Climbing rocks and cliffs normally using ropes, other apparatus and special footwear. In sports centres the 'rock' is artificial, and the climbing is normally done in pairs – with one person climbing and the other holding the rope. On natural cliffs climbers can climb singly, or in teams of up to four. In nearly all cases they are protected by a rope that prevents them from falling.	Physical benefits – rock climbing can develop strength, balance, flexibility, dexterity and stamina. Mental benefits – develops powers of concentration, problem-solving abilities, communication skills and decision-making abilities. Emotional benefits – gives self-reliance, confidence and the pleasure of being outdoors in a natural setting. Social benefits – teamwork skills.
2 Abseiling – this can be done on cliffs, old quarries, off bridges and off high buildings. The best places to do it are where rock-climbing is done.	Abseiling consists of lowering yourself down a cliff or building using a system of ropes and a harness. Normally you keep your feet against the face of the building or rock, but it is possible to abseil through thin air (e.g. off a viaduct). Somebody has to be at the top to control the ropes and to collect equipment after the abseil is over.	Physical benefits – develops balance and coordination. Mental benefits – communication skills (listening and following instructions). Emotional benefits – may help to overcome fear of heights and build confidence. Social benefits – none, really, but it is enjoyable and gives the pleasure of a challenge shared with friends.

Activity (and where it can be done)	Description of activity	How it benefits individuals
3 Mountain craft – in Britain this is done where there are hills and mountains, especially Wales, the Pennines, the Lake District and the Scottish Highlands.	Mountain craft means looking after yourself in the mountains. It includes knowing how to dress for comfort and safety, finding your way, planning walks and dealing with bad weather.	Physical benefits – good for endurance and cardiovascular fitness; also good for coordination and agility. Mental benefits – develops problem-solving, planning, orienteering, map-reading and communication skills. Emotional benefits – builds self-reliance and can be very enjoyable. Social benefits – good for team-building.
4 Camping craft – camping is normally done in the country, especially in or around national parks and areas of scenic beauty such as Wales and the Lake District. It can also be done in other countries, such as France. Camping is normally done on sites with showers, etc, but can be done in open country if you have permission.	This involves staying overnight in tents and looking after yourself. The aim is to be comfortable and well-fed while carrying a minimum of baggage. It is important to be prepared for bad weather and to have first aid.	Physical benefits – mainly coordination (e.g. pitching the tent and cooking). Mental benefits – developing skills and knowledge, solving problems, communication skills. Emotional benefits – confidence and self-reliance. Social benefits – teamwork, sharing and leadership skills. Camping is an enjoyable and cheap way of having a holiday.
5 Caving – this is done mainly in limestone areas where there are natural caves and potholes. Caves are horizontal so you can walk or crawl along them; potholes are vertical and have to be descended using rope ladders and other equipment.	This is a sport that is unsafe to do by yourself. It requires torches and is better done with protective clothing such as wet-suits and hard hats. Potholing is particularly difficult, since some of the 'pitches' using rope ladders can be up to 10 metres high, even in Britain, where potholes are smaller than they are in Europe. Potholing can be risky, especially in wet weather, and a good deal of special knowledge is needed.	Physical benefits – develops strength, endurance, flexibility, balance and coordination. Mental benefits – good for problem-solving, map-reading and the development of a range of special skills. Excellent for communication skills. Emotional benefits – builds self-reliance and confidence. It is an enjoyable challenge, and is different from all other sports. Social benefits – very good for teamwork and leadership skills.

! CHECKPOINT ...

There are many other outdoor activities such as skiing, boating, cycling, scuba-diving, paragliding and so on. Choose two of them and work out what the benefits of them are to individuals.

SUPERGRADE! *Merit*

Analyse the benefits of a series of outdoor activities, detailing the skills that individuals can develop.

- It improves flexibility because climbs are often done in narrow cracks where you have to twist your body to get the best grip.
- It increases dexterity because you have to learn to knot ropes and use clips and other equipment. You need skilled hands to do these things. Gripping the handholds on a climb also requires dexterity: the holds are all different shapes and sizes.
- It increases stamina, because many serious rock-climbs are over 50 metres high. The highest in Britain, on the Island of Skye, is about 700 metres!
- It develops your powers of concentration because you have to keep your wits about you at all stages of the climb. If you allow yourself to be distracted you could tie a knot or fix a rope in an unsafe manner, so that it will not hold you if you fall.
- It improves problem-solving abilities because climbs need advance planning. The planning is not only for the whole climb, it is also for the next few moves. The best rock-climbers move smoothly up the rock, not needing to pause because they have worked out what they need to do in advance, for each stage of the climb.
- It practises communication skills, because climbers work in teams and have to be able to shout clear instructions and advice to each other.
- It develops decision-making abilities – for example, if weather conditions get worse, decisions may have to be made about carrying on, or going back. The benefits have to be weighed against the risks, and lives may depend on making the right decision.
- It encourages self-reliance. You have to learn to know your own abilities and trust yourself when rock climbing. It is dangerous for yourself, and unfair on your team-mates, if you misjudge what you can do, and everyone has to turn back because you are 'the weakest link'.
- It increases confidence. The sense of achievement in climbing and overcoming a challenge is good for your confidence. It can also reduce your fear of heights.
- It gives the pleasure of being outdoors. People who spend a lot of time on outdoor activities do it partly because they enjoy being away from college or the office, in a natural and unpolluted

The sky's the limit with some outdoor activities

Rock climbing

This is an activity which uses a wide range of skills – all of which are useful in public service work – especially the more physical type of work in the fire service and the armed forces. Here is an analysis of the ways in which rock-climbing can develop your skills.

- It develops strength because it is a load-bearing activity – you have to lift your own weight up a cliff. At difficult points in the climb your whole weight can be hanging on your hands, or even your fingertips. Keen rock-climbers practise pull-ups and other activities designed to increase their arm and finger strength. Their aim is to increase their strength to weight ratio, i.e. get as much strength as they can without putting on weight.
- It develops balance because there are difficult sideways moves which have to be done cleanly and without hesitation. If you push too far away from the cliff you will fall off (though, all being well, the rope will hold you!).

environment. This is pleasurable, and an excellent way to reduce feelings of stress.

- It builds teamwork skills. You are working together on a shared task when climbing a cliff as part of a team. You get to know the people you are climbing with, and you learn skills of leadership and cooperation. You share the feeling of satisfaction when the climb is successfully completed.

Camping craft

Like rock-climbing, camping craft requires a wide range of useful skills – all of which are likely to be used in public service work at one time or another. Here is an analysis of the benefits camping craft can bring to these skills.

- It is good for coordination because you learn and practise complex tasks such as pitching tents and cooking in a confined space. These have to be done well, otherwise the tent may leak or blow down in the night, or the food you are cooking might get spilt on the ground or, worse still, in the tent!
- It gives you skills and knowledge linked to survival in wild environments. You learn about wind, weather, water-supplies, etc.
- It develops problem-solving skills. The essential problem in camping is how to minimise the weight you carry, yet maximise your comfort.
- It improves communication skills. When camping with other people you live close together and get to know each other's strengths and weaknesses.

Good communication helps you to get on with your team-mates, and carry out tasks quickly and safely – with everybody doing their share of the work.

- It gives you confidence and self-reliance. When camping you are looking after yourself – and this should give you confidence in other situations where you have to look after yourself.
- It builds teamwork skills. Your comfort in a tent depends on everybody doing their share of the work, and thinking about the well-being of others. Camping is a team effort, and an excellent chance to practise teamwork and cooperation. You learn how to share with others, how to follow instructions, and how to lead.

> **! CHECKPOINT …**
>
> ■ Choose another outdoor activity and do your own analysis of its benefits and the skills it can help you to develop.

Camping craft develops your communication skills

Evaluate a series of outdoor activities for an individual's skills development

skill POWER

For this outcome you need to look closely at the pluses and minuses of a number of outdoor activities – particularly from the point of view of how effectively they help individuals to develop their skills. You should also consider whether the skills developed are useful for public service work.

We will evaluate three outdoor activities here.

1 Caving

The skills which can be developed through caving are listed on page 144. They include manual skills, problem-solving, map-reading, building confidence and teamwork.

There are different ways of caving, and some of them are more useful for developing these skills and abilities than others. If you go caving with your college, it may be that you are caving for the first time. The skills you will practise will therefore include:

- listening skills, when you follow instructions about putting on and using wet-suits, torches, etc
- agility and balance skills as you follow your instructors through the caves
- coordination skills and strength if you are using rope ladders
- some teamwork skills (as you help, or are helped by, your fellow students).

Skills learned on a single caving trip

When you go caving for the first time you are introduced to new skills, but you do not have the chance to develop them. The experience is over in a few hours, and you have to do as you are told.

The main value of a single caving trip like this is to give you a new experience, in a new environment. You have the opportunity to decide whether you would like to go caving or potholing again, in the future.

Caving as a regular pastime

If you decide to go down more caves, then you will start to develop more skills. That will probably mean joining a club, since it is unsafe to go down caves alone, and real caving or potholing requires some expensive equipment. In a club you will get proper training in caving and potholing techniques, and you will, of course, make new friends. From these friends you will learn both practical and social skills.

Evaluation for skills development

Caving and potholing are done mainly for pleasure. But they have some value for people wanting to join the public services. As a new experience, caving increases your adaptability. You can overcome your fear of getting wet, being in the dark, or being enclosed in small spaces. It is like some claustrophobia tests in the fire service, and some assault courses in the armed forces. So it will prepare you for application and initial training in these services.

If you do more caving and potholing, it will improve your teamwork skills, and increase your stamina and strength, and your ability to withstand discomfort. As an individual you will benefit greatly.

2 Hill-walking

You may do this activity with your college, under a scheme such as the Duke of Edinburgh's Award, or simply for your own pleasure. In good weather, in areas you know, it is a safe activity – but it is unsafe for inexperienced people, in bad weather, in areas they do not know. It is dangerous in North Wales, parts of the Lake District, and parts of Scotland because the mountains are high and rugged, distances are long, and there are plenty of cliffs to fall off.

It is important to be properly equipped for hill-walking.

LINK! There's a list of hill-walking equipment on pages 281–282.

Evaluation of hill-walking skills

Some people do hill-walking on their own. This makes them self-reliant, helps their stamina, and gives them better skills in map-reading and orienteering.

Most people prefer to walk with friends, or in organised groups. This does not make them so self-reliant, because they tend to rely on group leaders. Being in a group may prevent them from learning how to use a map and compass if they leave all the navigation to the leader.

Skills developed in hill-walking include stamina, organisational skills such as setting your own goals, planning skills, map-reading skills, and teamwork skills – if you are walking in a group.

Hill-walking is also good because it makes people safety-conscious. You develop the skill of making

emergency plans to be used if the weather gets bad, or if somebody gets injured.

Relevance for public service work

Hill-walking teaches some skills that are useful in public service work – especially map-reading. It develops personal qualities such as determination and character, if the walks are long and difficult.

Hill-walking experience and skills are useful in the armed forces, especially the army. They are also essential for mountain rescue volunteers, but (apart from map-reading) they are not needed for most other public services.

3 Canoeing

There are different kinds of canoeing. Small canoes are called kayaks. They are light, manoeuvrable, and good for going down swift-flowing rivers. The long canoes which carry two people and turn up at the ends are called Canadian canoes, because they were used in the old days by fur-trappers and hunters in the Canadian wilderness.

Evaluation of canoeing skills

Skills learned in canoeing include using the paddles, moving the canoe in the direction you want it to go, and dealing with waves, rapids and the danger of capsizing. Since canoeing is done on water there are important safety rules to be learnt to avoid the risk of drowning.

In a wider sense, these skills include coordination, stamina, communication skills (especially listening), dexterity and some teamwork skills.

Long canoe trips down fast-flowing rivers can be a challenge and are therefore good for building self-reliance and confidence.

The social and personal skills developed by canoeing are useful in life in general, but can be developed equally well from other activities – such as doing a Saturday job in a garden centre. Canoeing is relevant to working in the armed forces but, like hill-walking, is not so relevant to most other public service work.

PASSGRADE

> Take part in, and record participation in at least two outdoor activities.

This outcome means you have to do an outdoor activity, and provide evidence that you have really done it.

> **LINK!** Evidence is discussed on pages 173–174.

Your college will almost certainly organise outdoor activities or residentials for you. So in order to pass this outcome you will need to:

- do two or more outdoor activities

- write or speak about what you have done afterwards – to a tutor or instructor (it might be an assignment, or some form of self-assessment)

- obtain feedback from your tutor (probably a feedback sheet with comments and a grade on it).

You will increase your chance of passing this outcome if you:

- arrive on time for the activity
- take part willingly and cheerfully
- ensure that you are properly dressed for the activity
- listen carefully to all instructions – and follow them
- put safety first
- enjoy the activity but take it seriously
- show consideration to classmates, tutors, and members of the public
- take care of the environment (e.g. don't drop litter).

If you record your participation in writing you should:

- describe what you did
- state what you enjoyed about it
- explain what problems you had.

The following points should be noted about safety. Tell your tutor if:

- you have a particular dislike or fear of any activity
- you feel ill
- you have recently been injured
- you are under any medication
- you haven't got any equipment or clothing you need
- you have any other doubts or worries about the activity.

Make sure you or your parents have filled in any permission or disclaimer forms needed for the activity before you do it. If you are asked for your doctor's name, phone number and address, make sure you give them!

SUPERGRADE! *Merit*

> Take part in at least two outdoor activities and review their benefits.

For this outcome you must attempt the activities, and explain what you got out of them. This could include:

- enjoyment

- coordination and some technical skills, e.g. using equipment

- practice in teamwork skills

- increased confidence

- development of personal effectiveness skills

- greater awareness of the natural environment.

A report on an outdoor activity, reviewing its benefits, might go like the following.

Profile

Name: Ayesha Sardar
Report of caving at Hawthorn Cave, Kingsdale
Date: 30.09.04

What we did

We put on wetsuits, helmets, electric torches and wellies and went into Hawthorn Cave. The entrance was very narrow, but after a bit it widened out. We had to walk bent double because the roof was very low, and we had to be careful not to bang our heads. After about a hundred metres we came to a stream which was quite fast and came up to our ankles. This went on till we heard a noise in front and then we came to a waterfall. The waterfall was about four metres high and there was quite a lot of water falling down it. Brian (the leader of the Army Youth Team) had fixed up a ladder and, after he had clipped a rope on to us, we went down in turn. There was a pool of water nearly waist deep at the bottom. We went on for a few hundred metres following a stream till the roof got too low. Then we turned back. We stopped to look at some stalactites and stalagmites. It was quite hard work getting back up the waterfall, and getting out again, but we had a great time.

Review of benefits

The first thing I can say about this is that I had never been caving before. It was very wet and muddy in the cave and I thought at first that I was not going to enjoy it. But in the end I did enjoy it and I actually think I got quite a lot out of it.

1   The cave was a new environment for me and at first I was a bit scared. But then I overcame my fear so I think it did quite a lot for my confidence. I thought I would suffer from claustrophobia, but after the first two minutes I was OK.
2   It was quite difficult even getting the wetsuits on and off, and I had some difficulty with my torch. But I think I learnt something about handling strange equipment and next time I will do better. So I think it was good for my coordination.
3   I learned how to climb down a rope ladder, and back up again, so this was good for my balance and helped me to be less afraid of heights.

4   I had to listen while Brian explained all about safety in the cave, so I benefited because I was practising my listening skills.
5   We had to pass instructions down the line when we got near the top of the waterfall, and that was good communications practice.
6   I had to help Samina with some of her equipment and give her some encouragement about getting down the rope ladder, so I think that helped me to improve my teamwork skills.

Conclusion

I think we all learned quite a lot from this caving expedition. We became more confident in a strange environment and we learned the importance of safety, especially as it would be very hard to get a stretcher into the cave to rescue an injured person. Because I would like to join the fire service I found it really useful since it gave me some experience of moving round in darkness, in a confined space, like firefighters sometimes have to do in a smoke-filled building.

! **CHECKPOINT ...**

Arrange to do an outdoor activity that you have never done before. With a friend:
(a)   discuss – before you've done it - what you hope to get out of it
(b)   discuss what you actually did get out of it, after you've done it.

Remember: You need to review the benefits of *at least two* outdoor activities for this outcome.

SUPERGRADE! *Distinction*

Take part in and evaluate the benefits of at least two outdoor activities.

For an evaluation you need to go into more depth than you do with a review. You can discuss the advantages and disadvantages of the activities you have done, and give reasons for their usefulness – or lack of usefulness – both for your own individual development and for a public service career.

For a distinction you will be graded on how enthusiastically and responsibly you took part in your outdoor activities, and how full and thoughtful your evaluation is.

You should bear in mind that evaluation, and self-evaluation, plays an important part in the training programmes of all public services. They want people who can think clearly about what they are doing and how well they are doing it.

Profile

Name: Simon Armitage
Evaluation of a hill walk from Greenfield to Black Hill and back
Date: 3 November 2004

What we did

Our group of five set off from Greenfield Station at 9.15 a.m. (it should have been 9 a.m. but some people were late!) and walked through Greenfield to the foot of Chew Valley. We took turns in map-reading, but I checked the map-reading of some members of the team who were less experienced at it than me. At about 10.15 it began to rain very hard and we stopped in a shelter to decide whether we should carry on or turn back. As the weather forecast had said the weather would improve at midday we carried on up Chew Valley, but we had a contingency plan to turn back at the top if the weather didn't get any better. By the time we got to the top the sun was shining, so we followed the track to Laddow Rocks, where we ate our packed lunches. We then turned left and followed the Pennine Way track to the top of Black Hill. We reached the top at 2 p.m., then we set off back by a different route, down Holme Clough to Ravens Rocks and then back down the unmade road to Dovestones Reservoir. We got back to Greenfield Station at 5 p.m.

Evaluation of the benefits of the walk

We practised a number of skills in connection with this walk, as follows:

- Communications skills, when we held a meeting, planned it as a group, and made out a route card. We gave one copy to Mrs Bryant, our tutor, and kept the other ourselves. We used speaking and listening skills when two of us went to the station to buy the train tickets in advance.
- Number skills. We used number skills when working out the distance we would have to walk, and the ▶ height we would have to climb from our starting point to the top of Black Hill. We used number skills when working out the overall cost, including the cost of sandwiches and snacks.
- Planning skills and goal-setting, when we worked out where we would go and set ourselves times to get to each stage of the walk. We also made lists of what we wanted to take with us, and had these checked by Mrs Bryant.
- Teamwork skills, when we planned together and walked together. When we had a disagreement about the contingency plan we discussed it and reached a compromise.
- Map-reading skills. We developed these when planning the walk, making our route card, and when we were on the walk. We took care to map-read in turn, so it wasn't all done by the same person.
- ICT skills. We used ICT skills when we used a computer to make our route card, print off copies and save it on disk.
- Problem-solving skills. These were used when planning the walk, deciding on our contingency plan, and in finding the way near the top of the hill when it got misty. We used a map and compass at this point.
- Fitness skills. Several fitness skills were improved by this walk. We improved our cardiovascular fitness by walking over rough tracks and bogs for 12 miles. We improved our coordination when going down a steep slope near Raven Rocks, where it could have been dangerous. We also improved our agility by leaping over bogs!

Conclusion

Although we were tired and muddy after the walk we thought we got a lot of benefit out of it, mainly because we enjoyed it and carried out our plan successfully. This increased our confidence. The walk was a challenge because some of us were not used to hill walking – especially in rain. But we did it in the time arranged, by the route we planned, and we did not take any unnecessary risks. In fact we were very careful about safety.

I think this kind of walk is useful preparation for the public services, because it helped to make us more self-reliant, yet it also showed us how to work effectively as a team. Both these skills are needed for all kinds of public service work.

Note that the writer links his evaluations with the things he did on the walk, e.g. linking problem-solving skills with when they got caught in the mist.

PASSGRADE

Explain how the public services can be involved in outdoor activities.

There are three ways in which the uniformed public services can be involved in outdoor activities:

1 On active operations such as fighting or peacekeeping
2 When training their own people
3 For recruitment and public relations.

There are also voluntary public services which get involved in outdoor activities – see page 153.

1 On operations

The job of the armed forces is to defend Britain. But this doesn't mean they sit on the beach waiting for an enemy ship to appear. They can go anywhere in the world, and either fight, or act as a peacekeeping force.

FOCUS

British soldiers hunting al-Qaeda and former Taliban fighters in the mountains of south-eastern Afghanistan have mounted 'the big push', military spokesmen said yesterday.

Hundreds of Royal Marines have spent the past five days moving into position. So far, the only trace of al-Qaeda has been a cache of small-arms ammunition hidden in a cave and some old defensive positions.

Source: *The Observer*, 5 May 2002

In places like Afghanistan they use special mountain and desert warfare skills, which have been learnt by outdoor training in wild and mountainous areas in various parts of the world.

2 Training

The armed forces use outdoor activities to train their troops. Their main reasons for doing this are:

- to increase fitness
- to develop survival, defence and fighting skills that could be used on operations
- to develop teamwork skills
- to raise morale.

The Royal Marines, a branch of the Royal Navy, use outdoor activities for all training purposes. In the Focus box below, 'fieldcraft, physical training and map-reading' are all outdoor activities.

FOCUS

The first phase for Recruits begins with Foundation and then Individual Training. The Foundation process is designed to help a recruit make the transition from civilian to service life. Individual training covers a wide spectrum of skills such as weapons training, field craft, physical training and map reading. During the initial 15 weeks the focus is on physically preparing Recruits for the arduous and challenging training ahead of them.

Source: MoD website (2000)

3 Recruitment and public relations

The armed forces run cadet schemes and Army Youth Teams, which provide outdoor activities for young people. Their reasons for doing this are:

- to show enjoyable aspects of army life to teenagers, in the hope that some of them will consider the army as a career
- to make links with the community, and to show young people what the army is like

! CHECKPOINT …

(a) Contact your local armed forces recruitment office, and ask them about 'Look at Life' days.

(b) Research a cadet scheme run by one of the armed forces.

- to give character, teamwork and outdoor skills training to young people
- to give a good image of the army to the public in general.

Volunteer public services which use outdoor activities

Mountain Rescue

In mountainous areas of Great Britain such as Wales and the Lake District there are mountain rescue teams. These are teams of local volunteers who encourage safe behaviour on the mountains, and who go out in all weather conditions to rescue people and animals. See the Focus box below.

FOCUS

Cockermouth Mountain Rescue Team

Registered charity no. 506956

Reproduced with kind permission of Cockermouth Mountain Rescue Team

The team responsible for rescuing people and animals from the Buttermere, Ennerdale, Lorton and Loweswater valley areas:

- Available 365 days a year, 24 hours a day
- Volunteers spend 1500 hours per year on rescues
- A registered charity solely funded by voluntary contributions
- Annual operating costs of £25,000.

Mountain rescue teams often work with other public services. The police sometimes use them in murder inquiries, when they are looking for a body.

> ! **CHECKPOINT …**
>
> ■ Research these if you are interested in sailing and boating!
>
> Lifeboat Services
> HM Coastguards

Non-uniformed public services

Most of these (except for people like National Park rangers or workers at environmental centres and nature reserves) do not regularly do outdoor activities – though they may arrange outdoor activities like footpath building for young volunteers who want a cheap working holiday.

Some of them arrange management training activities for team-building, which involve adventurous outdoor activities. These schemes are sometimes run by ex-army personnel.

PASSGRADE

> Compare a range of youth and community projects or groups, including their use of outdoor activities.

skill POWER

> When comparing, you should look at both *similarities* and *differences*.

There are many organisations for young people or for the community which use outdoor activities. They have a number of purposes:

- recreation, e.g. holidays and enjoyment
- education, e.g. environmental education
- character-building
- teaching outdoor skills, such as rock-climbing.

Some are based in one place; others are found all over Britain, and even in other countries as well. Here are some examples.

1 A recreational group – the YHA

The Youth Hostels Association started off as a chain of low-cost places for walkers to stay in. Originally people had to do their own cooking and cleaning up, but the image of the YHA has changed over the years, and now it provides accommodation for parties and families as well as young walkers. It also provides outdoor activities for educational purposes.

> **FOCUS**
>
> The place to stay for educational visits, outdoor pursuits, short breaks and conferences.
>
> Group leaders choose YHA for our:
>
> - 230 Youth Hostels
> - low cost
> - uncompromising standards in welcome, service, safety and security, including exclusive use of youth hostels
> - National Curriculum linked packages and GNVQ Tutor Information Pack
> - evening activities
> - having the place to yourselves
> - Group Activities (example Edale)
>
> Source: YHA (2002)

2 An educational community project

> **FOCUS**
>
> Canterbury Environmental Education Centre is located in the heart of the city of Canterbury on the 23-acre Broad Oak Nature Reserve. Our location has much to do with what we hope to achieve.
>
> 'That any student visiting the centre, be they child or adult, will leave us more aware of:

1 The variety and nature of our natural environment

2 An understanding that wildlife can flourish in urban and industrial areas

3 That they too have a part to play in informing, educating and persuading others to take a greater interest in the welfare of our environment.'

Canterbury Environmental Education Centre has a vital role to play in the promotion of environmental awareness in the local, national and global community. As a result of the partnership between Kent County Council and the National Grid Company we are able to manage a unique nature reserve and introduce thousands of children each year to the secrets that hide within.

Source: David Horne, Head of Centre, Broad Oak Nature Reserve. (2000)

3 Character building

FOCUS

The Youth and Community Service in Gloucestershire is a partnership between the many and varied voluntary youth organisations and the County Council. Youth workers are developing links with the county's schools, such as recent collaboration through the Duke of Edinburgh's Award Scheme and in project work with young people excluded, or in danger of being excluded, from schools. Schools are major users of the facilities available at South Cerney, the county's water based outdoor education centre in the Cotswolds, and at the Wilderness Centre in the Forest of Dean, which offers courses in environmental and outdoor education. The service has numerous inter agency links, such as those with the Health Promotion Unit, Social Services, Probation, Police, and County and Parish Councils, leading to jointly funded projects such as the drug project within schools.

Comparison

Here are three examples of youth and community projects. They are all similar because they all use outdoor activities to achieve their purposes. The Youth Hostels Association provides 230 places where people can stay fairly cheaply, and enjoy the countryside in any way they want. They have the choice of doing organised, group activities, or of going out on their own. Most people use youth hostels for walking or cycling, and many hostels are within a day's walk of another hostel. The YHA is an international organisation, and there are now youth hostels in many parts of the world.

Canterbury Environmental Education Centre is a single centre which has been set up for a specific educational purpose: to teach people about the environment. It has a 23-acre site – which is quite small – so the only outdoor activity is walking round the site looking at the flowers and wildlife.

Gloucestershire Youth and Community Service is concerned mainly with helping young people who may be at risk from crime or drugs or other problems. Its primary purpose is therefore to build the character of young people so that they are less likely to offend. It gives them adventurous outdoor activities at South Cerney so that besides enjoying themselves they can learn teamwork skills and become more aware of their rights and responsibilities.

All three organisations are non-profit-making. They are run as partnerships and helped by other organisations. For example the YHA has links with Barclays Bank. Gloucestershire Youth and Community Service is the only organisation that has links with the public services. This is because it is the only one of the three that is concerned with crime prevention.

> **! CHECKPOINT ...**
>
> (a) Find out about an outdoor centre or organisation which is run as a business, for profit.
> In what ways are these 'commercial' centres better or worse than the non-profit-making ones?
>
> (b) Using the Internet, or other research, find an organisation which trains you in the technical skills of outdoor activities.

SUPERGRADE! *Merit*

Compare and analyse a range of youth and community projects including their use of outdoor activities.

skill POWER

The best way to do this is as follows.

Collect information about three or more youth and community projects. Examples are: The Prince's Trust, the Scouts, the Duke of Edinburgh's Award Scheme, the Woodcraft Folk, Army Youth Teams. There are also many local ones, like the ones listed in the Cool Site.

Compare them – showing similarities and differences in:

- what outdoor activities they do
- the purpose of their outdoor activities
- who benefits from their outdoor activities
- who pays for the activities.

Analyse – go into more detail about the points listed above – as in the example on the right.

We thought Jenny ought to get out of the house a bit more, so we sent her to Kyrgyzstan -

C☉L SITE:
www.outdoor-learning.org/aoc/roguesgallery.htm

Analysis of the British Schools Exploring Society

FOCUS

BSES Expeditions
The British Schools Exploring Society, a charity based at the Royal Geographical Society. Aims to help in the development of $16\frac{1}{2}$–20-year-olds through the challenge of living and working in remote areas of the world. Does research and produces valuable scientific work. Welcomes those with physical disabilities. Many go on to attend leadership development courses and become leaders of future expeditions.

Source: www.bses.org.uk/

The aim of this society, which was founded in 1932, is 'to provide young people with an intense and lasting experience of self-discovery in a demanding and natural wilderness environment'. It arranges expeditions for 18–23-year-olds to places such as Patagonia, Greenland, Lesotho and Kyrgyzstan. The summer expeditions consist of twenty people and last about six weeks; gap year expeditions last 2–3 months.

There is a secondary aim: to 'do research and produce valuable scientific work'. This suggests that the scheme is targeted at young people who are very interested in subjects like biology, geology and geography.

The organisation is non-profit-making, but it does not offer a free service:

'Contribution excluding flight will be in the region of £4,400, including a deposit of £300 to be paid when accepting offer of a place.

An estimated additional flight cost of £1,100 will be invoiced separately.

Contribution will be confirmed in June and will include administration, in-country travel, freight, food, fuel, equipment and insurance.'

The expeditions tend to be to mountainous, remote areas of the world, so a high standard of fitness will normally be needed. The outdoor activities include mountain-climbing, long-distance walks and canoeing. But the organisation also invites physically disabled young people to go, so that they too can experience some outdoor activities, participate in teamwork, and carry out research.

This organisation gives a unique and valuable experience, not just in travelling and exploring a remote region, but also in teamwork and leadership development. It would be extremely relevant for young people wishing to become officers in the armed forces – and would look good on anybody's CV. It is, however, a scheme for 20 carefully chosen people only, so selection would be extremely competitive. And people selected would either have to come from wealthy families, or have the ability and contacts to raise at least £6,000.

SUPERGRADE! *Distinction*

> Evaluate a range of youth and community projects or groups including their use of outdoor activities.

For this outcome you will need details of at least three youth and community projects – probably ones you have already researched for the two previous outcomes.

SKILL POWER

When you evaluate, you do an analysis, then draw conclusions from it. You can make judgements (e.g. 'The project would be better if …') but you should always try to give reasons for your judgement – so that other people, such as tutors, will take your opinions seriously!

Your evaluation could include:

- picking out the differences between three or more projects

- making choices about which projects are best for different purposes (e.g. education, character building or fitness training)

- suggesting problems that some projects might have (e.g. lack of money; they don't benefit enough people; they cost too much)

- outlining how they might benefit society as a whole (e.g. by cutting down crime, increasing environmental awareness, giving cheap holidays)

- discussing where they get their money from, and saying what the advantages and disadvantages of different types of funding are (e.g. centres run by local authorities are free for many of the people using them, which is good; but they cost the taxpayer more money, which may be bad)

- asking – and trying to answer – the question: 'How do they know they are doing a good job?'

- finding out what the project does to ensure that its activities are safe for the people taking part

- discovering whether the projects provide equal opportunities for all.

PASSGRADE

> Examine the links one project has with the public services and explain the purpose of those links.

Many youth projects have links with one or more public services. These links have four main purposes:

- to benefit the youth project
- to benefit the young people in the youth project
- to benefit the public service
- to reduce crime or the risk of crime.

Let's look at the situation in a bit more detail by using an example.

FOCUS

Army Cadets – get some attitude!
Motto 'To inspire to achieve'

Get yourself some action with the Army Cadets!

Sleep out under the stars and cook your own meal – after finding your way over unknown countryside.

Try canoeing, rock climbing, abseiling, mountain biking and overseas expeditions.

Good at sports – or keen to have a go? We've got target shooting, football, athletics, cross country, swimming and many more.

Become proficient in map reading, first aid, fieldcraft, radios and weapons handling.

Get involved with your own town or village activities – parade in your uniform with pride on Remembrance Day, help with community projects.

The Army Cadet Force (ACF) is over 100 years old and is a national voluntary youth movement. It is sponsored by the Army and aims to provide opportunities for young people to build their personal skills and self-confidence so that they become responsible and caring citizens. Cadets and ACF adults are provided with army uniforms and ACF officers hold the Queen's Commission.

What we offer
- Adventure training, for example canoeing, abseiling and pot-holing
- Duke of Edinburgh Award Scheme
- Weapons handling
- Competition shooting
- Sports
- Camping
- Teamwork
- Map reading
- Leadership skills
- Citizenship
- Signal training
- Visits to military bases
- and even Foreign Travel

The Army Cadet Force is an organisation for young people between the ages of 13 and 18. It has over 50,000 members – including 10,000 girls. There are over 1,700 Cadet detachments around the country.

The cadets are linked to the army, but they are not part of the army. They were formed to give back-up to the army in the case of a national emergency, or if Britain was invaded. The modern Army Cadet Force was developed in World War II.

The ACF's links to the army benefit the army because:

- The ACF helps army recruitment. Many well-motivated cadets go on to join the army and have successful careers.
- The ACF provides a link between the army and the local community the cadets come from. The cadets will talk about what they do and give a good image of the army to local people. In other words, they act as a form of public relations.

The army's links to the ACF benefit the ACF because:

- The ACF can use army (or Territorial Army) buildings as their base.
- Army or TA instructors can help with the training of cadets.
- The cadets are able to use army camps, and get the help of army personnel, when they do activities such as their annual camp, or have days out with army units.

The cadets themselves benefit from army links because:

- They have exciting days out, free of charge.
- They develop a range of skills – teamwork, communication, shooting, rock-climbing, etc.
- They develop their confidence.
- They have the chance to find out about careers in the army, and whether they are suitable.
- They can join, or get help with, other schemes, such as the Duke of Edinburgh's Award and BTEC courses.
- They learn good citizenship.

COOL SITE:

www.armycadets.com

LINK! The Expedition Skills unit is all about the residential you may do as part of your BTEC 1st Diploma. See page 275 onwards.

! CHECKPOINT ...

■ Contact your local police and see what they do to help local projects for young people.

PASSGRADE

Describe the benefits to individuals of participating in outdoor activity residentials.

An outdoor activity residential is a period of time, usually two or three days, spent in the country doing adventurous activities such as rock-climbing, canoeing, hill-walking, mountain biking, orienteering, horse-riding or caving.

Residentials are:

- normally based in outdoor centres, army camps or camp sites
- designed for students, young people, or organised parties
- run by qualified people such as teachers and instructors
- governed by strict safety rules to reduce the risk of injury or death

- usually linked to some sort of certificate or qualification.

The benefits to individuals include:

- developing interpersonal skills – teamwork, leadership, communication, etc
- practising personal development skills – goal-setting
- learning practical skills linked to outdoor activities, e.g. canoeing, rock-climbing
- learning about health and safety outdoors
- increased confidence and sense of responsibility
- the enjoyment of doing new activities in natural surroundings
- making new friends, or improving the friendships you already have
- getting a cheap holiday.

! CHECKPOINT ...

■ Which of these benefits are also useful to people wanting careers in the public services? Why?

Unit 8 Sport and Recreation

Grading criteria

PASSGRADE	SUPERGRADE! *Merit*	SUPERGRADE! *Distinction*
To achieve a pass grade the evidence must show that the learner is able to:	To achieve a merit grade the evidence must show that the learner is able to:	To achieve a distinction grade the evidence must show that the learner is able to:
● describe the role of sports and recreational activities today **161**	● compare the uses of sporting and recreational activities by different public services **163**	● justify the uses of sporting and recreational activities by different public services **164**
● identify how different public services use sporting and recreational activities **162**	● analyse the safety practices applied to a range of sporting and recreational activities **167**	● evaluate some of the differences between safety practices that organisations are required to apply and that individuals should consider when participating in a range of sporting and recreational activities **170**
● investigate and describe how safety practices are applied to a range of sporting and recreational activities **165**	● specify some of the differences between safety practices that organisations are required to apply and that individuals should consider when participating in a range of sporting and recreational activities **170**	● evaluate the benefits to the individual from participation in sporting and recreational events **177**
● recognise differences between safety practices that organisations are required to apply and those that individuals should consider when participating in a range of sporting and recreational activities **169**	● explain the benefits to the individual from participation in sporting and recreational events **175**	
● outline the importance of planning and preparation when taking part in sporting or recreational activities **172**		
● record regular participation in a sporting or recreational activity **173**		
● identify a series of benefits to the individual from participation in sporting and recreational events **174**		

Public services are not the same thing as sport. But there is every reason why people who work in the public services should be interested in sport, and should enjoy it.

The work of the uniformed public services is mainly teamwork, and sport is an ideal activity for learning what teamwork is really all about. Much of the work of the uniformed public services is also active and physical – just like sport is. In the fire service or the army you would have to search a long time to find someone who was not interested in sport.

The situation with the non-uniformed public services is different. Council workers, HM Customs and Excise, teachers, nurses – these people may or may not be interested in sport. But since their jobs are fairly sedentary – jobs with plenty of sitting down and not much running about – there is a lot to be said for them doing sport in their spare time, for exercise and to get rid of stress. And the non-uniformed public services still work as teams.

So get out and do some sport and recreation! And, in between times, work your way through this unit.

> Describe the role of sports and recreational activities today.

A sport is an organised, physical, competitive activity which can be done for enjoyment.

A recreational activity is any form of leisure which may or may not be physical, but involves some kind of effort, achievement and enjoyment.

All sports can be recreational activities, but not all recreational activities are sports. For example, train-spotting or watercolour painting are recreational activities, but they are not normally thought of as sports!

The grading criteria for this unit do not mention physical recreational activity. This seems to mean that if you are disabled, or allergic to sport, you could still take this unit. If in doubt, talk with your tutor about it.

The role of sports

The government booklet 'A Sporting Future for All' (2001) points out: 'Sport is a booming industry, worth £12 billion of consumer spending every year and employing around 420,000 people.' But sport is also a leisure activity for millions who are either participants or spectators.

Sport, in fact, has many roles. Some of them are as follows.

Keeping fit

Participating in sport and most recreational activities helps us to keep fit. Swimming, walking, and running develop our aerobic endurance; weightlifting and similar exercises develop our strength; playing football or rugby develops agility and coordination – and so on.

Social practice

Sports and games are social activities which develop our awareness of ourselves, of other people and a number of interpersonal skills – such as teamwork and communication. They are a natural extension of the way we play as children – and psychologists believe that much of our learning is done by playing games.

Moral training

This is closely related to social practice. Sport teaches us ideas of honesty, fair play and hard work – all qualities which are valued in society as a whole, and in the public services in particular. We get this training from watching sports as well as playing them – for example, when a referee holds up a red card to a footballer who's just done a bad tackle.

A commercial activity

Professional sport is big business. And sports festivals such as the Olympic Games or the World Cup are major media events watched by many millions of people. People can make – and lose – billions of pounds broadcasting sport.

Crime reduction

Public services such as the police try to get involved in sporting youth clubs which attract young people who might otherwise be out on the streets committing crime or being disorderly. A number of famous sportspeople, e.g. Lennox Lewis, started in such clubs, and now say that sport saved them from committing petty crime.

Social activity

This is not the same as social practice. This is sport seen as a way of making friends, of meeting people and of having a good time. People can join clubs, travel with teams, or, if they prefer, they can join supporters' clubs and still enrich their social lives.

Reducing social conflict

Sport brings people of different races and cultures together, and has done a great deal to make diversity more acceptable to more people.

> **! CHECKPOINT ...**
>
> (a) Talk to someone who works in a local sports centre or other facility about the reasons why people take up sport, and the benefits it brings them.
> (b) Discuss with a friend why you – or they – support a sports team.

PASSGRADE

> Identify how different public services use sporting and recreational activities.

All uniformed public services and some non-uniformed ones take a keen interest in sporting and recreational activities. For this outcome you need more than one public service – but we only have space for one: the army.

The army

The army uses sporting and recreational activities in the following ways.

In basic training

A range of sporting and physical recreational activities are used to increase and assess the fitness of recruits. The activities are used in the soldier's professional development – to make him or her better at the job.

In specialised training

Many regiments train soldiers for arctic conditions, and this means that the army makes wide use of winter sports – especially cross-country (Nordic) skiing.

In maintaining fitness

Throughout their army careers soldiers need to keep fit. The army has gyms and physical training instructors to ensure that soldiers have regular fitness training in a top-class environment.

To develop team spirit

Recreational team games among people who know each other is very useful for this.

To develop sporting potential

The army takes sportspeople and puts them into 'athletic' regiments where they can achieve very high standards, taking part in international competition. The Focus box below illustrates what a sportsperson can get out of the armed forces.

> ### FOCUS
>
> **Kelly Morgan**
>
> The Olympic disappointment persuaded Morgan to give up her career as a physical training instructor in the Royal Air Force and concentrate on javelin. It was the wrong decision. 'I had a horrendous year,' she says. 'I didn't have a team around me and I had a bad injury with my shoulder – that's when it all flared up.'
>
> By the end of 2001 she was, she says, 'Pretty much at rock bottom'. She missed the camaraderie of the RAF and decided to re-join the services, this time opting for the Army.
>
> Source: International Association of Athletic Federations (2002)

For enjoyment and self-fulfilment

Competitive sport can be played in the army at a number of levels. They have a vast series of sporting fixtures each year. These are organised by the Army Sport Control Board. They play many other public services: for example, the cricketing fixtures for 2002 included matches against the fire brigade, Oxford University, a British Police team, the Stock Exchange and a range of county teams.

To make community links

Army physical training instructors sometimes work with school and college parties to give them a taste of the physical activities and sports done in the army. These events can inspire young people to apply to the army, or simply give them a better image of the army than they might have had. Equally important, it gives the young people a good day out!

___

C👓L SITE:

www.cssc.co.uk/pdf/eventorder.PDF civil service sports
___

To cover the next outcome it is probably best to compare only two public services. If you try to compare three or more your answer will be more complicated, but might not contain any more useful information.

Remember that when you are comparing two things you are looking at (a) the differences and (b) the similarities. You do not always need to look at the differences first – but it is easier in this particular case.

One way of doing it is to write three paragraphs. The first is a brief introduction, the second gives the differences and the third gives the similarities.

! CHECKPOINT ...

Talk to someone who works in (a) a uniformed service and (b) a non-uniformed public service about the use their public service makes of sport. What differences are there?

 Merit

Compare the uses of sporting and recreational activities by different public services.

Comparison between the uses of sporting and recreational activities in the army and the civil service

Introduction

The army is the biggest uniformed public service in Britain, and the civil service is the biggest non-uniformed public service. The army's job is to deal with major disasters or attacks on the country – in other words, things which do not happen very often. The civil service, on the other hand, helps to keep the government and the country running smoothly from day to day. Both organisations use sporting and recreational activities.

Differences

Everybody in the army does some sporting and recreational activities as part of their work – at least until they reach a certain age or rank. Soldiers and other army personnel spend much of their time training, and training involves getting fit and staying fit. Training includes long-distance walking, skiing, and other activities which are considered recreational for most people, but which are necessary work for many soldiers.

By contrast a large part of civil service work is done in offices, gathering information, giving out advice to the public, and so on. The work mainly involves talking to people, or using computers. Even if the work is active – such as going round inspecting buildings or examining environmental health problems – the activities are not what most people would call recreational or sporting.

The army encourages sport at all levels including the very highest. Famous sportspeople such as Kelly Holmes and Nigel Benn perfected their sport in the army. The army employs large numbers of physical training instructors (PTIs) who train soldiers and sometimes members of the public in sporting activities.

The civil service does not use qualified sportspeople except in the running of sports centres and a certain amount of work with the public. They are more interested in sports management than in sport for its own sake.

High levels of physical fitness are needed to get into the army, but this is not the case with most jobs in the civil service. In the army people are expected to do regular fitness training in the gym and outside so that they can be better at their job. In the civil service fitness is encouraged, and there may be gyms available, but they are used more to improve general health than to increase fitness for the job.

Similarities

The main similarity between the army and the civil service in their use of sporting and recreational activities is when they are used for leisure purposes. Both the army and the civil service have large numbers of recreational sports teams which are organised into a league. The army and the civil service have teams in most sports and games – even things like angling or chess, which are

Justify the uses of sporting and recreational activities by different public services.

recreational activities but not usually very physical. The value of sports and recreational activities for improving friendships and creating team spirit is recognised in both the army and the civil service.

'Justify' means 'give the reasons for' or 'explain'. In order to gain a distinction for this outcome you need to show clearly why sporting and recreational activities are used by different public services.

When justifying, you use words like 'because', 'so that' and 'in order to'. These are used when explaining reasons and purposes. You could fulfil this outcome while you are doing the previous one, because when comparing things it is normal to give reasons for the differences. And when you are giving reasons for differences (e.g. between the uses of sporting activities in two public services) you are justifying those differences.

Profile

Sporting and recreational activities are vitally important in the army because of the physical and strenuous nature of army work. Army people do sports, fitness training and recreational activities so that they will be strong enough to drive tanks, load heavy equipment on to lorries, or do long marches carrying their weapons.

They also use sporting and recreational activities in the army in order to develop their teamwork skills. Many sporting and recreational activities involve teamwork, and so do most jobs in the army. Even food preparation, as done by army cooks, is very much a team activity.

Sporting and recreational activities are especially important in the army because they help to build morale. Morale means 'a positive attitude', and if morale is good, soldiers work better and fight better. If morale is bad, courage goes down, and they are more likely to run away from a fight than to win it. Soldiers who never take part in sports or recreational activities are likely to become depressed and their morale will get worse.

Morale is raised by sporting activities because they are enjoyable. It is also linked to the fact that you make friends when playing sports. The army is made up of people from many different races and backgrounds, and sport is a way of bringing people together in spite of their diversity, and getting rid of racism, discrimination and bullying.

Some sporting and recreational activities are done by the army to raise money for charities such as Mencap. Usually this involves activities such as abseiling down the sides of tall buildings, or running assault course competitions which the public, too, can take part in and be sponsored for.

The special encouragement which the army gives to outstanding sportspeople can be justified by the fact that these people encourage all other army personnel to become fitter and more active. They also act as good public relations for the army, giving the army a better image with the public. The fact that a famous athlete such as Kelly Holmes has been an army sergeant is a good advertisement for the army.

In the civil service, sport and recreational activities are used mainly for pleasure and relaxation, and are not normally done during working hours; but they are still encouraged because they improve health and fitness. They also help to build team spirit and friendships within the civil service. As in the army, this raises morale, with the result that people work harder and more willingly; and, as with the army, sporting activities are valuable because they break down barriers and reduce discrimination in a diverse workforce.

> ## ! ■ CHECKPOINT ...
> Note down (taking no more than ten minutes to do it) all the ways in which sporting and recreational activities are used in your college or workplace.

PASSGRADE

> Investigate and describe how safety practices are applied to a range of sporting and recreational activities.

It's obvious from the previous outcomes that sporting and recreational activities are good for us as individuals, good for people who work in public services, and good for the performance of the public services themselves. So what's the catch? The answer is injuries.

This outcome asks us to look at what the sporting bodies, local authorities and other people such as coaches do to make sport safer. It does not ask us to look at what the individual sportsperson has to do. That comes in another outcome.

The table below gives some sports and the main safety practices that can be applied to them.

Sporting or recreational activity	Safety practices that can be applied
Football (safety of players)	These are some of the safety practices demanded by the Football Association for league matches: • Keeping the ground in good order, and only playing when weather conditions are fit • Keeping the public off the pitch • Checking players' footwear and making sure they have no jewellery • Having a doctor, a qualified physiotherapist and first aiders available • Having qualified referees and officials • Having good enough floodlights

Sporting or recreational activity	Safety practices that can be applied
	• Using separate dressing rooms • Having a medical treatment room • Ensuring protection from the crowd between the dressing rooms and the pitch
Football (safety of spectators)	These safety practices start with the design and building of the stadium, and include inspection by the fire service and the HSE, and crowd control by police and stewards: • Searching spectators before they come into the ground • Having good entrances and exits where people can be policed, and where they cannot be crushed • Using arrangements to keep home and away fans apart • Using closed circuit television and a police presence to detect violence or verbal aggression • Having crowd doctors • Having proper seating and lighting • Carrying out risk assessments and inspections of the stadium • Bans on alcohol and weapons
Javelin throwing	• Checking that the runway is not damaged • Making sure that the area is properly drained and free of standing water • Making sure that the throwing area is roped off • Checking javelins before being thrown – to ensure that the grip is right and that they are not bent • Ensuring that only authorised, trained people are in front of the throwing line • Giving clear signals to athletes before they can throw • Keeping spectators well away
Hill walking	• Planning the route to be walked beforehand, preferably as a route card giving estimated times of arrival • Having a contingency plan to get off the hill safely if something goes wrong • Carrying maps, compasses, whistles, mobile phones, etc • Wearing proper clothing and footwear • Finding out the weather forecast, and making sure the walk is appropriate for the weather • Telling someone where you are going, and sticking to the planned route • Not getting separated on the hills • Carrying the necessary food and drinks • Making sure that no one sets off on a hill walk unless they are in good health

CHECKPOINT ...

Do a survey of sporting injuries among your friends – and find out what caused each injury. Could all of the injuries have been avoided?

COOL SITE:

www.ukathletics.net/articles/additions/
risk%20assessment.pdf

Exciting – but fifteen times more dangerous than football

Analyse the safety practices applied to a range of sporting and recreational activities.

This outcome asks you to explain and give reasons for the safety practices applied to at least three sporting and recreational activities.

You may find that if you try to cover all the safety practices, this outcome will become too long. For each sport you should therefore pick out four or five that you consider important.

Here is an example of how you could do it.

Football

Safety practice	Analysis
1 Keeping the ground in good order, and only playing when weather conditions are fit	The ground must be kept in good order because players will be injured if they play on an unsuitable surface. Cans, bottles, litter and stones can cause serious cuts, gashes and grazes. The wounds will be dirty and the player may risk septicaemia or tetanus. Ground that is too wet could cause joint or muscle injuries through players slipping, and frozen ground can cause dangerous falls. Allowing dogs on the field can cause fouling, and a parasitic nematode worm called toxocara canis, which can cause blindness, may be in the soil. Heavy rain and snow mean that players risk more accidents, and may suffer from cold. If it is too hot there is a risk of dehydration.
2 Having a doctor, a qualified physiotherapist and first aiders available	In professional football the risk of injuries is high because players run fast and tackle hard. Injuries are a danger to the career of a professional player and must always be treated seriously. The sooner injuries are diagnosed and treated, the less the damage may be, and the quicker the recovery. With amateur players there should still be medical help available; unfit and unskilled players run a risk of injury or illness as well.
3 Having qualified referees and officials	The rules of football have developed over many years and exist (a) to make the game exciting; and (b) for the safety of the players. Referees and officials have to satisfy both these requirements. Most players' injuries happen through contact with other players and referees must monitor this carefully. They also have to make sure aggression doesn't flare up, leading to deliberate fouls or even fighting – which could lead to serious and even permanent injury.

167

Safety practice	Analysis
4 Having proper seating and lighting (in stadiums)	A number of terrible disasters in the past, such as the one at Bradford City in 1985 and at Hillsborough in 1989, have shown the importance of having stadiums that are designed for safety and built of safe materials. The Hillsborough disaster showed the danger of having too many people standing – nearly 100 people died.

In the last three outcomes we have been looking at how organisations can make sporting and recreational activities safer. But, as in all matters to do with health and safety, the individual has responsibilities too. People who take part in sporting and recreational activities can do a lot to make sure that they don't get hurt.

In this outcome we're going to look at the differences between organisations' responsibilities and those of the individual. The table below sets them out.

Sport or activity	Organisational safety practices	Individual safety practices
Tennis A fairly low-risk game if it is not played competitively, but professionals get impact injuries from sudden movements, changes of direction and falls.	• Building a suitable court, with the right kind of surface • Cushioning the posts holding the net • Keeping the court clean and free of gravel, broken glass, etc • Having safe fencing round the court • Ensuring that people keep out of the court unless they're playing • Keeping animals out of the court • Locking the court when it is not being used • Keeping an eye on games, especially if children are playing	• Warm up before playing – gentle jogging, etc until you start to sweat. • Make sure you know the rules of the game. • Check your style, e.g. serving. • Drink enough fluid. • Have good equipment, especially shoes that protect feet and ankles from shocks. • Bring your own first aid kit – with antiseptic and non-stick dressings for grazes; also use sun cream. • Don't play in unsuitable weather. • Avoid dangerous lunges that could cause ankle or knee injuries. • Don't fool about in a way that could be dangerous.
Hurdles This is a track event in athletics. There is some risk from cuts, bruises and strains, and collisions with other athletes.	• Signalling clearly when athletes are about to run • Ensuring that everybody keeps lane discipline • Arranging hurdles correctly – at the right height and facing the right way • Making sure the counterbalance is positioned so that the hurdle will fall over if struck • Maintaining hurdles • Replacing damaged hurdles • Making sure the track is safe, e.g. free of gravel, litter or standing water	• Do not train or run if in bad health. • Warm up before racing/training. • Wear suitable footwear. • Obey starter's and coaches' orders. • Keep in the right lane. • Learn safe techniques of hurdling. • Have the hurdles at the right height. • Do not start serious hurdling without getting fit first. • Do not compete if you are feeling unwell, or if you already have an injury. • Bring a first aid kit.

Sport or activity	Organisational safety practices	Individual safety practices
Recreational river bathing Risks include cuts, grazes, injuries from diving, drowning, sunburn and insect bites. Rivers are a natural environment and there may be no organisational safety practices unless the swimming place is near a campsite or under local government control. But the following may be relevant:	• Ensuring as far as possible that the water is unpolluted (environmental health; Environment Agency) • Cleaning litter and broken glass from the bathing area • Employing a warden or life-saver if the place is well used • Teachers, youth leaders or parents keeping an eye on children and checking that they are not doing anything dangerous • Teaching lifesaving techniques to everybody	• Bring footwear and swimming trunks/costume. • Don't try to swim in a river if you can't swim. • Avoid swimming alone. • Do not swim in polluted water. • Check for broken glass, etc in the swimming area or on the bank. • If you feel hot do not leap straight into cold water. • Do not dive without checking that the water is deep enough. • Do not swim above a waterfall, or where the current is too strong. • Do not swim in very cold water unless you are sure you can get warm again afterwards. • Protect yourself against sunburn or biting insects, if necessary. • Have a first aid kit and know about lifesaving techniques.

Recognise differences between safety practices that organisations are required to apply and those that individuals should consider when participating in a range of sporting and recreational activities.

In the table above organisations' safety practices and those of individuals are already specified for three sporting or recreational activities.

The job of an organisation – in sport or in work – is to do 'whatever is reasonably practicable' to reduce the risk of an accident. This means carrying out a risk assessment on the place where the sporting or recreational activity is done.

The job of the individual is to look after himself or herself, and not endanger others by careless or reckless behaviour.

LINK! Health and Safety at Work – page 100.

SUPERGRADE! *Merit*

> Specify some of the differences between safety practices that organisations are required to apply and that individuals should consider when participating in a range of sporting and recreational activities.

skill POWER — How to specify differences

'Specify' means give clear and exact examples or guidelines.

The differences between them can be seen from the table. If you wish to 'specify some of the differences' it is probably best to write sentences stating what the differences are. This means using words or phrases such as 'but', 'whereas', 'however' or 'on the other hand' to show where the differences lie.

Tennis

In tennis the organisation that runs the courts has a duty to make sure the court has the right kind of surface and is in good condition. On the other hand, the individual has to make sure that he or she is wearing suitable clothes and footwear for that kind of surface and for playing tennis. This means wearing loose clothes and sports shoes which have a good grip and can cushion the foot against impact.

Some of the danger in tennis comes from thoughtless behaviour or messing around on court. It is mainly the duty of the individual player not to do this – but the organisation running the courts should also employ someone to keep an eye on players – to make sure they are not doing anything unsafe.

Most of the safety practices of the organisation concern the design, construction and maintenance of the court, whereas those of the individual concern checking their own health and fitness,

warming up properly, and following the rules of the game.

If a game such as tennis turns out to be unsafe the governing bodies of the game can change the rules to make them safer. The use of tie-breaks to decide sets which would otherwise go on too long was an example of this. However, individuals who are playing for pleasure should stop playing anyway if they get too tired or think they are injured – whether the rules of tennis allow it or not.

! CHECKPOINT …

Make notes specifying the differences between organisational and individual safety practices for hurdling, river bathing – or for an activity of your own choice.

SUPERGRADE! *Distinction*

> Evaluate some of the differences between safety practices that organisations are required to apply and that individuals should consider when participating in a range of sporting and recreational activities.

skill POWER

In this outcome 'evaluate' means 'explain, and reach a reasoned opinion or judgement' about the differences between safety practices. You should say why you think some practices are more or less important than others, or why you think safety practices should be made stricter or more lenient. You will use words and phrases such as 'because', 'in view of', 'considering', 'provided that', or 'in my opinion'. You should also try to point out why there are more or less safety practices in different sports or recreations.

The differences between safety practices that organisations are required to apply and those that individuals should consider are based on the following factors:

- the nature of the sporting or recreational activity
- the responsibilities of the organisation
- the people taking part in the activity.

The general rules are as follows.

The nature of the sporting or recreational activity

Factors	Organisation safety responsibilities and practices	Individual safety responsibilities and practices
The sport has a governing body.	The governing body decides the rules and makes sure that professional players (and amateurs too, as far as possible) keep to them. The rules should encourage safety.	Participants should play the game according to the rules.
The sport takes place in a stadium.	The stadium must be designed and built to safety standards that will protect players and spectators.	Spectators and players must behave responsibly in the stadium.
The sport has referees and officials.	Officials should be trained and qualified; they should know the rules; and all of them should be present at the game or event.	Players must obey the referees.
The sport is being played professionally.	As the sport is making money there should be a full range of safety features, including stewards, supplied to protect spectators.	Players should behave professionally and responsibly.
The sport is a planned outdoor activity, e.g. skiing.	Organisers must supply safe equipment and be qualified instructors. They must take weather and terrain into consideration. They must know how skilled the skiers are, and give all necessary training in both technique and safety awareness. They should conduct risk assessments into all planned activities before doing them.	Participants must ensure they are healthy and fit, must bring the right clothing, must tell the instructors if they have any problems and must follow instructions.
The activity involves children, e.g. swimming at a beach.	Organisers must carry out a risk assessment on that beach, e.g. for dangerous currents. They must know if the children can swim. They must assess the weather. They must watch the children. They must be trained lifesavers. There must be enough organisers for the number of children. The party must be insured, and parents must have given consent.	Children should say if they are ill, can't swim, or don't want to swim.
The activity is being done by one person, e.g. climbing a mountain alone.	There are no organisation responsibilities.	The individual has full responsibility for safety – must be properly clothed and equipped, with map, compass, food, etc, should have a contingency plan, and should tell someone else where he or she is going.

General evaluation

Organisations have more safety responsibilities if:

- they have organised the sport or activity
- they are being paid
- the sport is professional
- the sport is a team sport
- there are many spectators
- there is a major risk of injuries
- the participants are children (or under 18)
- the participants are inexperienced, vulnerable or disabled.

Individuals have more safety responsibilities if:

- they have arranged the activity themselves
- they are doing the activity on their own
- they are in a wild environment, e.g. mountains
- they are playing for fun in a safe environment, e.g. playing cricket in the park
- no money is involved
- they are not part of an organisation.

! ■ **CHECKPOINT …**

(a) Discuss whether you think sports such as boxing – or any other sports – should be banned because of the risks.

(b) Look up the case of Bunmi Shagaya on the Internet. What lessons can be learnt?

LINK! Outdoor activities – girls drowning at Stainforth – pages 107–108.

PASSGRADE

Outline the importance of planning and preparation when taking part in sporting or recreational activities.

It is impossible to do a sporting or recreational activity without some planning. If your friend says, 'Let's skip college, and go and play football in the park,' you still have to plan to the extent of getting a football and knowing your way to the park. You may even have to plan an excuse for your course tutor!

skill POWER

One way to cover this outcome is to sit down (with or without a friend) and note down as quickly as possible all the ideas you can think of about why you should plan before taking part in a sport. Then join your notes together into paragraphs under headings like 'Health and Safety', 'Planning for Success' and 'Planning for Enjoyment'.

Suppose you are planning a five-a-side football competition for the end of term at your college. You need to:

- talk to your tutors to make sure that you and others will be free to take time off class
- decide who you are going to invite to take part in the competition (which classes, for example)
- publicise the event well in advance, so that different groups and classes can choose their teams
- make sure you have a referee, scorer and any other officials you might want
- find a sports centre and make arrangements with the person in charge to run your competition
- ensure that classes can be cancelled and that students (and tutors) can come and support the teams
- make safety arrangements
- buy in soft drinks or water in case people get dehydrated
- make sure you have a ball and any other equipment needed
- make sure everybody knows the way to the venue
- decide whether you need insurance
- make and put up posters if necessary
- choose your own class team and decide who is going to play in what position
- make sure everyone brings gym kit on the day.

CHECKPOINT ...

(a) Try running an event of this kind. Make notes of all the planning that was done – and why.

(b) Suppose you were going to take part in a marathon. What planning and preparation would you do for it?

(c) If you were arranging a sponsored walk for your favourite charity, what planning would you do to ensure the maximum amount of money was collected?

From this you can see that planning is needed:

(a) to ensure that the event takes place
(b) to ensure that everybody knows about it
(c) to avoid confusion and waste of time
(d) to have the event running smoothly so that people can enjoy it without worry or stress
(e) to ensure safety and comfort for those taking part – and for any spectators
(f) to ensure there are no money problems
(g) to get praise, rather than complaints, afterwards
(h) to encourage people to repeat the success at a later date.

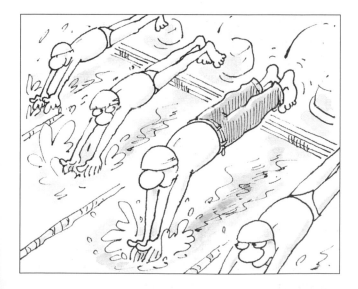

The importance of planning

LINK! Planning of a different sort – to maximise fitness before an entrance test – is discussed on page 50.

PASSGRADE

Record regular participation in a sporting or recreational activity.

There are two sides to this outcome. One is regularly doing a sporting or recreational activity. The other is recording it: in other words making notes and getting proof that you have done it all the times you say you have done it.

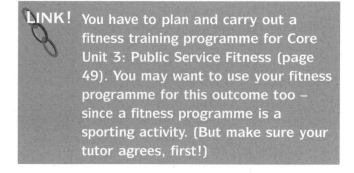

LINK! You have to plan and carry out a fitness training programme for Core Unit 3: Public Service Fitness (page 49). You may want to use your fitness programme for this outcome too – since a fitness programme is a sporting activity. (But make sure your tutor agrees, first!)

You may already regularly participate in a sporting or recreational activity. You might play football every Saturday, you might train cricketers or umpire for them, or you might go rock climbing at the sports centre every Thursday night. If this is the case you will have no problems – *provided you record what you do and get witness statements*. We will look at that on the next page.

You will also have no problems if you participate regularly in course sporting activities – the lessons you have in Sport and Recreation. You and your tutor will be able to record what you have done.

But suppose you don't participate regularly in sporting and recreational activities. Suppose your bus is always late for the lesson, or you have an ingrowing toenail which has been getting worse ever since September. What do you do?

You see your tutor – preferably with a box of chocolates.

Recording

This will be no problem if you are covering this outcome in your weekly Sport and Recreation lessons. It will be arranged by your tutor. But if you want to use another activity, such as a weekly football match, you should prepare a form which looks like the following.

Evidence of regular participation in a sporting or recreational activity

Name: Daniel Bowker   **Course:** BTEC First Diploma in Public Services

Date	Times	Activity	Comments and progress	Signed and dated by
6.11.04	2.30–4.00 p.m.	Goalkeeper for Slack Top United	We were beaten 6–0 by Slack End Academicals. I made a number of remarkable saves – they were remarkably bad!	Andy Slack (Coach) 6 Nov 04
13.11.04	2.30–4.00 p.m.	Goalkeeper for Slack Top United	We beat Slack Bottom Terriers 3–2. I realise where I went wrong last week and only let two in, and they were scored by a bloke who used to play for Halifax Town.	Andy Slack (Coach) 13 Nov 04
20.11.04	2.30–4.00 p.m.	Goalkeeper for Slack Top United	We played Slack Wood Bulldogs. The score was 6–0 to us at half time, but then the game had to be abandoned because a herd of cows was driven onto the pitch.	Andy Slack (Coach) 20 Nov 04

PASSGRADE

> Identify a series of benefits to the individual from participation in sporting and recreational events.

As far as this outcome is concerned, 'events' means the same as 'activities'. The benefits to the person taking part include the following.

- **Increased fitness**. The type of fitness and the amount of increase depend on different factors such as the type of sport, how often you do it, and how fit you were to start off with.

> **LINK!** See page 67 for much more on different types of fitness.

- **Health**. Sport speeds up breathing and heart-rate, makes you sweat, and is good for all the main body systems. In moderation it strengthens the immune system and helps protect against illness.

- **Self-esteem**. This means 'feeling good about yourself'. People who take part in sport often have greater confidence than those who don't. They may be more optimistic, less moody, less likely to feel depressed or tired, and more likely to enjoy a good laugh.

- **Stamina (endurance)**. This is increased by sports such as long-distance running, swimming or aerobics. Activities such as jogging which use a moderate amount of strength and last for some time are best for developing stamina.

- **Strength**. This is increased by short bursts of intense activity – such as lifting heavy weights, or sprinting very fast over a short distance.

- **Understanding yourself and others**. When you take part in a sporting activity you often test yourself and find your limits. If it is a team sport you learn about what other people can do as well – and this can motivate you to do better.

- **Relaxation**. Although sport may seem like hard work at the time, it is an excellent form of relaxation. This is because it makes a change from normal work and study, and refreshes our minds as well as our bodies.

- **Friendship**. Most sports are social activities. They may be competitive, but the competition is done in a spirit of friendship (e.g. in tennis). In team sports you play with other people who share an interest (the sport) with you.

- **Skills**. Sporting and recreational events are one of the best ways of developing teamwork, communication and leadership skills.

- **Confidence**. Confidence is a general word for most of the benefits listed above. It means you can trust yourself better, both physically and mentally, and you can trust others, because you understand them better.

 SUPERGRADE! *Merit*

Explain the benefits to the individual from participation in sporting and recreational events.

For this outcome you explain why the things you said for the last outcome are true.

skill POWER

You use words such as 'since', 'because', 'although', 'the reason why' and 'as' when explaining things. You should also give some examples. You can use the same headings you used for the last outcome, but you should go into more detail.

Increased fitness

There are many types of fitness. The basic one is cardiovascular fitness, which means having a good heart and circulation system. This kind of fitness has a big effect on people's lives. People who do not exercise and become unfit cannot work as hard as fit people, nor can they play as hard. Their lives may become less exciting. Also, they may be treated with less respect and interest by other people. Unfit people, on average, have less success at work, earn less money, have fewer friends, and don't live as long as people who keep fit.

Health

Health is defined as 'a state of physical and mental well-being'. Taking part in sporting or recreational activities makes you feel good – while you are doing it. This is partly due to natural drugs called endorphins produced inside the body. After some time, though, pains and stiffness can set in due to the accumulation of a waste chemical called lactic acid in the muscles. With regular exercise the stiffness lessens, and the health benefits are greater. The immune system works better and the body is better able to fight off illnesses like colds and flu. Finally, many of the effects of ageing are slowed down by remaining active. It should be stressed, however, that regular participation in sport or physical recreation must be linked to a good, balanced diet taken from all five food groups.

 **LINK!** **See page 69 for food groups.**

Self-esteem

Self-esteem is a complex subject, but sporting and recreational activity makes you feel happier and more at ease with yourself. This is partly due to the competition, which uses up aggression and changes it into an enjoyable and purposeful activity. Self-esteem is also raised by playing a sport or doing an activity that you are good at. The interactive nature of many sports is good for self-esteem, because of the communication and respect which comes from it. And the fact that participation is active (in contrast to watching, which is passive) has an effect of 'empowerment', of being in control, which is good for self-esteem.

Stamina (endurance)

This is a sign of cardiovascular fitness, and is linked to the healthy action of the lungs and heart. When you exercise, your heart and muscles work overtime, while parts of the body which are not needed – such as the digestive system – stop working for the time being. The lungs fill and empty rapidly, bringing more oxygen into the body. This – together with nutrients in the blood – helps the development of muscles in the heart, the blood vessels and the muscles you are using. 'Slow-twitch' muscle cells get stronger and more effective. Exercise produces heat, so the sweat glands are used to keep the body at the right temperature. All these body systems benefit from sport and recreational activities, and stamina – the ability to work or be active for long periods of time without getting tired – increases.

Strength

Sport using sudden bursts of intense energy, together with a diet high in protein and carbohydrate, increases strength – especially when you are young. There is no other way of increasing strength except by exercising the muscles and pushing them to the limit. This is what happens in various sports, especially weightlifting but also sprinting and some field athletic events such as shot put and hammer throwing. Sports such as rugby union, and American football, in which there is a lot of pushing and shoving, also develop strength. Strength is needed in some public service jobs, and tends to get respect from other people.

Understanding yourself and others

Sporting and recreational activities help you to understand your physical limits – how much endurance and strength you have. When you are young you are also able to discover how your endurance and strength are growing. But sporting and recreational activities are also intellectual – they use the brain. Planning, decision-making and problem-solving play a major part in sports – and may happen in a split second. There is humour as well in sport. In fact many of the emotions we have in everyday life are intensified in sport. Sport tells us what our brains – and other people's – are capable of.

Relaxation

Sport and recreation de-stress us. They tire us out so that afterwards we can sleep deeply and refreshingly. They purify the body by helping us to sweat and get rid of urea and other waste chemicals. They exercise our minds and get rid of the frustrations of ordinary life. And they let us use our natural aggression in ways that are not harmful to other people.

Friendship

In ordinary life we often use other people for our own purposes. We are nice to the teacher so that we can get a decent grade. We obey the police because we don't want to find ourselves in court. We are pleasant to our parents most of the time because they feed us, wash our clothes and give us a roof over our heads – and perhaps we want to thank them for taking the trouble to bring us up. Sport and recreation, however, are not done for a purpose – they are simply done because we like doing them. In other words, they are done for their own sake. And in sport or recreation we make friends because we enjoy the other players' company, and because they share our pleasure in the sport.

Skills

Sporting and recreational activities are the ideal way to develop a whole range of teamwork, interpersonal and personal development skills.

LINK! See pages 33–37 to find out more about these skills.

CHECKPOINT ...

(a) With a friend, discuss and note down as many ways in which sport develops confidence as you can think of.

(b) Think about how participating in a sport or recreational activity has helped to develop your own confidence.

 **SUPERGRADE!** *Distinction*

Evaluate the benefits to the individual from participation in sporting and recreational events.

skill POWER

For this outcome you have to decide how important or valuable the benefits of participation in sporting and recreational events are to the individual.

It may help you to consider the following points.

Signs that the benefits of sport are important

- All societies and cultures, in all parts of the world, value sports and games. Some of these sports are traditional; others have been learned in more recent years (e.g. football in South America). The biggest television and other media events are the major sporting contests.
- The public services are keen to recruit people who enjoy sports. This must mean that the skills and qualities that people use in sporting and recreational activities are the same skills and qualities that are needed in public service work.
- Most public services have gyms, and many of them, such as the army, have repeat fitness tests. The civil service and the army run a vast range of

recreational sporting events, from angling and archery through to tennis and telemark.
- The police use sporting and recreational youth clubs when helping young people who are at risk of becoming criminals. And sport and exercise are important aspects of prison life.
- The Prime Minister, Tony Blair, recently had a gym installed at 10 Downing Street.
- If a football team does well in the league, local businesses are said to benefit.
- Football hooligans are generally not people who actually play the game.
- There are now Olympic Games and other major sporting events for disabled people.
- Sports and recreational activities can cause serious injuries – even deaths.

Some possible drawbacks of sport

- What about the problem of drugs and sport?
- When sport turns into big business, does it harm the people who participate?
- In what ways can participation in sporting and recreational events be bad for us, as individuals?
- Many children dislike or even hate sport at school.

CL SITES:

Safety for outdoor activities
www.teachernet.gov.uk/docbank/
index.cfm?id=2577

www.dfes.gov.uk/h_s_ev/index.shtml

Football rules and safety
www.football-league.co.uk/
fans/view/third_feature/0,,10794,00.html

Athletics rules and safety
www.saf.org.uk/uka-safety3.pdf

www.ukathletics.net/articles/additions/
risk%20assessment.pdf

CHECKPOINT ...

Suppose you met someone who hated sport. How would you try to make them change their mind and start to enjoy it?

Unit 9 Land Navigation with Map and Compass
Grading criteria

PASSGRADE	SUPERGRADE! _Merit_	SUPERGRADE! _Distinction_
To achieve a pass grade the evidence must show that the learner is able to:	To achieve a merit grade the evidence must show that the learner is able to:	To achieve a distinction grade the evidence must show that the learner is able to:
● explain the purpose of a range of maps and identify conventional signs **179**	● calculate accurately distances between points on an OS map **185**	● calculate accurately distances and timings, taking into account terrain and gradient **187**
● use grid references to reach two different destinations and be able to calculate distance **182**	● demonstrate the ability to work with bearings in degrees and mils **190**	● produce a route card with emergency escape routes included **194**
● explain the main features, use and care of a lightweight compass and demonstrate its use for taking bearings from both map and ground **188**	● produce a route card with bearings and distances accurately recorded **194**	● explain the procedure to be adopted on becoming lost **198**
● explain magnetic bearings and variation and demonstrate ways of determining direction without a compass **191**	● describe how the requirements of the Country Code would be incorporated into a route card **197**	
● explain the safety and other considerations required for planning a route using route cards **194**		
● describe the action to be taken to minimise the effects of land navigation on the landscape **197**		

Map reading and navigation play a big part in public service work. The police, fire and ambulance services all need to have full knowledge of the areas where they work, in order to cut down attendance times at emergencies. They get this knowledge partly from following directions, and partly from reading and understanding maps. And if they don't know the place they're going to, they must use a map.

The armed forces use maps even more. The army uses maps of the land, the Royal Navy uses maps of the sea, and the RAF uses both. They also use the compass – an old but clever invention which enables you to find your way even on the open sea, in thick fog, or at dead of night.

In this unit we are going to look at some of the basics of maps, the compass and navigation – especially for travelling on foot.

Explain the purpose of a range of maps and identify conventional signs.

The purpose of maps

The purpose of a map is to show us how to get from A to B without going through Z. But maps differ according to the kind of transport we are using. Maps used by motorists are very different from maps used by walkers. And maps used to find your way round town are quite different from maps for finding your way round in the country.

A map is like a picture of a place seen from outer space. If you have ever looked at a satellite photograph, you will have noticed that it is hard to tell where or what you are looking at. Things are not easy to recognise when viewed from above.

So maps are not photographs. They are drawings. And they are simplified so that they give you only the information you want to know.

Conventional signs

This information is given using conventional signs. These are lines, dots or little shapes which show things like roads, rivers, railways, buildings and electricity pylons. Most maps have a key showing all the conventional signs and what they mean.

There are two things you need to know to read a map. One is the meaning of the conventional signs; the other is the scale of the map.

FOCUS

Conventional signs

There are large numbers of conventional signs on maps, and to know them all you need to use maps frequently. However, some of these signs are more important than others – for the kind of land navigation (walking) that you will probably do for this unit:

Contours. These are brown lines on OS 1:25,000 and 1:50,000 maps, joining places of equal height. The height above sea level in metres is marked on some of them. If contours are close together, it means there is a steep slope. If they are widely spaced, there is a gentle slope. And if there are no contours, the land is flat.

Streams and rivers. A stream narrow enough to jump across is a single blue line. A river is a double blue line with blue shading between the lines.

Rocks and cliffs. These are shown by black spots or lines on the map. Higher cliffs, which might be dangerous, are shown by signs that look like tiny broken combs.

Map scale

All maps are drawn to scale, so you can measure distances on them accurately. On a street map, five centimetres on the map equals one kilometre on the ground. On an Ordnance Survey 1:25,000 map, four centimetres on the map equals one kilometre on the ground. On an Ordnance Survey 1:50,000 map, two centimetres on the map equals one kilometre on the ground. On a motorists' map which is three miles to one inch the scale is 1:190,080. On this kind of map two centimetres on the map equals roughly four kilometres on the ground.

Figures such as 1:50,000 mean that everything on the ground is fifty thousand times as long as it is on the map. A road 1 cm long on the map would be 50,000 cm long in reality – which is 500 metres or half a kilometre.

Maps like motorists' maps which cover a big area are called small-scale maps. Maps like street maps which cover a small area are called large-scale maps – because they are in a sense 'magnified' and everything looks bigger on them.

If you are not quite sure what the scale of a map is, there is usually a line like a little ruler at the bottom of the map, which represents how long a kilometre or a mile is.

Here are four examples of different kinds of map.

1 Street map

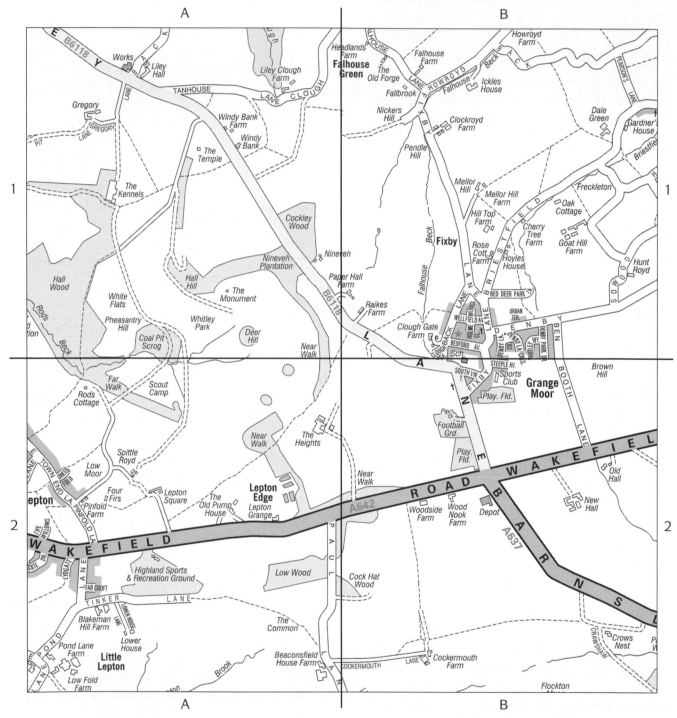

The purpose of this map is to help you to find any street in the Kirklees area. If you wanted to find someone who lived at 55 Bedford Avenue, Grange Moor, this is the kind of map you could use. But it would only be useful to you once you were within a few kilometres (a mile or two) of the village of Grange Moor.

This is a large-scale map. That means that roads, rivers and other features appear quite big on it.

Each square has sides representing one kilometre, so if you walked along a road which was the length represented by one of the sides of a square, you would have walked one kilometre.

You will notice that only the roads and a few other landmarks are put on this kind of map. This is so there is room to put in the street names. The aim is to produce a map that is simple and easy to read.

The conventional sign for a road is a pair of parallel lines. They are continuous if the road has fences, walls, hedges or buildings running along it. The lines are dashed if the road or track is unfenced. These maps are normally used by motorists. The roads are therefore drawn so that they stand out clearly.

Attached to the original map is a street index – part of which looks like this:

Bedale Drive	(V)C1
Beddington Edge Road	(X)C3/D3
Bedford Avenue	(O)B1
Bedford Close	(N)E2

If you want to find Bedford Avenue in Grange Moor you will see that it is at (O)B1. (O) is the map and B1 is the square. You will find B at the top of the page, and 1 at the side.

2 Ordnance Survey 1:50,000 map

This map is a medium-scale map. Everything looks much smaller on this map than on the street map. You will see that Grange Moor, which looks quite big on the street map, looks small on this one.

This map – like the street map – has squares on it. Though these look so much smaller, they still represent 1-kilometre squares. If you were to cut 50,000 squares each 2 cm in size (like the ones on the map) and put them in a line, with their sides just touching, that line would be 1 kilometre long. That's why the map scale is 1:50,000. The real world is fifty thousand times as big as the features on the map.

Though this map is a smaller scale map than the street map, it contains more information. It tells

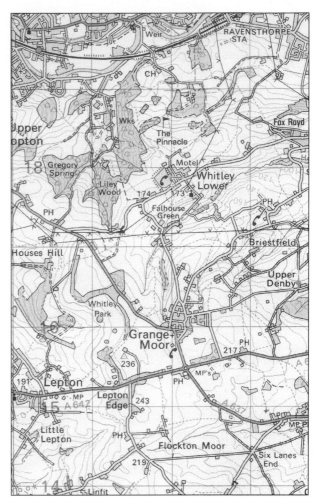

you which areas are built up, and where the hills are (using wavy lines called contours). But it doesn't give you the names of the streets. If it did, you would need a microscope to read them!

This is a multi-purpose map. You can use it for motoring and for walking, because it shows both roads and paths. But it isn't very good for finding your way round a town, and if you need to go more than about 20 miles, you will probably go off the edge of this map.

3 Ordnance Survey 1:25,000 map

This map is on page 186 and is on a larger scale than the 1:50,000 map. That means the squares are bigger – though the real distance along each side is still one kilometre.

This is a very detailed map, and contains much more information than the 1:50,000. It has features like walls and springs and rock outcrops marked on it, and plenty of footpaths are marked. But it isn't easy to read at a glance, because it looks very complicated.

This is a walker's map. It doesn't cover such a big area of land as the 1:50,000, but it tells you much more. Though it shows roads, they don't stand out very clearly because of all the other detail. It would not be useful for a motorist because it only covers a small area.

LINK! See page 186.

4 Ordnance Survey Motoring Atlas

This is a small-scale map (actually 1:190,080). On this map one inch equals three miles. You can see that everything looks much smaller on this map than it does even on the 1:50,000 map. The squares are 10-kilometre squares.

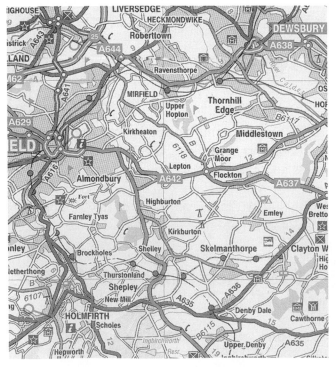

There is not much information given – there are no tracks and very few contours. But the main roads stand out clearly. This is because it is a motoring atlas. It tells you what you need to know on a long car journey, and no more. And because of the small scale, you might be able to go 50 miles before you even have to turn the page!

> **CHECKPOINT …**
> (a) Why are these maps called Ordnance Survey (OS) maps?
> (b) Find an example of a weather map. This is a kind of map which is used a lot by some public services, such as the armed forces and HM Coastguards. Find out what the main conventional signs mean.

> Use grid references to reach two different destinations and be able to calculate distance.

Grid references

If you look at an Ordnance Survey 1:25,000 map, or 1:50,000 map, you will see that the map is covered with faint blue squares. The squares are bigger on a 1:25,000 map than they are on a 1:50,000.

Along the top of the map all the vertical lines are numbered (from left to right), and up the side of the map all the horizontal lines are numbered (from bottom to top).

These blue lines are called grid lines, and you can use these to pinpoint any place on any of these OS maps, anywhere in Britain. The row of letters and numbers pinpointing a place on a map is called its grid reference. A national grid reference has two letters and six figures, but provided you know which map you are on, you don't have to bother with the letters.

Letters on a grid reference

(You may be able to ignore this section!)

Instructions on how to write grid references are given near the key of an OS map. If you need to put letters at the front of your grid reference, you will see them on a small square next to the instructions.

If the square has two or more pairs of letters in it you will have to decide which part of the map your pinpointed place is in, before deciding on the letters to go before your grid reference.

SE
SK

In the figure above, if the place you have pinpointed is in the southern (bottom) half of the map, your six-figure reference will begin with SK.

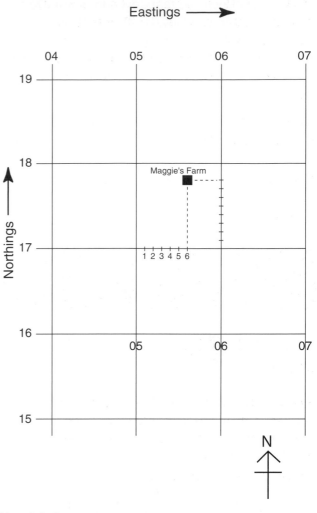

Maggie's farm

The numbers on a grid reference

(Don't ignore this!)

Opposite is a simplified map of a place called Maggie's Farm.

To give a six-figure grid reference you:

1 Read along the line numbers from left to right ('eastings') and put down the number of the line to the left of the farm. This is 05.

2 Estimate tenths of the distance across the square from left to right, starting at line 05. These are shown on the bottom of the square in the simplified map. Maggie's Farm is six tenths of the way across the square, so the next figure in the grid reference is 6.

3 You have now done the first half of your grid reference, and it is 056. Write this down.

4 Read up the line numbers from bottom to top ('northings') and put down the number of the line below the farm. This is 17.

5 Estimate tenths of the distance up the square from bottom to top, starting at line 17. These are shown to the right of the square on the simplified map. Maggie's Farm is eight tenths of the way up the square, so the next figure in the grid reference is 8.

6 You have now done the second half of your grid reference, and it is 178.

7 Put the two halves of your grid reference together and you have the 6-figure grid reference for Maggie's Farm, which is 056178.

Remember:

(a) Always read eastings before northings (i.e. 'along the passage and up the stairs').

183

(b) Don't write on the map, even in pencil. Do the estimates in your head – it's easier and quicker!

(c) The method is exactly the same whether the OS map is 1:25,000 or 1:50,000. But the squares are smaller on the 1:50,000 map.

(d) Since the squares are 1 kilometre in size, a six-figure grid reference gives the position of the place you have pinpointed to the nearest 100 metres.

> ! CHECKPOINT ...
> Choose ten places on an OS map and
> ■ write 6-figure grid references for them.

Calculating distance

One of the main uses of a map is to work out the distance between two points, or the distance of a journey. It should be possible to do this with any map which is drawn 'to scale' (see above).

Motoring maps

Some maps, such as motoring maps, tell you the distance between most places. They use conventional signs which look a bit like tiny lollipops, and then they print the distance – either in kilometres or miles – along the road between the two 'lollipops'. For a long journey you have to add up the figures between all the lollipops you pass on the journey to reach a total.

Motoring maps also tell you the scale in simple words, e.g. 'three miles to the inch'. If you have a ruler, lay it on the map, and you find that two towns are five inches apart, the distance between the towns on the ground is 5 x 3 = 15 miles.

Calculating distances without a ruler

It is, of course, annoying carrying a ruler about with you every time you think you might have to read a map. Fortunately, the hand is a natural ruler. If you know how long or wide your finger is, you can use it for calculating distances on maps. A finger is not

the world's most accurate measuring device, but it is very easy to carry about.

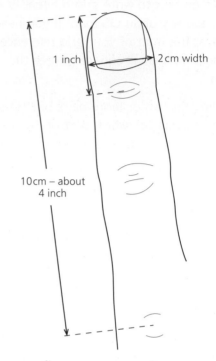

How does your finger measure up?

Distances on the OS 1:50,000 map

The OS 1:50,000 map is often used as a good, general-purpose map. It is easy to calculate distances roughly on this map, because it is covered with blue squares – and the side of each square is 2 centimetres in length. On the ground, this translates into 1 kilometre.

If you put a ruler down between two places on a map, and discover that the distance is 13 centimetres, you know from this that the real distance on the ground is 6.5 kilometres.

Distances on the OS 1:25,000 map

The OS 1:25,000 map, which is often used by walkers, is a larger scale map. It still has blue squares on, but they are much bigger – 4 centimetres each side. But on the ground these squares are still 1 kilometre. If you put a ruler on the map and find that two places are 13 centimetres apart, the real distance on the ground is 3.25 kilometres.

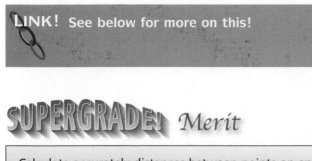

LINK! See below for more on this!

SUPERGRADE! *Merit*

Calculate accurately distances between points on an OS map.

The OS map we are going to use for this outcome is the 1:25,000. It is the type of map you are most likely to use for this unit.

At present the calculation of distances on British maps is complicated by the fact that some people think in miles, and others think in kilometres. Road signs are still in miles, but for OS maps it is easier at a glance to see distances in kilometres.

On the next page is an example of part of one of the OS maps. As you read the explanation, remember that the real map is in colour.

Calculating distances in kilometres

On the original version of this kind of map there are blue numbers along the top of the map which rise as you go from left (west) to right (east). On this extract the numbers along the top are 43, 44, 45, 46, 47. Up the side of the map are numbers which rise from the bottom (south) to the top (north). On this extract the numbers are 05, 06, 07, 08, 09, and 10.

Each of these numbers is at the end of a line: 43 to 47 are at the ends of vertical lines; 05 to 10 are at the ends of horizontal lines. On the map the lines are printed in blue. These lines are called grid lines, and every OS map in the country has them.

The lines are at right angles to each other and make squares on the map. On the map the sides of each square are exactly 4 centimetres long. The same distance on the ground is exactly 1 kilometre.

So on this kind of map (1:25,000) 1 kilometre equals the distance along the side of any of these blue squares. This fact makes it easy to calculate distances on the map.

Accuracy

To find out the distance between two points in a straight line there are two methods you can use.

Ruler

The first method is to place a ruler between the two points and measure the distance in centimetres. For example, the distance on the map between Brockstones and Kentmere Reservoir is 12.5 centimetres. Since 4 centimetres on the map equals 1 kilometre on the ground, 12 centimetres equals three kilometres.

Other distances:

On the 1:25,000 map	On the ground
4 cm	1 kilometre
2 cm	1/2 kilometre (500 metres)
1 cm	1/4 kilometre (250 metres)
0.5 cm (5 millimetres)	1/8 kilometre (125 metres)
0.1 cm (1 millimetre)	25 metres

You have 0.5 of a centimetre (5 millimetres) left over. You can see from the table above that on the ground this equals 125 metres. So your accurate measurement of the distance between Brockstones and Kentmere Reservoir is 3 kilometres and 125 metres.

Compasses or pair of dividers

The second method is to use compasses or a pair of dividers to do this sort of measurement. You put one point of the dividers (or compasses) on Brockstones and the other point (or the pencil point, if you are using compasses) on the edge of Kentmere Reservoir. Then, taking care not to change the distance between the divider points or the compass point and the pencil point, you place the dividers (or compasses) against the ruler and read off the distance in centimetres. Then you do the same calculation as you did with the ruler.

The problem with this method is that it generally ends up with people digging holes in the map. That's good news for the Ordnance Survey, because someone has to buy a new map.

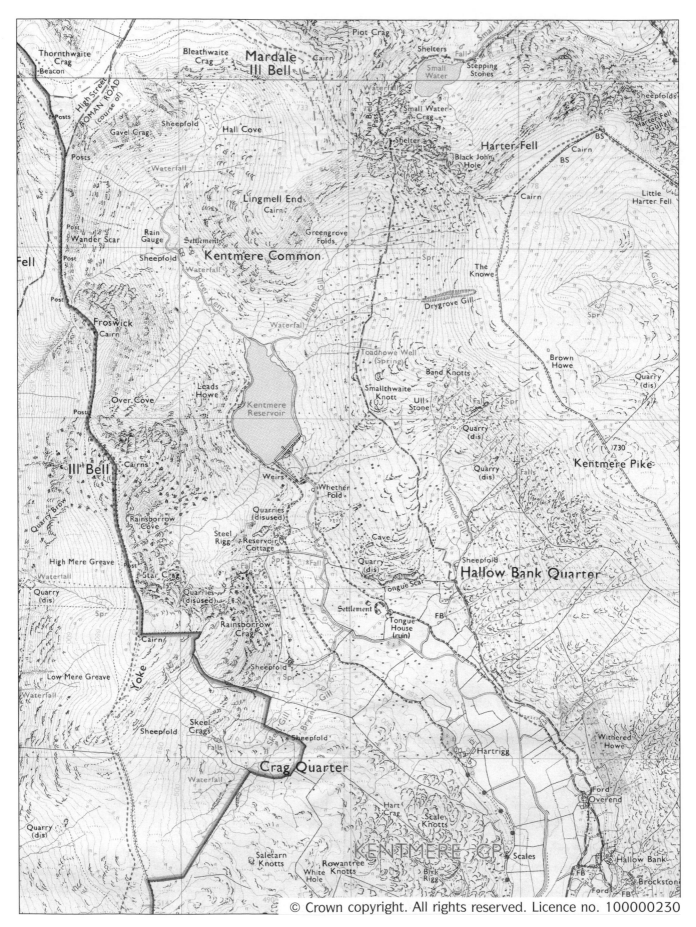

Calculating distances which are not straight lines

Unless you are driving a tank you are unlikely to go in a straight line. When walking you often have to follow winding footpaths or zig-zag up steep hillsides. What's more, if you are walking from a centre or a campsite and coming back in the evening, your walk will be a circular one anyway.

To calculate accurately the true length of a route there are two methods.

String method

Materials needed: map, thread, ruler.

(a) Get a piece of string or thread about 60 cm long.
(b) Place one end on your starting point on the map.
(c) Lay it along your route, following every wiggle.
(d) When you have finished, grip the finishing point on the thread between your fingernails so that you don't lose it.
(e) Lay the thread along the ruler.
(f) Read off the length in centimetres and millimetres.
(g) Do the same calculation as the one above, remembering that 1 millimetre on the map equals 25 metres on the ground, and that 4 centimetres equal one kilometre.

Paper method

Materials needed: map, sheet of A4 paper, pencil, ruler.

(a) Put the corner of the sheet of paper on your starting point on the map.
(b) Place the edge of the paper along the route of your walk, on the map, until you come to the first bend in the track.
(c) Mark the edge of your piece of paper by the first bend.
(d) Turn the paper so that the side runs along the next part of the track, and put a mark at the next bend.
(e) Keep doing this until you reach the end of your walk. You should have as many marks on the

side of your paper as there are bends in the route.
(f) Place the marked edge(s) of your paper against a ruler (metric side).
(g) Measure the length between the corner where you started, and your last pencil mark.
(h) To find the walking distance, in kilometres, do the same calculation as that given above.

Distances in miles

You or your instructor may prefer the calculation to be done in miles. This is possible, but it won't be as accurate as a calculation done in kilometres.

At the bottom of an OS 1:25,000 map you will see a scale giving distances in kilometres and miles. This will help to remind you that the scale of this kind of map (in inches) is two and a half inches to a mile. That means a road two and a half inches long on the map will be a mile long when it comes to walking it.

To accurately calculate distances in miles you can use thread or paper just as you did with kilometre measurements. But when it comes to the calculation at the end, place your thread or marked paper against the 'inches' side of the ruler. Measure the length in inches and tenths of an inch. Let's suppose your piece of thread is 16 inches long. To get the distance in miles you have to divide 16 by 2.5. That comes to 6.4, which means that your planned walk is six and four tenths miles long.

SUPERGRADE! *Distinction*

Calculate accurately distances and timings, taking into account terrain and gradient.

This outcome is about planning walks in hilly or mountainous country. It links with outcomes in Outdoor Activities, pages 149 and 150; and Expedition Skills, pages 277–279.

Calculating distances and timings is important, otherwise you might plan a walk which is too long and tiring and have to spend a night out.

Remember that on an OS map close contours mean a steep gradient (slope), and that the OS 1:25,000 gives detailed information about terrain – rocks, scree, bog, moorland, vegetation, walls and trees. Make sure you know about these when calculating timings.

Timings

To know how long a walk is likely to take you need to know:

- the average walking speed of the group
- the distance (length) of the walk
- the terrain – the kind of surface you are walking on
- gradient – the steepness and heights of any hills
- the fitness, experience and motivation of the party doing the walk
- weather conditions
- the number of rests or breaks taken
- the equipment of the party.

When planning your route you should try to take all these factors into consideration. We will look at these in more detail.

Average walking speed

A fit person walking fast along a level road goes at about 4 miles/6 kilometres an hour. A 'normal' person walking at a steady, comfortable speed along a road goes at about 3 miles/5 kilometres an hour. A normal person walking over open country should plan on going at 2 miles/3 kilometres an hour. This is the most likely speed for a group to walk at.

Distance

An all-day walk for a party of students is likely to be about 10 miles or 15 kilometres. Motivated, keen walkers may go much further than this – 30 miles (45 kilometres) or more in a day.

Terrain

This is the nature of the ground underfoot. Rough or boggy ground will slow you down. It is hard to go faster than 2 miles/3 kilometres an hour over rough ground.

Gradient

People walk fast on flat ground or on gentle downhill slopes. They walk slower going uphill, and the steeper the hill, the slower they go. They also walk slowly down some steep or rocky slopes. An average speed of 1 mile/1.5 kilometres an hour is likely on very steep ground. Add an hour for each 1,000 feet (305 metres) that you climb.

Fitness, experience and motivation

Ideally, parties should be made up of people of equal fitness. If there are differences, plan for the slowest person in the group.

Weather conditions

Sunny, cool days, with light winds and dry conditions underfoot are best for walking. In wet, foggy or windy weather you are unlikely to go faster than 2 miles/3 kilometres an hour unless you are on paths and roads.

Rests or breaks

You should allow 10 minutes every hour for rests, plus half an hour for lunch. You may take more rests on steep or difficult terrain.

Equipment

Anything other than good walking boots or (in dry conditions) trainers will slow you down.

PASSGRADE

Explain the main features, use and care of a lightweight compass and demonstrate its use for taking bearings from both map and ground.

Main features of a compass

A compass is a device for finding which direction you are travelling in. It consists of a balanced steel needle which has been magnetised so that one end of the needle always points north and the other end (a different colour) always points south. The reason why the needle always points north and south is that the earth itself is a giant magnet.

The needle is contained in a case. Behind the needle is a face on which directions and bearings are marked.

The compass is light so you can easily carry it with you on a walk.

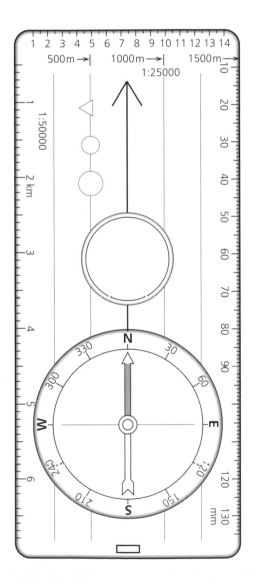

A lightweight compass

Cardinal points and bearings

There are two ways of describing direction. One is to use the cardinal points, North, East, South and West, and the intermediate directions: North-east, South-east, South-West and North-west. These can be further divided into directions such as North-north-east or East-north-east.

The other method is by taking bearings. The armed forces often use this method, because it is more accurate. Bearings are explained on page 190.

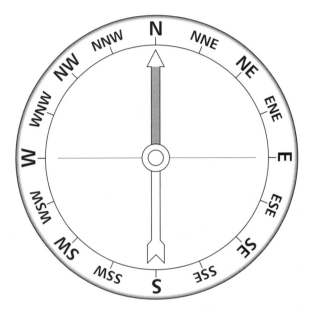

Taking compass directions from a map

(a) First find where you are on the map – and also find the place you wish to go to.

(b) Place the compass so that the centre is over the point where you are on the map.

(c) Turn the compass so that the north point of the needle is pointing to North on the face of the compass.

(d) Turn the map so that North on the compass is pointing straight at the top of the map.

(e) Then see which of the directions on the face of the compass is pointing towards the place you wish to go to.

(f) The direction pointing most nearly towards the place you wish to go to is the direction you should follow on the ground.

Direction-finding using the map is used for:

- planning your walk, and
- finding the way in foggy weather or darkness.

Taking compass directions on the ground

If you want to find the compass direction of a landmark (e.g. a hill) that you can see, do the following.

(a) Face in that direction.
(b) Hold the compass level in front of your chest.
(c) Turn the compass carefully until the north end of the needle is pointing to North on the face of the compass.
(d) Read the direction on the face of the compass which is straight ahead of you – pointing towards the landmark.

Taking compass directions in fog

(a) Hold the compass level in front of your chest.
(b) Turn the compass until the north end of the needle is pointing to North on the compass face.
(c) Read the direction you are pointing towards from the face of the compass.

Taking bearings

What is a bearing? You may remember from school geometry that a circle is made up of 360 divisions called degrees. Imagine that each one of these degrees has a number, starting at 0 for North and then counting up as you move clockwise round the compass face. When you get to east you have gone 90 degrees round the face, so East is 090. South is therefore 180 and West is 270. It's as simple as that.

With this system all the intermediate directions round the face of the compass have numbers as well. For example North-east is 045.

Bearings are usually given as three figures, so they should have 0 as the first figure if they are less than 100.

To find your bearing using a map you use exactly the same method as the direction-finding using a

map given above. The only difference is that the direction is given in degrees instead of words. So instead of saying, 'We need to go west,' for example, you say, 'We need to follow a bearing of 270.'

To find your bearing on the ground, use the same method as the one given above. But give your answer in degrees. And never forget that:

- North is 000
- the degrees are counted clockwise.

CHECKPOINT ...

Directions and bearings may sound complicated until you have practised them. Buy or borrow a cheap compass and practise reading direction, using the methods shown. You don't have to go on a mountain to do it – a playing field will give you good practice.

SUPERGRADE! *Merit*

Demonstrate the ability to work with bearings in degrees and mils.

To cover this outcome you will need to take part in a practical exercise in which you use bearings. To do this you should be able to use compasses which already have bearings marked on the compass face. Remember that the bearings are numbers going clockwise round the compass face, starting at 0 and going up to 359.

Mils

Mils are a measurement of angles rather like degrees, only more accurate. They are used mainly by the armed forces for aiming guns and missiles. There are 6,400 mils in a full circle. This means there are roughly 17.8 mils to a degree. This kind of angle measurement is much more accurate than the degrees system, and can be divided by four, which is useful for military purposes. Mils are shown only on expensive compasses and are counted, like degrees, in a clockwork direction. They are not needed when finding your way around on British mountains.

FOCUS

Angular measure
One full turn =

4 right angles

2 pi radians (scientific)

360 degrees

400 grads (continental)

6400 mils (military; artillery)

Explain magnetic bearings and variation and demonstrate ways of determining direction without a compass.

There are three different types of North.

FOCUS

Different types of north
1 True north – this is the shortest distance to the North Pole.

2 Grid north – straight up – or parallel to – the vertical lines on the National Grid (in other words, pointing to the top of the map).

3 Magnetic north – the direction the compass needle points to. In Britain this is 4 degrees to the west of true north.

(1 and 2 are almost exactly the same.)

The difference between grid north and magnetic north is called magnetic variation.

When we use a compass we get magnetic bearings. To convert these bearings to bearings based on true north, we have to make the changes shown in the table showing magnetic variation differences.

Bearings based on magnetic north (i.e. taken from the compass)	Bearings based on true north (the direction of the north pole) or grid north (north on the map)
358	354
359	355
000	356
001	357
002	358
003	359
004	000
005	001
006	002
007	003
008	004
009	005

All magnetic bearings are 4 degrees more than bearings based on 'geographical' north, *except for the four bearings close to due North between 000 and 003* as shown on the table above.

FOCUS

How to remember the difference between magnetic and grid north

Grid to mag(netic) – ADD (i.e. add 4 degrees to the grid bearing).

Mag to grid – GET RID (i.e. subtract 4 degrees from the magnetic bearing).

NB These figures only apply to the UK.

Compass troubleshooting!

On rare occasions a compass won't work properly, or may lead you astray. This could be for the following reasons.

1 Objects made of iron, steel or nickel close to the compass. These will stop the compass from working properly. Magnets should always be kept away from a compass. In certain places, the rocks themselves hold so much iron that they may affect the workings of a compass. But this is rare in Britain.

2 Movement of the magnetic poles of the earth. The centre of the earth is liquid, and for this reason the north and south magnetic poles of the earth are moving slowly. The movement is very slow and will hardly be noticed in a person's lifetime.

3 Being outside Britain. Compass needles do not point north in all parts of the world. In some places they point east or west! If you use a compass in a foreign country, get local advice.

4 A fault in the compass. Always test a compass before you set out on a walk, and **make sure you know which is the NORTH end of the needle!**

Determining direction without a compass

There are several ways of determining direction without a compass. Not all of them are accurate.

1 Using the sun

The sun is a useful way of telling the direction – provided that it is shining! But you also need to know the time, so you need a watch as well. In British Summer Time the sun is at its highest at about 1.30 p.m. So at 1.30 it is due (exactly) south. Six hours before this, i.e. at 7.30 a.m., the sun is due east, and six hours later, at 7.30 p.m., the sun is due west. Around midsummer (21 June) the sun rises well to the north of east, and sets well to the north of west. In fact the sun moves about fifteen degrees every hour, so at 4.30 p.m. in summer it is south west, or at a bearing of 225.

2 Using a watch and the sun

If you hold a watch so that the hour hand is pointing towards the sun, and you bisect (halve) the angle between the hour hand and the twelve, the line forming the bisection points south.

The drawback of this is that it does not work with a digital watch.

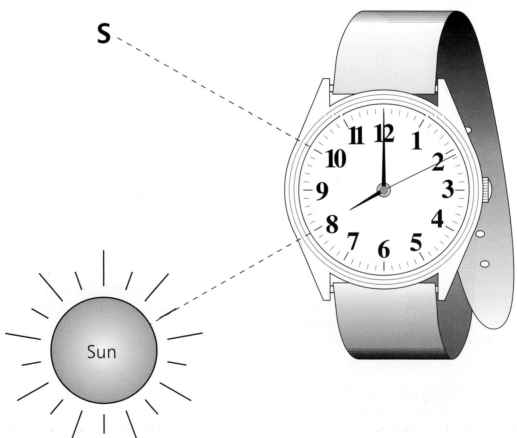

Watch and sun

192

3 Using the stars

On a clear night the stars will give you an accurate pointer towards north, at any time of the year. This is because the Pole Star ('Polaris') is straight overhead at the North Pole. The Pole Star is quite bright and can be found by following the last two stars of an easily recognisable star-group, the Great Bear (sometimes called 'The Plough') – as in the diagram.

This does not work south of the Equator.

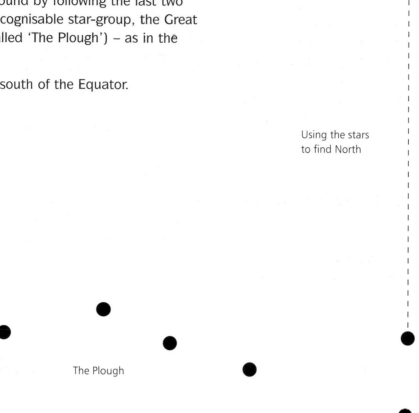

How to find the Pole Star, using the Great Bear as a 'signpost'

4 Using the wind

If you have watched a weather forecast and know which way the wind is blowing, this can be useful especially if you can see which way the clouds are moving, or if you are standing in an exposed place where the wind is not affected by obstacles such as hills or trees. This method is not reliable, because wind directions can change rapidly, especially in bad weather.

5 Looking at the ground

Experienced navigators can tell directions by looking at grass or snow on the ground. In Britain mountain and moorland grass is usually beaten down by the west wind, so the stems and blades tend to point eastwards. Snow comes from the north or the east, and drifts usually form on the southern or western sides of stones, etc. Trees often bend towards the east because of the prevailing wind. These methods are unreliable, but better than nothing.

6 Moss and lichen on trees

It is said that trees are greener on the north side, because this side stays damp away from the sun. Unreliable.

Look at this picture. Can you tell which way is North?

 *Merit*

> Produce a route card with bearings and distances accurately recorded.

 *Distinction*

> Produce a route card with emergency escape routes included.

These two outcomes will be dealt with together.

A route card is a piece of paper which outlines, in table form, the route of a walk (see page 195). It gives all the information that the walkers need, and which rescuers would need if they had to set out, even in darkness and fog, to find them. Here is a specimen route card, followed by explanation. It is based on the extract from the OS 1:25,000 map on page 186.

NB (a) A 'leg' is a section of a route. (b) Because bearings are accurate they do not correspond exactly to directions.

> **! CHECKPOINT …**
>
> Follow this route on the map on page 186.
> (a) What possible risks might the walkers face?
> (b) What could happen which might make the walkers take their escape route?
> (c) What risks are there on the escape routes?

PASSGRADE

> Explain the safety and other considerations required for planning a route using route cards.

Route Card Date: .... Expedition members: .... Telephone numbers: ....

Start + grid reference: Ford, Brockstones 466053   Starting time: 9.30 a.m.

Leg	To + grid reference	Details of route	Direction & bearing	Distance	Height	Walking Time	Rests	Estimated time of arrival	Total Time	Escape
1	Overend 464058	Follow walled lane, turn right.	N 350	0.5 km	Level	10 mins	None	9.40 a.m	10 mins	
2	Ullstone Gill 457071	Wide track follows valley side to where it crosses a big stream.	NNW 330	1.5 km	+ 50 m	40 mins	10 mins	10.30 a.m	50 mins	
3	Smallthwaite Knott 451081	Track climbs long, stony hillside. View of Kentmere Reservoir to left at top.	NNW 330	1 km	+ 180 m	50 mins	None	11.20 a.m	50 mins	Follow path back
4	Shelter 452096	Track continues rising. Keep high ground on right. Shelter is on a pass between two mountains: Harter Fell and Mardale Ill Bell.	N 008	1.6 km	+ 150 m	1 hr 5 mins	10 mins	12.35 p.m	1 hr 15 mins	Go down to Kentmere Reservoir SW – follow stream
5	Mardale Ill Bell 448101	Follow track up steep stony slope to cairn and top of hill. Small Water (lake) down on right.	NW 310	0.7 km	+ 100 m	35 mins	30 mins lunch	13.40 p.m	1 hr 5 mins	Kentmere Reservoir S
6	Posts 433095	Walk west, then south-west, to High Street Roman road, keeping steep slope and Kentmere Reservoir down to left.	WSW 260	1.5 km	No change	45 mins	10 mins	14.35 p.m	55 mins	Kentmere Reservoir SE
7	438065	Walk south along ridge path over Froswick and Ill Bell, then over Yoke and down hill till paths level out.	S 175	4 km	+ 170 m	2 hrs 25 mins	20 mins	17.20 p.m	2 hrs 45 mins	Left (east) down steep slopes
8	Tongue House ruins 452069	Turn left and follow stream down into valley past waterfalls and sheepfold. Ford River Kent. Meet track at Tongue House.	NE 055	2.2 km	– 320 m	1 hr 10 mins	10 mins	18.40 p.m	1 hr 20 mins	Follow path SE back
9	Overend 464058	Follow track along flat fields, down the valley.	SE 120	2 km	– 330 m	40 mins	10 mins	19.10 p.m	50 mins	
10	Brockstones 466053	Follow same path we started on.	S 170	0.5 km	– 10 m Level	10 mins	10 mins	19.20 p.m	10 mins	

British hills and mountains are not particularly high, but each year people die on them.

To avoid becoming a statistic, the following safety measures should be included when planning a walk in British hills or mountains.

1 **Be in a party**. It is not safe to walk alone on the hills unless you are an experienced walker. **A party must not split up**.

2 **Know how to navigate**. At least one person in a group must be able to read maps and navigate. This includes being able to use grid references.

3 **Carry safety equipment**. Map, compass, whistle, torch, and watch should all be carried. Many walkers now carry mobile phones as well. Don't forget your route card!

4 **Dress for safety and comfort**. The best clothing is light but warm (and warmth is more important than lightness). Mountains are much colder, windier, wetter and snowier than valleys. Wear or carry extra T-shirts, pullovers or fleeces, and a windproof and waterproof outer layer for rain. A woolly hat or balaclava and gloves are needed at most times of the year.

5 **Have safe footwear**. Walking boots are best. Get advice before you buy them. Wellies are OK – and cheap. Get boots which are slightly too big for you, and wear at least two pairs of socks (preferably wool) to prevent blisters. Gaiters to stop water or snow going down your boots are a good idea.

6 **Know the weather forecast**. You can have four seasons in one day on British mountains. If the forecast is bad, consider not going out, or keeping below 300 metres. If you go out when the forecast is bad, take extra clothes and have an 'escape' planned (see route card above).

7 **Have a rucksack**. A small one of the 'day-sack' type is best for one-day walks. In it, carry your spare clothes and items 8, 9 and 10 below.

8 **Carry first aid**. Plasters, bandages, antiseptic cream, sunblock, safety pins and perhaps painkiller tablets like paracetamol (not aspirin) should be carried – by at least one member of the group.

9 **Carry food**. Carry more food than you need in case something goes wrong. Some items should be high calorie, e.g. cheese sandwiches, chocolate bars, fruit cake. Don't carry heavy items with little food value, such as large amounts of fruit.

10 **Drink**. In some places, such as the Lake District, Snowdonia or the Scottish Highlands, you can often drink safely from streams. In most other areas, streams might be polluted by farm manure and sewage. It's best to carry bottled water or soft drinks when in doubt. Never take alcoholic drinks on a mountain.

11 **Say where you're going**. Tell someone (e.g. a tutor) where you are going and when you hope to be back. Leave a copy of your route card, medical information, doctors' phone numbers, and your own mobile numbers (if you have them).

12 **Illness**. If you feel ill, don't go out on the hills. Get medical advice, then put your feet up.

13 Finally, the group leader should personally check that everybody has what they need. If the weather looks too bad, stay low. Don't leave the planned route unless you have good reason.

FOCUS

Special hazards

1 **Steep slopes**. Avoid these unless you have good walking boots. Don't run down them, and pause from time to time if you're going up them. Don't dislodge stones – especially when people are below you.

2 **Cliffs**. Keep away from cliffs, especially in fog – they can be killers.

3 **Screes**. These are steep slopes covered with stones. They are unsafe for inexperienced walkers.

4 **Bog**. Flattish wet areas that are best avoided – you can sink into them!

5 **Heatstroke**. Symptoms are heat, dehydration and feeling ill. On hot days carry plenty of water, drink plenty, and have a sunhat and sunblock. Don't try to do too much.

6 **Hypothermia** (getting too cold). Symptoms are shivering, then confusion. Keep off the hills in very cold weather. Carry plenty of spare clothes and use them. If you get very wet cut the walk short and go home!

PASSGRADE

> Describe the action to be taken to minimise the effects of land navigation on the landscape.

The purpose of this outcome is to ensure that when you go into the country on navigation exercises or outdoor activities, you cause as little damage as possible.

The rules for this are given in the Country Code. This is not a law, but if you do not follow its advice, you may end up being prosecuted for criminal damage.

FOCUS

Countryside Code

1 Enjoy the countryside and respect its life and work.

2 Guard against all risk of fire.

3 Fasten all gates.

4 Keep your dogs under close control.

5 Keep to public paths across farmland.

6 Use gates and stiles to cross fences, hedges and walls.

7 Leave livestock, crops and machinery alone.

8 Take your litter home.

9 Help keep all water clean.

10 Protect wildlife, plants and trees.

11 Take special care on country roads.

12 Make no unnecessary noise.

Notes

1 The countryside in Britain is not purely natural. It has developed over centuries as a partnership between nature and farmers. Respecting the countryside means respecting the people who live and work there as well as the plants and animals.

2 In dry weather, grass, forests and peat moorland can burn – and there are no fire hydrants in the country. Fire causes long-term damage to trees, plants and wild animals. Avoid lighting fires, and be careful when using outdoor cooking stoves.

3 Animals need to be kept enclosed for their own safety, and because farmers' livelihoods depend on them.

4 Farmers have the right to shoot a dog on sight if it is attacking livestock.

5 Crops and even grass are valuable. If you keep to the path you don't trample them.

6 Fences, hedges and walls can be damaged by people climbing over them.

7 Animals can be dangerous. The same is true of machines.

8 Litter is dangerous for animals and unsightly for other users of the countryside.

9 In mountain areas many farms get their drinking water supply from springs and streams.

10 Much of Britain's wildlife and plants are under threat from human activity – this includes walking in the country.

11 Country roads don't have pavements, so take care.

12 People go to the countryside to get peace and quiet.

SUPERGRADE! *Merit*

> Describe how the requirements of the Country Code would be incorporated into a route card.

The main ways of doing this are:

- by planning routes which do not go across farmland, and which follow footpaths wherever possible
- avoiding walled and fenced areas (walls and fences are marked on the OS 1:25,000 map)
- avoiding planning routes in nature reserves
- being careful about planning walks during the grouse-shooting season
- being aware of diseases such as foot and mouth or swine fever, and not planning walks in areas where restrictions might apply
- not planning routes near reservoirs that are used for drinking water
- not planning to swim in lakes, streams and reservoirs that might be used for drinking water
- avoiding planning walks along tarred roads, where there might be traffic hazards.

SUPERGRADE! *Distinction*

Explain the procedure to be adopted on becoming lost.

It is surprisingly easy to get lost on Britain's hills – and this can happen even to experienced walkers who have planned their route carefully.

The procedure to follow depends on the circumstances.

! CHECKPOINT ...

Ask a mountain rescue expert what you should do if you get lost.

Circumstances	Procedure
1 If nobody is injured, if the party feels good, if it is daylight and the weather is not too bad and if the area is not too remote	(a) Stay together and walk downhill until you reach a stream. (b) Walk downstream until you reach a road, track, buildings or a place you recognise. (c) Telephone base if you think you are going to get back late.
2 If the weather is bad, the place is remote, and it is getting dark	If you are going to a remote area you should carry survival bags and spare clothes in case this happens. (a) Find a sheltered place. (b) Get into your bags with all your dry clothes on, eat some of your spare food, huddle together, and prepare to spend a night out. (c) If there is deep snow, dig yourself a hole to shelter in before you get too tired. (d) Telephone the emergency services if you can and ask their advice. In most places you can reach mountain rescue by dialling 999 for the police and then asking the police for mountain rescue.

Circumstances	Procedure
3 If someone is injured, or you badly need help	(a) If there are more than four of you, two can go and get help while the other stays with the injured (or ill) person. Otherwise, do not split up! (b) If you have a whistle but no phone, blow six long blasts on the whistle, then wait for a minute, then repeat the six blasts. A torch or bright clothing can be used to attract attention. (c) If you telephone the emergency services you should • give your exact location, using a six-figure grid reference if possible • describe the accident, the time it happened, and the injuries • mention any first aid or other relevant action.

C👓L SITES:

Mountain safety

www.trossachs.org.uk/activity/safety.html#cloth

www.scotlands-best.com/
lomondtrossachspark/activities/hillwalking/
hill_walking_safety.html

A very useful site! It's got nearly everything.

www.scoutbase.org.uk/activity/outdoor/
exped/index.htm

More advanced navigation

www.thebmc.co.uk/safety/train/skill_2.htm

Canadian

www.discoverjasper.com/RMHiking/navigat.htm

Irish

http://indigo.ie/~rpmurphy/Wild/navig.html

Unit 10 Law and the Individual

Grading criteria

PASSGRADE	SUPERGRADE! *Merit*	SUPERGRADE! *Distinction*
To achieve a pass grade the evidence must show that the learner is able to:	To achieve a merit grade the evidence must show that the learner is able to:	To achieve a distinction grade the evidence must show that the learner is able to:
● identify the key features of the English legal system **201**	● explain how the key features of the English legal system promote fairness for the accused **202**	● compare different types of courts and offences **205**
● identify four different types of law, few [sic] different types of court and three different types of offences **203**	● explain the rights of a person under arrest and of an accused person in court with reference to the provisions of PACE and HRA **210**	● apply detailed knowledge and understanding to explain the legal process of a criminal case in the magistrates court, using appropriate language **212**
● describe the rights of an accused person whilst under arrest and in court **209**	● apply good knowledge and understanding to describe the legal process of a criminal case in the magistrates court **212**	
● describe the legal process involved in a criminal case in the magistrates court **212**		
● describe the process of making a claim in the civil courts **216**		

The law is not something we can close our eyes to. As citizens we need to understand what is right and wrong, and what actions will lead to arrest by the police, or punishment by the courts.

The job of many of the public services is to help uphold the law. So for people who wish to join the public services knowledge of the law is often a professional requirement, without which the job cannot be done properly.

Finally we can all get into trouble of one sort or another. We may do something which is against the law, or we may be victims of crime. What do we do in these situations?

The purpose of this unit is to give you a first step towards understanding the law.

Knowledge of the law is sometimes a professional requirement

Identify the key features of the English legal system.

We are looking here at the English legal system. The Scottish legal system is slightly different.

European law is beginning to affect the English legal system. But most of the key features are likely to stay the same. Some of them are as follows.

Key features

1 Equality under the law

This means that the courts, the police and the prison service must treat everybody the same whatever their race, sex, religion, family background or wealth.

2 Presumption of innocence

In a British court it is up to the prosecution to prove beyond reasonable doubt that a person is guilty of a crime before they can be sentenced (punished).

3 Open court

This means that courts – with the exception of some children's courts, or trials involving some sex crimes such as rape – are open to the public, who can sit and watch. The public can see for themselves that the law is being used fairly.

4 Cross-examination

The English court system is 'adversarial' (it has two sides like a football match). The prosecution wants to show that the defendant is guilty, while the defence wants to show that he (or she) isn't. Each set of lawyers calls witnesses who support their point of view.

In cross-examination, defence lawyers can question prosecution witnesses, and prosecution lawyers can question defence witnesses.

5 Previous record not known

If an accused person comes to court, lawyers cannot mention any previous crimes that person has committed.

6 Trial by jury

In serious cases, in the Crown Court, a jury is called in. A jury consists of twelve people aged between 18 and 70. Their job is to listen to the evidence in an unbiased and commonsense way and decide whether the person on trial is guilty of the crime they are accused of.

Types of law

Common law

This is the English name for old, traditional law which was never written down but which it was the custom of people to believe in. Major crimes such as murder, rape, robbery and theft are all common law offences, and were crimes thousands of years ago.

Arson has always been a crime

Statute law

This is the name for laws that have been decided by Parliament and written down. All new laws since the seventeenth century have been of this type (though they may be based on earlier ideas that were found in common law). The laws about drugs, driving or education are all statute laws.

Civil law

This is law about buying, selling, compensation and the ownership of property. If a couple get divorced and go to court about access to the children, or division of property, it is civil law. Consumer law – about buying and selling goods – is civil law. So is most law about sex and race discrimination, unfair dismissal from work, and human rights. Civil lawsuits are started by the people involved in them.

Criminal law

This is the kind of law which the police enforce. It is to do with crimes such as murder, robbery, rape, theft and many others. Criminal cases are started by the police, then passed to the Crown Prosecution Service, a public service made of lawyers who help the police to prepare their cases for court.

Types of court

Magistrates court

The magistrates court is the court which tries over 90 per cent of all criminal law cases. It also does some civil law, such as issuing drinks licences. Even people accused of the most serious crimes, such as murder, have to go first to the magistrates court. The magistrates are three people who listen to the cases and make decisions on them. Many magistrates do not have much legal training (though they are trained how to be magistrates). The trials are usually short – often less than an hour. There are no juries, and no judges (though some magistrates are now, confusingly, called 'district judges'). The maximum sentence is six months' imprisonment or a £3,000 fine.

Crown Court

The Crown Court (always with capital letters, and singular) tries major crimes such as robbery, murder and rape. There is a judge and a jury. The judges have high legal qualifications, and so do the lawyers – called barristers – for the prosecution and defence. Trials can last for weeks.

Youth courts

Youth courts are like magistrates courts, only they deal with defendants under 18. Unlike magistrates courts they are not open to the public. A parent, guardian or youth worker must attend if the person being tried is under 16. The magistrates in youth courts are trained in youth justice.

Court of Appeal

The Court of Appeal deals with cases where someone – either the prosecution or the defence –

is unhappy with the outcome of a Crown Court or County Court case.

The Court of Appeal has two parts. The Civil Division hears appeals against the decisions of a county court or a High Court. The Criminal Division hears appeals from the Crown Court.

County courts

County courts are civil courts. They deal with problems brought by an individual or organisation, not by the police. Typical cases involve broken contracts, road accident compensation and arguments about who owns land. They also deal with bankruptcy and some divorce cases. They can decide compensation or damages to be paid to the person or organisation that has been wronged. There are 250 County Courts in England and Wales.

Coroner's court

Coroner's courts are used when people have died for a reason that is not clear. Their job is to find out why the person has died. They can order a post-mortem – and can say if somebody may have been murdered. But they cannot give any sentences.

Tribunals

Industrial (now called Employment) tribunals deal with cases where things have gone wrong for an employee at work. If someone suffers discrimination, or is sacked without good reason, the tribunal will examine the case and decide what compensation should be paid by the employer to the employee.

Family courts

These courts exist to deal with problems involving children and their care. They protect children against abuse, and in cases of divorce, where there is disagreement, they decide who should look after the children and how much access the other parent should have. They also arrange mediation (trying to get people to agree without going to court). They work with an organisation called the Children's and Family Court Advisory Support Service (CAFCASS), which provides links with other organisations working with families who are in difficulty.

Types of offences

As far as the court system is concerned there are three types of offences.

1 Summary offences

These are 'minor' offences which are tried in a magistrates court. There are no judges or juries. The maximum fine is £3,000 and the maximum imprisonment is six months.

2 Triable either way

These are more serious offences, where the accused can be tried at a magistrates court or at the Crown Court. They include some assault cases and serious thefts.

3 Indictable offences

These are serious offences such as murder, rape, armed robbery, major frauds and grievous bodily harm (GBH), which must be tried at a Crown Court. Sentences go up to and include life imprisonment, and in rare cases (if the Home Secretary is involved) there may be no upper limit.

SUPERGRADE! *Distinction*

Compare different types of courts and offences.

skill POWER

When you compare you should give differences and similarities.

Every type of court in the country does a different job. As you can see from the diagram, some are civil courts and some are criminal courts.

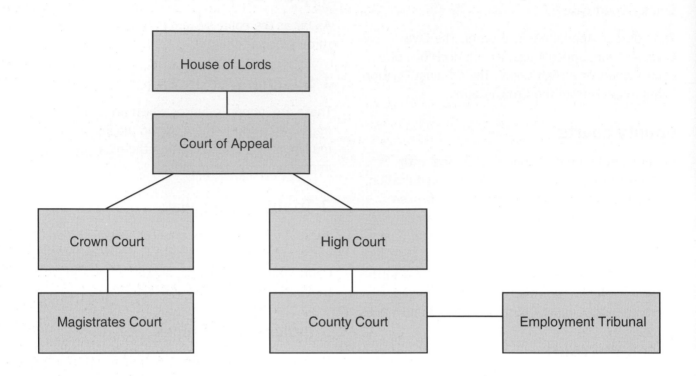

The court system of England and Wales

Differences between civil and criminal courts

Civil courts

- Deal with civil law, e.g. buying, selling, family law, business, contracts, compensation, problems with employment, most discrimination cases.
- Adversarial, but the people are the claimant, who complains about something, and the defendant – whom the complaint is about. Both claimants and defendants can be organisations, e.g. firms or public services, as well as individuals. The police are not usually involved.
- The main civil court is the county court – though there are also 'small claims courts' which can deal with minor cases quickly.
- County courts are run by a judge. There are no juries.

Criminal courts

- Deal with criminal law – evidence for cases is collected by the police and handed to the Crown Prosecution Service.
- Criminal cases are also adversarial, but the names of the adversaries are the state (i.e. the prosecution) and the defendant, who is usually an individual or a group of individuals. The prosecution is organised by the Crown Prosecution Service but done in the name of the Queen ('Regina v ....').
- The main criminal court is the magistrates court – because it deals with most cases. Instead of having judges they have magistrates. Magistrates are cheaper and have a commonsense view of the law, which makes them rather like judge and jury combined. Major crimes are dealt with at the Crown Court.

Civil courts	Criminal courts
• Penalties at civil courts are almost always in the form of compensation, paid by the defendant to the claimant if it is shown that the defendant wronged the claimant. Huge sums of money can change hands in major cases – especially libel cases where someone has lied about someone famous in public, or cases involving accidents such as train crashes.	• Penalties at criminal courts take the form mainly of sentences (see section on magistrates courts). Defendants can be fined, sent to prison, given community service or attendance orders, put on probation and so on. There is a wide variety of different sentences and they are changing all the time.

Comparisons between courts

Within the civil or criminal systems, each court is different. Below is a comparison between the magistrates court, the Crown Court and the coroner's court.

Magistrates court	Crown Court	Coroner's court
• Deals with all minor crimes.	• Deals with major crimes.	• Finds cause of death when person has died without a clear cause.
• Decisions are made by three magistrates, one of whom, the 'stipendiary magistrate' or 'district judge', may be paid.	• Verdict (decision) made by jury, but the sentence is decided by the judge.	• The coroner gives a decision on how the person died, based mainly on forensic (scientific/medical) evidence.
• Adversarial system – the cases are outlined for prosecution and defence by solicitors.	• Adversarial system – cases are outlined by barristers, who are more highly qualified than solicitors.	• The system is not adversarial. The coroner's job is not to give official blame, but to establish cause of death.
• Deals with local cases. There are magistrates courts in most towns.	• Deals with cases from a wide area. The Crown Court is only found in large cities.	• Only 24 coroners' courts in England and Wales.
• Does no appeals.	• Deals with appeals against decisions made in magistrates courts.	• Does no appeals. If findings suggest a crime, files go to the Crown Prosecution Service.

Comparison of offences

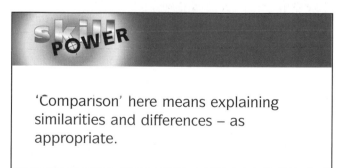

'Comparison' here means explaining similarities and differences – as appropriate.

There are many different ways of classifying offences, so it is not easy to compare them. We have already seen that indictable offences are those which are tried in the Crown Court, while summary offences are tried in magistrates courts. The difference between these is that indictable offences are more serious and carry heavier penalties.

Another way of classifying offences is to divide them into offences against the person, and offences against property.

 **BOOK**:

A–Z of Policing Law (2nd edn), by Roger Lorton (The Stationery Office, 2001)

Offences against the person

These are crimes in which a person is harmed or killed. The harm is usually physical (wounding, for example) but it can also be psychological (as when threats are given). Often the harm is of both types – as in rape cases.

A crime such as robbery is treated as a crime against the person, even though property is stolen. This is because there is violence or the threat of violence in all cases of robbery.

Crimes are defined in law, in order to make sentencing easier.

Here are some definitions.

> I don't even know what day it is, your honour, so how could I be a murderer?

which did not use writing still regarded murder as a very serious crime.

The definition given dates from the eighteenth century (which explains the funny English). It is not an attempt to define a new crime, but to explain what people already meant by the word.

If you read the definition carefully you will see that to murder someone you have to be an adult, and to kill the victim deliberately. If you kill somebody accidentally it isn't murder. 'Unlawfully' excludes war – it isn't murder to kill people in war. It also excludes self-defence: if you kill someone in self-defence, it isn't murder. This definition of murder was changed in 1997 to end the 'within a year and a day' rule.

FOCUS

Murder

'Murder is when a man of sound memory and of the age of discretion, unlawfully killeth within any county of the realm any reasonable creature in rerum natura under the King's peace, with malice aforethought, either expressed by the party or implied by law, so as the party wounded, or hurt etc. die of the wound or hurt etc. within a year and a day of the same.'

Rape

A man commits rape if:

(a) he has unlawful sexual intercourse with a person who at the time does not consent to it, and

(b) at that time he knows that they do not consent to the intercourse or he is reckless as to whether they consent to it.

Theft

The basic legal definition of theft is 'the dishonest appropriation of property belonging to another with the intention of permanently depriving that person of it'.

Robbery

The legal definition of robbery is where 'a person steals and immediately before or at the time and in order to do so, uses force on any person or puts or seeks to put, any person in fear of being, then and there, subjected to force'.

Comparison

Murder

Murder is possibly the oldest of all crimes, and it has always been a crime in common law. Societies

> ! **CHECKPOINT …**
>
> Why do you think the government decided to change the legal definition of murder?

Rape

Rape is also an old crime dating from common law. Like murder and robbery it is a crime against the person. Crimes against the person are more serious than crimes against property.

The definition of rape does not mention the sex of the victim – though it used to do.

Nor does it define what is meant by 'intercourse', though this is taken to mean penetration. There is no mention of whether ejaculation takes place or not. The definition does make it clear that only men can be guilty of rape.

Robbery and theft

Robbery and theft are often confused, but robbery is a much more serious crime. This is because force or the threat of force is used – which makes it a crime against the person. The same principle applies in comparing theft from an empty house with theft from a house when someone is in the house at the time of the theft. The courts take a more serious view of theft when there is someone in the house, even if the person in the house is not aware that they are being burgled at the time. This is because there is the possibility of causing fear or getting into a violent situation.

When sentencing offenders judges and magistrates take into account various key questions about the offences. These include:

- Was anybody killed or injured?
- Was there an intention to hurt or kill someone?
- Had the offender committed the crime before?
- Is the offender a risk to the public?
- Has the offender shown regret or remorse?
- Did the offender plead guilty?

! CHECKPOINT ...

What other factors might judges or magistrates consider before sentencing someone?

Describe the rights of an accused person whilst under arrest and in court.

When arrested

1 When the person is arrested they have the right to know why they are being arrested.

At the police station

2 At the police station they have the right to see a solicitor, to ensure that someone knows where they are, and to read a copy of the Codes of Practice, which explain what the police must do when they have arrested someone.

3 The person arrested must be cautioned before being questioned.

FOCUS

The caution

'You do not have to say anything. But it may harm your defence if you do not mention when questioned something which you later rely on in court. Anything you do say may be given in evidence.'

---

4 An arrested person cannot normally be held for more than 24 hours without being charged or released. If the offence is serious, a senior police officer can allow the person to be held for a further 12 hours, which can be extended up to a maximum of 96 hours, with the approval of a magistrates court.

5 The person has a right to be questioned fairly. There must be regular food breaks, the cell and interview room must be clean and warm, and the questioning must not put unreasonable pressure on the suspect. Interpreters or signers must be provided if needed.

6 The person has a right to free legal advice from a solicitor (except in special cases).

7 All the questioning must be tape recorded.

8 The person must allow fingerprints to be taken but can refuse to be photographed.

9 When the questioning is over the arrested person must be either charged or released. When a person is charged with an offence they are given a charge sheet, saying what the offence is, when and where they are due to appear in court and the conditions of bail (release but with a promise to return on the day of the hearing).

Before the trial

10 The arrested person should hear within six months if they are going to be prosecuted.

11 They should get a written summons telling them what offences they have been charged with and saying when they have to be at court and the address of the court building.

In court

12 If the accused person does not have a solicitor, the court must provide one, free of charge.

Explain the rights of a person under arrest and of an accused person in court with reference to the provisions of PACE and HRA.

The table below shows some of the main rights of an arrested person and how they are referred to in the Police and Criminal Evidence Act 1984 and the Human Rights Act 1998.

Right of accused person	Provisions of PACE	Human Rights Act
The right to know why they are being arrested	PACE section 37 – the police have to let the arrested person know the relevant section of the Act under which they are being arrested, and must let them see the PACE Codes of Practice.	Everyone who is arrested shall be informed promptly, in a language which he understands, of the reasons for his arrest and of any charge against him. (Article 5:2)
The right to have someone informed of the arrest	This is included in PACE section 56. The arrested person also has the right to have someone know where they are.	Not mentioned.
The right to see a solicitor	58–(1) A person arrested and held in custody in a police station or other premises shall be entitled, if he so requests, to consult a solicitor privately at any time.	Everyone who is deprived of his liberty by arrest or detention shall be entitled to take proceedings by which the lawfulness of his detention shall be decided speedily by a court and his release ordered if the detention is not lawful. (Article 5:4)
The right to read a copy of the Codes of Practice	See above.	Not covered in HRA.
They must be cautioned before being questioned	Yes, section 34.	The lawful arrest or detention of a person effected for the purpose of bringing him before the competent legal authority on reasonable suspicion of having committed an offence. (Article 5:1(c))
Cannot normally be held for more than 24 hours	Sections 41–43 – yes, but can be held up to 96 hours in extreme circumstances.	No one shall be subjected to torture or to inhuman or degrading treatment or punishment. (Article 3(e))

Right of accused person	Provisions of PACE	Human Rights Act
Has a right to be questioned fairly – interpreters or signers must be provided if needed	Yes.	To have the free assistance of an interpreter if he cannot understand or speak the language used in court, (Article 6:3(e))
The right to free legal advice	Section 58 – yes, the duty solicitor must be available.	To have adequate time and facilities for the preparation of his defence. (Article 6:3(b))
All the questioning must be tape recorded	Must be recorded – preferably on video.	Not covered.
The right to refuse to be photographed	Section 39 – yes.	Not covered.
The person must be either charged or released	Not covered by PACE.	Shall be entitled to trial within a reasonable time or to release pending trial. (Article 5:3)
Should hear within six months	Not covered by PACE.	Everyone is entitled to a fair and public hearing within a reasonable time by an independent and impartial tribunal established by law. (Article 6:1)
Should get a written summons	Not covered by PACE.	Entitled to trial within a reasonable time. (Article 5:3)
Court must provide a solicitor free of charge		To defend himself in person or through legal assistance of his own choosing or, if he has not sufficient means to pay for legal assistance, to be given it free when the interests of justice so require. (Article 6:3(c))

Differences between PACE and HRA

There is general agreement between the Police and Criminal Evidence Act and the Human Rights Act on the rights of an arrested person. The main difference is that the Human Rights Act does not speak about tape recordings and photographs. This may be because these are technological methods, and may (for example) be entirely replaced by video recording or some other electronic process in the near future. There is also a difference in viewpoint.

The Police and Criminal Evidence Act looks at arresting from a police point of view, and is intended to be a fairly exact guide as to what police officers can and cannot do. It is also designed to protect the police from accusations of unfairness. The HRA is a more general guide, and is designed to protect the arrested person rather than the police.

Rights under PACE and HRA

The rights covered by the two laws come under two categories.

1 Rights intended to ensure that arrested people, and people on trial, are treated humanely

This applies both to the physical conditions in which they are kept (for example, that cells should be clean and warm), and to the way they are questioned (they should not be threatened or intimidated). The aim is to avoid unnecessary physical, emotional and mental stress to people accused of crimes.

2 Rights intended to ensure that the truth about the crime and the suspect's involvement in it will come out

Though some parts of PACE have been criticised on the grounds that they make it harder for the police to do their job, there is a big advantage. That is, that if evidence is collected honestly, and without bullying or cheating, the case is more likely to stand up in court, and the right person will be convicted. If PACE is not followed there is a greater danger of the wrong person being convicted and the real criminal being let off. If the crime is serious an innocent person may waste years in prison, while the guilty person is free to enjoy life – and to commit more crimes.

PASSGRADE

> Describe the legal process involved in a criminal case in the magistrates court.

SUPERGRADE! *Merit*

> Apply good knowledge and understanding to describe the legal process of a criminal case in the magistrates court.

SUPERGRADE! *Distinction*

> Apply detailed knowledge and understanding to explain the legal process of a criminal case in the magistrates court, using appropriate language.

These three outcomes will be dealt with together in this section to avoid repetition. Subheadings are used to help you distinguish between the types of knowledge or explanation needed for a pass, merit or distinction grade.

Has he got too many rights?

skill POWER — Court visits

There is no substitute for going to a magistrates court and seeing what goes on for yourself. The public – including students – are welcome to sit in a court and watch the trials as long as they keep quiet and don't distract anybody. If there are several courts there is nothing to stop you from moving quietly from one court to another in order to get a 'feel' for what is going on. The only courts you may not be allowed into are those dealing with young people or some sensitive family matters.

If you are in a court do not be afraid to take notes. In addition you can ask at reception to see whether an officer of the court is free to explain some details of the legal process to you. The more details you get, the more likely you are to get a distinction for this outcome!

If you don't feel like visiting a court yourself, or with friends, ask a tutor to arrange visits for you. They will be well worth it.

Introduction

The legal process of a criminal case in the magistrates court involves the following people.

1 The defendant

This is a person who has been charged with committing a crime.

2 The magistrates

These are the three people from the community who sit on 'the bench', listen to the information on the case, and decide whether the defendant is guilty and what sentence to give.

3 The Clerk of the Court

This person – a qualified solicitor – is responsible for the smooth running of the court and for giving legal advice to the magistrates. The clerk also plans the work of the court for the days and weeks ahead, and keeps in contact with all the people outside the court who need to know what is going on.

4 The Prosecution Solicitor

This solicitor outlines what the defendant is supposed to have done wrong. If the defendant pleads not guilty, the prosecution has to supply witnesses to try to prove that the defendant is indeed guilty – even though they have said that they are not.

5 The Defence Solicitor

The job of this solicitor is to speak up for the defendant. First he or she gives reasons why the defendant has either done nothing wrong, or has done something less serious than the prosecution is trying to claim. The defence solicitor can also talk about the defendant's background, giving personal or other reasons why the court should take a sympathetic view towards the defendant.

6 Ushers

These are people who ensure that all the people who need to be in court at a given time are there. They go backwards and forwards leading people in and out, so that time is not wasted.

Other people in court

Other people who sometimes use the court are:

- police officers, who escort people who are being kept in custody in and out of the court
- other police officers to help to ensure security
- social workers who stay with some defendants to make sure they understand what is going on
- probation workers who prepare pre-sentence reports and discuss cases with the solicitors and others who may want to use their special knowledge of sentencing or defendants
- guardians, parents and others who may accompany young people in the youth courts
- journalists
- family and friends of defendants
- members of the public.

The legal process for the defendant

Stage 1

The defendant is told to come to the court on a certain day, at a certain time, through a summons (letter).

The defendant is likely to discuss the case with a solicitor at this stage, and to try to decide whether to plead guilty or not guilty.

A probation officer or social worker may write a pre-sentence report about the offence, the circumstances and the reasons behind it. The pre-sentence report will probably look at the family background and personal life of the defendant. Depending on the offence, a psychiatric report may also be asked for by the Clerk of the Court.

During this period the Crown Prosecution Service will be preparing the case for the prosecution. Its job is to make sure that the case has a reasonable chance of succeeding, and that the police have provided the right evidence.

Stage 2

If the case appears to be serious there will be a preliminary hearing at a magistrates court. The defendant will be identified and make a plea of guilty or not guilty. A decision is also made at this stage about whether the trial should be at a magistrates court at all, or whether it should be referred to the Crown Court. If the offence is serious ('indictable') it will be tried at the Crown Court. If the offence is possibly too serious to be dealt with by a magistrates court, i.e. if it could carry a sentence of more than six months in prison or a fine of more than £3,000, but they aren't sure, the offence will be classed as 'triable either way'. In this case the defendant can choose to be tried at the Crown Court or at the magistrates court. If the offence is less serious, it is always dealt with by the magistrates court.

Stage 3 – the main court hearing

A 'hearing' is a trial. If there is a plea of guilty the trial will be much simpler than if there is a plea of not guilty. There will be no need for witnesses, and once the magistrates have heard the basic facts of the case and read the pre-sentence reports they will be able to make a decision.

If there is a plea of 'not guilty' the prosecution has to prove its case in court, in front of the magistrates. This means the Crown Prosecution Service solicitors have to get witnesses who will tell, clearly and believably, the facts of the case as the prosecution sees it. In other words, these witnesses must say that the crime is what the prosecution (i.e. the police) say it is.

Where the plea is 'not guilty' the defence will also try to find witnesses who will show that the defendant is telling the truth and is not guilty of the crime he (or she) has been accused of.

When the trial starts the defendant goes to the dock (a special place in the room reserved for defendants) and gives their name. The prosecution solicitor then outlines the crime, naming the exact law that has been broken. After this the defendant's solicitor explains why the defendant is not guilty.

The prosecution then calls witnesses, who swear to tell the truth. They stand, or sit, in the witness box and say what they know, saw and heard. The defence solicitor then asks them awkward questions, in order to weaken their evidence. This is called cross-examination. The defence does not have to prove that the defendant is definitely innocent – only that there is some reasonable doubt about whether the defendant is guilty.

The defence can also call witnesses, who tell their side of the story. The prosecution solicitor is allowed to cross-examine these witnesses, and try to pick holes in their stories.

All this time the three magistrates have been listening. When they have heard enough they go into a side-room to discuss the case.

Stage 4

When the magistrates have made their decision they come back into the courtroom and announce the sentence. There are many kinds of sentence they can give, depending on how serious the offence is. These include (in rising order of seriousness):

- Acquittal – this is not a sentence. It means the defendant has done nothing wrong (or at least that it's not proved beyond reasonable doubt).
- Absolute discharge – the defendant did something wrong, but it isn't serious enough to be punished. It does, however, go on the accused's criminal record.
- Conditional discharge – this is slightly more serious, because if the accused re-offends, it will be taken into account in deciding the next sentence.
- Fine – a sum of money paid to the court as a penalty. This is often used in motoring offences. Fines can be paid in instalments. This penalty can cause problems if the accused can't afford to pay.
- Community penalties. This means working for the community, under close supervision by a probation officer, for a period of time.
- Custodial sentence. This means imprisonment or something else which restricts the offender's freedom – such as electronic tagging.

Further explanation

About 95 per cent of all criminal cases in England and Wales are dealt with in the magistrates courts. This means that magistrates have a very heavy workload, and the Clerk of the Court is kept busy trying to organise everything.

Much of the legal process goes on outside the court. This is particularly true of the report-writing, which is done to help the magistrates decide what kind of treatment or sentencing an accused person should have. Many people who appear before the magistrates have mental health, drugs or drink problems, and since the aim is to stop people offending, the magistrates have to think about the causes of the offence as well as the offence itself. For this reason, when giving sentences, they often link them with things like drugs rehabilitation programmes.

All accused people, even those accused of terrorism or murder, go to a magistrates court for a preliminary hearing. But if the crime is very serious they are tried in the Crown Court.

skill POWER   Appropriate language

This means technical or specialised words to do with the work of the magistrates court. To achieve a distinction for these outcomes, you need to show that you can use such words when talking or writing about the magistrates courts and their work. Here are some examples.

- Adjourn
- Admissible/inadmissible
- Aggravated
- Assault
- Bail
- Bench
- Community service
- Compensation
- Conditional
- Contempt of court
- Custody
- Defaulter
- Discretion
- Dock
- Evidence
- Guilty/Not guilty
- Magistrate
- Mitigation
- Offence
- Offender
- Order
- Plea
- Pre-sentence report
- Public gallery
- Remand
- Reparation order
- Sentence
- Standard of proof
- Suspended sentence
- Theft
- Trial
- Verdict
- Witness

Grading criteria

To achieve a pass grade the evidence must show that the learner is able to:	To achieve a merit grade the evidence must show that the learner is able to:	To achieve a distinction grade the evidence must show that the learner is able to:

You only have to switch on the television or open a newspaper to know that crime matters. Much of the news is about crime, and many television programmes and films are about crime as well.

Our towns are now full of CCTV cameras, neighbourhood watch signs, security grilles on shopfronts, and street-names fixed high above the reach of the spray-can artist. The signs of crime, and of the defences we put up against crime, are all around us.

Then there are the police stations, the courts, the prisons – not to mention the banks and the insurance industries – all effects of crime.

If we could look into the landscape of the mind, we would see a lot more signs of crime. We would see people's fear and anger. But we would also see hopes – the hopes of probation and social workers, all those professionals and volunteers who work to cure people of the criminal habit, to help both criminals and the victims of crime to put the shattered pieces of their lives together again.

That is what this unit is about.

PASSGRADE

> Explain the fear of crime and the measures to be taken to reduce those fears.

Fear of crime

The fear of crime is very complex. It comes from:

- the feeling that any of us could become criminals if we allowed ourselves to be tempted into crime
- the teachings of religions such as Christianity and Islam, which tell us that crime is wrong, and threaten punishments from God
- the fact that we are taught from our earliest years, through the influence of the family, friends, school, religion, the law and the media that crime is wrong, and is to be feared
- the perception that, despite all the advances of civilisation, crime seems to be getting worse; the media – newspapers and TV particularly –

constantly publicise crimes, rising crime rates, and run huge stories on murders
- people's own experience, or what they see around them; if someone is a victim of crime, or knows someone who is, this adds to the fear
- the stress laid by the police and other public services on the importance of crime prevention.

FOCUS

Crime on a Sheffield estate
Friday, 11 January, 2002, 16:29 GMT

Head to head: Our fear of crime
Youth worker, Sheffield:
'Our area is one of the least safe. Near us, the Parkhill development is rife with drugs and vandals.

I have only been a victim of crime through vandalism. My house was attacked and vandalised and my windows broken.

One elderly woman on our estate was mugged a couple of hundred yards away from where she lived. Another was mugged outside her front door.

We are the only tenant management co-operative in Sheffield – we run the estate for the council. Our concern is damage which is being done by gangs of youths.

We haven't had an exodus from the estate, but we have had people leave the area.

For old people it is the same old adage, they go in at night and vanish from view.

When we ask them to take diaries and report crime to us in our office they don't do it. They are too scared to get involved.

We are trying our damnedest, putting in a number of CCTV cameras using money we've saved over the years.

I used to be a great believer in English justice but over the last few months my confidence in the police in Sheffield is down to zero.

Police forums
We get no response whatsoever. When we call them about the number of cars being stolen, they just don't want to know.

We used to have police forums on a neighbouring estate but they stopped about 18 months to two years ago. We have not seen a police person since. They never walk around the estate.

> They have got statistics to prove me wrong but when you talk to the tenants of the city they are all of the same mind.
>
> There is no crime reduction – things are still the same.'
>
> Source: BBC website

Fear of crime is called a *perception*. It is how we see crime, or feel about it. It is not directly linked to the crime rate – though there is a relation between the amount of crime and the fear of it.

The British Crime Survey of 2001–2002 shows how fear of crime is linked more to how crime is reported in the media, than it is to the actual crime statistics.

Ways of reducing fear of crime

Reducing fear of crime is not the same thing as reducing crime. But it is linked.

Fear is already being reduced in the following ways.

1 Having more police on the beat. The complaint about the police in the passage above: 'They never walk around the estate' shows the importance people give to 'visible' policing.

This reduces fear of crime both for the individual and for the local community.

2 Neighbourhood watch schemes, or patrolling by community 'forces' who liaise with the police. People are less afraid to go out at night because they know there are systems in place to deter crime.

3 Protecting the home. Good locks, burglar alarms, neat gardens with low fences, security lighting, keeping dogs – all these and other protective measures reduce the fear of burglars getting into the house: the fear of crime.

4 Technology such as CCTV and better lighting in town centres. People feel less afraid of being mugged in bright surroundings that are also protected by cameras.

5 The insurance industry exists to reduce our fear of crime. We know that if we pay our premiums, and report thefts to the police, we have a good chance of getting money back.

The following methods might also reduce fear of crime.

6 The media could reduce fear of crime by giving less space to crime on TV news and broadcasting fewer dramas and soaps in which horrific crimes are dealt with. (They will probably not do this because people like watching crime programmes, and they will lose money if they stop broadcasting them.)

7 Newspapers could give less space to crime (but they would sell fewer copies).

8 Politicians could spend less time talking about crime (but they might get fewer votes).

9 The police could stop encouraging crime prevention (but if there was less fear of crime, then crime rates would probably go up).

10 Publicising crime statistics might make fewer old people fear crime as much as they do – it is mainly the young who are victims of crime, especially violent crime.

11 There could be less encouragement for people to spend money and buy things; then there would be less to steal, and people wouldn't want consumer goods as much (but this would seriously damage the economy and lower people's standard of living).

PASSGRADE

> Identify the vulnerable members of society, describing the types of crime to which they may become victim.

Not everybody is at equal risk of becoming a victim of crime. And different kinds of people are more likely to suffer different kinds of crime. For example, a person who doesn't own a mobile phone is never going to be a victim of phone theft!

How do we know who is vulnerable? There is a classification of residential neighbourhoods called ACORN. It is as follows.

> # FOCUS
>
> **Thriving** – affluent home-owning areas, suburban and rural, commuters and older people.
>
> **Expanding** – affluent working couples and families with mortgages, plus home-owners.
>
> **Rising** – well-off professionals, students and single people, living in town and city areas.
>
> **Settling** – established communities, home owners, skilled workers.
>
> **Aspiring** – mature communities, some new home owners and multi-ethnic areas.
>
> **Striving** – council estates with elderly, lone parent or unemployed residents.

Examples of vulnerable groups

The following chart, from the British Crime Survey, shows how people in some kinds of neighbourhood are more vulnerable to certain crimes than those who live in other kinds of neighbourhood.

A 'striving' area

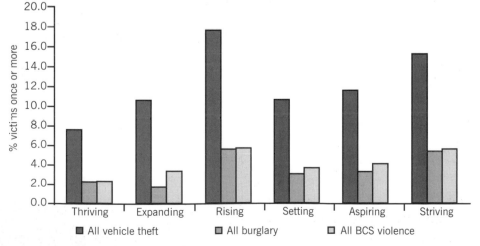

British crime survey 2001–02

C**L SITE:

British Crime Survey

Other vulnerable groups

The old

The old are less at risk from most kinds of crime than the young. They go out less and have fewer obvious possessions (e.g. mobile phones). They feel vulnerable because they are less able to run or fight than younger people. They can be victims of 'distraction crimes', e.g. fake telephone engineers and others who 'con' their way into the house.

The young

Young men are the group most likely to commit crimes and to be victims of crimes, especially violent crimes such as assault. This may be due to biological factors (hormones), cultural factors (admiration of strength and aggression, which is encouraged by the media), and the fact that young people, especially men, spend more time on the street. Drinking and drug-taking sometimes encourage violence of men against men – so the young men are victims as well as aggressors. Young

women are most likely to be victims of rape and sexual assaults by men. Children are often victims of abuse or assault, either by family members or their peers.

Ethnic minorities

These are vulnerable to race-hate crimes – and the law has been strengthened to take account of this (Crime and Disorder Act 1998).

Gays

Homophobic crime still exists and gays and lesbians are still targeted for harassment, abuse and physical attack.

> **!** CHECKPOINT …
>
> (a) In a group, pool your knowledge of crimes that have happened to people you know. Can you draw any conclusions about what kinds of crime are most common, and who is most likely to suffer from them?
>
> (b) Talk to someone in the police about who is most likely to become a victim of crime – and why. Don't forget to make notes!

Merit

> Explain the impact crime has on the lives of its
> victims and identify appropriate preventative
> measures.

All crimes are different, and all individuals are
different. So there is some danger in generalising
about the impact of crime on victims. However,
many surveys on the impact of crime on victims
have been carried out, and people are becoming
more and more aware of how great this impact
can be.

Main kinds of impact

Some of the main kinds of impact (effects) crime
can have on the lives of victims are as follows.

Physical injury

Violent attacks can kill or wound victims. Injuries
can be life-threatening, for example if someone is
struck by a hit-and-run driver, or stabbed in the
course of a mugging. In the case of rape, infection
with a number of serious diseases, including
HIV/AIDS, can result.

Psychological damage

Attacks on the person, and some burglaries, leave
lasting psychological effects. These include things
like panic attacks, exhaustion, depression,
flashbacks, nightmares and inability to concentrate.
If these effects last for a long time they are called
post-traumatic stress disorder (PTSD) and are
difficult to treat. Victims may, for example, be
unable to hold down a job, and their families may
break up as a result of the psychological strain.

Even without PTSD, many crime victims suffer lack
of confidence, or are afraid to go out at night. Their
quality of life is downgraded because they feel
worried and insecure. This worry and insecurity may
spread to their families or friends. The situation is
made worse by the fact that people who have been
crime victims are statistically more likely to become
victims again.

Economic effects

Crime against property, such as theft, causes
financial loss – especially if the stolen property was
not insured. Insurance premiums can go up, and
businesses may lose money if essential equipment is
stolen – especially computers which contain
valuable business information.

Preventative measures

In crime, prevention is better than cure. There is a
great deal that people can do to avoid becoming
victims of crime.

> **!** CHECKPOINT ...
>
> All police forces have crime prevention
> officers. Crime prevention is a subject
> which is much more interesting than it
> sounds! Invite a crime prevention
> officer to talk to you.
> There are also plenty of useful police
> leaflets. Visit your local police station
> and ask for some.

 C**L SITE:

www.homeoffice.gov.uk/crimprev/
personalsafety.htm

Some preventative measures intended to reduce
crime or the impact of crime are as follows.

In the home

Strong doors, good locks, properly fastened
windows, security lighting, dogs, prickly bushes and
front gardens clearly visible from the street all
discourage burglary. They reduce the fear of crime
and therefore, indirectly, its impact.

On the street

Keeping to well-lit streets, carrying an alarm,
watching out for people following you, keeping
away from rowdy gangs, avoiding talking to
strangers or meeting their eyes, and being prepared

to make a loud noise if you are attacked are all ways of reducing the risk of becoming a victim of violent crime on the street. Hiding mobile phones and carrying bags in such a way that they can't be snatched cut the risk of being robbed.

In cars

Keeping windows closed or nearly closed, locking the doors, not stopping if people flag you down, not picking up hitch-hikers, parking in well-lit places and using car locks are all ways of reducing car crime. It is also important to drive defensively and show respect to other road users.

Education and youth work

The police and social services are involved in many local projects to reduce the risk of young people participating in crime. These schemes, sometimes called 'divert' or 'diversionary', are designed to occupy young people in interesting and worthwhile activities which replace the idleness and boredom that might lead to crime. Activities such as sports clubs, which may seem to have nothing to do with crime, are effective ways of cutting crime since they give intelligent and active young people a constructive, non-criminal, outlet for their energies.

Education itself cuts crime levels by keeping young people occupied for many hours each day, and by giving them goals in life.

> **! ■ CHECKPOINT ...**
> (a) Review your own home and your lifestyle. What avoidable crime risks do you – or your family – face?
> (b) What do the family and the media do to help prevent crime? How successful do you think they are in crime prevention?

PASSGRADE

> Explain the role of organisations who offer support to victims of crime.

There are more and more organisations for protecting the victims of crime, and so reducing the impact of crime. These include:

- **Victim Support** – a voluntary organisation for counselling and helping people who have been victims of crime. See the Focus below.
- **Witness protection services** – these protect crime victims and witnesses at the court, so that they are not threatened or attacked by the criminals or their friends for giving evidence for the prosecution. These effective and far-reaching services are run at the Crown Court and at magistrates courts, with the collaboration of the police.
- **The Samaritans** – an organisation for counselling people (often over the phone) who feel depressed or upset – for whatever reason.
- **Social groups** such as those linked to Neighbourhood Watch, which aim to bind the community together and make it a more friendly place.

It is perhaps worth mentioning that in the past most of this victim support was given by friends and family of the victim. However, as society changes and more and more people are living on their own, away from their families and friends, there is a greater need for community organisations to step in and help.

Below is an example of an organisation which offers support to victims of crime.

> ### FOCUS
> **Witness Service – a branch of Victim Support**
> For many witnesses and victims, going to court can be a frightening and bewildering experience. Problems may include: not knowing what is expected; receiving inadequate information about court procedures, court layout or the role of various court personnel; and having to wait, often for long periods, in the same area as the defendant and his/her supporters. Giving evidence itself can be difficult and may mean a public airing of unpleasant events, including accusing another person of serious crime and the resultant fear that this may produce. Witnesses may also not understand or feel prepared for the process of cross-examination.

Victim Support's Witness Service offers information and support to any witness who needs it, in every Crown Court centre in England and Wales and an increasing number of magistrates courts. The Witness Service can also help victims and the families of witnesses and victims in court.

The Witness Service can offer:

- someone to talk to in confidence

- a visit to the court and where possible, a look round a court room before you are called as a witness

- information on court procedures

- a quiet place to wait before and during the hearing

- someone to accompany you into the court room when giving evidence

- practical help, for example, with expense forms

- to put you in touch with people who can answer specific questions about the case (the Witness Service cannot discuss evidence or offer legal advice)

- a chance to talk over the case when it has ended and to get more help or information.

Source: © Victim Support (2002)

This extract shows the kind of help that organisations which support victims of crime can give. Their roles include:

- giving information
- giving comfort and reassurance
- giving help or putting people in touch with others who can help
- arranging protection.

 Distinction

Carry out independent research to explain the effect crime has on the local community within a chosen area, e.g. the borough, local authority area.

Independent research means finding out about something on your own. It is also possible to do independent research as part of a small group. But you must be able to demonstrate that each individual within the group has done independent research, even if the findings have then been put together by the group as part of a group assignment.

If you are in any doubt about this, ask your tutor!

Ways of doing independent research:

- talking to community police officers about crime and its effects within their area

- talking to local councillors about local crime and its effects (especially if the councillor sits on the local police authority)

- talking to crime prevention officers about the effects of crime

- talking to youth divert officers about the effects of crime on young people, and the effects of youth crime on a community

- meeting members of neighbourhood watch committees.

In any of these cases be prepared to take notes – the more detailed the better!

You can also:

- get publications from your local government area about society, ethnicity, industry and other local information

- get details of crime and community partnerships run by the local authority

- obtain copies of your local policing report and policing plan – these are normally published each year by the police, and in some cases they are able to send out multiple copies; they give detailed information about local crime and local crime trends

- get ideas about local crime from the internet, for example on http://www.burnley.gov.uk/community/auditpart1.pdf

However, remember that the information you research must come as nearly as possible from your own area.

Your tutors may be able to help you arrange meetings with people, or obtain publications, but sometimes it is a good thing to make the contact yourselves.

Your research will probably take the form of either a report or presentation. See the Links below.

LINK! See pages xv–xvi – How to contact the public services.

LINK! See pages 32, 42–43 – Reports and presentations.

Whether you write a report, give a presentation, or use some other format for your work for this outcome, it may help if you break your work up into:

- collecting information
- describing the crime occurring in the local community
- describing the effects: (a) on the physical environment; (b) on people's lives; (c) on the public services
- indicating the cost of crime to the taxpayer or the householder

- explaining links between aspects of crime, e.g. truancy, criminal damage, shoplifting, car crime, drugs
- outlining schemes to reduce local crime and its effects.

A brief example explaining how antisocial behaviour in the street affects people is given below.

FOCUS

The problem

Anti-social behaviour destroys lives and shatters communities. It is a widespread problem but its effects are often most damaging in communities that are already fragile. If left unchecked it can lead to neighbourhood decline with people moving away and tenants abandoning housing. It can seriously damage the quality of life of vulnerable people through the fear of crime and the long-term effects of victimisation. It also incurs costs to a wide range of people including individuals and families, schools, local authorities, social landlords and business.

Source: www.saferlancashire.co.uk

Criminals or victims?

PASSGRADE

Give a detailed analysis of the systems used to report and record crime.

For statisticians there are five main types of crime. These are:

1 **Unreported crime**. A crime takes place but it is not reported to the police by the victim or anybody else.
2 **Reported crime**. This is crime that is reported to the police.
3 **Unrecorded crime**. This is crime which has been reported to the police, but they have not written down the details.
4 **Recorded crime**. This is crime which is reported to the police, written down by the police, and put on computer.
5 **Detected crime**. This is crime where the culprit has been identified.

It is only for type 4, recorded crime, that the police take any action.

Systems for reporting crime

The following are the systems used by the Metropolitan Police.

1 Calling 999.
2 Phoning the police using a non-urgent number.
3 Visiting the police station and giving information about the crime at the front office.
4 Report the crime on-line at http://www.online.police.uk/.
5 Use special ways of reporting crime for:
   • computer and internet-related crime. See http://www.met.police.uk/computercrime/index.htm
   • domestic violence. Contact a local Community Safety Unit (or phone 999 in an emergency). A good website for more detail is www.met.police.uk/csu
6 For frauds and scams contact www.icstis.org.uk – the Independent Committee for the Supervision of Standards for Telephone Information Services (ICSTIS). Other types of fraud can be reported through other sites. One of these is http://www.met.police.uk/fraudalert/ 419how.htm
7 Anonymous crime reporting can be done through an organisation called Crimestoppers.
8 Information on possible terrorism. This can be reported to the anti-terrorist hotline: 0800 789 321 – besides using 999.
9 Racial crime can be reported by the normal methods, or through the local Community Safety Unit.
10 Other charitable organisations, e.g. ChildLine.

FOCUS

In an emergency you should phone 999. The emergency service is for use when an immediate response is required. You should use this service to contact police in situations where a crime is happening now or if anyone is in immediate danger.

The 999 system handles calls for the fire brigade and ambulance service as well as the police so you should try to be clear about which service it is that you need. The following is what happens when you make a call:

• When your call is first answered you will be speaking to a BT or Cable & Wireless operator who will ask you which service you require.

• The operator will connect you to the service you request. The operator stays on the line with the caller until satisfied that communication has been established.

• Once you are connected to the police there are two things we will want to know straight away:

   1 Exactly where is it that police are required?
   2 Why do you want the police?

• You will also be asked for your name and the number that you are calling from.

Source: Metropolitan Police (2002)

FOCUS

Crimestoppers Trust, set up in 1988, is the only UK charity aimed at putting criminals behind bars through an anonymous Freephone number: 0800 555 111. Callers with information on crime are not asked their name. This anonymity is the key to the scheme's success, because it provides callers with complete safety from any reprisals.

Crimestoppers Trust works in partnership with the police. Operating through 31 UK regions, each call centre is supported by a board of volunteers drawn from the local business community and the media.

The Trust's job is to make sure that the phone keeps ringing, by promoting and explaining the scheme to the public at large.

The main reasons why there are so many ways of reporting crime are as follows.

- There is a danger that if non-urgent crime is reported through 999, someone with an urgent crime to report will not be able to get through when they need to.
- With many kinds of crime, e.g. sex crimes and fraud, victims feel ashamed of what has happened. If they report their crimes to, say, a fraud unit or a Community Safety Unit they can be sure their report will be dealt with sensitively and in confidence.

Recording crime

Crime is recorded in two ways: by the police, and by the British Crime Survey. The two systems are quite different.

By the police

Police crime recording is an essential part of their job, without which no crimes could be reliably detected.

In the past, the 43 police forces in England and Wales have had differences in their methods of recording crime. Though these differences have not been vast, they have been enough to affect crime figures for different parts of the country, and make it difficult:

- to get a clear picture of whether crime rates are going up or down
- to do a fair comparison between the success rates of different forces
- to get true figures for crimes such as robbery and assault, which were often not recorded under the old system
- to see underlying patterns of crime that might help in the detection of crime.

For these reasons, in April 2002 the government introduced a nation-wide system for recording crimes. It is called the National Crime Recording Standard, and has to be followed by all police forces.

The flow chart on the next page shows what happens.

The main things to notice about this are that there are crime reports and incident reports. A report is a crime report if a victim or witness says it happened, and if what happens is a crime in the sense of being a 'notifiable offence'.

An incident report is a report of a possibly criminal act which cannot be confirmed, where there is no clear victim, or where the victim refuses to confirm that a crime took place.

Once a crime is recorded it cannot be removed from the list.

The disadvantages of the new system are that it will take people time to get used to it, and it will be hard to compare crime statistics from before 2002 with those after 2002.

The advantages of the new system are that it makes use of up-to-date computer technology, produces more reliable statistics, and will eventually make policing more effective.

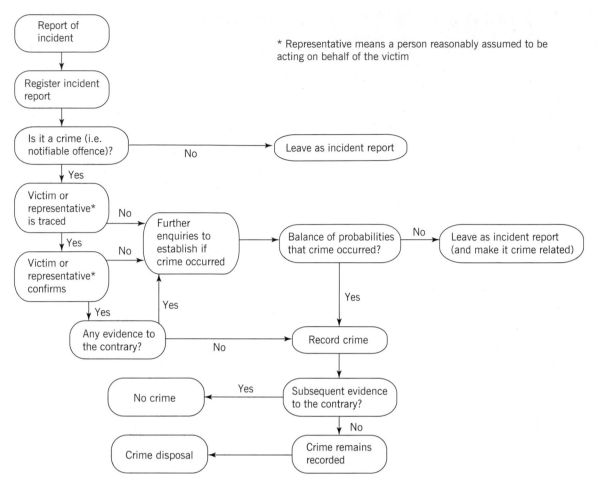

* Representative means a person reasonably assumed to be acting on behalf of the victim

The recording process for crimes

Source: © Home Office (2002)

The British Crime Survey

This survey, conducted every few years, tries to find out the real numbers of crimes in society, rather than simply those which are reported to the police. A team of investigators, employed by the Home Office, interviews large numbers of people (33,000 in 2001/02) and asks them if they have been victims of crime. If they have, they answer other questions as well – even if they never reported those crimes to the police.

The people questioned are chosen at random by a social research company, and once they are chosen, they cannot get someone else to answer the questions for them (though they can refuse to answer them).

Questions categorise crime in much the same way as the police do – by type – but they are not completely the same. 'Victimless crime', such as drug possession, is left out of the British Crime Survey, but would be included in police crime figures.

The crimes included in the British Crime Survey are:

- Violence against the person
- Sexual offences
- Burglary – dwelling
- Burglary – other
- Robbery
- Vehicle theft
- Non-vehicle thefts
- Criminal damage
- Other notifiable offences.

Merit

Analyse and evaluate the alternative methods available to report crime.

For this outcome we need to look at the different methods of reporting crime to the police, to other organisations linked with the police, and to the British Crime Survey.

This is a subject where you can do some of your own research, for example discussing with police officers how crime

is reported in their experience, and what they consider to be the best ways of reporting different kinds of crime.

Remember that 'analyse' means 'give some in-depth information or ideas', while 'evaluate' means 'give a reasoned opinion or judgement of the method(s)' that you have chosen.

Below are examples of analysis and evaluation of methods available to report crime.

Method of reporting	Analysis	Evaluation
1 Calling 999	This method of reporting crime in an emergency has existed for a long time. You are asked what service you require, though in some cases, e.g. car accidents, all three blue light services – police, fire and ambulance – are immediately notified by the switchboard.	This method is easy to remember and gets a quick response. Sometimes it fails because the person phoning is too shocked to get the details right. Because it is the easiest way of reporting crime, people use it for things that are not urgent, and risk blocking up the system.
2 Phoning the police using a non-urgent number	This is useful for reporting criminal damage, or theft, when it is clear that the culprits are no longer around, and when there is no immediate danger.	This system works well because the police do not usually keep you waiting. Sometimes it might be hard for a person to find the right telephone number – they may not have a phonebook nearby or may not want to use directory enquiries.
3 Visiting the police station and giving information about the crime at the front office	This means going into the police station and talking to the officer at the desk, and either filling in forms or answering questions so that your information about a crime can go straight into the computer.	The police are normally good at dealing with the public. But it takes time going to the police station, and you may have to wait when you get there. Filling in forms is time-consuming.
4 Report the crime on-line	This means getting onto the internet and using the website given on page 227.	This system is not straightforward because there are lists of crimes that cannot be reported by this method, and the website says that reporting the crime will take ten minutes.

- The National Automated Fingerprint Identification System
- The Criminal Names Index
- Home Office Large Major Enquiry System.

CHECKPOINT ...

Choose other ways of reporting crime, and do your own analysis and evaluation of them – following a system like the one used above.

SUPERGRADE! *Merit*

Describe how crime records are used to produce statistical data.

The total number of crimes recorded by the police in 2001/02 was 5,527,082. Each was entered into a computer which was linked with other police computers all over the country. The crimes are entered in such a way that different aspects of the crime go under different headings, e.g. type of crime, location, etc.

Using these headings, and special computer software, the information on all these crimes is sorted out into categories.

Crime statistics are figures about crime, put in such a way that we can learn something from them. Statistics do not tell us about individual crimes, but about numbers of crimes, types of crimes, types of offenders and crime trends.

Statistics come in various forms – tables, graphs, charts, pictograms and coloured maps. They highlight different kinds of information, and make it clear to us almost at a glance. They reveal hidden problems, and enable both the government and the police to plan forward in the never-ending battle against crime.

Statistics on crime are produced by each of Britain's 43 police forces, and by the Home Office (central government). Major crimes are kept on various national and even international databases.

These include:

- The Police National Computer
- The National Criminal Intelligence Service
- The National DNA database

Example of local crime statistics – Burnley

All crime	Records	Percentage
Burglary in a dwelling	1512	13.69
Theft from vehicle	1332	12.06
Burglary of a non-dwelling	876	7.93
Criminal damage to vehicles	847	7.67
Other theft or unauthorised taking	828	7.50
Stealing from shops and stalls	720	6.52
Criminal damage to dwellings	529	4.79
Stealing motor vehicles or UMTV	455	4.12
Criminal damage to other buildings	351	3.18
Other wounding	322	2.91
Drugs, possession of drugs	319	2.89
Harassment	293	2.65
Cheque and credit card fraud	285	2.58
Common assault	260	2.35
Other frauds	221	2.00

Source: Lancashire Constabulary

PASSGRADE

Analyse the methods of offender management and the effectiveness of these.

The main methods of offender management are:

- custodial sentence (prison)
- community sentence

- fines
- conditional or absolute discharge
- supervision under probation service.

Analysis

Custody

The youngest age at which someone can be imprisoned in England and Wales is normally 15 (though there have been younger people, such as the boys who killed Jamie Bulger). The shortest prison sentence available is five days and the longest is 'life' – which typically means 25 years but with some time off for good behaviour.

Custody is the severest kind of sentence and is used for serious crimes. The aim is to keep people who are a danger to society out of circulation, punish them for their crimes, and rehabilitate them if possible so that they can re-enter society and lead worthwhile, non-criminal lives.

Escapes are rare in British prisons, so they are effective in keeping people locked up. The punishment is effective in the sense that prison life is less enjoyable than life outside, and freedom is strictly limited. The threat of prison may well deter people from crime, but it is hard to prove this. Prison is not very effective in preventing re-offending. Over 70 per cent of prisoners aged under 21 reoffend, but the rates get lower with age.

Prisons have some big drawbacks. They are expensive – it costs about £24,000 to keep a prisoner locked up for a year. If women are imprisoned it causes major problems for their children, and if men are imprisoned their families often suffer emotionally and financially.

Community sentences

These sentences involve closely supervised work in the community. Their aim is to punish but also to prevent reoffending. These sentences are useful for people who are less of a threat to society, and are not likely to harm the people they are working with. They are less expensive than imprisonment, since offenders live at home, rather than getting board and lodging at the government's expense!

Unfortunately reconviction rates are very similar to those for prisoners. However, community sentences have the advantage of being less likely to prevent offenders from getting work. They may even keep their present jobs.

Fines

A fine is a sum of money paid to the court by an offender who has been found guilty. In a sense this is not offender management because once the fine has been paid the offender is able to lead a normal life, and is not managed (controlled) in any way.

Fines are the main penalty used for motoring offences, and for offences in the magistrates courts. They are not used as much in the Crown Court. Major fines can be used in a few cases where the defendants are companies or corporations. The amounts paid in fines vary, but are usually a few hundred pounds.

Fines are an effective deterrent for motoring offences, because most drivers are employed and can afford to pay fines. There can be problems collecting them, because sometimes the offender can only pay in instalments. If the person refuses or fails to pay the fine, a further sentence – perhaps in prison – is possible. Fines do not work if the offender has no money.

> **! ■ CHECKPOINT ...**
> (a) Talk to someone who works in the probation service about the methods of offender management which they use; or
> (b) Research conditional or absolute discharge and supervision under the probation service.

SUPERGRADE! *Merit*

> Explain the role of one public service within offender rehabilitation programmes.

Probation Service

The aim of the probation service is to put offenders through structured programmes of 'intervention' so that they will not reoffend in the future. This work has many aspects to it.

Social learning programmes

These are courses of counselling, training and activities, which are intended to make offenders behave more responsibly and find a constructive role for themselves in society. They are highly structured and designed to make offenders stop and think before they act. This work is done with offenders on community sentences and also with prisoners who have been released 'on licence', i.e. under supervision.

Domestic violence programmes

In these programmes the probation service works with the police, the prison service and other agencies to correct the behaviour and attitudes of people who have been convicted of violence in the home. These programmes aim to correct 'a misuse of power and control' by the offender, and usually last 24 weeks.

Substance-related offending programmes

These are designed to stop illegal drug and alcohol use, and the crime linked with drug dependency. The programmes teach self-control, problem-solving and ways of avoiding returning to drugs when the programme is over. They aim to change the lifestyles of offenders so that they no longer need drugs, excessive alcohol or crime.

Work programmes

Much probation work is linked to finding jobs for offenders. Research has shown that employment reduces reoffending by 37 per cent. Probation officers aim to make offenders more employable by improving their communication and other skills. The probation service also works with employers so that they overcome their fear of employing ex-offenders.

Offender assessment

The probation service tries to find out how likely it is that offenders will reoffend. To do this they work with the prison service. They do a risk assessment on each offender, looking at past and present behaviour. In the event of reoffending, they produce pre-sentence reports and supervision plans.

PASSGRADE

Identify and describe in detail local crime and disorder multi-agency partnerships.

The Crime and Disorder Act 1998 has a basic aim of attacking crime and disorder (bad or rowdy behaviour on the street) at a local level. It aims to involve the community by getting all crime prevention organisations in an area to work together in partnerships. This law also makes local authorities draw up a 'crime audit' – a survey to

Main aims	Priorities for action	Input resources	Measure of achievement	Target 2000/01
• Maintain the local community policing initiative	• Monitoring effectiveness • Encouraging individuals, groups and agencies to liaise with community constables	• Police	• Reduction in recorded crime • Reduced number of nuisance calls to police• • Community survey	• 1% per year • 5% per year

Neath Port Talbot County Borough Crime and Disorder Partnership Action Plans

find out what local people think are the main crime problems. Then they have to produce plans for fighting crime in their area.

A small extract from such a plan is given below.

COOL SITE:

www.neath-porttalbot.gov.uk/
crimeanddisorder/cd_action_plan.html

Crime and disorder multi-agency partnerships usually contain the following:

- Local government
- Police
- Fire service
- Hospitals
- Ambulance service
- Victim Support

- Housing department
- Probation service
- Neighbourhood Watch
- Mediation service
- Town planning dept
- Community Safety Unit

- Social Services
- Youth Service
- Local business
- Local media

These agencies are all partners, working together to reduce the amount of crime and disorder. They do this by:

- holding planning meetings
- setting targets
- exchanging information and ideas
- working with offenders and people who are at risk of offending
- working to make the environment less encouraging for crime (e.g. better design of buildings)
- raising and allocating money to deal with specific problems
- communicating with the public.

! CHECKPOINT ...

Check out the internet for crime and disorder action plans in the UK.

SUPERGRADE! *Merit*

Provide appropriate examples of how crime and disorder legislation impacts upon public services and local authorities.

The law makes it clear that there must be partnership.

Here is an example showing how public services are expected to work together:

Main aims	Priorities for action	Input resources	Measure of achievement	Target 2000/01
• Develop and extend consultation with young people	• Establish a youth council • Extend Youth Action Group (YAG) approach	(public services) • Education • Voluntary sector • Community safety • Police • Private sector	• Establishment of the youth council	By 2001
			• Number of occasions young people consulted	No data
			• Percentage increase of young people in YAGs	By 1999/2000 (72%)
			• Percentage increase of young people consulted	By 2000/01 (84%)

Impacts of this approach on public services and local authorities are as follows.

- They need to be more aware of the government's ideas on 'joined-up government' – that organisations should work together for the benefit of society.
- They need to communicate well at all levels.
- There will be more bureaucracy (office work) involved in arranging and attending meetings, and a risk of more paperwork.
- There may be problems with the Data Protection Act (protecting people's privacy) because information about individuals will be put on computer and passed from agency to agency. Public services will need to be aware of the details of privacy laws.
- Different agencies will have to understand and sympathise with other people's way of working. The police will become more caring, like social workers, and social workers will have to be somewhat stricter or more 'hard-nosed' in their approach.
- To cope with the increased workload there will be more investment in information technology (ICT), and much more pooling of information.
- There will be greater effectiveness in dealing with problems such as malicious false alarms – a multi-agency problem involving youth behaviour, fire service working practices and police detection.

skill POWER

'Assess' means something very like 'evaluate'. It means you should give your own opinions about the 'implications' (= 'possible effects') of crime and disorder laws on public services and local government. Your opinions should be backed up by reasons and examples where appropriate.

There is a great deal of 'crime and disorder legislation', but the main law is now the Crime and Disorder Act of 1998.

The police may be the best people to tell you about the effects of this law. Perhaps your tutor could invite a Youth Divert Officer or Community Constable to talk to you as a group – and answer questions at the end. When you give your own opinions about crime and disorder legislation and its effects, it is a good idea to take into account the views of the professionals!

SUPERGRADE! *Distinction*

Assess the implications of crime and disorder legislation on public services and local authorities.

Other implications

For the police

The police will have to continue to increase their contacts with the community. This will be done through organisations such as Neighbourhood Watch, youth organisations, and organisations involving ethnic minorities such as the Indian Workers' Association. There is an important section in the 1998 Act about race-hate crimes and the police will need to find more ways to deal with this problem. In the past the law on race hate was vague, and if there was no law, the police could not do as much about it. The police now have an opportunity to deal more positively with a major crime problem.

At the same time, if new laws are made, and new crimes defined, the police workload goes up. This means the police and local communities will need new resources – more staff and more money – from the government if they are to deal with the problem effectively.

For other public services

The fire service should get more help in dealing with arson and malicious calls. But it will also have to reach out to the community so that it can get more cooperation in preventing and dealing with arson. In many parts of the country over 60 per cent of the fires the fire service put out are started deliberately. Many of these fires are started by the young people who are being targeted by the Crime and Disorder Act.

For education

Education has a large part to play in preventing crime. At schools and colleges there is a 'hidden curriculum' in which young people are taught good citizenship. With the Crime and Disorder Act this hidden curriculum becomes less hidden, because the education service becomes a partner with the others in working to reduce crime and disorder. Citizenship is becoming part of the school curriculum, and the government is working hard to limit exclusions from school because excluded pupils are more likely to commit crimes and become habitual offenders. So one implication for schools and colleges is that they must stop excluding so many pupils.

Youth offending teams

Youth offending teams, under the Crime and Disorder Act, include a probation officer, a social worker, a police officer and someone chosen by a health authority. The implication here is that members of different public services will spend much of their time working with a team like this rather than with their normal public service. Public service workers will have to develop their communication skills to work together effectively.

CHECKPOINT ...

How will the Crime and Disorder Act affect employment prospects in the public services?
What problems might there be in sharing information within or between multi-agency crime and disorder partnerships?

COOL SITE:

www.crimereduction.co.uk/partnerships9.htm

Unit 12 Community and Cultural Awareness
Grading criteria

PASS GRADE	SUPERGRADE! Merit	SUPERGRADE! Distinction
To achieve a pass grade the evidence must show that the learner is able to:	To achieve a merit grade the evidence must show that the learner is able to:	To achieve a distinction grade the evidence must show that the learner is able to:
● contribute to a discussion showing basic knowledge of communities and cultures **238**	● summarise key information on community and culture **240**	● evaluate the social and cultural problems in communities across the UK and suggest improvements that could be made **252**
● identify the differences between local and national communities **241**	● compare one local and one national community, assessing the costs and benefits of each **243**	● evaluate the differences between local and national communities **253**
● explain the costs and benefits of living in communities **242**	● explain why and how social and cultural problems exist within communities in the UK **250**	
● outline the positive and negative aspects of cultural diversity **246**		
● identify a range of social problems within communities in the UK **248**		
● identify a range of cultural problems within communities in the UK **249**		

For over twenty years the biggest single criticism of the public services has been that they have not recognised the diversity of British society. This criticism has been loudest since the end of the 1990s, with the publication of the Macpherson Report on the police response to the death of Stephen Lawrence, and the statement that the Metropolitan Police was guilty of 'institutionalised racism'. Many police officers were deeply hurt by this accusation, for they had been working hard since the Brixton Riots of 1981 (and even before that) to build bridges with all communities and prove that they were not racist.

The purpose of this unit is to develop your understanding of this controversial area of public service work. Issues of race, ethnicity, community and culture – together with issues of gender – are now deeply rooted in the public services, and people who have a closed mind on these subjects are not welcome in public service work – nor would they be likely to enjoy it anyway.

Despite this, community and cultural awareness is not something to be frightened of. It opens the door to a deeper understanding of people. And if public service work was easy, it wouldn't be worth doing. So read on …

Contribute to a discussion showing basic knowledge of communities and cultures.

skill POWER

A discussion is usually an organised conversation between two or more people, in which information and ideas are exchanged. Discussions

- normally have a purpose, e.g. to reach a shared understanding or to plan a course of action

- are 'rational' – in other words you can give reasons and examples to support what you say.

In discussions you should speak, but you should also listen to others.

To have a discussion about communities and cultures you need to do some research on them. Useful types of research would include:

- talking with friends and classmates who come from different ethnic and cultural backgrounds from yourself

- listening to police, social workers or teachers who have wide experience of diversity (which means different communities and cultures living together)

- collecting local authority booklets on diversity

- looking for library books on community and culture

- looking at community newspapers

- visiting websites about community and culture such as the CRE website.

If your discussion is going to be taped you may find it useful to make notes beforehand. However, it is not a good idea to read your notes aloud during the discussion.

Here are some basic ideas about communities and cultures.

Communities

A community is any group of more than, say, twenty people who feel they have something in common. The word 'community' comes from the idea of 'sharing'.

Examples of communities are:

- the people who live in a village, suburb or small town
- the people who work together in an institution, such as a factory or a public service
- ethnic minority groups who come from the same area and share languages and customs
- people who share interests, lifestyles and a social life, such as bikers, gays, etc
- some larger groups of people (there are elements of community in a nation like Britain).

The word 'community' can also mean something like 'togetherness'. A 'sense of community' is a feeling of loyalty towards other people in the same group. If somebody lives in a village but never talks to the other people in the village, that person is sometimes disliked because they are 'not one of us' or 'not part of the community'.

The word 'community' has a sense of living together in peace. However, gangs and armies are also communities, since they share norms and values (ways of behaving and thinking). However, because they are on the move, or because they are aggressive, they would not normally be called communities.

Examples of communities in Britain are:

- local neighbourhoods, estates, villages, suburbs and small towns, e.g. Notting Hill in London, Boston in Lincolnshire, and thousands more
- areas such as valleys where people share the same facilities (e.g. pubs, churches and schools), e.g. Rhondda Valley, Swaledale
- ethnic minorities who share languages, beliefs, customs, societies, organisations, etc, e.g. Kashmiris, Gujaratis, Afro-Caribbeans
- religious organisations or groups of believers who have a clear identity and shared social life, e.g. monasteries, Quakers, the Ahmadiyya Movement, Orthodox Jews, Rastafarians – and many others
- people whose work gives them a sense of identity and togetherness, e.g. firefighters, farmers
- subcultures or lifestyle-based communities, e.g. travellers, hippies.

There can be communities within communities. Afro-Caribbeans are a community on a wide scale, but

A community of people who share the same interest

within that community people whose families come from, say, Grenada or Cariacou are themselves communities.

A community need not necessarily live in the same area, but they must be able to communicate easily. 'On-line communities' are groups of people who share similar interests and communicate easily through websites, message boards, chatrooms, etc on the web.

CHECKPOINT ...

We all live in one or more communities. For example, a Rastafarian whose family came from Jamaica and who works as a hospital porter at Huddersfield Royal Infirmary would be a member of:

- the Rastafarian community
- the Afro-Caribbean (Jamaican) community
- the hospital community in which he works
- the community in the suburb of Huddersfield where he lives.

What communities are you part of? Discuss this in groups.

LINK! There's more on this in Unit 4: Citizenship, page 80 and Unit 6: The Individual and Society, pages 121–125.

Cultures

A culture is a collection of behaviours and beliefs shared by a group of people.

Cultures are made up of the lifestyles, beliefs, languages and customs shared by people within a community. We all belong to one or more cultures, just as we all belong to communities.

The behaviour patterns in a culture are called its **norms**. Examples of norms are:

- wearing the colours of your football team when you go to support them
- taking off your shoes when you go into a mosque
- not swearing in front of a woman
- swearing in front of your mates, when they all swear
- students wearing trainers
- Catholics taking communion
- Londoners speaking with a London accent
- soldiers keeping their hair short.

The beliefs of a culture are called its **values**. Examples of values are:

- it is wrong to kill people except in self-defence
- dropping litter is anti-social
- it's OK to steal – if you aren't found out
- it's not OK to steal even if you aren't found out
- it is good to be unselfish
- it is wrong to drive in the middle of the road
- a doctor's job is to limit the patient's suffering
- work should always be done before the deadline.

To sum up: Norms are what we do; values are what we think.

> **!** **CHECKPOINT ...**
>
> Choose two cultures.
>
> (a) List their norms and values
>
> (b) Say which norms and values are **the same** and which are **different**
>
> (c) Do you think one of the cultures is better than the other?
>
> (d) What would a public service, such as the police, think?

SUPERGRADE! *Merit*

> Summarise key information on community and culture.

For this outcome you should keep your information brief – otherwise you could end up doing a long presentation or piece of writing – because there is a great deal to say about culture.

You could use a table, as in the example below.

Summary of two communities and their culture	
Name of community	
• Birstall	• Pakistani origin, Huddersfield
Type of community	
• Small town	• Ethnic minority group
Locality	
• West Yorkshire	• West Yorkshire
Size of community	
• 11,000 people	• 17,500 people
Ethnic group	
• Mainly white British	• Pakistani (south Asian)
Occupations	
• Factory workers, office workers, etc	• Originally factory workers, but now a range of occupations
First language	
• English	• Mainly Punjabi
Family structure	
• Nuclear family or one-parent families	• Extended family, but forced into nuclear families by housing
Food	
• Bread, potatoes – ordinary British diet with too much sugar and fat	• Chapatis and traditional foods (mainly halal)

Religion	
• Church of England, Methodist, Baptist, Salvation Army – or none	• Mainly Muslim, with a few Christians and agnostics

Clothes	
• Jeans, trainers, working clothes, etc	• Some traditional clothes such as shalwar and kameez

Customs	
• Ordinary British customs	• Different customs for weddings, funerals, etc

Taboos	
• Appearing 'stuck up'	• Eating pork or non-halal meat

Sport	
• Prefer to watch sport than play it; support Leeds United	• Traditionally keen on cricket; now enjoy all sports

Views on education	
• Some think it's a waste of time – varies	• Either keen on education or alienated from it

Law and order issues	
• Concern about petty crime	• Concerned about crime, but may prefer Sharia law to English law

Culture clashes or tension	
• Dislike 'comers-in'	• Some conflict between older and younger generations; some discrimination from other ethnic groups

Economic status and problems	
• A working-class area; environmental problems caused by traffic and factories	• Has a lower standard of living than the average for the area

> Identify the differences between local and national communities.

A local community is one that lives within a limited area. A national community is one which is spread out over the whole country. In between the local and national community are other communities which are more than local and less than national. And beyond the national community there is an international community.

For this outcome we're going to ignore some types of community and look at local and national communities only.

Local communities

These can be defined in the following ways.

- They cover a small area.
- They include most or all of the people who live in that small area, whatever their interests, family background or personal wealth.
- They are defined or described by the area, so they are linked to the name of a village, suburb, estate, ward, town, valley or similar geographical area.
- They are often linked to local government areas such as boroughs, councils and local authorities.
- They have a history which goes back hundreds of years, and which is often linked to old buildings, landmarks, industries, etc.
- They have a culture which shows itself in the local accent, local names, local foods and some local festivals.
- They are considered as 'home' by people who have lived there long enough, or whose families are also there.
- They have many local amenities such as pubs, churches, playing fields, shops and parks.
- They are small enough for people to meet people they know, or recognise people in the street.
- They often regard people born outside the area as 'outsiders' or 'comers-in' – but are not normally hostile to them.

National communities

National communities come in two types. One type is defined by interest or lifestyle, and might include train-spotters, football supporters, gays or travellers.

The other type of national community is the country itself. England is a community and so is Britain – but of course they are not quite the same community.

National communities defined by lifestyle and interest

These may be said to have the following characteristics.

- They have members who could live anywhere in the country.
- They only include people of a certain type (those who share the main interest).
- They are sometimes formal (such as churches) and sometimes informal (such as paragliding enthusiasts).
- They may have existed for a long time, or may have appeared recently.
- They may be secret or even criminal, e.g. cult members or paedophiles.
- They communicate in ways that other members of their community would recognise (through dress, etc).
- They have a special feeling of friendliness towards other members of the community, but are not usually hostile to outsiders.
- They meet each other and keep in touch through magazines, societies or the internet.
- They are usually divided into core members, for whom the community is very important, and hangers-on, who have a part-time interest.

National communities – the nation itself

The nation may be defined in the following ways.

- It includes everybody who has permanent right of abode in the country, and excludes everybody else.

- It is linked by ethnic and cultural factors, so immigrants and ethnic minorities may not feel as if they really 'belong'.
- It is reinforced by the media, particularly the right-wing press, who are often nationalistic (i.e. encourage the idea of the nation).
- It has political leaders, laws and institutions which are the same all over the country.
- It has a flag, name, head of state and other symbols round which national feeling can be built.
- It sees itself as different from other nations.
- It is a focus of loyalty and emotion for its members.
- It is prepared, in extreme cases, to go to war with other nations.
- It has a long history, which many people feel very strongly about.
- It has a language and culture which is taught in schools and of which many people are very proud.

> ## ! CHECKPOINT ...
>
> Visit this nifty website to get the statistical low-down on your local community!
>
> www.neighbourhood.statistics. gov.uk/ward.asp?la=CZ

PASSGRADE

> Explain the costs and benefits of living in communities.

'There is no such thing as a free lunch.' Communities are the same. You only get out what you put in. What you put in is the cost. What you get out is the benefit.

Take a loose-knit national community such as that of paragliders. This is a community of people who share the same leisure activity. Paragliders like to hang about in the air on 'wings' made of light cloth, rising on columns of hot air called 'thermals' till they reach cloud level (if there are any clouds) and then they come down again. If they can afford it they go off to places like the Alps, Turkey or beyond, where the thermals rise higher and they can fly further.

The costs

The costs of belonging to this particular informal community can be listed as follows.

Money

- The cost of buying the equipment – wings, protective clothing, bag, etc.
- The cost of transport to carry you and your wings to the flying sites – in the UK and abroad.
- The cost of learning to fly and any other courses (safety, etc).

Time

- The time spent flying, travelling to sites, waiting for suitable weather or wind, buying and sorting out equipment.
- The time spent meeting and making friends with other paragliders.
- The time spent reading and learning about paragliding.

Effort

- The effort of obtaining the equipment.
- The effort of going to the flying sites and flying.
- The effort of flying.
- The effort of socialising with other flyers.

Emotional energy

- Picking up the courage to start the sport.
- Dealing with the stress of waiting for good flying conditions.
- Coping with fear of accidents – and the accidents themselves if they happen.

The benefits

The benefits of being in the paragliding community include the following.

- Practising a unique 'extreme sport' which costs no more than about £2,000.
- Meeting others who understand, enjoy and practise the sport themselves.
- Making new friends.
- The exhilaration of it.
- Seeing new places.

You will notice that in this example there are many costs and and perhaps fewer benefits. You will also notice that the costs are more than just money. But for those who enjoy paragliding, the sheer excitement and 'buzz' of the sport and the delight of being in the air in beautiful places, the costs are well worth paying. In addition the sense of community with others who enjoy the sport is a major plus.

Costs and benefits applying to other types of community

The costs of living in a community in Britain include things like paying tax and carrying out the duties of a citizen. In return you get security, the trust and companionship of other people, and all the social life that the community can offer. You also get education, employment and medical care.

! ■ CHECKPOINT ...

(a) How far would you say a public service, such as the police, or a place such as a prison, is a community?

(b) Talk to someone in the armed forces and ask about the communities within the army, navy or RAF (e.g. the regiment and its role).

SUPERGRADE! *Merit*

Compare one local and one national community, assessing the costs and benefits of each.

To cover this outcome you should pick a local community which you belong to, or know something about, and a national community which you can easily get information about, e.g. from the internet.

When making a comparison it is probably easier to state the differences between the communities before discussing their similarities.

Communities can be compared in many ways. Some of them are listed as follows:

- geographical position and geographical size
- numbers of members
- the main factors binding the community together (e.g. geographical closeness; shared interests; lifestyle of members)
- the role of the community
- different types of members (e.g. different ages, jobs or roles within the community)
- what duties the members have to keep the community going (costs of the community)
- how the community benefits its members (benefits of the community)
- relationship with other communities.

Comparison between a further education college (local community) and the gay community (national community)

Descriptions

FE College

Anytown FE College provides a wide range of education for people living in and around Anytown. It has 500 teaching staff – full and part-time – and about 20,000 students (though only 2,000 of these are full time).

The college is a community because in addition to providing education and employment, it provides a wide range of services for its employees and users. These include canteens, sports facilities, societies, teams and clubs, counselling services and access to accommodation and financial help. It has social workers and others who can find accommodation for homeless students, and give help with a wide range of educational and social problems. The college also gives careers help and guidance, and has extensive links with employers and other useful organisations in the Anytown area.

The national gay community

This includes anybody in the country who is gay and wishes to communicate with other gay people. It tends to reflect national society as a whole, because in this community there are gay politicians, gay organisations of all kinds, gay recreational groups, gay football teams and so on. Through the gay community people can, if they wish, lead a full and varied life among gay people and institutions. One of the main roles of the community is to spread information about where and how gay people can meet other gay people for the kinds of relationships that they would like to have.

Differences

There are obvious differences between Anytown FE College and the British gay community. One caters only for local people; the other caters for people throughout the country (though it has many local branches and organisations). In Anytown FE College people meet in their classes, in the corridors of the building, or in the social areas. In the gay community people meet in known bars that are advertised in magazines or on the internet. In the college people meet face to face – while in the gay community people are much more dependent on the media for meeting.

Similarities

All communities educate or influence their members about norms and values (behaviour and beliefs) and these two communities are no exception.

The college educates and trains people so that they can take a full, productive and satisfying role in society. Through the college they can fulfil their own needs and those of society as a whole, which needs reasonably skilled people to carry out its work. Students learn how to behave in study and work situations; they also learn ideas, principles and theories, which come under the heading of values.

The gay community educates its members about aspects of gay life, such as 'coming out', gay rights, gay culture, how and where to meet people, and safe sex. In other words, it provides the norms and values that people need if they are join the community, and that people need to have if the community is to survive.

The college is divided into sub-communities, such as departments or non-teaching staff, and each class or group of courses (e.g. BTEC Public Services) is in itself a little community. In the gay community there is a similar fragmentation, for example between the activists such as members of OutRage (who form a politically motivated sub-community), regional groups such as the Scarborough and Ryedale Gay Community Network, and occupational groups such as the Lesbian and Gay Police Association (LAGPA) (http://www.lagpa.org.uk).

Assessment of costs and benefits

Anytown FE College

Costs

- Money. The college costs £6 million a year of public money, including the fees of some students. The money goes to paying staff, buying materials and maintaining the buildings.
- Time. All the time spent by staff and students in the building, learning, teaching or otherwise working is part of the costs of this community. This also includes time spent socialising with other students or staff.
- Effort. All the work spent in teaching and learning, and all the work done by support services, is an additional cost in maintaining this community.
- Emotional energy. Students, lecturers, administrative staff and the rest sometimes have to push themselves and suffer stress so that they and the college perform well.

Benefits

- Learning what we need to know, or want to know.
- Achieving qualifications which are needed for further progress in study and work.
- The pleasure of meeting and making friends with people (often people whom we have plenty in common with).
- The hope of making more money and getting professional success in the future.

The gay community

Costs

- Money. The cost of going to gay clubs and pubs, of buying gay magazines, of surfing the internet, etc.
- Time. The time spent finding and making gay friends.
- Effort. The effort of being sociable, and of being with other people.
- Emotional energy. The stress of being gay in a 'straight' society; the struggle to be accepted and the fear of being attacked or despised.

Benefits

The pleasure of meeting, and relating to, other gay people, and of being able to react naturally to people.

Costs and benefits in common

All communities have costs and benefits, and these two, which appear so different, are alike in this respect.

It is worth noting that communities only benefit their members – or those people who want to be in them. A person who does not want to learn would get no benefit from being a student at Anytown FE College. And a person who is not gay would get no pleasure or benefit from being a member of the gay community.

> LINK! There is more about diversity in Unit 4: Citizenship, pages 79–82; and Unit 6: The Individual and Society pages 121–125.

PASSGRADE

> Outline the positive and negative aspects of cultural diversity.

Cultural diversity means the variety of different cultures that exist in the UK at the present time. We have already seen that cultures are: (a) ways of behaving (norms); and (b) ways of thinking (values).

Different cultures are linked to:

- different communities
- different ethnic groups
- different occupational groups (jobs)
- different social classes
- different age groups
- people with different lifestyles
- people with different recreational interests.

Where all these different groups exist in the same society we have diversity.

Positive aspects of cultural diversity are those features that are considered good. The negative aspects are those that are considered bad.

It should be stressed that not everybody agrees on what the positive and negative aspects of cultural diversity are. And people are different. Young people who like getting out and about, enjoy meeting people and are not afraid of new experiences usually enjoy cultural diversity. Older people, or people who fear change and are set in their ways, often fear and dislike cultural diversity.

The positive and negative aspects of cultural diversity suggested below are based on the kind of views that might be acceptable in a modern public service.

Positive aspects

- People have more choice about what they want to believe in and how they want to live. They don't have to follow the old traditional ways which nearly everybody followed before about 1960.
- There is more variety in music, films, entertainment, food, and drink.
- We can meet people from different backgrounds and cultures and learn more about the world and more about how other people think.
- People are more tolerant of people who are different from themselves than they used to be.
- The country has benefited from the talents of people from ethnic minorities who have settled here. Some public services such as the NHS depend greatly on people from a diverse range of backgrounds and cultures.
- Public figures from diverse backgrounds – sportspeople and musicians, for example – have enriched the cultural life of Britain.
- The world as a whole is being 'globalised' and diversified, and it is inevitable that Britain should reflect this trend towards greater diversity.
- Britain needs to become more diverse and outward-looking to increase her prosperity and influence in the world.

Negative aspects

- Diversity includes having a wide gap between the rich and poor in our society, and the income gap between the lowest and the highest earners is widening.
- At present, diversity is not working very well, and people from ethnic minorities still suffer from various kinds of discrimination.
- Diversity is a worry to the white working class in places like Oldham and Burnley, and there is a risk that the far-right politics of the National Front or British National Party will gain a foothold in these places.
- Diversity is causing problems for many uniformed public services, as they struggle to employ more people from ethnic minorities, and to accept gays and lesbians.
- Problems of ethnic and cultural conflict are thought by some to be a threat to public order.
- Asylum seekers and illegal immigrants have become a hot political issue, linked in some people's minds with the dangers of terrorism.
- Some laws and customs of minority ethnic groups – such as the right to have more than one wife, or the custom of forced marriage – are illegal according to British law.
- There is a risk of religious as well as racial discrimination in a culturally diverse society.

Not everybody likes diversity

Social problems are situations in which large numbers of people suffer and require help from the government and the public services or from charities. Some major social problems are: poverty, unemployment, racism, mental illness, domestic abuse, drug abuse and alcohol.

Poverty

Poverty is hard to define, but the government has an official 'poverty line' – this means an income for one household of less than half the average household income for the country as a whole. The average household income is about £24,000 a year, so a household which gets £12,000 or less is at or below the poverty line.

In 1998 the government identified the 44 poorest districts in England (DETR analysis). They discovered that poverty was linked to a number of other problems, which are listed in the Focus box below.

> ## FOCUS
>
> **Poverty**
> Compared with the rest of England, these 44 districts have:
>
> - nearly two thirds more unemployment
> - almost one and a half times the proportion of lone-parent households
> - one and a half times the underage pregnancy rate
> - almost a third of children growing up in families on Income Support (against less than a quarter in the rest of England)
> - 37 per cent of 16 year olds without a single GCSE at grades A–C, against 30 per cent for the rest of England
> - more than twice as many nursery/primary schools and more than five times as many secondary schools on special measures (OFSTED correspondence).
> - roughly a quarter more adults with poor literacy or numeracy
> - mortality ratios 30 per cent higher, adjusting for age and sex
> - levels of vacant housing one and a half times elsewhere

- two to three times the levels of poor housing, vandalism and dereliction

- more young people, with child densities a fifth higher

- nearly four times the proportion of ethnic minority residents.

Source: www.socialexclusionunit.gov.uk

PASSGRADE

Identify a range of social problems within communities in the UK.

Unemployment

Unemployment is defined by the government as being out of work and receiving benefit. According to this definition, 3.1 per cent of people of working age in Britain were unemployed – 943,300 people in July 2002. The figures change by a few thousand every month.

Unemployment is a social problem because:

- it leads to poverty for unemployed people and their dependants
- it is linked to depression and mental illness
- it is a waste of resources for the country, since if unemployed people found work they could benefit not only themselves but also the country as a whole
- it costs a lot of taxpayers' money to pay out unemployment benefit to nearly a million people.

Racism

Racism is a general word for discrimination against people because of their race or ethnic group. 'Race' is sometimes seen as the biological differences between people (e.g. skin colour and average physical appearance). 'Ethnic group' refers to people's culture. The issue is complicated and 'racism' – as the word is normally used – relates to discrimination on grounds of both race and culture.

Racial discrimination is illegal in Britain, but it still exists.

There are several types of racism:

- direct racial discrimination, as for example when someone is refused a job because they are black
- indirect racial discrimination, where conditions, e.g. for employment, are laid down which affect one ethnic group more than another; an example would be if all female employees at a supermarket had to wear skirts
- institutionalised racism – this is the 'unconscious' racism practised by organisations such as public services.

Racism is a social problem because:

- it causes suffering to the victims
- it leads to economic disadvantage (i.e. poverty) for the minority group
- it is linked to crime.

Mental illness

Schizophrenia, manic depression, Alzheimer's disease and many other mental illnesses are not in themselves social problems. It is more that society treats mentally ill (and disabled) people often unfairly, sometimes condemning them to poverty and insecurity. The problem is, however, very difficult to deal with. If mentally ill people are kept in hospitals and institutions – which used to be the case – they lose their freedom and may lack rights. But if the hospitals are closed, as happened in the 1980s, mentally ill people have nowhere to go and many wander the streets and join the homeless. The situation is made worse by the fact that people in general are frightened of mental illness and the mentally ill.

Mental illness becomes a social problem when:

- it is linked to poverty and homelessness
- it is linked to unemployment
- it causes suffering to the ill and to the families and friends of mentally ill people
- it is linked to crime, alcoholism and drug abuse
- it costs a lot of money to the taxpayer to deal with it.

Domestic abuse

This takes a number of forms: violence, mental and emotional abuse and sexual abuse. Normally the violence is by men against women and children, but some of the violence is by women too. The old can also be victims of domestic abuse.

Domestic abuse is a social problem because:

- it causes suffering
- it causes physical injury and can cause death
- it can cause long-term psychological damage to victims
- it breaks up families
- it makes a heavy workload for the public services, and costs a huge amount of money to deal with it.

Drug abuse

> # FOCUS
>
> The major legislation dealing with 'controlled' drugs is the Misuse of Drugs Act 1971. It classifies drugs according to their relative harm and makes it a criminal offence to possess, produce or deal in them. Class A drugs include cocaine, crack, ecstasy, and heroin; Class B includes amphetamines (speed), barbiturates and cannabis; Class C includes mild amphetamines, anabolic steroids and some tranquillisers. Possession of some of these is not illegal if prescribed by a doctor.
> The maximum penalties for possession and supply of controlled drugs are:
>
> Class A – 7 years + fine (possession) and Life + fine (supply)
> Class B – 5 years + fine and 14 years + fine
> Class C – 2 years + fine and 5 years + fine
>
> Source: www.ukonline.gov.uk

Drug abuse is the taking of illegal drugs. It is a social problem because:

- many drugs are addictive and become a habit
- drugs are expensive and addicts often need to steal in order to afford them
- drugs are linked to physical and mental illness
- the supply of drugs is controlled by mafia-type criminal gangs

- it costs the taxpayer a lot of money to deal with drug-related crime.

Alcohol abuse

Drinking too much alcohol is a social problem because:

- it is linked to antisocial behaviour such as fighting and drink-driving
- it can cause serious illnesses such as liver disease
- it is linked to mental illness
- it can cause poverty for alcoholics and their families
- the effects of drink are expensive for the taxpayer.

PASSGRADE

> Identify a range of cultural problems within communities in the UK.

This is a complex topic. Many of the complaints people make about other people are culture based. If you say, 'I can't stand the way he talks!', or 'I think that hairstyle's horrible!' or 'That **** music does my **** head in!' – you are saying something about your own culture and someone else's culture.

Problems with culture occur mainly

- when one group of people doesn't like the culture of another group of people
- when rapid culture change causes problems within families or communities.

Let's look at some of the different cultural problems found in our communities today.

Mainstream and alternative cultures

A mainstream culture is the culture (norms and values) followed by the majority of people. In Britain there are at least two mainstream cultures linked with social class. The middle-class people who read *The Times* or *The Guardian* and work as lawyers, engineers, teachers, doctors, architects, etc have a lifestyle and collection of beliefs and attitudes that are different from those of most people who read *The Sun*, *The Daily Star* or *The Mirror* and work as cleaners, bus-drivers, council-workers, factory workers or farm labourers. These class differences are also culture differences, and affect the nature of communities in Britain. But they are mainstream cultures because most people belong to one or other of them.

An alternative culture is a subculture – a culture followed by far fewer people than a mainstream culture. People who are not average – for example, very religious people, hippies, skinheads, people who are homeless, travellers, drug-users, criminals, gays and some others – belong to alternative cultures which have somewhat different norms and values from mainstream cultures.

Mainstream and alternative cultures have nothing to do with ethnicity. Any ethnic group, such as people of Pakistani descent, has a mainstream culture. Its norms and values include working hard, being Muslim, speaking languages such as Punjabi and Kashmiri at home, eating chapattis and parathas – and so on. But a person of Pakistani descent who is also part of the gay community does not entirely belong to mainstream culture – since mainstream Pakistani culture, like mainstream British culture, does not really accept homosexuality.

Cultural problems

In the UK these include:

- problems to do with the 'generation gap' where the young and old do not understand each other
- problems with 'deviance' – non-mainstream lifestyles – such as crime, drug-taking or the gay lifestyle
- differences between mainstream British cultures and mainstream cultures of ethnic groups
- cultural problems linked to poverty and the strains that poor people live under, in an increasingly rich mainstream society
- the problems of belonging to more than one culture, e.g. young British Muslims who may find themselves in conflict with both their parents' culture and mainstream British culture

- class differences and inequalities within mainstream society
- professional 'cultures' such as the culture of the police or the culture of the fire service, where this seems to work against equal opportunities
- racism (see page 247 under social problems); in some ways this is a cultural problem.

Explain why and how social and cultural problems exist within communities in the UK.

This is a highly complex subject. Many books have been written about it and a great deal of government work by civil servants is being done to try to understand these social and cultural problems. Here there is only room to hit the high spots.

Inequality of income

Some people in Britain earn a lot more than others. The poorest 10 per cent of families get under £11,000 a year while the richest 10 per cent get over £44,000 a year. Some effects of this are as follows.

- It may encourage theft, because some people have a lot of property, while other people sometimes feel that they will never get what they want if they don't steal.
- Some people have an enjoyable or even luxurious lifestyle, which is good for their health and relatively stress-free, while poor people have a worse lifestyle, worse health, more stress and a shorter life expectancy.
- Rich people have more power, so that they influence the government and media to reflect their culture, while ignoring the culture of the poor.
- A culture of consumerism is encouraged, which can discriminate against the poor because they are less able to afford to be consumers.
- Political problems occur, since helping the poor means taxing the rich, and the rich often resent high taxation.
- Environmental problems may result from too much car ownership and too much of the wrong

kind of industry (which mainly pollutes the areas where poorer people live).

Diversity

If there was no diversity there would probably be fewer social and cultural problems. Most cultural problems exist because of diversity.

Without diversity:

- everybody might be equally rich
- there would be less discrimination because everybody would be roughly the same
- ethnic groups would all have the same or similar cultures.

But people are different, and not having diversity is not an option. Attempts have been made in the past (e.g. in Communist Russia and Nazi Germany) to stamp out diversity. Nazi Germany brought about the Holocaust in which six million Jews were murdered by the German authorities.

The problems that diversity causes are nothing compared to the problems there would be if there was no diversity.

Is there room for diversity in the armed forces?

Crime

Crime is a social problem and occurs for many reasons. Some reasons for it are listed below.

- Some people find it easy to break the law – either on purpose or because they lack the self-control to stop themselves.

- Some people are brought up without the right values, lack moral conscience or because they are influenced by their friends to break the law.
- In a modern consumer society there is plenty of opportunity to commit crimes.
- The influence of alcohol and drugs.
- The inequalities in society between rich and poor.
- Mental illness leading to criminal behaviour.
- Conflicts between individuals, leading to violence.
- Society defines some actions as criminal (for example, if cannabis was decriminalised it would no longer be a crime to possess it).
- People do not take precautions to prevent crime.

> **! CHECKPOINT ...**
>
> Discuss this question: In a case of rape, is it possible for the person who is raped to be partly to blame?

Drug abuse

Drug abuse exists for the following reasons.

- Drugs are available, and give people pleasure.
- Many drugs are addictive, so once people start taking them they can't stop.
- It is socially acceptable or even expected to use drugs in some sections of society.
- There are apparent rewards of money and status for drug-takers in some sports.
- Some people find life boring and unsatisfying, and take drugs because they think they will give their lives more meaning and purpose.
- Drug taking is a way of rebelling against mainstream culture.

> **! CHECKPOINT ...**
>
> Take any other social problem and research its causes. Then note the causes down. Distinguish between causes which are the fault of the people involved, and causes which may be attributed to society or economics (money or lack of money).

For this outcome you have to judge the seriousness of social and cultural problems in communities – and suggest ways of reducing those problems.

It is worth remembering that not all communities are the same, and that different communities may suffer from different problems.

It will help you to talk to (or listen to) a police or probation officer, or a social worker.

We have already seen that it costs billions of pounds to tackle social problems each year. For example, it costs over £7 billion a year to finance the police, and their job is to deal with only one social problem – crime. If we think of the other social problems – poverty, poor housing, racism, inequality, mental illness, domestic abuse, drugs and alcohol and the money it costs to tackle these – we can see that social problems are, in money terms, an astronomical cost for society.

But money is only part of the cost of social and cultural problems. The real cost, which cannot be calculated, is the cost in the suffering of individuals who encounter these problems. If someone loses their job, if they become mentally ill, if their son or daughter becomes a heroin addict, if their parent suffers racial discrimination, all these are major causes of grief. We should also not forget the links between social and cultural problems and ill-health, and early death. In Britain the poor die, on average, seven years younger than the rich.

What can be done about social and cultural problems?

Some people think that (as it says in the Bible) 'the poor are always with us' – and there is not much to be done about social or cultural problems. But this is not the view of the government or the public services, whose main job is to try to reduce these problems, and ensure that everybody in the country can lead happier and more satisfying lives.

Some improvements could be made by doing the following.

Work

The government is doing work to find out what the underlying causes of social problems are. Setting a national minimum wage, running the New Deal Scheme, and working on 'urban regeneration' (improving the quality of life in towns) are attempts to lessen poverty and its effects. Schemes to lessen unemployment, give benefits to those who need them, and improve the environment should all help to reduce social problems linked to poverty.

Crime reduction

To reduce crime the Crime and Disorder Act will have to be put into operation. Building more prisons may not help, because prisoners tend to learn about crime from other prisoners and may come out of prison worse than when they went in. Educating children about the risks of crime, and giving children more things to do out of school, e.g. running holiday clubs and arranging activities, entertainment or holiday camps, might make life more interesting for them and cut down on vandalism and petty crime.

Another good way of reducing crime is to teach people more about security, and design estates and other housing schemes so that they offer fewer opportunities to criminals – without becoming too bare or bleak.

Drug-related crime

Drug-related crime could be tackled differently – perhaps by restricting smoking still further, since smoking may be the first step towards drug use for many young people. Legalisation of some drugs could be considered, because this would prevent mafia-type gangs from developing, and by monitoring the quality of drugs it might ensure that fewer people died of overdoses. But if this was done, some way would have to be found to protect young people, who might be at even greater risk of drug addiction than they are at present.

Cultural problems

Cultural problems linked to religion – such as 'Islamophobia' – might or might not be reduced by having more 'faith schools'; at the same time having more lessons in citizenship in schools should help to teach people to respect other religions even if they do not agree with them. In general, anti-racist education is an effective way of tackling some of these problems. It is also helpful in tackling the problem of institutionalised racism, which still exists in the public services and in many schools and colleges.

> **! CHECKPOINT ...**
> Which is the worst social problem in your immediate neighbourhood? If you had the power, what steps would you take to tackle the problem?

SUPERGRADE! *Distinction*

> Evaluate the differences between local and national communities.

SkILL POWER

To evaluate the differences you should (a) identify them and (b) say why the differences are important, either in our daily lives or for the public services.

You could do this under the following headings.

Differences in power and influence

Local communities have little power or influence over national communities, but national communities may have influence over local communities (e.g. the national community, through Parliament, can make laws that affect local people, for example banning hunting).

Differences in how communities are governed

The national community (i.e. British people as a whole) is run from London by central government, while local communities are run by local government, or by their own members. It is easier for an individual to contact a local councillor about a problem than it is to contact, say, the Prime Minister.

Differences in organisation

The organisation of many national communities is far more complex than that of many local communities. This is because national communities are sometimes made up of local communities which all come under the same 'umbrella' or leadership. An example of this is the Anglican Church.

Differences in communication

Members of local communities can usually communicate by meeting each other, often informally as friends and neighbours. National communities have to communicate more formally, through the media, using the Internet, or by letters, phone calls, magazines, e-mails or advertisements. Many magazines serve a particular national community; for example, *New Scientist* serves the 'community' of scientists, students of science and people who are interested in science.

Criminal communities

Some communities are criminal. Local examples are drug-users within a particular area, or football hooligans. National criminal communities include paedophiles who communicate using the Internet, or criminal gangs such as Triads, which may have links in a number of cities. National criminal communities are much more dangerous, and pose a much greater problem for the police, than local

criminal communities, who are more likely to carry out petty crime. However, most of the work of an average police officer is concerned with local, small-scale crime.

Differences in our daily lives

Although national communities are often much more powerful and influential than local communities, they are not always more important in our daily lives. Local communities provide our friends and our daily social life. National communities (including the public services) protect and help us at times of crisis, but we may hardly be aware of them at most other times.

> **! ■ CHECKPOINT ...**
>
> Choose a local community and a national community and list as many differences between them as you can. Then pick the three most important differences you have found, and say why you think they are important.

Grading criteria

PASS GRADE	SUPERGRADE! Merit	SUPERGRADE! Distinction
To achieve a pass grade the evidence must show that the learner is able to:	To achieve a merit grade the evidence must show that the learner is able to:	To achieve a distinction grade the evidence must show that the learner is able to:
● describe the procedure for obtaining driving documents, the requirements and criteria for driving lessons and the advantages of advanced driving **256**	● summarise the legal requirements placed on a driver to obtain a driver's licence and to drive a motor vehicle on a road **258**	● critically evaluate the process of driving, drivers' responsibilities and the causes and costs, financial and personal, of collisions **265**
● explain the causes of collisions **260**	● interpret and analyse the causes of collisions and the solutions, and responsibilities of the driver and employer **262**	● critically evaluate the success or failure of a local and a national campaign in accident prevention **270**
● outline the responsibilities of the employer and employee whilst driving and the cost, both financially and psychologically, on families and employers when an individual has been involved in a collision **261**	● evaluate the cost of collisions, both from a personal and a financial point of view **264**	
● explain the role of the Health and Safety Executive and the emergency services in collisions, comparing national and local involvement in road safety campaigns **266**	● assess the importance of local and national campaigns in accident prevention **269**	
● prepare a road safety strategy for your locality **271**		
● monitor the success or failure of local campaigns **273**		
● explain the different attitudes and behaviour of drivers and why they are prone to attitudinal behaviour **273**		

In Britain over 90 per cent of men and 60 per cent of women are drivers. You should aim to join them at the earliest possible opportunity. Not being able to drive is a personal, social and professional disadvantage.

This is especially true in the uniformed public services. A hundred years ago armies travelled on foot. Not any more. And firefighters no longer use a horse and cart to go off to a 'shout'. In most of the non-uniformed public services it is also very useful to be able to drive.

The main aim of this unit is to prepare you for learning to drive. It also looks at road safety, and what the public services do to save lives on the road.

! CHECKPOINT ...

Pester a generous relative for the cost of driving lessons. Failing that, get a part-time job and spend some of the proceeds on learning to drive. And if you can't do either of those, and you're old enough, join the Territorial Army – and get stuck in with their free driving lessons!

PASSGRADE

Describe the procedure for obtaining driving documents, the requirements and criteria for driving lessons and the advantages of advanced driving.

It is illegal to drive without a licence. When you want to learn to drive you must get a **provisional** licence and have it while you are learning. When you pass your test this can be converted to a **full** driving licence.

Procedure for obtaining driving documents

There are different licences for different types of vehicle. The procedure given below relates only to cars. If you want to know more about different kinds of licence you should visit the DVLA website.

FOCUS

(from the Driver and Vehicle Licensing Agency (DVLA) website)

1 How To Apply For Your Driving Licence
First Applications/Provisional Licences

If you have never held a driving licence before you will need to apply for a provisional licence. You must complete driving licence application form D1 and photocard application form D750 and the appropriate fee. You must also enclose original documentation confirming your identity and a passport sized colour photograph taken against a plain light background. Send your completed application and fee to DVLA, Swansea SA99 1AD.

Driving licences are now in the photocard format. To get one you need to prove your identity and supply a suitable photograph.

To prove your identity you need one of the following:

- Full Valid Current Passport
- Birth Certificate
- Certificate of Registry of Birth (provided your name is on the certificate)
- Adoption Certificate
- ID Card issued by a member state of the EC/EEA
- Travel Documents issued by the Home Office
- Certificate of Naturalisation or Registration

(The first four of these apply to British citizens.)

You must provide a colour passport photograph, full face, and without hat, helmet or sunglasses. If you do not send a passport the photograph will need to be certified on the back by a teacher, police officer, or other professional person.

The cost of a first provisional licence is (in 2000) £23.50. When you pass your test it will cost another £8.50 to convert it to a full licence.

Your licence will need renewing every ten years.

Once you have passed your driving test (theory and practical) you should exchange your test pass certificate for a new licence as soon as possible. **If you do not claim your test pass within two years of the date of your test, the entitlement conveyed by the test pass will be lost and you will have to pass a further driving test (theory and practical) for that category of vehicle if you wish to have it included on your driving licence**.

If you hold a **provisional driving licence** you must complete the declaration on your test pass certificate and send it together with your photocard licence, paper counterpart and the appropriate fee to DVLA, Swansea, SA99 1BJ.

Requirements and criteria for driving lessons

Before you start to drive:

- you must hold a valid, signed, provisional driving licence
- ensure that any car you drive is properly insured for you to drive.

Your eyesight is also important. Your instructor will check your eyesight before you start to drive. It is important to learn safe driving practice from the beginning of your driving career, because bad habits are hard to break.

FOCUS
To help you study
Books
The Highway Code is essential reading. It explains the rules of the road and gives sound advice about best driving practices.
The Official Theory Test for Car Drivers contains all the questions in the theory test and explains the answers.
The Official Driving Manual explains best driving practices in greater detail.
The Official Driving Test covers what is required during the driving test and explains the full test syllabus.
The Official Guide to Accompanying L-drivers gives very useful information to anyone who is supervising you while you practise.

Other media
The Driving Test – an inside view is a video explaining what the examiners expect to see and gives some practical tips.
What If – an interactive video and workbook designed to improve your ability to think ahead to boost your hazard awareness.
The Official Theory Test – your licence to drive is a CD-Rom providing interactive fun and a modern way of learning.
Your ADI will be able to advise you where you can obtain these.

Source: Driving Standards Agency website

When learning to drive it is best to use an Approved Driving Instructor – who will have passed strict tests in driving and instructing. Approved Driving Instructors also know about the test, and

the kind of things the examiners are looking for in the practical part.

About 40 hours of driving lessons are needed, on average, before a person passes their driving test. The time needed varies from person to person. You need to book the test some time in advance, but there is no point in taking the test until you are ready for it.

FOCUS
'You must be able to drive consistently well, with confidence and without assistance or guidance from your instructor. If you can't, you aren't ready for the test.' (Driving Standards Agency)

The advantages of advanced driving

This part of the outcome refers to a driving test for experienced drivers set up by the Institute of Advanced Motorists (IAM) whose address is 510 Chiswick High Street, London W4 5RG; Tel: 020 8996 9600. The test is called the Advanced Driving Test.

FOCUS
Who conducts Advanced Driving Tests?
Today's advanced tests are conducted by the IAM and also the RoSPA Advanced Drivers' Association. Becoming a full member of either of these two active motoring clubs involves your passing their respective 90 minute tests which cover up to 35–40 miles in varying conditions. RoSPA ADA test results are graded 'Gold', 'Silver', 'Bronze' or 'Ungraded' and to remain a member you have to take regular refresher tests.

Both organisations use driving examiners who hold the Class One Advanced Driving Certificate awarded to traffic patrol police officers who've passed a specialised and demanding training course lasting up to 6 weeks at one of Britain's Police Driving Schools. It is testimony to this training based on the 'system of car control' that police drivers covering high mileages, often at speed, have very few serious accidents. Their day-to-day work puts them at the sharp end of traffic problems, giving them the relevant experience and understanding to conduct advanced tests.

Source: www.driving.co.uk

The IAM gives free advanced test guidance. The test is used by professional drivers, including police and other public service drivers, to upgrade their skills and increase their safety on the roads. The more hours a week a driver spends on the roads, the more likely it is that they will have an accident – simply because there is an accident risk whenever you are out on the road. Passing the Advanced Driving Test reduces this risk.

> Summarise the legal requirements placed on a driver to obtain a driver's licence and to drive a motor vehicle on a road.

Most laws relating to driving and vehicles apply only on public roads. If you own a field, or a private lane or drive, you can do what you like on it (provided you don't set out to harm, hurt or kill people).

Legal requirements for vehicles

The following are the legal requirements for vehicles on public roads.

1 Driving licences

All drivers must have a licence to drive. If they have passed their test it is called a full driving licence; if they haven't passed their test it is called a provisional licence.

Motorcycles, cars, medium/large vehicles and minibuses/buses all have difference licences with different costs. They can be either provisional or full.

There are age limits. You cannot drive a car until you are 17, and you cannot drive a large vehicle or a bus until you are 21.

2 Learning to drive

While learning you must have someone aged at least 21, who has held a full licence for at least

three years, in the passenger seat. You must have the red L-plates on the car while driving.

3 Insurance

You must be insured, so that you and others can be compensated if you are in an accident.

There are three main types of insurance:

(a) **Third party** – this covers anyone you injure or whose property you damage. It does not protect you or your vehicle.
(b) **Third party, fire and theft** – like (a) but it also protects your vehicle against being stolen or damaged by fire.
(c) **Comprehensive** – this protects you and your vehicle, as well as other people and their property.

An insurance is sometimes called a policy. When you get insured you are given a policy document explaining exactly what is insured. You pay a sum of money each year – called a 'premium' – to protect you. If you have no accidents, you lose the money but you may get a 'no claims bonus', which means that you pay less next year. If you have an accident you can make a claim and, all being well, the insurance company will pay the costs.

When you are insured, your insurance company gives you a certificate which you must show the police if they ask to see it or you have an accident. The police may also ask to see your policy document.

4 The Vehicle Registration Document

This gives details of your vehicle, and should be completed by both the buyer and the seller of the vehicle.

5 Road tax disc

This shows that you have paid a tax which goes towards the upkeep of the roads. It is normally renewed each year and must be stuck to the windscreen.

What difference does insurance make?

6 MOT (Ministry of Transport) test certificate

All vehicles over three years old and lorries, buses, ambulances and taxis over one year old must be given a mechanical test at a vehicle testing station run by a government organisation called the Vehicle Inspectorate. If the vehicle fails this test it must be repaired and brought up to standard without delay.

Other legal requirements relating to the vehicle

1 It must have good brakes, lights and tyres, all correctly fitted and in working order.

2 The exhaust must have a silencer, and pollution from it must not be above the legal limit. Thick black smoke, for example, is against the law.
3 Instruments on the dashboard must work properly and give correct readings.
4 Horns and windscreen wipers must be in good working order.
5 Mirrors must be up to standard.

Legal requirements when driving

1 Drivers must follow the Highway Code, especially the instructions worded 'MUST' and 'MUST NOT' in red in the official booklet.
2 Drivers must obey:
   • all road signs and markings
   • all traffic lights and other signals, beacons and warning lights
   • signals or instructions given by the police, traffic wardens, school crossing wardens
   • road workers giving authorised directions.
3 Drivers must drive:
   • safely
   • with 'due care and attention'
   • with 'reasonable consideration for other road users'.
4 The vehicle must not be overloaded – either with too many people or too much luggage. Any trailer must be safely packed.

The vehicle must not be overloaded

Seat belts

The following is a table showing the seat belt laws.

	Front seat	Back seat	Legal responsibility
Driver	Adult seat belt	Adult seat belt	Driver
Child under 3	Must have a child restraint	Child restraint if available	Driver
Child aged 3–11 (under 1.5 m height)	Child restraint if available or adult seat belt	Child restraint if available or adult seat belt if available	Driver
Child aged 12 or 13, or younger child over 1.5 m in height	Adult seat belt	Adult seat belt	Driver
Passenger aged 14 or more	Adult seat belt	Adult seat belt	Passenger

PASSGRADE

Explain the causes of collisions.

A collision is a crash between two or more vehicles, between a vehicle and a person or animal, or between a vehicle and a stationary object.

Collisions don't just happen to road vehicles. Trains, boats and planes can also collide, but they are not studied in this unit.

There are some road traffic accidents which would not normally be described as collisions. If a vehicle skidded off the road and rolled down a bank, it would not normally be called a collision. But it may well have similar causes and effects to a collision.

Under this outcome we are going to look only at road collisions.

In the Focus box are the main causes of accidents recorded by the Metropolitan Police in the year 2000.

FOCUS

1 Driver disobeying 'Stop' or 'Give Way' signs or road markings	10.7%	4030
2 Driver turning right injudiciously	8.9%	3355
3 Driving too fast having regard for the road environment	8.3%	3123
4 Driving too fast having regard for other road users	7.6%	2856
5 Driving too close to the vehicle in front	6.1%	2289
6 Driver swerved or braked to avoid an accident	3.9%	1484
7 Driver changing lane injudiciously	3.5%	1337
8 Driver making a U turn injudiciously	2.5%	937
9 Driver disobeying Traffic Light	2.2%	847
10 Driver overtaking on the offside injudiciously	2.2%	838
11 Other Driver or Rider factor	2.0%	750
12 Driving when drunk	1.9%	716

Source: www.driving.co.uk/3a2.html#

'Injudiciously' means carelessly or unwisely.

The statistics given are interesting, but they refer only to London, where driving conditions are different from many other parts of the country.

Basic causes of collisions

The basic causes of collisions are given below.

1 Bad driving which can either be:
   - deliberate (e.g. speeding on purpose)
   - accidental (carelessness)
   - due to bad driving skills (bad teaching, or lack of practice).
2 Bad vehicles (poor design or mechanical condition).
3 Bad roads (poor surfaces or poor design, e.g. too narrow, rough surfaces, unsuitable road markings).
4 Distractions such as other accidents, passengers, mobile phones or bad driving by other people.
5 Bad weather (snow, fog, heavy rain, strong wind, black ice) or bad light.
6 Medical or other factors affecting the minds of drivers or their passengers: drink, drugs, illness, 'road rage', suicide, poor eyesight, age and gender factors.
7 Inadequate policing or control of traffic; wrong speed limits given the nature of the road.
8 Too much traffic (this must increase the number of accidents, but not necessarily their seriousness, since if there is too much traffic it moves slowly, and therefore accidents are less likely to be fatal).

All these factors place strain on the driver or undermine the driver's control of the vehicle. Reaction times are slower, and there is less chance of foreseeing or avoiding a collision.

Outline the responsibilities of the employer and employee whilst driving and the cost, both financially and psychologically, on families and employers when an individual has been involved in a collision.

Much of the driving on Britain's roads is done professionally – that is, by people who are working. Often they are working for someone else. The legal responsibility for safe driving falls, in these cases, both on the driver (the employee) and on the employer.

Employer's responsibilities

This is a complicated area of law and the responsibilities (duties) of the employers depend on the kind of driving that is being done. For example there are differences in the regulations for lorry drivers, coach drivers, taxi drivers and for the emergency services.

Goods vehicle operators (employers of lorry drivers) need a licence from the government. The main requirements are given in the Focus box below.

FOCUS

Responsibilities of employers of lorry drivers

1 For any type of licence, you will have to satisfy the Traffic Commissioner that:

- you and, if you have any, your partners or directors, are fit to hold a licence;

- you will have proper maintenance facilities of your own, or arrangements with a garage and enough money to keep your vehicles fit and serviceable;

- you will have an operating centre suitable for your vehicles, bearing in mind such things as its size, location, availability and means of access;

- you will have proper arrangements to ensure that the rules about drivers' hours are followed and that vehicles are not overloaded – more details can be found in the guide "Drivers Hours and Tachograph Rules for Goods Vehicles in the UK and Europe".

Source: www.tan.gov.uk/ TANEngCS/procedure/gvweb4.asp

They also have to ensure that the drivers they employ are fully licensed to drive that type of vehicle.

Drivers' hours

Professional drivers such as lorry drivers are normally not allowed to drive regularly for more than 10 hours a day on a public road.

The time spent driving is recorded on an instrument called a tachograph, which by law has to be fixed to lorries.

Similar but more complicated rules apply to coach drivers. If you are interested you can read about them on the website of the Guild of British Coach Operators – http://www.coach-tours.co.uk

These rules do not apply to the emergency services.

> **! CHECKPOINT ...**
> **■** Find the information below, and note down the relevant details.
> Department for Transport
> Drivers' Hours and Tachograph Rules
> for Goods Vehicles in the UK and
> Europe (GV262)

Employees' responsibilities

The employees are the drivers themselves. Their responsibilities are:

- to drive safely, following all rules and advice given in the Highway Code
- to ensure that they do not drive for longer than they are allowed
- to check their health and eyesight from time to time
- to stop driving if they are sleepy
- to report all mechanical defects
- to avoid all alcohol or drugs before and during driving.

The costs of collisions

The costs of collisions and vehicle accidents take two forms.

1 Financial cost

FOCUS
Costs (£) of road traffic accidents (1998 figures)

Average cost per casualty for Great Britain
Fatal
1,047,240
Serious
117,670
Slight
9,070
Average all casualties
33,630

The costs for the police and ambulance services are relatively low, normally less than £5,000 even for a fatal accident. But the cost for the country as a whole, in terms of lost output and property damage, is very high.

COOL SITE:

www.scotland.gov.uk/library2/
doc05/ras-31.htm

2 Psychological costs

This means the cost in terms of the suffering of accident victims, families and friends. These costs cannot be counted in money – as medical care can – but they are very great. Bereavement, disability and post-traumatic stress disorder (i.e. long-term mental illness) can all result from road traffic accidents.

SUPERGRADE! *Merit*

> Interpret and analyse the causes of collisions and the solutions, and responsibilities of the driver and employer.

In this outcome you are asked to look in more detail at the causes of collisions, and possible ways of preventing them – from both the point of view of the driver, and of the employer of the driver.

We have already outlined some causes of collisions on page 261. We can examine some of these more closely.

Causes of and solutions to collisions

Cause – bad driving

Bad driving is either deliberately bad – for example when a driver is showing off – or careless, when a driver is not paying enough attention. Either way it can result in collisions. One of the main danger factors is speed. Speed results in more collisions, because the braking distance is greater, and more serious collisions, because the impact is greater. In addition, speed is dangerous because it gives other drivers less time to react to mistakes. The slogan 'speed kills' is entirely true.

Solutions

The solution to bad driving is to drive well. This means drivers must be properly trained, and understand driving well. They must know their priorities – which means that safety must come first. They should drive considerately, following the rules of defensive driving.

The key points of defensive driving are as follows.

1 Take care not to anger or frighten other road users.
2 Watch other road users.
3 Watch the road.
4 Watch traffic behind.
5 Look sideways when changing lanes.
6 Look round before you start.
7 Safe behaviour at traffic lights.
8 Give clear signals to other road users.
9 Only flash your headlights as a warning.
10 Only use the horn as a warning.

Drive according to the weather

11 Keep a proper space between you and the next driver.
12 Keep an eye open for all dangers and obstructions on the road.
13 Be especially careful when overtaking.
14 Take care when overtaking horses and cyclists.
15 Never cut in front of other drivers.
16 Don't let yourself get angry.
17 Drive according to the weather.
18 Never drive under the influence of alcohol or drugs.

What employers can do

Employers can do a good deal to reduce collisions by:

- ensuring that all vehicles in their fleet are in top mechanical condition; some very serious collisions have been caused by runaway lorries and other vehicles that were not roadworthy
- having systems in place to make sure lorries are safely loaded
- carefully checking that they employ good drivers
- enforcing the law about driving hours, and encouraging good driving by their employees, for example by putting signs on the backs of lorries with a phone number through which members of the public can report dangerous driving.

Cause – bad roads

Many roads have 'accident black spots' – places where accidents happen time and again. These are places such as awkward junctions or places which drivers cannot see properly. The Department of Transport is responsible for the safe design and quality of major roads, while local highways departments look after smaller roads.

Solution

The solution to accident black spots is to:

- keep proper records of where and why collisions happen
- redesign junctions, etc that are dangerous – if possible
- put up signs which warn of dangers well ahead
- use traffic calming devices such as humps and chicanes to slow traffic down
- put up traffic lights if necessary
- remove obstructions to driver's view, such as hedges and trees
- discourage the use of short-cuts ('rat runs') taken by drivers through residential areas to avoid traffic lights, etc.

COOL SITE:

There is a very interesting analysis of factors causing accidents on the Department of Transport's website at www.roads.dft.gov.uk/roadsafety/dbrgroup/02.htm

! CHECKPOINT …

How many reasons can you think of why young drivers are more likely to have collisions than older drivers?

SUPERGRADE! *Merit*

Evaluate the cost of collisions, both from a personal and financial point of view.

The table below shows the average cost of different kinds of road accident, classed by how serious they are.

FOCUS

Costs per accident by element of cost and severity for Great Britain (£) at 1998 prices				
	Accident severity			
	Fatal	**Serious**	**Slight**	**Damage**
Casualty-related costs for GB				
Lost output	399,540	16,430	1,930	
Medical/ambulance	4,730	9,840	820	
Pain, grief, suffering	794,870	111,700	9,170	
Police and damage to property costs for GB				
Police/administration	1,220	170	40	2
Damage to property				
Motorways	10,804	9,218	4,663	1,626
Rural roads	8,494	3,872	2,566	1,692
Urban roads	5,007	2,684	1,584	1,133
Total costs per accident for GB	**1,207,670**	**141,490**	**13,940**	**1,250**

Source: Scottish Executive – figures 1998

Financial costs

The table shows how the cost of an accident is calculated. Lost output means money lost because the accident victims cannot work for a period of time. If someone dies, their entire future earnings are lost.

The costs to the public services (medical, ambulance and police), though significant, are far less than the cost to the victims and their insurers. In serious collisions the vehicles involved are usually write-offs.

There is significant cost to the taxpayer in putting right the damage to roads.

Personal costs

The cost of pain, grief and suffering is calculated on the basis of insurance claims. They are hard to describe except in terms of money, because suffering is such a personal experience. The suffering caused by collisions can be as bad as any that can be imagined.

There are personal costs to rescue workers as well. Firefighters, police and ambulance workers who attend a bad collision may need counselling afterwards.

Is driving necessary?

The government already encourages people to share journeys into work, and is now trying to reduce the amount of driving done by means of developing park and ride systems near big cities, more school bus services to reduce rush-hour traffic, and more internet shopping so that people don't have to drive to supermarkets every week.

Cutting down driving reduces the number of accidents. If there are fewer cars on the road there are fewer vehicles to collide with.

SUPERGRADE! *Distinction*

> Critically evaluate the process of driving, drivers' responsibilities and the causes and costs, financial and personal, of collisions.

Is driving necessary?

The increasing pressure of traffic on the roads and the effect of traffic on the environment is making everybody – the government, ordinary people, industry and the public services – look more closely at driving and the responsibility of drivers. Because of the risks of global warming there are reasons why every country in the world should ask whether so many people should spend so much of their time driving.

Britain's good safety record

Nevertheless the rate of collisions and road accidents in general is much lower in Britain than in most other European countries. For example, Britain and France have a similar size of population and roughly the same number of cars and lorries, but over 8,000 people a year die on French roads, as opposed to 3,500 on English roads. This is despite the fact that French roads are less crowded than British roads.

Part of the reason for lower death rates on Britain's roads seems to be that the roads are so crowded that most drivers can't go fast most of the time, so collisions are less serious. There are also more road safety campaigns in Britain, and stiffer penalties for drink-driving. In any case, the culture of Britain is different and people are less likely to drink with their meals. A further factor is that Britain's roads are wider than French roads, and not lined with trees or old buildings which people can easily crash into.

Who are the dangerous drivers?

Young drivers have more accidents than older drivers. This is partly due to inexperience, since inexperienced drivers of any age have more collisions than experienced drivers. But all young drivers are inexperienced in the sense that they are still young. This is one major reason why young drivers have more collisions. But there may be psychological reasons – especially where young men are concerned. The culture of young men encourages excitement, risk-taking – and fast driving. Young men have fast reflexes, but the drivers they collide with may not.

The main danger of cannabis is that it distorts people's sense of distance

Drivers who drive under the influence of drugs and alcohol are much more dangerous than other drivers. The main danger of cannabis is that it distorts people's sense of distance and therefore increases the risk of road accidents. Alcohol impairs judgement and affects a driver's mood, and is still the cause of many accidents. Young drivers now drink less than they used to: the main group of drink drivers now are middle-aged men who think they can take their drink.

Women are safer drivers than men.

Costs of collisions

We have seen from the statistics above that the financial and personal costs of collisions are very great. But they are nothing compared to the importance of driving to the economy and to people's personal lives.

For this reason there is a limit to what people are prepared to do to stop collisions from happening. The government is prepared to make roads safer, and the car industry is prepared to make vehicles safer. In recent years the driving test has been made more difficult, by adding a theory paper – and only 43 per cent of people tested in a given period of time pass the test. But to stop accidents and collisions you would have to ban all traffic – and nobody is going to do that in the foreseeable future.

PASSGRADE

Explain the role of the Health and Safety Executive and the emergency services in collisions, comparing national and local involvement in road safety campaigns.

LINK! See more about the Health and Safety Executive on page 102.

The role of the HSE

The Health and Safety Executive is an organisation that was set up by the government as part of the Health and Safety at Work Act 1974 to ensure that workplaces were as safe as possible. The Executive is concerned with collisions where drivers or others are 'at work' – in other words driving for a living.

The following is part of a statement from the HSE about its role in reducing or investigating collisions.

FOCUS

Each year about 3,500 people are killed on our roads and 40,000 are seriously injured. Each one results in terrible pain and suffering. A significant proportion of these deaths and injuries can be connected with work. Accidents involving heavy goods vehicles, buses, company car and van drivers, and despatch riders are obvious examples. Pedestrians at work such as postal workers, refuse collectors or utility workers are also at risk from traffic.

The Task Group

The number of at-work road deaths could number over 300, more than the figure for deaths in workplaces. [The HSE has set up] a Task Group to recommend measures to reduce at-work road traffic incidents. The Terms of Reference for the Group are to:

- establish accurate casualty and incident statistics for work-related activities on or near roads;

- establish the main causes and methods of preventing at-work road traffic incidents;

- promote a public debate on best practice in relation to preventing at-work road traffic incidents;

- agree minimum management standards for employers, the self-employed and others for work-related journeys and other work activities on the highway;

- propose, if possible non-legislative, ways to bring together road traffic law with health and safety at work law;

- propose ways in which those who enforce road traffic law and those who enforce health and safety at work law can work together.

The Group includes representatives from the Police, Traffic Commissioners, employers, workers, safety professionals, local authorities, driving standards, passenger transport, motorcyclists, freight transport, motorists and policy makers.

Source: HSE

The role of the emergency services in collisions

The three main emergency services dealing with road collisions are the police, the fire service and the ambulance service.

The police

Drivers have a duty to inform the police if they have had a collision, however slight. If the accident is a minor one and there are no injuries reported, only the police will attend. Their role in a minor collision is to:

- ensure that no one is injured
- ensure that the collision area is safe
- warn other drivers and direct them appropriately
- take statements from witnesses and drivers
- give advice or reassurance if needed
- make a record of the position of the vehicles after the collision
- make a preliminary breathalyser test if drink-driving is suspected
- ascertain whether drugs might be involved
- decide who, if anybody, is to blame for the collision
- decide whether any charges should be brought.

The fire service

In a serious collision, i.e. if there are injuries, or if people are trapped, or if there is fire or a risk of fire, the 999 service should be used and all three blue light services will attend. The role of the fire service is:

- to prevent further injury or death by warning other drivers and getting people out of the way, if possible
- to put out any fires, and deal with other serious hazards such as chemical spills
- to rescue people trapped in vehicles. To do this they use special cutting and separating equipment. Unless there is an immediate risk of fire or explosion the fire service will give emergency aid to injured people, e.g. fluid, painkillers, etc, and try to stabilise their condition before cutting them out; they have to take great

care that they do not make injuries worse while doing this

- to work with paramedics
- to help with accident investigation.

The ambulance service

The role of the ambulance service is:

- to sort out the casualties, if there are many of them, and make sure the most urgent care goes to those who most need it; this process is called 'triage'
- to give primary medical care, as quickly as possible (i.e. in the 'golden hour'); this may save life more effectively than rushing a badly injured person straight to hospital
- to rush people to hospital as soon as their conditions are stabilised
- to treat people who are suffering from shock – and take them to hospital
- to remove dead bodies (in collaboration with the police) to a morgue.

!■ **CHECKPOINT …**
Talk to people in any of the 'blue light' services about their role in a collision.

National and local involvement in road safety campaigns

For many years road safety campaigns have been used to make driving safer. The organisations involved in these campaigns include:

- central government (collecting information and organising national campaigns)
- local government (local campaigns)
- advertising agencies (they provide words and images for campaigns)
- public services such as the police, fire service and bus companies (they provide information about road dangers and help to spread leaflets and educate the public)
- organisations such as the Health and Safety Executive (pay for and organise research into dangers)

- charities such as RoSPA – the Royal Society for the Prevention of Accidents – (research and publicise dangers).

Road safety campaigns are a form of advertising and they highlight road safety problems and try to make people more aware of them. Like advertising, road safety campaigns use psychological techniques – such as shock tactics or humour – to get themselves noticed and remembered.

National

National road safety campaigns change from year to year or month to month so that people don't get tired of them. They may be seasonal – for example, anti drink-drive campaigns are usually run before Christmas, when more people are tempted to drink and drive. They are organised by the Department of Transport. National campaigns normally use high-profile media like television to get the message across, though many safety leaflets are produced on a national scale as well.

You don't think you'll kill someone, so think about 6 months in prison.

What will it take to stop you drink driving?

THINK!

Drive under the influence of alcohol or drugs and you will also face a 12 month ban and a fine of up to £5000.

Source: Department for Transport

Local

Local road safety campaigns are organised and financed by local authorities. They may concentrate on particular accident blackspots – for example, notices saying 'This is a kidzone' placed at the entrance to an estate. Local road safety campaigns often concentrate on the risk to children. This is because Britain's record – though better than most countries for road accidents as a whole – is bad when it comes to accidents to children.

Media used

Road safety campaigns use various media to get their message across. These include:

- television
- radio
- posters
- newspapers and magazines
- leaflets
- stickers
- the internet.

Television, radio and newspapers also carry many news stories about collisions and other road accidents. Often these stories give information about the cause of the accident, which would have the effect of warning motorists about dangers on the roads.

C👓L SITES:

www.think.dft.gov.uk/drinkdrive/

www.think.dft.gov.uk/campaigns/index.htm

www.lhc.org.uk/members/pubs/factsht/74fact.pdf

www.hants.gov.uk/roadsafety/

www.solihull.gov.uk/wwwes/roadsafety.htm

 **SUPERGRADE!** *Merit*

Assess the importance of local and national campaigns in accident prevention.

The importance of both local and national road safety campaigns can be seen in the increasing number and variety of campaigns. Forty years ago when the first campaigns came out they were few and far between – and usually only appeared in the run-up to Christmas. Now they are a multi-million pound industry involving both the public and private sector.

Road safety campaigns are linked to a greatly increased use of signs, road markings, traffic lights and other 'street furniture' associated with safety. In addition they are backed up by increasing numbers of traffic laws, designed to improve road safety. There are far more traffic police and a much greater awareness of road safety on the part of vehicle manufacturers, who carry out research on collisions using dummies, pigs and (in France) dead bodies.

Because of the large number of children killed on British roads, many safety campaigns, especially local ones, are targeted at children. Road safety is taught in schools, and leaflets and websites explaining safety in words and styles that appeal to children of different ages are being distributed by many local authorities. Cute images – such as cartoon hedgehogs – are used. New kinds of road safety campaign are being invented all the time, to try to reach parts of the population that haven't yet been reached, or to overcome the boredom that happens when the same campaign runs on and on without changing.

C👓L SITE:

www.badjobs.co.uk

There is no doubt that road safety campaigns are important, because there are so many of them, but it is harder to know how effective they are. This is what we shall look at in the next outcome.

Critically evaluate the success or failure of a local and a national campaign in accident prevention.

Local campaign

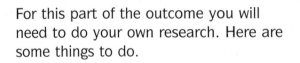

For this part of the outcome you will need to do your own research. Here are some things to do.

Research

- Choose a local road safety campaign – preferably one linked to a particular area such as an estate, or a town centre.
- If you don't know what your local safety campaigns are, ask the police. They will have a road safety officer who will be able to help you, or who will know where you can get help.
- Consider contacting the local council or any local safety organisations.

- Take a wide view of what a road safety campaign is. It might involve speed cameras, new lights or street crossings, parking restrictions, introducing one-way systems or traffic calming devices, CCTV, leaflets, posters on buses or hoardings, stickers, cycling proficiency tests, police visits to schools, adverts on local radio or in local newspapers, changes in sentencing at magistrates courts – and so on.
- If you have any doubts about whether you have chosen the right kind of campaign, check with your tutor before you have done too much work!
- Get information about local accident statistics before and after the road safety campaign you have chosen.
- Ask the police what changes in accident rates have happened as a result of the campaign you have chosen to study.

Evaluation

Your critical evaluation of a local campaign might take the form of a report or a presentation. It should contain some or all of the following features.

Introduction

- Describe the main features of the campaign.
- Say where you got your information from, or how you did your research.

Critical evaluation

- Try to find out how much your local road safety campaign cost.
- Where did the money come from – the local taxpayer, private business, or some other source?

- Are ordinary people (or local councillors) in favour of the scheme?
- Is there any statistical evidence that accident rates have gone down since the campaign started?
- Do the police think the campaign is working?

Conclusions

Your aim in this outcome is to relate the cost of the campaign with its success. Your conclusions might include the following points.

- A campaign which costs little but reduces accidents must be a success.
- A campaign which costs a lot and has little or no success is a failure.
- Any reduction in the rate of collisions, accidents or injuries is a good thing.
- Some safety campaigns such as speed humps are disliked by motorists because they damage cars.
- Some more things might need to be done, e.g. opening playing fields so that children don't have to play in the street.

National campaign

Mobile phones

FOCUS

No driver should use a mobile telephone or any similar piece of telecommunications equipment (whether hand-held or hands free) while driving. Such use is likely to distract the driver from the main task of managing the vehicle in a safe and competent manner and be prejudicial to road safety. Calls should not be made or received while on the move.

Source: RoSPA

The law says ...

Drivers must have proper control of their vehicles at all times. You can also be prosecuted for careless or inconsiderate driving, or even dangerous driving, if using a phone causes you to drive in this way. The penalties include an unlimited fine, disqualification and up to two years imprisonment. It can also be an offence for employers to require their employees to use mobile phones while driving.

Source: www.think.dft.gov.uk/mobile/

The national campaign to try to stop drivers making or receiving phone calls while driving is an interesting one. There is little evidence that it has worked. On almost any road trip you can see drivers talking on the phone while they are driving.

There have been a few high-profile prosecutions by the police of people who are driving while talking on the phone, but it normally becomes an issue only when it is clear that an accident – or dangerous driving – has been caused by the fact that a driver was on the phone. Scientific experiments have been carried out which show that phone calls distract drivers and slow their reaction time. (This is true whether the phones are hand-held or not.) But the law itself does not prohibit the use of a mobile phone in the car.

The Department for Transport – the government department in charge of road safety – says that it is a good thing to have a mobile phone in the car. It can be useful in emergencies and provides protection when travelling alone, and at night. This undermines the idea that you shouldn't use a mobile phone in the car; nevertheless mobile phones should only be used when the vehicle is stationary.

The mobile phone industry is a vast one, and nearly everybody wants a mobile phone. The prosperity of Britain and many other countries depends on its electronic industry, and mobile phones have been one of the most profitable branches of that industry. If governments start banning the use of mobile phones in cars it could cause economic problems and unemployment. And since the police would have to enforce any laws, it would greatly add to their workload, and reduce their popularity with drivers – a large and important section of the population.

The safety campaign to stop people using mobile phones in cars is therefore unsuccessful at present. But it may have stopped some people from using phones in their cars and lorries – and may well have saved some lives.

Prepare a road safety strategy for your locality.

Local road safety strategies are a popular new idea for getting people involved in road safety and at the same time improving the environment. They can be linked to other plans for improving the local quality of life – such as Neighbourhood Watch.

The government is encouraging local road safety strategies under the heading of 'home zones'. These were put forward in the Transport Act 2000 (England and Wales) – a new law.

The following is an example of some points to be considered in preparing local road safety strategies.

FOCUS

Home Zones should have these key design features in order to be successful:

- The desired speed within the Home Zone should be decided from the start; 10 mph is a recommended speed limit. Speed should be self-enforced within the design, using chicanes, planters and parking positions to slow speeds.

- Lack of separate raised pavements.

- Surface treatments suited to a pedestrian environment that blur the distinction between road space and social space.

- Traffic calming features should not be more than thirty metres apart.

- Road lane width of three metres with four and a half metres for passing vehicles at intervals.

- Use of trees, planting, and street furniture to define and screen car parking.

- Use of bollards and street lighting to define space.

- Gateways at entrance with the Home Zone entry and exit signs.

- Parking/landscape features that don't allow vehicles too close to residential buildings.

- Controlled parking zones are valuable tools for controlling the location of parked cars, and are essential in areas where there is parking pressure. Parking spaces should be clearly defined in the design of streets.

- High proportion of homes with an active front onto the street with few or no front gardens.

- Stopping sight distance of twelve metres maximum; longer views encourage drivers to increase speed.

Source: Department for Transport

Remember to choose a suitable locality. A few streets should be enough. If the area is too big your strategy will get too complicated.

If you know a place where a safety strategy has already been carried out, visit it and make notes.

Contact your local authority to see what schemes they have set up and how they work.

Talk to the police about local road safety strategies.

Think of the kinds of local support you would need – residents, police, etc.

Use maps and plans. You could photocopy the street maps, enlarge them, and then add your own alterations.

If you are doing a presentation, think of visual aids, and ways to persuade an audience to get more interested in the idea of a local road safety strategy.

Below are various websites and links to give you further ideas and information.

C👓L SITES:

www.roads.dft.gov.uk/roadsafety/
safeside/03/index.htm

www.hants.gov.uk/environment/ltp/
section5/rdsafety/1.html

www.local-transport.dft.gov.uk/
walk/walka.htm#aa1

www.sustrans.org.uk

www.homezonenews.org.uk

www.homezoneschallenge.com (site of the 61 Home Zones challenge)

www.ncb.org.uk/cpc (Children's Play Council)

www.transport2000.org.uk

Monitor the success or failure of local campaigns.

There are various ways to monitor (check) the success of local safety campaigns.

1 Find out whether people have heard of it. If they haven't, it's not working. If people know a lot about it, it may be working well.

2 Find out whether people like the campaign. You can do this by asking local residents, or even going round with a questionnaire. If the campaign consists, say, of road-bumps or speed cameras, or the threat of wheel-clamping, it may be very unpopular. If it's popular, the idea is probably working well. If it's unpopular, it may be only unpopular with bad drivers, or people who like speeding. In that case it's working.

3 Ask the police or a road safety expert if the campaign is working. If you do this you will get an expert's opinion. But it may be that the expert doesn't know whether it's working or not.

4 Try to get accident statistics for the area for both before and after the campaign. If accident figures have gone down, and if there have been fewer collisions, the campaign is working. (Even so, it may not be working as well as everybody hoped!)

5 You could spend some time at the roadside in the area covered by the campaign, watching the traffic. Do vehicles (or pedestrians) seem to be doing what the campaign wants them to do, e.g. driving slowly? If lorries are excluded, are they keeping out of the area, or are they still using it?

6 Get information from local newspapers about the campaign and whether it is considered successful. This may mean looking up the paper on the internet and going through the archives.

C👓L SITE:

www.roads.dft.gov.uk/roadsafety/
goodpractice/06.htm#2

Explain the different attitudes and behaviour of drivers and why they are prone to attitudinal behaviour.

We have all heard drivers swearing at other drivers, and seen drivers making rude gestures through the windscreen. There is a reason for this. Drivers are human. And, being human, they are all different.

They show their differences in *attitude* (their feelings about driving and other drivers) and in *behaviour* (the way they drive and their communication with other road users).

Some research on driver attitudes and behaviour has been done at Huddersfield University.

Findings include the fact that company car drivers are twice as likely to have collisions as other drivers. Researchers also found that:

'Company car drivers are the most likely to speed, tailgate (drive too close), use alcohol and drive, show aggression, take risks, lose concentration and hold their mobile phone whilst driving, as well as

park in illegal places. They also have the worst lane discipline (particularly excessive use of the outside lane on motorways) and commit more traffic offences (particularly speeding and illegal parking).'

Their other research findings show that:

- road rage is caused by tailgating, queue-jumping, aggressive driving, 'hogging the overtaking lane', passing on the inside and driving too slowly
- one in five drivers has some form of defective eyesight.

The Department of Transport has also researched these issues and found that:

- gender, age and lack of experience make collisions more likely
- male drivers have more serious crashes
- young drivers have more fatal accidents
- inexperienced drivers have more accidents
- violations (deliberate law-breaking such as drink-driving or racing other drivers) cause many collisions. Errors and mistakes, though dangerous, are much less likely to cause collisions.

Some explanations of these findings are as follows.

- Company car drivers have bad attitudes and behaviour because they drive for too long, get tired and impatient, and are not driving their own cars.
- Road rage causes bad driving, and bad driving causes road rage. It is 'a vicious spiral'.
- Male drivers are attracted to speed for hormonal and cultural reasons. Although, mile for mile, they do not have many more collisions than female drivers, their crashes tend to be more serious.
- Young drivers suffer more fatalities because: (a) they are young and reckless; (b) they are inexperienced; and (c) they drive older cars which are mechanically less safe and give less protection in a crash.

CL SITES:

www.roads.dft.gov.uk/roadsafety

Driving Standards Agency

www.dsa.gov.uk/

DVLA

www.dvla.gov.uk

Accidents

www.rospa.co.uk/

Unit 14 Expedition Skills

Grading criteria

To achieve a pass grade the evidence must show that the learner is able to:	To achieve a merit grade the evidence must show that the learner is able to:	To achieve a distinction grade the evidence must show that the learner is able to:
● explain leadership, interpersonal and organisation skills needed when taking part in a multi-day expedition **276**	● analyse the planning and preparation required for a multi-day expedition **282**	● evaluate the planning and preparation required for a multi-day expedition, justifying the preparation required to fulfil and achieve objectives **284**
● contribute to the planning and preparation required for a multi-day expedition **279**	● explain own roles and responsibilities and those of other team members whilst participating in a multi-day expedition **287**	● justify own roles and responsibilities and those of other team members whilst participating in a multi-day expedition **288**
● identify and list the equipment required for a multi-day expedition **280**	● describe individual performance and that of group members, identifying weaknesses and areas for improvement **290**	● critically evaluate individual performance and that of group members, identifying weaknesses and areas for improvement **292**
● participate in a multi-day expedition, identifying own roles and responsibilities **285**		
● record individual performance and that of group members, identifying strengths and weaknesses **289**		

'Expedition' comes from an old word meaning 'going out on foot', but now it means any adventurous or strenuous journey lasting more than a day. In the wildest parts of the world such as the Arctic, the Antarctic, the great deserts, and parts of Africa and South America, expeditions can be carried out in vehicles, and on the oceans an expedition could use a motor boat. But most expeditions demand physical effort, and use alternative forms of transport such as sailing boats, horseback, canoes, bicycles, skis or foot.

Much of the training in the armed forces consists of expeditions. Long-distance skiing in Norway or Canada, river journeys in kayaks, survival exercises in Kenya – these are expeditions using a range of special skills. These skills, which are mainly to do with travelling, survival and teamwork, are expedition skills.

In other public services expedition skills are not an essential feature of the work. But expeditions are used, in non-uniformed public services, education and industry, as an excellent way of developing team spirit and motivation. Running expeditions is a multi-million pound industry, and the people who go on these expeditions get value for money.

If you do this unit you too will go on an expedition. There might be a bit of effort and discomfort and you might get wet and cold. If you aren't used to the outdoor life, it might seem a little masochistic at first. But stick with it, and you'll find you enjoy it. You'll make friends, gain new experiences, have a few thrills and spills, and a lot of laughs. And you'll come out more confident and self-assured than you were when you went in.

PASSGRADE

> Explain leadership, interpersonal and organisation skills needed when taking part in a multi-day expedition.

Expeditions can be dangerous, and good leadership is essential.

For this unit your leaders will be qualified professionals, many of whom have specific qualifications in expedition, survival and leadership skills. If you understand and follow their instructions nothing much should go wrong.

But you will also be asked to do supervised group activities which will give you a chance to develop your own leadership, interpersonal and organisation skills.

> **LINK!** These skills are discussed in detail in Unit 2, pages 33–34.

Leadership skills in multi-day expeditions

1 Hard skills

Leaders need to have 'hard skills' – these are the technical skills and knowledge to run an expedition. Examples of hard skills are:

- how to use caving and potholing equipment
- being able to do safety procedures in a canoe
- being able to survive a night out in a blizzard using the correct equipment
- being able to find your way around a mountain in thick fog
- pitching a tent correctly without having to look at the instructions
- knowing the best thing to do in an emergency.

2 Soft skills

Leaders also need 'soft skills'. These are to do with understanding the team and working effectively with them. Examples of soft skills are:

- being able to give instructions before an abseil so that people know what they have to do and don't feel too scared to attempt the exercise
- encouraging someone who has never done a rock-climb before to have a go
- cheering up someone who is feeling homesick
- knowing how long to spend on an activity before people get bored, tired, cold or wet.

Interpersonal skills

Cooperation – the willingness and skills to work with other people in order to make a team effort a success.

Understanding – being able to look at people and, through what they say or their body language, have an insight into what they are really thinking and feeling; an example of this is understanding how far a group can walk in a day by assessing their fitness and motivation.

Patience – the ability to wait for other people to complete what they are doing. A leader with good 'hard skills' may get impatient and 'ratty' with people who are less skilled. This kind of impatience would show a weakness in interpersonal skills.

Motivation – the ability to make other people keen and enthusiastic. This can be done by humour, liveliness, commitment and offering appropriate rewards (usually praise).

Working as a member of a team – good listening skills, the willingness to help others, putting forward ideas – and so on.

 LINK! There's plenty about teamwork on page 28 onwards.

LINK! Interpersonal skills are soft skills. They are discussed in detail on pages 33–34.

Organisational planning

The planning for an expedition – which is the responsibility of the expedition leader(s) – includes the following.

- Researching or visiting the area where the expedition is to take place, and carrying out a risk assessment to find out what special dangers there might be, and how those dangers can be controlled or reduced.
- Planning finances, i.e. working out the overall cost, deciding who is to pay for it, when and how.
- Deciding who is to be in charge, and how closely other expedition members will need to be supervised. (If the expedition consists of experienced people very little supervision may be needed. But if people are inexperienced or

vulnerable in any way, there will have to be much more supervision.)
- Ensuring that activity leaders are fully qualified.
- Planning activities which are safe and appropriate yet challenging for the people going on the expedition.
- Preparing the expedition members and informing them of what they will need to bring with them.
- Getting written consent for the expedition (from parents or guardians if expedition members are under 18, or from members themselves if they are 18 or over).
- Getting information about people's medical needs and health, so that everybody who goes on the expedition is fit enough to carry out the activities, and so that organisers know if anybody can or should be exempted. Contact numbers for doctors should be obtained.
- Arranging insurance which is suitable for the activities (for example, insurance for skiing is more expensive than insurance for hill-walking).
- Arranging transport to the expedition base or starting-point.
- Planning a range of emergency procedures for things that might go wrong, e.g. bad weather, illness or injury.
- Arranging activities for evenings or other spare time.
- Organising all documentation and keeping records secure.

Navigation skills

LINK! There is information on map-reading, grid references, contours and some aspects of compass use in Unit 9: Land Navigation with Map and Compass, starting on page 179.

There are some extra navigation skills which are useful on long expeditions – or in orienteering exercises. These are as follows.

Handrailing – following a feature such as a stream, ridge or wall which is marked on the map and goes in the direction you want to go in.

Aiming-off – this means not taking the shortest distance to your objective, but taking the route which is least likely to get you lost. This may mean going to the left (or right) of your target destination till you reach a track which you know leads to it. If you went straight towards the destination and you reached the track you might not know which way to turn on the track to reach your destination.

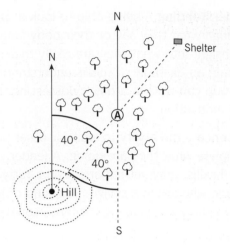

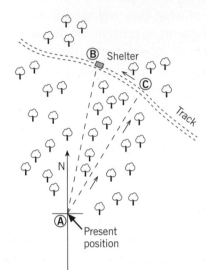

Aiming off

It is better to go from A→C→B than A→B.
A→B means walking further through the forest, and if you reach the track and cannot see the shelter, you won't know whether to turn left or right.
A→C→B is longer but you are less likely to get lost.

Attack points – landmarks which you visit on the way to your target.

Catching features – landmarks which are beyond your destination but which show that you are walking in the right direction. (If you reach the catching feature it means you have gone too far and ought to turn round!)

Tick-off features – landmarks which you pass (on your left or right) on your way to your target.

Backbearings – these are landmarks behind you which you aim away from (using compass bearings) to get to a destination which is in front of you.

Relocation techniques – these are ways of finding where you are if you are lost. In England and Wales the simplest and best relocation technique, in thick fog or darkness, is walking downhill until you reach a stream, then following the stream down. Another technique is to retrace your steps to the last place where you definitely knew where you were.

Backbearings

Backbearings are used if you can see where you are coming from, but not where you are going to.
From A to the shelter the bearing is 040.
The bearing of the hill behind you is 220.
By checking that this stays at 220 you can ensure that you are walking in a straight line towards your destination (the shelter).

Navigate your way through the Web to these cool sites!

CL SITES:

www.air-cadets.org.uk/aircadets/admin/acps/ACP%2032%20Volume%202-Basic%20Nav.pdf
www.go4awalk.com/bunk/tales/gnashjargon.htm
www.rankin.com.au/navigat1.htm
http://users.ox.ac.uk/~oxdoe/navigation1.html

PASSGRADE

> Contribute to the planning and preparation required for a multi-day expedition.

In Expedition Skills it is likely that your expedition will be organised by your college. It will probably take the form of a few days' camping or staying at an outdoor centre. The overall planning will therefore be done by the college. But you will need to make your own contribution as well. This will mean doing the following.

Planning your expedition

1 Find out where you are going

Find out when you are going, where you are going, and how long you will be staying there. If you are under 18, or living with your parents, make sure your parents know where you're going – and show them all the forms, letters and other documents you may be given at college.

2 Money

Sort out the money! You will need money:

(a) to pay the people running your expedition; this may be your college, the army, a private provider or some other organisation

Your honour, he was trying to raise money for his residential.

(b) for your own food and clothing, and equipment if you are taking your own tent, cooking utensils, stove etc.

If you think you are going to have problems paying for your expedition, see your tutor or the organiser as soon as possible to discuss the problem. (It may help if the discussion is private.)

3 Accommodation

Plan with your colleagues/classmates if you are going to be sharing a tent or working as a group. Get to know them and make sure you get on with them. You may want to pool your food resources and plan meals, etc together. This is certainly a good idea if you are sharing a tent.

4 Food

Buy food – if you are expected to provide it yourself. Before you buy food, you need to know:

- how long the expedition is
- what time of year it will be
- whether you will be staying near any shops
- what kind of cooking facilities you will be using
- whether you will need to provide your own packed lunches.

If your expedition is being planned by an organisation like the army, they may well provide all the food.

The food you buy must be:

- **easy to carry**, *if you are going to carry it*. This means that 'dry' food like oatmeal, dried milk, raisins, chocolate, cheese, etc should be taken. (You can last many days on those items, and they weigh very little.) If you are not going to carry your food, you have far more choice.
- **high in energy** – especially carbohydrates. Bread, potatoes, rice and beans will give you plenty of energy, steadily through the day, and will not make you put on weight if you are active.
- **easy to cook**. Cooking in tents is hard work and you don't want to spend any longer doing it than you have to. Items such as bread, dried potatoes and baked beans are good from this point of view. Food that doesn't need cooking, but gives

plenty of energy, such as sardines, is useful. Other people prefer a good fry-up with sausages, etc. If you are staying in a centre, you may well be sharing a kitchen. It is best to have food you can cook quickly so that other groups also have time to use the stoves and cook their meals. If you haven't got time to cook vegetables you can eat bananas, apples and oranges instead.

5 Clothes

Sort out your clothes. If you are carrying clothes in a rucksack, you can't take very many. But it is vital that you are able to keep warm. The following is a list for four days which you could carry on your back (but it might not be enough in midwinter or on high mountains):

- two changes of underwear
- two changes of shirts
- two pairs of trousers (jogging-bottom types)
- three fleeces or pullovers
- two pairs of thick socks
- one pair of leggings
- woolly hat
- waterproof top and leggings
- one pair of gloves.

If the weather is likely to be cold put in extra thermal T-shirts. To keep warm on an expedition it is better to have many light layers of clothing than a few heavy layers of clothing.

For footwear, if you are camping, one pair of boots is all you need. They should be waterproof, and you must test them beforehand to make sure they don't give you blisters. Walking boots should be a size bigger than your normal shoes, e.g. size 9 instead of 8 – and you should wear two pairs of socks with them.

If you are staying in an outdoor centre, or returning to the same place every night, you can take extra clothes, food and other equipment because you will not be carrying them far.

6 Other belongings to take

- A torch
- A tin opener

- Knife, fork and spoon
- Plastic cup and plate
- Pen, pencil and notebook
- Pocket money
- Water bottle
- Completed consent forms, etc (if you haven't given them in already!)

If your expedition is not arranged by the college you should also take:

- first aid – especially dressings for blisters, bandages, antiseptic ointment
- a small pocket knife
- map, compass, whistle
- money
- watch
- travel tickets
- two bin liners.

Optional items:

- mobile phone
- camera
- walkman.

Don't take anything valuable which could get lost or damaged.

PASSGRADE

Identify and list the equipment needed for a multi-day expedition.

skill POWER

Listing equipment is easy, but the list must be complete and well laid out.

Identifying equipment means (a) researching what equipment you need; and (b) knowing what the equipment is. For example, if you think that gaiters are something you wear on your head, then you have not identified them!

Personal equipment

This is equipment which you are likely to own yourself, and which you could take from home. It is listed above, under the previous outcome. It includes clothes, footwear and personal belongings.

On a BTEC First course the personal belongings you are expected to bring with you on an expedition will be much the same wherever your expedition is (if it is in Britain).

Specialist equipment

This is equipment which is used for activities done on expeditions. This may be loaned to you by the organisers of your expedition. The specialist equipment you need depends on the type of expedition you are going on, where it is, and the activities you will be doing.

You should be able to get full information on specialist equipment from the organisers of your expedition. An example of the kind of information you need for this outcome is given in the section on hill walking below.

Hill walking

Walking boots. These are strongly-made boots with soles that will protect your feet and grip steep slopes. They protect the ankle from twists and sprains. Good boots are expensive, and if you do not want to walk regularly you should try to borrow some from the expedition organisers. Wellies are a cheap alternative if they fit you but may be slippery on steep grassy slopes. Walking boots should be a size bigger than your normal shoes.

Socks. Thick wool socks are the best. You should wear two pairs.

Thermal underwear. Thermal vests and T-shirts are light and give a lot of warmth. They can be worn at night, in tents, instead of pyjamas.

Fleeces. These warm, light, elastic garments are worn as pullovers. They work best if you wear something windproof over them, as a 'shell'.

Waterproof jacket. These are expensive and can often be borrowed from organisers. The best ones are made of breathable fabrics; cheaper ones may be waterproof but cause condensation – so you get damp anyway. Waterproof jackets are also windproof.

Waterproof trousers. These are normally cheap leggings that you pull on over your other trousers. They protect against heavy rain and wet vegetation.

Gaiters. These are tubular waterproofs which stop water and snow from getting into your boots. They are essential on wet, snowy days on the mountain.

Rucksack. A day-sack is a small rucksack in which you carry a packed lunch and spare clothing. An expedition sack holds at least 60 litres and has attachments for carrying things like tents and sleeping bags. Good rucksacks are expensive to buy, and it is likely that you will be able to borrow them from your expedition organisers.

Rucksack liner. A waterproof sack to put round your clothes in a rucksack. A bin-liner will do, as long as it's not torn.

Compass.

LINK! See page 189.

Flask/hydration system. Many people, including the army, feel it is good for morale to have a hot drink on the mountains, and so they carry thermos flasks. If the weather is hot, plenty of water should be carried to avoid dehydration. Soft drinks are also good, since they contain glucose for energy, but avoid carrying heavy glass bottles.

Food. Sandwiches, cake, cheese and chocolate are good for a midday packed lunch. If you need food for several days cut down the weight by carrying dried food (see page 279).

Watch. It should be cheap, reliable, not too heavy and have a fresh battery.

Trowel. Useful in a camp if there are no toilets. But on the hills you can dig a hole with your boot, or place a stone on top of the result.

Map. Absolutely necessary in country you don't know. 1:25,000 is the best scale for walkers in Britain – though 1:50,000 is quite usable.

Whistle. A loud plastic whistle is the best.

Head torch. Used for potholing rather than hill walking.

Survival bag. You will probably not need one for your BTEC First expedition. A survival bag is typically a big orange sack made of heavy-duty polythene. With a survival bag and a sleeping bag you can sleep out without a tent in most weathers. If you are tall check that your survival bag is long enough for you!

Camping equipment

For this unit it is likely that camping equipment will be provided by your college or by the organisers of your expedition. But if you intend to use your own equipment, make sure it's suitable.

Tents

Most expedition tents are ridge or dome tents. Dome tents are used the most. If you are carrying a tent it must be light, give good protection and be easy to pitch and dismantle. Most tents have two layers, an inner tent and an outer flysheet, to protect against rain – and a sewn-in groundsheet, to protect against draughts and insects. You will find good technical information on tents on the internet.

C**OO**L SITES:

www.antarctica.co.uk/

www.amg-outdoor.co.uk/lichfield/

Sleeping bags

These are like duvets shaped in the form of a sack. They have 'tog' ratings for insulation, so if you are camping in cold weather check that your bag is warm enough. In any British weather you will be cold if you try to camp without a sleeping bag.

Stoves

Most campers use stoves – though they are not strictly necessary. They work mainly with butane or methylated spirit. Stoves are best used outside the tent – as they can cause fires. Practise using them before you go on your camping expedition.

C**OO**L SITE:

www.gear-zone.co.uk/acatalog/
Online_Catalogue_Stoves_56.html

Carry-mats

These light plastic mats go under the sleeping bag to stop the cold from striking up from the ground. They weigh very little and add to your comfort, especially in areas like Scotland where the ground is always wet.

> **! CHECKPOINT ...**
> Research the equipment needed for other kinds of expedition, e.g. pony-trekking, rafting, sailing, cycling or caving. Make lists and brief explanations like the ones given above.

SUPERGRADE! *Merit*

> Analyse the planning and preparation required for a multi-day expedition.

Planning for a multi-day expedition has to be appropriate for the kind of expedition you are carrying out. It depends on:

- who is going (age, interests, numbers, etc)
- how long you are going for
- where you are going
- how experienced, motivated and fit everybody is
- what the main activities will be (a kayak or a cycling expedition is clearly different from a walking expedition)

- what time of year it is
- what the weather is likely to be
- what kind of back-up you have (e.g. how you're getting to the expedition area and whether you'll have vehicles to back you up when you get there)
- the amount of money available
- the real purpose of the expedition (e.g. pleasure, team-building, exploring).

General rules

General rules are as follows:

- the greater the number of people going, the greater the planning needed
- the longer the expedition lasts, the more planning you need
- the further you go, the more you need to plan, and the more it will cost
- the more experienced and motivated you are, the easier the planning will be
- the planning must be geared to the main activity
- expeditions in winter or in bad weather need more planning – for both safety and comfort
- planning is easier if you have vehicles to back you up, or if you are staying in a centre; if you are carrying everything on your back, and going from A to B, planning is more difficult
- if there are money problems they should be sorted out well in advance to avoid worry or disappointment
- the planning should maximise the benefit to the individuals going on the expedition.

Safety

Whatever happens, expeditions should be safe. Never take unnecessary risks. Safety planning includes:

- making sure that everybody going on the expedition is well and fit
- being aware of any disabilities or medical problems
- ensuring that weaker members are looked after and helped where necessary
- ensuring that everybody has the right clothing, footwear and equipment

- ensuring that equipment is in good condition and working order
- ensuring that people know how to use their equipment, e.g. pitch tents and use stoves
- planning for possible bad weather, including contingency plans, e.g. getting off mountains or out of caves and making contact with the emergency services
- ensuring that first aid skills and equipment will be available
- carrying out a risk assessment to ensure that routes and activities are safe and suitable for the people doing them
- making parents, partners or relatives aware of what is planned
- planning evening activities if necessary to keep people occupied
- giving training to inexperienced expedition members about safe and environmentally acceptable behaviour, and about resolving possible conflicts.

Enjoyment

Expeditions should be enjoyable. Expedition planning should:

- take into account the age, abilities and interests of expedition members
- give choices and responsibility wherever possible (without risking safety)
- combine discipline and freedom
- be planned in a way that avoids any risk of discrimination, dangerous horseplay, harassment or bullying
- enable people to learn and experience outdoor activities which they may not have known about before
- allow for cultural differences such as special dietary requirements
- develop an informed love of the countryside.

Be environment friendly

Expeditions should respect the environment. Inexperienced members should be trained in litter disposal, the avoidance of fire risks, toilet procedures, and the country code (see page 197).

 *Distinction*

> Evaluate the planning and preparation required for a multi-day expedition, justifying the preparation required to fulfil and achieve objectives.

For this outcome you need to show that you understand how important expedition planning is, and know the reasons for the preparation you have to do.

Objectives

The objectives for an expedition are some or all of the following:

- to travel certain distances and reach certain places – by whatever means of travel the expedition uses; for example the objectives might be to kayak down a river from A to B, to climb a mountain, to walk 10 or 15 miles
- to develop certain technical skills such as climbing, caving, skiing, canoeing, navigation, mountain biking, hill-walking and campcraft
- to carry out investigation or research (e.g. about wildlife, geography or weather)
- to develop individual, teamwork and social skills.

These objectives could be summed up as physical challenges, technical skills, gaining knowledge and social and personal development.

Fulfilling objectives

This outcome could be fulfilled by:

(a) Planning and preparing for your BTEC First expedition, keeping a record of what you have done and why you are doing it. For example you could list all the food you have bought, explaining to your tutor why it is suitable for the expedition.

(b) Evaluating your planning during and after the expedition. For example, you could do a chart relating your planning to what you did, and assessing how good your planning was – like this:

Item/preparation
1 Tent – borrowed from college
How it was used
Shared by me, Andy, Sam and Ashok for two nights
How useful it was
The tent itself was OK but there were some guy-ropes missing. Had to use Ashok's bootlaces!
Any improvements or changes needed for next time
Check any tent properly by pitching it before going on expedition.
Item/preparation
2 Wellies – cost £5 at Anytown Market
How it was used
Worn all the time except in bed
How useful it was
They were good for all walking except running down steep slopes. Slipped on Helvellyn – luckily not hurt.
Any improvements or changes needed for next time
Might save up and buy some proper boots, because I want to go on some more expeditions!

When doing this outcome it will help you if you show a keen understanding of the importance of planning, and if you are not afraid to point out where – or why – you made a mistake.

PASSGRADE

> Participate in a multi-day expedition identifying own roles and responsibilities.

The key feature of this unit is *taking part in an expedition yourself*. There are two main ways you could do this.

The first way is take part in an expedition arranged by your tutors to achieve this unit. This is much the best way of participating in a multi-day expedition, from the point of view of passing Expedition Skills. This is because your tutors and instructors are also your assessors. These are the people who understand you, understand expeditions and understand your BTEC course. They can monitor what you are doing, collect all the evidence they – and you – need, and (provided you do what is expected of you) can ensure that you will pass.

An additional advantage is that you will be working with other members of your class, so that the expedition should be an enjoyable group experience. Your learning will be shared, and will probably be more successful because you will be working in teams with people you already know.

The second way is to take part in an expedition with another organisation, such as the Scouts, the Cadets, or as part of the Duke of Edinburgh's Award Scheme. Provided you can get the expedition organisers to confirm in writing that you have really covered the outcomes needed for the unit, then you should gain accreditation for this and should pass.

But even if you have done these things, it would still be best to go on an expedition with your class. You can then share your skills (which will probably be better than theirs) with them – and you might get a distinction as well!

Warning: Think ahead!

If you think you cannot go on an expedition for any reason, you must talk about it, in confidence, with your tutor at the earliest opportunity.

Some people go on expeditions with family, friends or by themselves. This is a good thing to do, provided you follow safety rules. But though you may learn excellent skills by doing this, you won't get evidence for this unit which will be accepted by BTEC. You cannot be assessed by members of your own family.

You cannot be assessed by members of your own family

285

skill POWER

Here is some advice for getting the most out of your multi-day expedition.

Before

- Inform the organisers if you have any worries or problems as far in advance as possible before the expedition. This includes health problems, disability, phobias, lack of money, possible clash of dates with something else you need or want to do, family difficulties, worries about food, problems with other classmates or problems with staff members.

- Be certain how you are travelling to the expedition base (e.g. coach, minibus, train group travel, etc). Follow your tutors' instructions about this (for they will be based on safety and insurance requirements).

- Pay for the expedition – if you need to pay – at the earliest possible date.

- Tell your parents or other people all about it well in advance, and keep them in the picture.

- If you are asked to form groups (e.g. to share tents) choose people you are friendly with, but take care not to exclude or be don't like.

- Arrive at the right place and time for setting off.

- Don't pack anything you shouldn't take – alcohol, drugs, valuables, dangerous knives, etc!

- Work as a team at all times.

- Have a positive attitude to tutors and instructors – remember your aim is to get a good grade!

- Make lists of what you need and check them off while you do your packing.

- Arrange well in advance to borrow equipment if you need to do so. If you need to borrow clothes or footwear, be sure of your sizes.

During

- Be pleasant and cooperative with other students and tutors.

- Follow instructions.

- Participate enthusiastically in all activities.

- Do your share of chores, e.g. washing up.

- Be tidy and considerate in the tent or in the outdoor centre/bunk-house/hostel.

- Be punctual – don't keep other people waiting.

- Make sure you understand and follow all safety instructions.

- Never wander off without telling people in charge where you're going.

- If you are walking, never separate from your party.

- Check your equipment before setting out each day.

- Be prepared for cold, wet or horrible weather.

- If you are camping, pitch your tent with the door downwind.

- Don't try to carry too much.

- Remember that a chain is only as strong as its weakest link. Don't force anyone to do more than they are capable of.

- Carry out any exercises, paperwork, record-keeping or self-assessment connected with passing the unit.

- Keep out of pubs unless you have permission to go in.

- Follow agreed sleeping arrangements.

- Avoid quarrelling with other people.

- Tell a tutor if you feel unwell, or have any worries or problems.

After

- Tidy the campsite and pack all your stuff away properly.

- Make sure you give back everything you borrowed, to the person you borrowed it from.

- Don't leave your belongings on the coach or train home.

- Carry out all self-assessments set by your tutors so that you get the best possible grade for the unit.

- Thank your instructors and tutors for the effort they

SUPERGRADE! *Merit*

Explain own roles and responsibilities and those of other team members whilst participating in a multi-day expedition.

On a BTEC expedition your roles and responsibilities, many of which are listed above, exist for five main reasons:

1 to ensure that the expedition achieves its objectives
2 to ensure that the expedition is safe and environmentally friendly
3 to ensure that the expedition is enjoyable for all
4 to improve your skills and those of others
5 to ensure that you get good grades.

Roles and responsibilities in an expedition can also be explained in a table form, as below.

Note that the roles and responsibilities you are asked to explain are those that you have during the expedition. Some of these are listed on page 286.

skill POWER

You may be asked to explain roles and responsibilities, e.g. who is doing what in a particular team, group or (say) tent, during the expedition itself. If this is the case, tutors or instructors will interview you, and make notes about your answers on the spot. Later, they will put these notes together to give you a grade for this outcome.

This means you should (a) carry out your roles and responsibilities, e.g. cleaning a kitchen or pitching a tent; and (b) explain what you are doing and why you are doing it.

Role/responsibility	Explanation
• Be pleasant and cooperative with other students and tutors.	This means being willing and helpful when carrying out team activities with other expedition members. You should be cheerful, help people who are in difficulties or falling behind, and give encouragement. You should not get into unnecessary arguments with other students, instructors or tutors.
• Follow instructions.	Some instructions, e.g. those given during an abseil, are for your own safety. Others, such as keeping quiet after, say, 11 p.m., are for other people's comfort.
• Participate enthusiastically in all activities.	This means having a go at any activities available during an expedition. If you get a chance to go canoeing or mountain biking, take it. Try not to make excuses. If you have a really serious reason for not doing an activity, tell your tutor and make it clear why you cannot do it.
• Do your share of chores, e.g. washing up.	Some of your roles and responsibilities will be chores like washing, tidying, packing and so on. If three people are sharing a tent, it is best if each person does the same amount of work.

Role/responsibility	Explanation
• Never wander off without telling people in charge where you're going	Sometimes you might be tempted to leave the others and go off by yourself, either on a mountain or from the campsite. It may sometimes be difficult to be surrounded by people for 24 hours a day, which you might be on an expedition. If you need time on your own, tell your tutor first.
• Keep out of pubs unless you have permission to go in.	Your expedition organisers will probably lay down ground rules on the subject of pubs. Your responsibility is to obey those rules!

Participate enthusiastically in all activities ...

As with the last outcome, your justification (giving reasons why you do something) may be done orally, talking to tutors or instructors during the expedition.

On the other hand you might be asked to write down your justifications, as in the example below.

! CHECKPOINT ...
Work out some explanations of your
■ own for some of the other roles and responsibilities listed on pages 287–288.

! CHECKPOINT ...
Discuss the following situations:
■ • An instructor put a raw egg down the back of a student as a joke. What should have happened next?
• Four male students shared a room in a bunkhouse. Tutors inspecting the room at lights out found a female student hidden under a duvet.
• Five students set on a sixth at an army camp and shaved off his eyebrows.
• A student had a panic attack on the top of a mountain and couldn't move. It was getting dark.

 *Distinction*

Justify own roles and responsibilities and those of other team members whilst participating in a multi-day expedition.

Role/responsibility	Justification
• Be pleasant and cooperative with other students and tutors.	Quarrelling and hassle are not useful in an expedition. They spoil people's pleasure and prevent them from concentrating on things that matter. If people get angry they cannot think clearly, and as a result they may do something dangerous, or forget safety precautions. In addition, you need to show that you are good at teamwork in order to get a good grade for this outcome.
• Follow instructions.	You must do this because instructors know more about expedition skills than you do. You learn by following instructions. Many instructions are to do with safety and if they are disobeyed people (including yourself) could be put at risk.
• Participate enthusiastically in all activities.	By taking part in everything you learn more. You also demonstrate good personal qualities – confidence and enthusiasm – which are needed in the public services. Finally, you and others will enjoy the expedition more if everybody is enthusiastic.
• Do your share of chores, e.g. washing up.	This will show that you are a team player, and an unselfish person. It will also show that you are capable of looking after yourself. An expedition is more successful if everybody pulls their weight – and it saves time too.
• Never wander off without telling people in charge where you're going.	It is dangerous and inconsiderate to disappear during an expedition. If you get hurt it is hard to send help or a rescue party because no one knows where you are – or even that you are hurt! It forces the expedition organisers to call the police and, if you are under 18, to contact your parents. If you are unhappy it is much better to tell someone than keep it bottled up.
• Keep out of pubs unless you have permission to go in.	Unauthorised pub visits by underage students is one of the main causes of problems on expeditions with young people. It can lead to unsafe or antisocial behaviour, embarrasses expedition organisers, breaks the law – and causes insurance problems. Why risk your qualification for the sake of a drink?

PASSGRADE

Record individual performance and that of group members, identifying strengths and weaknesses.

To meet this outcome you need to work in a group with other students on your expedition.

This outcome asks you to do some *self-assessment* and *peer assessment*.

For self-assessment, you have to record (note down clearly) your own performance on the expedition. You will need to do this under various headings (see below).

For peer assessment you need to do the same thing with other group members.

A 'group' should be 3–6 members, ideally. If the group is more or less than this, ask your tutor's advice about how many people's performance you should record. If you have too few, you may not be covering the outcome. If you have too many, the chances are you weren't around when some of them were doing their activities, and you won't be in a position to record what they did, or identify their strengths and weaknesses.

You must decide what you are going to record. And, to be on the safe side, you should check with your tutors or instructors about what aspects of performance you should record. Obviously, if you go on a sailing expedition you will not be recording the same things as you would on a walking expedition.

Your tutors may provide you with a form for this outcome. If not, you may find it useful to design one yourself. An example is given on the next page.

Being objective

You may find it hard identifying the strengths and weaknesses of your own and other people's performance. It is not particularly easy for tutors – and they get paid to do it! However, you must try to be as honest as possible.

You should take your tutor's advice as to whether this should be done as a group exercise or not.

Your record of performance might end up looking like the one on page 291.

Note that to achieve a pass grade your comments do not have to be very detailed.

Describe individual performance and that of group members, identifying weaknesses and areas for improvement.

This outcome is similar to the previous one, but you should go into more detail. This may mean

describing people's performance in more detail and with more analysis to your tutor or instructor. Or it might mean writing a self-appraisal, and an appraisal of your group.

An appraisal is a description of the strengths and weaknesses of someone's performance. A self-appraisal is about your own performance, and a peer appraisal is about your team-mates' performance.

You should practise writing appraisals – it is useful when planning interviews and when training in the public services. A great deal of police training, for example, consists of role plays and simulations followed by a self-appraisal of your own strengths and weaknesses.

Profile

Expedition Record Sheet – BTEC First Diploma in Public Services

Name: Simon Wu

Other Group Members: Ahmed Bashir, Stephen Knight

Date: 15 March 2004

Performance recorded	Simon Wu	Ahmed Bashir	Stephen Knight
CAMPCRAFT			
Pitching tent	Good – knew how to do it. Organised pitching of tent.	Put in pegs – followed instructions.	Did his share – knew about positioning door downwind.
Cooking	Made sandwiches, assembled and lit stove.	Cooked spaghetti – very good.	Gave advice and did washing up.
Dismantling tent	I organised this and packed tent.	Took out pegs, etc.	Cleaned inside of tent and cleared litter.
WALKING			
Map-reading	OK	OK	Good – explained it to the rest of us.
Compass	Found bearings hard at first.	Good once he got the hang of it.	Showed us how to use compass.
Timekeeping	Good.	Good but slow uphill.	Good.
Route card	Gave advice.	Wrote it because he has best handwriting.	Good – understood how to add time for uphill bits.
Contigency plan	Agreed with Stephen.	Agreed with Stephen.	Made the contingency plan.
Environment	Dropped litter.	Dropped litter.	Picked litter up.
ACTIVITIES			
Abseil	Scared but did it.	Refused to do abseil.	Good at abseiling. Has done it before.
Caving	Enjoyed it.	Scared – but did it.	Did it but didn't enjoy it.
General Comments	I was quite cooperative and also a good leader.	Ahmed worked well and is a good cook.	Stephen was a good team member but could be a bit bossy.

When doing a self-appraisal do not be too hard on yourself, and mention your strengths as well as your weaknesses.

You could use a similar format to the one given above. Below is an example of one of the same aspects of performance, but with more analysis of weaknesses and areas for improvement.

Performance recorded

Simon Wu

Ahmed Bashir

Stephen Knight

CAMPCRAFT

Pitching tent

The tent was a Lichfield dome tent and I knew how to pitch it because we have a similar one at home. I explained to Ahmed and Stephen how to do it. It was quite windy so I made Ahmed hold the tent down while Stephen and I put in the poles and then while I held it, Ahmed and Stephen put in the pegs.

Ahmed had never put up a tent before so he needed some guidance from me and Stephen. He wanted to be helpful but he didn't always listen to what I said. When we had got the poles in he was very active putting in the pegs, and did it very well. He also organised the layout inside the tent so that we all had enough room.

Stephen did not know much about this sort of tent because he normally uses an old-fashioned ridge tent belonging to his dad. He gave very good advice about where to pitch the tent (against a wall to protect it from wind) and about having the door facing downwind. He showed us how to lock pegs and align guy-ropes.

Areas for improvement

I might have been a bit bossy when telling Ahmed and Stephen how to pitch the tent. I might have given too many instructions and not enough help!

In my opinion Ahmed should try not to panic and get confused when given instructions. When he gets the idea he is careful and well-organised.

Stephen knows a lot about expeditions because of walking in Scotland with his dad. But like me he is a bit bossy!

Notice that weaknesses are clearly identified and that Simon puts forward areas for improvement for himself and his team-mates. But notice too that he has a positive attitude and looks for good points as well as faults.

SUPERGRADE! *Distinction*

Critically evaluate individual performance and that of group members, identifying weaknesses and areas for improvement.

For this outcome it would be useful to look at aspects of individual performance that are a bit more complex and demanding than whether or not a person can pitch a tent.

You may not need to do this critical evaluation in writing, but if you do, it could look something like the passage below.

Profile

Evaluation of Individual and Group Performance by Simon Wu

Method of travel

Ahmed Bashir, Stephen Knight and I took part in a camping and walking expedition where we camped for two nights and walked for two half days and one full day in the Lake District.

Route and environment

The route we planned was agreed upon by our tutor, but it turned out to be too long, and we had to miss out one section – otherwise we would have reached the second campsite after dark. This would have given us problems setting up camp.

Apart from the length, the route was a good one which gave us experience in walking on footpaths, moorland and scree slopes. We took care to avoid dropping litter and damaging walls and fences – which we did have to climb when we missed the way at one point.

Navigation skills

Our navigation was not always successful, partly because of fog and partly because our map-reading skills were not very good. Only Stephen read the map without making any mistakes. Stephen was best at compass reading as well.

Physical, social, moral and spiritual benefits

We found that the expedition benefited our physical, social, moral and spiritual development. We felt fitter after walking for so long (though tired as well!) so it was good for us physically. Before doing this expedition Ahmed, Stephen and I didn't really know each other very well, but now we are good friends, despite the fact that Stephen took up more than his fair share of space in the tent, and Ahmed snores! This means the expedition helped us socially. Morally and spiritually it helped us to work as a team, to be less selfish, and to enjoy the beauty of nature (when it wasn't foggy).

Spiritual healing

Health and Safety

We took care to minimise risk by staying together and not walking too fast for Ahmed, who was a bit slow. We also carried whistles, a compass, and spare food in case we had to spend the night out. The only problem was

that I forgot my mobile phone, which would have been very useful if one of us had broken his leg.

We were comfortable and well equipped because we had good sleeping bags, carry-mats and a stove which worked well. We checked the stove before we set out, though Ahmed was the only person who really understood how it worked.

On the whole we enjoyed the expedition a great deal and felt we got a lot out of it. But we did learn some things about ourselves, and our expedition skills, which need improvement.

Areas for improvement

Simon

I understood the tent but I wasn't very skilled at map-reading or route-finding. I led the group into a bog at one point, and another time we got into a field which had a bull in it. My teamwork was OK because I didn't quarrel with anybody but Stephen said I talked too much and was sometimes bossy. He said I didn't listen to him when he was trying to explain map-reading. I need to think more about other people when I am in a team, improve my listening skills, and try not to act as if I know it all, when I don't.

Ahmed

Ahmed was brilliant at cooking spaghetti and thanks to him we had a really good meal. I think we all slept well in the tent because we were full of food. He was rather a slow walker and kept complaining about his feet. I think his boots were too small for him. He should have checked them properly before we set out. He had no experience of camping but he was very tidy and once he understood how to put tent pegs in and stuff like that he did it very well. He was a good team member because he was funny and good-natured. He can take a joke. I think his areas for improvement are fitness, and perhaps confidence. He said he was no good at cooking and he turned out to be brilliant.

Stephen

Stephen was the best of us because he knew more about expeditions and walking and map-reading than the rest of us. I didn't think he was well prepared because he was wearing wellies but he had no problem with his feet. Though he didn't understand the tent, he made us pitch it in a good dry place, out of the wind, and facing away from the wind. This was a good thing because Wednesday night was quite windy. Stephen was a good team member because he was cheerful and active. When going uphill he was a bit too active and we had to ask him to slow down a few times. His areas for improvement, in my opinion, are taking more interest in equipment like tents, and trying not to talk so much about things he knows nothing about, like politics.

Conclusion

We would like to arrange another, similar expedition, for a bit longer at the end of the summer term.

CHECKPOINT ...

(a) Write a careful self-appraisal in relation to any aspect of your expedition.

(b) Make an action plan for improving your own expedition skills.

Index